FREEDOM FAITH

FREEDOM FAITH

The Womanist Vision of

PRATHIA HALL

by COURTNEY PACE

The University of Georgia Press | Athens

A Sarah Mills Hodge Fund Publication
This publication is made possible in part through a grant
from the Hodge Foundation in memory of its founder,
Sarah Mills Hodge, who devoted her life to the relief and
education of African Americans in Savannah, Georgia.

Paperback edition, 2021
© 2019 by the University of Georgia Press
Athens, Georgia 30602
www.ugapress.org
All rights reserved
Designed by Melissa Bugbee Buchanan
Set in Sentinel

Most University of Georgia Press titles are
available from popular e-book vendors.

Printed digitally

The Library of Congress has cataloged the hardcover edition of this book as follows:

Names: Pace, Courtney, 1984– author.
Title: Freedom faith : the womanist vision of Prathia Hall / by Courtney Pace.
Description: Athens : The University of Georgia Press, [2019] | Includes bibliographical references and index.
Identifiers: LCCN 2018053137 | ISBN 9780820355061 (hardcover : alk. paper) | ISBN 9780820355054 (ebook)
Subjects: LCSH: Hall, Prathia LauraAnn. | Hall, Prathia LauraAnn—Religion. | Hall, Prathia LauraAnn—Political and social views. | African American civil rights workers—Biography. | African American women civil rights workers—Biography. | African American Baptists—Biography. | Baptists—United States—Clergy—Biography. | African American feminists—Biography. | African Americans—Civil rights—History—20th century. | Civil rights movements—United States—History—20th century.
Classification: LCC E185.97.H246 P33 2019 | DDC 323.092 [B]—dc23
LC record available at https://lccn.loc.gov/2018053137

Paperback ISBN 978-0-8203-6171-0

For Stanley. May you live by Freedom Faith.

CONTENTS

Preface ix

Introduction 1

Chapter 1. "I See Africa Rising" 6

Chapter 2. "Living in the Face of Death" 25

Chapter 3. "In Jail for a Just Cause" 62

Chapter 4. "Equality Now" 89

Chapter 5. "Black, Preacher, Baptist, Woman" 110

Chapter 6. "I'm 5'6", but I Should Have Been Taller" 133

Chapter 7. "The Living God Is Not a Bigot" 153

Chapter 8. "The Baptist Church Is Going to Have to Deal with Me" 185

Chapter 9. "One of the Founding Mothers of the New America" 212

Appendix. Who Had the Dream? Prathia Hall and the "I Have A Dream" Speech 221

Notes 235

Bibliography 289

Index 305

PREFACE

In my first year of graduate school, I sought a dissertation topic addressing the intersections of race and gender, largely because of my own educational and ministry experiences. Homiletician Tom Long suggested Prathia Hall as a potential research focus based on her civil rights activism and alleged origination of "I have a dream." I was instantly drawn to her, beyond what I could fully understand at the time. I left no rock unturned in my quest to find primary sources from which to tell her story. This work has in many ways been like putting together puzzle pieces without the picture on the box as a guide. New sources offered snippets of information, and as a historian, I had to figure out how the pieces fit together.

An added challenge to this work is the fact that I am white. Womanism is a liberation methodology rooted in the experiences of black women, affirming the equal humanity of all people, with concern to oppose every form of oppression, including racism, sexism, and classism, and offering black women's correction to white feminism that isolated gender, often ignoring race and class. While some of Hall's friends were delighted that a scholar was focusing on Hall, some hoped Hall's first biographer would be a womanist scholar. Historians have always been both insiders and outsiders to their work, typically choosing topics that are somewhat autobiographical but that extend beyond our understanding. While I can relate to some of the adversity Hall faced—I am an ordained, Baptist woman in ministry who juggled child-rearing, divorce, and a mix of part-time and full-time jobs while earning a PhD—my understanding is limited by my context as a white scholar. My earnest hope is that this book and the ground it covers make future study of Hall more accessible. My book title is not an attempt to produce womanist scholarship, but to accurately reflect the way Hall described her work. I offer my research as a resource, but I respect and celebrate that critical engagement with Hall's life and work must be led by womanist scholars.

To honor Hall and do justice to her story, I present Hall telling her story in her own words wherever possible, including referring to her by the surname

Hall throughout the narrative, as she recovered her maiden name following her divorce. I have immersed myself in this work—listening to her recorded sermons, attending SNCC reunions, singing freedom songs, worshipping with black congregations, reading womanist scholarship, building relationships with her friends and family, spending time in the neighborhoods where she lived and worked, mining archives, and welcoming critical feedback on my work. My scholarship is rooted in primary sources and informed by an embodied understanding as much as possible. I have spent nearly a decade listening more than speaking, reading more than writing, and building trust rooted in relationship.[1]

No historical figure is ever beyond critique. As a researcher and author, I wrestled with whether to include certain pieces of Hall's story, particularly the details of her divorce, the long process of completing her PhD, and her difficult job search. I ultimately opted to include those details, though sensitive, to do justice to her story, her character, and her desire that the truth be known. The causes for such events are complex, and one can as easily fall into the unfortunate trope of blaming the victim as one can into the trope of justifying every action, both of which I tried not to do. Some interviewees mentioned that Hall could be a difficult colleague, but that, too, can often become an oppressive trope perpetuated by the predominantly white, male academy that targets black women in order to limit black women's influence and significance within the church and in academia.

This project would not have been possible without the guidance and support of so many. Thank you to my editor, Walter Biggins, and to Deborah Oliver and Jon Davies, who worked closely with me throughout the final editing process, and the other University of Georgia Press staff, for believing in this project. Thank you for your support, your thoughtful feedback, and your commitment to publishing this book.

Baylor University also offered tremendous support for my research. Generous fellowships from the Baylor University Institute for Oral History, the Glen Hillburn Dissertation Travel Award, and the National Association of Baptist Professors of Religion Dissertation Fellowship aided my work. I am grateful to the Baylor University Graduate School for supporting me—and now others—by establishing a parental leave policy for graduate students and for funding research and conference travel. The Baylor Department of

Religion has likewise offered a community of support and resources. Thanks to my dissertation committee and other Baylor faculty who have guided my work along the way: Bill Pitts, Stephen Sloan, Rosalie Beck, Bruce Longenecker, Beverly Gaventa, James Sorrelle, David Whitford, Bill Bellinger, Jim Nogalski, and especially to my advisor, mentor, friend, and *doktorvater*, Doug Weaver. Thank you also to my faculty colleagues at Memphis Theological Seminary for supporting this project, for being understanding of the time needed to complete the writing, and for encouraging me in the final steps of the process.

I am grateful for the helpful archivists at Temple University's Urban Archive Collection who assisted me in my research of Fellowship House. Princeton Theological Seminary's libraries also provided valuable records about Hall's theological education. I am grateful to the Student Nonviolent Coordinating Committee for opening its fiftieth anniversary celebration to students, allowing me to form relationships with so many who knew Prathia Hall: Martha Norman Noonan, Joan Browning, Judy Richardson, Bob Zellner, Mary King, Penny Patch, Peggy Dammond Preacely, Faith Holsaert, Sheila Michaels, U.S. Representative John Lewis, John Perdew, Peter DeLissovoy, Charles Sherrod, Bernice Johnson Reagon, Rutha Harris, Larry Rubin, Jack Chatfield, Chuck McDew, Connie Curry, Courtland Cox, Don Harris, Charles Nesbitt, James Lawson, Joyce Ladner, Dorie Ladner, Julian Bond, Frank Smith, Betty Garman Robinson, Ivanhoe Donaldson, Danny Lyon, Bernard Lafayette, Harry Belafonte, Joanne Christian Mants, Bob Mants, Benjamin Chavis, and Wyatt Tee Walker. I was fortunate to locate several of Prathia Hall's colleagues and friends, who welcomed me and offered invaluable resources: Jeremiah Wright, Charles Adams, Evelyn Brooks Higginbotham, Leah Gaskin Fitchue, Cheryl Townsend Gilkes, Edith Kimbrough, Jeriann Harris, Frank Thomas, Martha Simmons, Cleophus LaRue, Daryl and Vanessa Ward, and Presttonia Davis Brown. I must give a special word of gratitude to Rev. LaGretta Bjorn, and her son Akil, for granting me access to Dr. Hall's papers, for blessing my research, and for pastoral encouragement throughout the project.

Thanks are due to my nonbinary and sister scholars, preachers, and activists who labor alongside me, committed to social justice. In some way each of you has inspired me, and I'm grateful for you and your friendship: Tamura Lomax, Valarie Kaur, Emilye Crosby, Wesley Hogan, Tiyi Morris,

Barbara Ransby, Allyson Dylan Robinson, Sinda Vanderpool, Tami Sawyer, Terri Freeman, Noelle Trent, Essence Jackson, Betsy Flowers, Eileen Campbell-Reed, Karen Seat, Susan Shaw, Melva Sampson, Wil Gafney, Keri Day, Amy Jill-Levine, Melody Maxwell, Mandy McMichael, Molly Marshall, Kate Bowler, Laine Scales, Pam Durso, Laura Ann Rogers Levens, Isabel Docampo, Jann Aldredge-Clanton, Sheila Sholes-Ross, Andrea Clark Chambers, Christine Smith, Patricia Hernandez, Judith Liro, Christine Wiley, Susan Newman Moore, Lynn Casteel Harper, Virginia Marie Rincon, Joanne Chadwick, Alphonetta Wines, Amy Butler, Pamela Smoot, Natalie Webb, Kyndall Rothaus, Emma Wood, Jewel London, Irie Session, Kamilah Hall Sharp, Yvette Blair Lavallais, Felecia LaVant, Gina Stewart, Jeralyn Major, Virzola Law, Vahisha Hasan, Katie Bauman, Floridia Jackson, Ashley Coffield, Aimee Lewis, Sarah Wallett, Whitney Hardy, Dorothy Wells, Rebecca Luter, Jen Dziura, Eileen Kuo, Kate Richards, Kyndra Frazier, Becky Fox, Rachel Donohue, Amanda Fisher, Lindsey Trozzo, Laurie Scott, Karoline Lewis, Emmy Kegler, Eliza Tweedy, Margaret Aymer Oget, Valerie Bridgeman, Amanda Tyler, Taryn Deaton, Jennifer Hawks, Sofi Hersher, Aurelia Pratt, Kristen Neilsen Donnelly, Sharyl West Loeung, Suzanne Holsomback, Candace Shaw, Emily Hunter McGowin, Leah Grundset Davis, Meredith Holladay, Nancy Sehested, Emily Peck-McClain, Robyn Henderson-Espinoza, Dorisanne Cooper, Latrice McLin, Saadia Khan Omer, Sehrish Siddiqui, Sara Dorrien-Christians, my sister-in-love Meredith Owen, and my bestie through thick and thin and back again, Elizabeth Grasham.

The fight for gender equality cannot be won without brothers standing alongside sisters in solidarity, and I am grateful for supportive, affirming brothers in the struggle: Broderick Greer, Earle Fisher, Andre Johnson, Peter Gathje, Byron Forester, David Weatherspoon, Patrick Jones, Thomas Sugrue, Charles Watson Jr., Kendall Harris, Christopher Hutson, Craig Henry, Will Christians, Brandon Morgan, David Breckenridge, Steve Montgomery, Nabil Bayakly, Micah Greenstein, Steven Sprinkle, and U.S. Representative Steve Cohen.

Outside of academia, I am blessed to have a wide community of support and encouragement. Thanks to Young Clergywomen International, the Bullish Society, the Alliance of Baptists, the Baptist Joint Committee for Religious Liberty, Equity for Women in the Church, Nevertheless She Preached,

Planned Parenthood of Tennessee and North Mississippi, Baptist Women in Ministry, Together We Will West Tennessee, my theater friends, my figure skating family, my workout buddies at the Memphis Jewish Community Center, and my church family at First Baptist Church of Memphis.

Finally, and most importantly, none of this work would be possible without my family. I cannot adequately thank my parents, Roger and Janyce Pace, or my grandmother, Colyne Johnson, for the countless ways they helped me over the past decade as I researched and wrote this book. Thanks to my Papa Stanley (of blessed memory) for always believing in me. And most of all, I thank my husband, Michael Owen, and my son, Stanley, for loving me so well and for believing in me and in this work.

FREEDOM FAITH

INTRODUCTION

A key leader in the Civil Rights Movement and a pillar of the black church in the United States, Rev. Dr. Prathia LauraAnn Hall (1940–2002) began her work by assisting her father, Rev. Berkeley Hall, in his social gospel–oriented church ministry. As her primary spiritual and intellectual mentor, he shaped her initial understanding of Freedom Faith, the belief that God wants people to be free and equips and empowers those who work for freedom. This was the central guiding principle of her life, her activism, and her ministry, and it offers the most appropriate lens through which to understand her life's work. Instilled by her father, contextualized and matured in the movement, and nurtured by her scholarship and preaching, Freedom Faith found its ultimate expression in her womanist vision of liberation for all people. Prathia Hall spoke strongly against layered forms of oppression—sexism, racism, classism, ageism, heterosexism, denominationalism—and called her hearers to work in cooperation with others and in affirmation of human rights. The gospel, as she proclaimed it, involved both the liberation of individuals and the redemption of systems so that all of God's people could be free.

Rev. Dr. Prathia Hall was one of the most profound, prophetic, and influential preachers of the twentieth century. A man with her talents and successes would have been a nationally recognized civil rights leader, held a prestigious pulpit, and served as president of a major denomination. That path was not open to Hall, despite the influence she held. Even Martin Luther King Jr. so admired Hall's preaching that he once described her as "the one platform speaker I would prefer not to follow."[1] In 1962 after a string of church burnings, King visited an Albany, Georgia, prayer service. There, Hall reportedly used the phrase "I have a dream," a phrase that would then have great significance in King's own preaching. While Hall modestly withheld this information for most of her life and praised King's own work and preaching, her closest friends knew her to be a major source of his "I have a dream" speech.[2]

That scholarship has largely ignored Hall is unsurprising, however. The history of the Civil Rights Movement has often fallen for the Great Man Theory, emphasizing figures like King, John Lewis, and Malcolm X. In spite of the fact that women comprised 80 percent of laborers in the movement, and even as the literature has expanded to include local figures, such as Fred Shuttlesworth and Medgar Evers, the focus has remained predominantly on men, which neglects—even erases—the thousands of women who supported the movement through local activism. This exclusion also denies the rightful place of women at the center of any history of religion in the United States. Historians since about 2000, however, have begun to correct this exclusion, publishing biographies of more familiar names such as Ella Baker, Coretta Scott King, and Fannie Lou Hamer. And many movement veterans, such as Joanne Gibson Robinson, Mary King, and Judy Richardson, have recognized the importance of telling their own stories. Recent memoir anthologies by the women of the Student Nonviolent Coordinating Committee (SNCC) have added more nuance to the importance of local women's activism. Hall's story, however, has remained untold.[3]

Hall is a significant figure of the Civil Rights Movement for several reasons. She was one of the few women field workers in SNCC; because of the real and present danger involved in door-to-door voter registration, women in the movement predominantly helped with secretarial work or through education programs at churches. Hall was also Charles Sherrod's second-in-command of SNCC's Southwest Georgia Project in Albany, Georgia. When Martin Luther King Jr. or any other high-profile civil rights leader visited Albany, Sherrod frequently chose Hall to speak at the mass meeting. She later became the leader of SNCC's Selma, Alabama, voter registration project as well as the multiorganization Atlanta, Georgia, project and was among the very few SNCC leaders who traveled to Africa in 1964 on invitation by the Guinean government. She was a well respected leader and organizer, and her activism directly challenged racism, sexism, and classism as she advocated for people's right to vote and exercise their full rights as citizens. Looking back on all she did, Hall described her time in the movement as the best education she ever received. It was in Southwest Georgia that Hall's Freedom Faith was contextualized and achieved maturity.

That Hall became a firebrand for the Civil Rights Movement is somewhat surprising given her early experiences. Growing up in Philadelphia, she attended predominantly white schools and did not experience Jim Crow segregation until age five on a journey to Virginia to visit her grandmother. As an adult, Hall had joined the Civil Rights Movement, in part, to wrestle with her vocational calling, but her experiences in the movement helped her discern and confirm her call to ministry. Hall became one of the first black Baptist women to be ordained by the American Baptist Churches USA (1977) and was the first woman accepted into the Baptist Minister Conference of Philadelphia and Vicinity (1982). She completed her MDiv (1982), ThM (1984), and PhD (1997) degrees at Princeton Theological Seminary and became a well-respected professor, primarily teaching womanist theology, Christian ethics, and black church history.[4] She served as associate dean of Spiritual and Community Life, director of the Harriett L. Miller Women's Center, and dean of African American Ministries at United Theological Seminary in Dayton, Ohio (1989-98), Visiting Womanist Scholar at the Interdenominational Theological Center in Atlanta, Georgia (1998-99), and the Martin Luther King Jr. Chair in Social Ethics at Boston University School of Theology (2000-2002). In 1997, *Ebony* magazine placed her at the top of its "15 Greatest Black Women Preachers" list, and she was the only woman considered for its "10 Greatest Black Preachers" list, ultimately placing eleventh. She pastored Mount Sharon Baptist Church in Philadelphia for twenty-five years in addition to serving in an international itinerant preaching ministry. She served among the leadership of the Progressive National Baptist Convention, American Baptist Churches USA, the New York Board of Education, the Children's Defense Fund, the Association of Black Seminarians, and domestic and international advocacy for liberation for all people. Her public leadership and prophetic preaching, rooted in Freedom Faith, challenged black churches to model a new, inclusive humanity.[5]

Hall's racial justice activism sheds light on the long Civil Rights Movement and the differences between activists of various faiths, ages, races, regions, and organizations. Her activism spanned demonstrations, social justice education, urban race riots, economic justice campaigns, voter registration drives, and freedom schools. Though her name recognition has been limited until now, she shaped the work of SNCC across three states: Georgia, Alabama, and Mississippi. She trained hundreds of SNCC volunteers to work across cultures for social justice. A sage beyond her years, she reminded SNCC of the importance of its nonviolent beginnings and profoundly articulated the realities of faith, of fear, and of the dream that would emerge from the nightmare of Jim Crow. Hall's story also showcases several aspects of the relationship between religion and culture in the post–World War II United States, particularly the ways in which many religious groups became polarized between conservative and liberal constituencies as they addressed the social issues of the 1960s: racial and economic justice, feminism, and foreign policy. Hall's exit from SNCC coincided with the rise of movement leaders who abandoned nonviolence, SNCC's expulsion of its white members, and a growing distrust of government leaders, intensified by the Vietnam War.

Hall's transition to ministry and education following the movement also demonstrated the ways those in the movement continued their activism into their later lives, mostly as politicians, educators, and social activists. As a community organizer and pastor, she worked for justice rather than self-promotion. She mentored a generation of black clergywomen, many of whom rose to national prominence. She weathered sexism within black churches to oppose all forms of oppression, both within and beyond black churches. Throughout her life, she developed her understanding of Freedom Faith, most fully expressed through her womanist vision of liberation for all people.

The fact that Hall's preaching against any form of oppression—including sexism, classism, and heterosexism—was considered radical even forty years after the Civil Rights Movement began demonstrated entrenched prejudice within black culture and religion. In response to her context and her own experiences, she boldly confronted injustice with a womanist vision of liberation for all people, emerging from a long tradition of black women's intellectualism, addressing her context and organizing black churches and black people toward liberation. She stood on the foundation built by enslaved black women who organized black people to resist slavery and its oppressive pathology. She followed in the footsteps of Harriet Tubman, forging paths to freedom as guided by the ancestors, ever widening the path for the liberation of others. She echoed the prophetic proclamations of Sojourner Truth and Maria Stewart, fearlessly decrying sexism and racism as twin evils of patriarchy. She harnessed the power of poetic language, like Frances E. W. Harper and Pauline Hopkins, to capture the essence of human experience and envision a liberated future for all people. She came of age as a race warrior, as did Mary Shadd Cary, promoting information literacy and lifelong learning in the struggle for gender and racial justice. She continued the international, revivalist preaching ministry of Amanda Berry Smith, advocating for an engaged community and educational opportunities for black children. She emulated Anna Julia Cooper's scholarship, community organizing, and unapologetic pride in black womanhood as key in the struggle for a just society. She boldly named racist double standards endangering the lives of black men, pioneered by Ida B. Wells-Barnett. She carried on the work of Mary Church Terrell, organizing people for activism for women's rights and desegregation of public businesses. She reached across racial and class divides to organize people of faith in the struggle for human rights, as Violet Johnson and Florence Spearing had done. She extended the trail blazed by Nannie Helen Burroughs, harnessing the power and influence of black Baptist clubwomen's organizing for missions, institution building, education, and racial uplift. She confronted sexism within black institutions as part of her civil rights activism, as Pauli Murray modeled, and continued this work through ordained ministry. She served in and led civil rights organizations like Ella Baker, leading them to collaborate for greater impact and mentoring the next generation to carry on the work. Working on the building constructed by these women and thousands more, Prathia Hall's activism, ministry, community organizing, brilliant scholarship, prophetic preaching, and pastoral leadership honored the historic legacy of black women's intellectualism as she added her own legacy of Freedom Faith.[6]

Through Freedom Faith, the belief that God wants people to be free and equips and empowers those who work for freedom, Hall's life's work proclaimed truth to power, mobilizing thousands to do the same.

CHAPTER 1
"I SEE AFRICA RISING"

"Daughter, do good"

Prathia LauraAnn Hall was born in Philadelphia on June 29, 1940, to Rev. Berkeley L. and Ruby Hall. The Hall family was originally from Virginia, but Berkeley and Ruby moved north to Philadelphia as a young couple to protect their future children from Jim Crow segregation. Their first child, a son, did not survive infancy. Prathia was the second child, followed by Berkeley Jr. and Teresa. Her parents also raised Ruby's sister's daughter, Betty, whom Prathia called "sister."[1]

Berkeley's family of origin was from Florence, South Carolina, and Richmond, Virginia. They moved frequently, looking "for the best work." Prathia's paternal grandfather died when her father was thirteen years old, positioning her father as the breadwinner and parent figure for his siblings. He quit school to work full-time but still made time for occasional classes. By his eighteenth year, he moved the family to Philadelphia. There a train accident severed his leg through the bone. Doctors wanted to amputate his leg, but he refused. Recalling that family story later in life, Prathia admired his fortitude at such a young age: "He left this world with a limp, but he had two legs." She often wondered what he might have accomplished without the constrictive racial barriers of his day. Through his "incredible strength," he raised and supported his siblings, his sister's three children, and his own children.[2]

Ruby Johnson Hall's family lived on a small farm in northeastern Nelson County, outside of Charlottesville, Virginia. One of six children, Ruby was highly intelligent and enjoyed literature and poetry. The Johnson family attended St. James Baptist Church in Roseland, Virginia, where Ruby and her children would make their professions of faith.[3] Ruby's parents wanted to give her every opportunity for a better life, so they sent her to school in the county seat, where she boarded with her teacher in order to finish the eighth grade. Her parents then sent her to Baltimore to attend Frederick Douglass High School, an admirable accomplishment for the time. Throughout, Ruby worked odd jobs to supplement her parents' contributions toward the cost of her education.[4] Ruby attended the Coppin Normal School, later renamed Coppin State Teachers College, also in Baltimore. There she joined the Bethlehem Baptist Church, which called Rev. Berkeley L. Hall its pastor in 1926.

After marrying, Rev. Hall and Ruby moved to Philadelphia. Rev. Hall founded Mount Sharon Baptist Church in 1938 as a mission church of the National Baptist Convention, pastoring there until his death in 1960.[5] The church originally met in the Hall residence; the living and dining rooms were arranged as a small chapel, and the Halls lived on the second and third floors. He was known as a "phenomenal preacher," but he declined offers to pastor larger churches because he was committed to social ministry through Mount Sharon and to raising his family in the North Philadelphia neighborhood.[6] The church also offered a ministry of education to children considered unteachable by the local public schools because of disability or behavioral issues.[7]

Looking back as an adult, Prathia saw her father's specialized ministry in North Philadelphia as ahead of its time, "focused primarily upon the needs of children and youth," meeting the "bread and butter" needs of families in their community, where the poverty otherwise led to numerous "petty economic crimes."[8] The entire Hall family participated in the church's ministry, assisting with its food pantry, clothes closet, visitation, and discipleship programs. Every week, after Hall's parents visited wholesale grocers or producers to gather food, the children divided the food into boxes they then distributed to needy families.

The Hall family opened their three-story Victorian row house on West Girard Avenue to extended family and friends needing a place to stay. Prathia remembered their home being "large and always full" and akin to a "New Testament household" because they held "everything in common."[9] The composition of the household embodied her parents' willingness to care for others: "They were the parents of four children: Betty, Prathia, Teresa, and Berkeley, Jr, and surrogate parents of numerous other children who needed to share the love, guidance and protection of their home."[10] Remaining at home to manage the household, Ruby was both strict with her children and held high expectations of them.[11]

In 1945, when Prathia was five years old, she, and her younger sisters Teresa and Betty, took a train from Philadelphia to Virginia to visit their grandparents. This was Hall's first time traveling by train unaccompanied by her parents. The girls were dressed in their finest clothes and filled with excitement as they found seats, unaware of Jim Crow: "The conductor just literally snatched us up by the collar, you know, and what are you doing here? You can't sit here." Without giving the girls time to respond, he shoved them from car to car forward in the train. He pushed them into the car immediately behind the engine, filled with smoke. Hall later recounted her disillusionment in that moment: "The whole trip we sat there looking out the window, hurt far less by the pushing and the shoving, than in the psyche. The train ride had lost all its excitement. There was a message in the rhythm of the wheels on the tracks. The message was: you're not good enough, you're not good enough, you're not good enough."[12]

Prathia learned a great deal about church leadership from her mother. Ruby taught children's Sunday School at Mount Sharon Baptist and led the children in poetry recitation and dramas performed for the congregation. Hall's mother was instrumental in providing opportunities for Hall to speak before the congregation of Mount Sharon Baptist Church, directing programs for the children to perform. Mrs. Hall "had taught children to read who the school system had said couldn't be taught, and taught them to speak and to perform plays and do poetry." Hall remembered, even when she was "too small to be seen," being lifted onto a chair or tabletop to recite her lines in children's productions at church. "We'd always forget it and mess it up, and they would just applaud and say, 'You're wonderful. You can do anything you want to do.'" Hall's parents both stressed the importance of learning "to speak well and to handle the language well."[13] Prathia remembered gaining her love for poets such as Paul Laurence Dunbar, Langston Hughes, Countee Cullen, and Henry Wadsworth Longfellow from her mother.[14] Reflecting on Ruby, Hall observed that "since her early childhood, two personal characteristics have earned for her the respect of family and friends—her keen intelligence and her devotion to her Lord." Presttonia "Prestie" Brown, a childhood friend of Prathia's, remembered Mother Hall as "extremely bright" and good at managing money, especially in helping the church stretch its budget to meet its ministry goals. Ruby could also be controlling and quick to ask people when she wanted something from them.[15]

Prathia's primary spiritual and intellectual mentor, however, was her father. Rev. Hall impressed on his elder daughter that she was destined for great things, for which she would need a strong work ethic. Prathia recognized that he "never let the fact that I was a woman be an excuse for not being the very best I could be, whatever it was I would be doing." She cherished memories of him taking her to see excellent preachers: Paul Robeson, Mordecai Johnson, and Nannie Helen Burroughs.[16] When Prathia would later listen to herself preach, she heard her father, more than any other preaching mentor. As a tangible reminder of his influence on her, she carried his handkerchief in her Bible the rest of her life.

He told her of a vision he had the year she was born, of God taking him to "a high mountain" and saying to him, "This is the year that marks the rising up of the colored peoples of the world. I see Africa rising, Asia rising, India rising." This story instilled in young Prathia that she was "nurtured for the Freedom Movement."[17]

In many ways, Rev. Hall did raise Prathia for the freedom movement. He shared with her his passion for issues of faith and justice, particularly as concerns race. He frequently talked about "the struggles of black people, history of Africa, African Americans, Asia." He was passionate about solidarity between the oppressed, "colored peoples of the world." Mount Sharon frequently held Black History celebrations, in which the entire church participated.

Prathia remembered that her childhood friends would share how much they loved her father because, when children were visiting their home, Rev. Hall would regale them with his stories of black history.[18] Brown described Rev. Hall as a tall, "no-nonsense" kind of man, with a professorial manner. Though he was very loving, as a child, Brown still felt that she should sit respectfully, with her hands folded in her lap, when she was with him.[19] When Rev. Hall would begin to "wax eloquent" in a teaching moment, Prathia's siblings would "flee for the hills," but Prathia would "draw closer" to hear his teaching. She laughed as she reflected: "Part of the reason he poured all those things into me was not gender—it was access. I was the one who was there." While her siblings received "the mandatory," she "went for more."[20]

Brown remembered Prathia as "always an excellent speaker," even as a young girl, skilled in elocution and speech writing. As the girls played at each other's houses, Prathia encouraged Brown to improve her own skills. Prathia frequently read for church services, and as a preteen she was a regular participant in Mason, Eastern Star, and Elk Club debates, which Hall won in 1955.[21] As far back as Brown remembers, Prathia was a woman of conviction, determined to work hard for what she considered important: "If she believed in something, she didn't move off of it."[22]

Prathia attended predominantly white public schools in Center City Philadelphia, including the Philadelphia High School for Girls, one of the top secondary schools in the city. Her outspokenness against the omission of black history in her junior high and high school curriculum led several of her teachers to dock her grades.[23] She felt the support of her community with her as she pursued her education: "I'll never forget the woman who used to watch me walk to school with my books as she waited for the bus to go to her job as a domestic. When I would come past her on my way to school, her own shoulders would straighten up and every now and then she would press a crumpled dollar in my hand and say, 'Daughter do good. I'm prayin' for you.'"[24]

As a junior in high school, Prathia started to tell her guidance counselor that she wanted to attend law school to "become a civil rights attorney like Thurgood Marshall and Constance Baker Motley."[25] The counselor interrupted her, insisting she abandon this plan, because asking her family to finance law school was selfish. Knowing nothing about Hall's family when giving this advice, the counselor assumed that all black people were poor, destined for continued poverty. Prathia never forgot this conversation, nor did she let it derail her goals.[26]

At the same time, Prathia was determined not to become a preacher.[27] She felt as if "a war [was] being waged in [her] consciousness against the compelling call to the ordained ministry."[28] Prathia realized the difficulty she would face as a female minister, "a terrifying prospect," since she "knew almost no ordained ministers who were women who were taken seriously by the church"—except Mary Watson Stewart, an itinerant African Methodist Episcopal (AME) preacher whom she had observed.[29] In many ways, she searched for alternative ways to follow her call "by fighting racism at home and in the South."[30]

In no uncertain terms, even as an adolescent, Prathia knew she was expected to "have an identity" and not "be a domestic." She and her sisters were raised to be self-sufficient and independent. Her father rejected excuses of race or gender for any level of underperformance. Not only did he invest his wisdom into her, but she saw him regularly help other women become independent.[31] Though she had traits of both of her parents, she was in many ways her father's daughter.[32]

"You'll have a hard time convincing her that she should be in class"

During high school, Hall joined Fellowship House (FH), an interfaith, interracial organization established in 1931 and led by Marjorie Penney. Raised in a middle-class home in Philadelphia and a graduate of what was then known as the Pennsylvania Museum School of Art, Penney understood the potential for young people to combat segregation through "a handful of young church folk, Negro and white, convinced that peace in the world must" come from local people taking action in their communities. In 1929, these "church kids" met at the Quaker school Pendle Hill to address church segregation. After much struggle to find a willing church host, Penney's congregation, the First Baptist Church of Philadelphia, first allowed them to meet, and thereafter "the church was always packed."[33] By 1931, FH held interracial worship services across Philadelphia.

In 1942 FH established its headquarters in a home at 1431 Brown Street, in "a conflict neighborhood." FH relished the opportunity to test its ideas in that atmosphere. The house, colloquially known as Bums' Castle, had previously functioned as a firehouse, coffin factory, and hideout for fugitives.

The windows were painted black, the floors were so "thick with scum" that they were cleaned with an acetylene torch, and the building itself "was big and cheap." Having outgrown the Brown Street house, FH moved to 1521 West Girard Avenue, less than a block from the Hall family home, in 1957. FH eventually expanded into eleven multistate locations. In 1964, Little Fellowship House opened at Columbia Avenue and Twenty-Seventh Street in Philadelphia under the direction of Prathia Hall and Diana King, "to build hope and strength in a clearly disadvantaged and dilapidated neighborhood"; the neighborhood had erupted into a three-day race riot earlier that same year.[34]

As early as the 1930s, Penney had been leading people to test segregation in restaurants, theaters, and other public places in Philadelphia using nonviolent demonstration techniques, long before Martin Luther King Jr. would popularize this approach.[35] When anti-Semitism swept Philadelphia circa 1939—with eighty-three hate groups, even the KKK, operating across the Delaware Valley—Jewish leaders sought Penney's collaboration. Even the FBI sought Penney's collaboration, since FH was "the only Christian group prepared to fight anti-Semitism."[36]

During her time at FH, Hall observed competent, professional women in public leadership. The leadership of FH was predominantly female. Penney, who mentored Hall in nonviolence, served as executive director of FH for nearly forty years (1931–68). In addition to exhibiting exceptional wisdom and an enchanting sense of humor, Penney was "an all-purpose mother-prophet-friend-confidante-adviser."[37] "For Philadelphians," living in the city of brotherly love, she was "the epitome of sisterly love."[38] Penney frequently published articles in journals and magazines to promote FH's teachings. She twice received the Philadelphia Award, presented annually to the "Philadelphian who has made the greatest contribution to the city"—"a kind of local Nobel prize"—accompanied by a $5,000 award funded by the Curtis Bok family. Penney married Dr. Victor Paschkis, a science professor at Columbia University and founder of the Society for Social Responsibility in Science, of which Albert Einstein was also a member. When Penney retired, she and Paschkis volunteered at the FH Farm outside of Pottsville for the rest of their lives.

FH was both an agency and a movement, and on both counts, gave Hall exceptional preparation for her later work in the Civil Rights Movement.[39] FH intended to give its surrounding neighborhood "the vision, the hope, the courage, the determination, and the training to make changes," rather than to just address the "social ills that beset people at the bottom."[40] The house offered educational resources for school teachers, community members, and churches, such as its doll library of historic figures, and accredited teacher in-service and community workshops on the philosophies of nonviolence and religious, racial, and political reconciliation. FH commissioned speakers and a choir for local and traveling presentations and organized ministers of various local congregations in its work. It also supported the Civil Rights Movement in the South, raised awareness of injustice locally and internationally, and trained upcoming leaders to be "movers, shakers, and changers of the status quo."[41] FH offered housing to civil rights activists fund-raising in the North, including Medgar Evers and many SNCC workers.[42]

FH viewed itself as a training center for "good human relations," promoting "the American faith in brotherhood" and "social justice through Fellowship." The organization praised democratic process, "equal rights," "equal treatment," and "equal opportunities," aiming "to point the way for everyone to get equality of treatment and equality of opportunity."[43]

In addition to promoting nonviolence ahead of its time, FH led the way in inclusivity and ecumenism.[44] Baptist pastor A. Herbert Haslam coordinated its ecumenical and interracial worship services and minister's alliance. Haslam also organized home-based small groups "in strategic areas" of Philadelphia to discuss FH ideas and plan outreach for its neighbors and communities. The FH Speakers Bureau served hundreds of engagements annually, often sending a trio of speakers: "Negro, White Christian & Jew."[45] The operation became so influential that large denominational and parachurch bodies, including the National Council of Churches, the NAACP, and the American Friends Service Committee, sought Haslam and FH for "guidance and program."[46]

FH played a critical role in the modern Civil Rights Movement, even beyond its own activities. In 1952, young Crozer Theological School student Martin Luther King Jr. attended a FH event in Philadelphia to hear Howard University president Dr. Mordecai Johnson speak. Johnson had just returned from visiting the widowed Indira Gandhi in India, and his talk introduced King to Mahatma Gandhi's nonviolent approach. The experience revolutionized King's theology. He recounted the influence of that lecture, and FH, in his *Stride toward Freedom: The Montgomery Story* (1958):

One Sunday afternoon I traveled to Philadelphia to hear a sermon by Dr. Mordecai Johnson, president of Howard University... for the Fellowship House of Philadelphia. Dr. Johnson... spoke of the life and teachings of Mahatma Gandhi. His message was so profound and electrifying that I left the meeting and bought a half-dozen books on Gandhi's life and works.... It was in this Gandhian emphasis on love and non-violence that I discovered the method of social reform that I had been seeking for so many months.... I came to feel that this was the only morally and practically sound method open to oppressed people in their struggle for freedom."[47]

King maintained a connection with FH from this moment forward. Throughout the Montgomery bus boycott (1955–56), Penney and King frequently corresponded as she quasi-mentored King in nonviolence and interfaith, interracial cooperation. Penney also strongly encouraged King to bring the movement to the North, which he eventually did. Penney described that particular conversation: "I went to Atlanta. We met in the airport; I was going one place, he was going another. I sat for an hour with Dr. King and Coretta and the children, and he felt that his place was in the South; he didn't want to come to the North. I argued, she argued, and at the end I got his willingness to come." Penney also kept FH volunteers well-informed and engaged with the movement, with open doors to those from the South who had come north to raise funds and awareness.[48]

Participating in FH through high school and college, Hall was formed by the same community that shaped King's understanding of nonviolent direct action. She was able to hear world-class speakers, among them Mordecai Johnson, Howard Thurman, Reinhold Niebuhr, Abraham Heschel, Raymond Pace Alexander, Leon Sullivan, Fred Shuttlesworth, Frank Sinatra, Ralph Bunche, Harry Belafonte, Norman Thomas, Frank Laubach, Septima Clark, Mary McLeod Bethune, Dorothy Height, Margaret Meade, Dorothy Day, and Eleanor Roosevelt. She heard King and Thurman on multiple occasions.[49]

Hall was also influenced by FH educational programs that offered theoretical, historical, and practical instruction in the philosophy and theology of nonviolence, ideas that King would later popularize: nonviolence as not just the absence of violence but also the "presence of justice," the choice of love and forgiveness rather than hate, willingness to suffer, and concern for the redemption of the oppressed and the oppressor. Nonviolence was rooted in insisting on one's right to be treated as a human being, not letting hate compromise one's inner peace, and refusing to use violence no matter the provocation, with the goal that such an example would compel the other person to recognize one's humanity. After King's recognition in the South grew, FH remarketed its nonviolence training as "King's Way." FH materials would include taglines such as "King's Way is Soul Force! He had it, you can have it!"[50]

Hall became well versed in practical strategies for nonviolent demonstration, including withstanding physical injury without retaliation (external nonviolence) rooted in a spiritual commitment to loving others (internal nonviolence) long before such training became standard for student activists. While many other student activists were not introduced to nonviolent philosophy or strategy until they joined the movement, Hall was as well trained in the techniques and strategies of nonviolent direct action as the southern students training with James Lawson, who catalyzed the student movement through the Nashville demonstrations and the Freedom Rides in 1960–61.[51]

FH gave Hall opportunity to reflect on her father's teachings in new ways. Just as Rev. Hall taught her African and African American history, FH introduced her to the larger manifestations of racism worldwide, namely the processes leading to social sanction of systematic mistreatment of racial minorities and citizens of Third World countries around the world.[52] Hall further recognized the global consequences of prejudice and the relevance of the struggle for social justice for everyone, particularly the parallels between the struggles of nonwhite and non-Christian peoples, all dominated and oppressed by the West.[53]

While Hall already had experience in public speaking through her church and high school debate club, FH added to her oratory skills, particularly making and supporting arguments, using inclusive language, and connecting religious and philosophical ideas. FH also strengthened her gifts for building relationships within the community.[54] Speakers were trained to handle hostile audiences and to evaluate the success of projects.[55] These ideas closely resonated with the modus operandi of SNCC, further demonstrating how Hall's involvement in FH prepared her exceptionally well for activism in the movement.

Hall remained involved with FH throughout high school and into college. One group of which she was a member, the High School Fellowship:

By Youth Itself, met on Tuesdays at 3:45 p.m., led by Mitzy Jacoby Barnes, a graduate of Philadelphia High School for Girls and Temple University. This group held work camps and conferences at the farm, weekly meetings, "action-training sessions for peaceful change," and musical-drama productions promoting social justice and human equality. Members also produced a newsletter, *Viewpoint*.[56] Deeply involved with High School Fellowship's music-drama team, Hall often spoke at their programs. Dale Phalen, secretary of FH, remarked in a 1957 board meeting that "Joyce Barrett and Prathia Hall presented revealing and inspiring pictures of their participation in the work of the House in their well-delivered talks on 'What High School Fellowship Did for Me.'"[57]

Her father's tutelage, Penney's mentorship, and her work at FH did not satisfy Hall's desperation to go south. Because she attended predominantly white schools, she had never taken a Black history class, something commonly offered in black schools. On finishing high school, she asked her parents for permission to study at Tuskegee University for the summer of 1960, but after a racial incident in that area, her father forbade her to go, fearing for her safety. She later reflected: "So this race warrior, this minister with a passion for justice, who had groomed me for the movement, when it came down to seeing me in danger, was not able to handle that." As much as he had trained her to bravely oppose injustice, he could not let her go south for fear that she might be hurt, or worse.[58]

Rev. Hall was a "very sheltering father," particularly when it came to the safety of his children, though Hall never discerned gender bias in his protective nature—she felt that she and her sisters were raised no differently than her brother. She believed that her father's affection for her—as the oldest child and as the child most like him—was the main reason his rules for her were so strict. Rev. Hall hoped his son would continue his ministry legacy, but Berkeley Jr., the second born and only son, did not share his father's hopes. Recognizing Prathia's maturity and giftedness, Rev. Hall groomed her, in part, as the son he never had. Indeed, Berkeley Jr. was the only Hall child *not* to become a pastor. Later in life, Berkeley Jr. did express a sense of call and an adamant desire to run from it.[59]

In 1958 Hall enrolled in Temple University, a fifteen-minute walk from her family home. She majored in political science and minored in religion. She attended from 1958 to 1961 but withdrew in the summer of 1960, reenrolling later. Low grades placed Hall on academic probation in June 1959 and again in June 1961.⁶⁰ Throughout her time at Temple, Hall remained active in the FH college group, founded by Joyce Barrett. That group met weekly across the city but focused its efforts on work in North Philadelphia, particularly with children.⁶¹

Hall would later reflect that her parents taught her that a right relationship with God meant that death would never sneak up on you. According to Hall, in October 1959, her father became seriously ill, during which time he said to his children, "I have walked through the valley and the shadow of death. I made it through the summer, but the winter will take me home." Asked why he said that, Rev. Hall responded: "Because the Lord came for me. But I asked for time to set some business in order for you and your children and your mother. But I am on my way home."⁶²

Rev. Hall was driving his 1949 Cadillac in North Philadelphia when a trolley car hit him in early February 1960. Though the particulars are unclear, somehow the accident ejected Hall from his vehicle, after which he was dragged by the trolley for several blocks and was completely underneath the trolley by the time police and other emergency workers arrived on the scene. Desperate for her father to recover, Prathia stayed by his bedside at Temple University Hospital until her mother told her that she had to let her father go. He died shortly after Prathia said good-bye, less than a week after the accident. Her father's death was extremely difficult for her, and she never fully recovered from this loss.⁶³

Reading news about the February 1, 1960, sit-ins at Greensboro, North Carolina, intensified Prathia's desire to join the movement in the South, an effect felt by many others who eventually joined SNCC. Grief of losing her father compounded with this powerful student activism gave Hall the sign to go. Howard Zinn, then professor at Spelman College, a black women's college in Atlanta, and an adult advisor on the executive board of SNCC, echoed: "For so many in SNCC, the Greensboro sit-in—more than the Supreme Court decision, more than the Little Rock crisis, more than the Montgomery Bus Boycott, more than the recent declarations of independence by a host of African nations—was a turning point in their lives." Similar demonstrations erupted nationwide after Greensboro: "The sit-ins had begun a new phase of the Negro upsurge, in which students—matured overnight into social revolutionaries—started to play the leading role. These same students, in the brutal training ground of the Freedom Rides, became toughened, experienced."⁶⁴

Hall later reflected on how the movement filled the hole in her life left by her father's death: "The movement was the healthiest, the most therapeutic thing for my grief."[65] As much as she would have liked to share her movement activism with her father, she knew how difficult it would have been for him to see her in jail or to know she was in danger. Difficult as her father's death was, its timing at the beginning of the student movement gave her the freedom to pursue activism without reservation.

Having closely followed the student-led Civil Rights Movement and energized by its momentum, a team from FH—Joyce Barrett, Marjorie Penney, and Claire Maier—traveled to Raleigh, North Carolina, in April 1960 for a meeting led by King's Southern Christian Leadership Conference (SCLC), at King's invitation, on the topic of students in the movement. His speech at this meeting echoed his lessons from FH: "I believe with all my heart that the prejudiced mind of America can become a kind and loving mind if enough of us are willing to sacrifice and suffer for it. I believe that every man has a heart and conscience and can be reached, and we will never stop trying to reach them, no matter what they do to us. All the great turning points of history have been made by small, determined groups, and I am grateful that my life has been set down at this time and under these circumstances."[66]

FH had financed the journey to Raleigh for Barrett, Penney, and Maier, eagerly awaiting news from the southern movement, including its "insight and real wisdom as to how to proceed in the battle for human rights, using love as a weapon." While in Raleigh, the three heard moving testimonies from student sit-in veterans, and Barrett visited five campuses where sit-ins had occurred. They even recruited some of the SCLC workers to visit FH. Their trip extended beyond King's meeting to include eight days of touring civil rights projects throughout the Atlantic states of the Deep South—North Carolina, South Carolina, and Georgia.[67]

At this meeting during Easter weekend 1960, the Student Nonviolent Coordinating Committee (SNCC) formed. Certain that they wanted to join SNCC as soon as they could, Hall and Barrett stayed in correspondence with several of the SNCC workers they had met at SNCC's founding. They kept FH up to date with the movement in the South and coordinated northern efforts to help SNCC.[68]

Hall had a difficult time concentrating on her Temple University classes because "the pull of the Southern movement upon [her] heart was so powerful." Nevertheless, she remained at Temple until she finished her coursework in 1962, even taking a few seminary classes in her senior year. Temple would not award her bachelor's degree until 1965, however, because of a dispute over one credit hour.[69]

Since Hall could not yet join SNCC's work, she took advantage of opportunities for nonviolent demonstrations through FH. She participated in integration demonstrations at local department stores and other locations across Philadelphia. She contributed to FH's support of the movement, most notably its Kingsway campaign—promoting nonviolent social justice activism through sit-ins, boycotts, and other justice-conscious civil disobedience.[70] She also collaborated with students from the Congress of Racial Equality (CORE) to join weekend Freedom Rides to the Eastern Shore of Maryland for demonstrations.

When the Philadelphia Commission on Human Relations received complaints about racial discrimination in the city, they would often ask FH students to "test" the location, report their findings, and be available as witnesses if the incident moved into litigation. FH first sent white students to the location, then a group of black students, then another group of white students, to assess whether the business in question discriminated against black patrons. For example, in October 1960, the Chez-Vous skating rink in Upper Darby in Delaware County denied entry to an FH group, permitting only white skaters with membership cards to skate. Barrett challenged the inconsistency of this rule since white nonmembers were regularly admitted. The group of nine sat-in in the rink lobby reading aloud from the Bible and from the works of Gandhi and King until they were permitted to skate. The rink's patrons fled as the group entered, and many of the demonstrators reported being tripped, shoved, or otherwise harassed in the lobby.[71]

Hall picketed with FH at Woolworth's and Cresky's stores. They met at FH prior to each demonstration to practice nonviolence techniques: picketing, shielding their bodies, falling safely, and not responding to hateful insults.[72]

After the 1960 SCLC conference, FH had remained in communication with King, who agreed to speak at FH's thirtieth anniversary celebration, October 22–24, 1961. Hall and a select group of college students joined him for a question-and-answer session on October 22, at which King defended civil disobedience as a foundational principle in U.S. history.[73] FH organized study groups and issued press releases, radio and television advertisements, and over twenty thousand copies of materials on Kingsway of nonviolence. King received warm hospitality in Philadelphia, including an official resolution of the city council welcoming him to the city. Mayor Richardson Dilworth declared October 23, 1961, to be Kingsway Day.[74] Religious, civic, and educational organizations collaborated to promote and attend the event, and the influx of phone calls and correspondence to FH following King's visit suggests that these three days were significant in promoting awareness of racial justice throughout the city.[75]

On the weekends, Hall and other FH students traveled to Baltimore—Freedom Rides—to stage demonstrations at segregated restaurants.[76] CORE and Juanita Jackson Mitchell of the Baltimore NAACP organized hundreds of college students along the Eastern Shore to sit in. Students dressed "properly" for the demonstrations: men in ties, and women in dresses, hats, and gloves.[77]

To justify arresting demonstrators, Maryland state officials drafted a statement that restaurant owners were required to read aloud to desegregation demonstrators. In order for someone to be arrested, the owners had to ask demonstrators to leave, and the demonstrators had to audibly refuse to leave. Barrett later joked that demonstrators would often select restaurants owned by non-English speakers so that they could not be arrested, or the demonstrators would read the statement on the owners' behalf. Those who wanted to be arrested stayed for the reading, while those who were not prepared for arrest would advance to the next restaurant.[78]

On November 11, 1961, police arrested Hall and ten other demonstrators for sitting in at Barnes' Drive-In Restaurant in Annapolis. This was the first of a series of demonstrations held on November 11 along U.S. Route 40 in Annapolis, Baltimore, and Ferndale, designed to force Maryland's governor to push for desegregation of all public facilities.[79] Twenty-two others, including future SNCC leader Stokely Carmichael, were arrested for making "the rounds of restaurants refusing service to Negroes" and released November 12 on $157 bail a head for trespassing and disorderly conduct. Hall was released on $100 bail alongside seven others awaiting their requested jury trial, while Diana King, Joyce Barrett, and Larsine Sirizotti refused bail, opting to remain in Arundel County Jail. Antisegregation leaders met a few days later at Cornerstone Baptist Church to plan subsequent demonstrations for continued pressure against segregation in Maryland.[80] Hall described this as her "baptism and initiation into the movement of nonviolent direct action," after which she and others continued to support the student movement and conduct local demonstrations.[81]

Another interesting presence in these November 11 arrests was *Afro-*

American reporter Elizabeth Oliver, who had been with the demonstrators at the restaurant but left before the anti-trespass "readout." Oliver's coverage of the events included detailed accounts of dialogue between restaurant staff, police, and the demonstrators. Despite her having identified herself as a reporter on multiple occasions, police required that she produce documentation, not believing a black woman could be a reporter. The restaurant owner demanded she be arrested for violating the anti-trespass law, even though as a member of the press she should have been permitted to be on the scene. She and the nine student demonstrators filled their cell with the sounds of freedom songs. Within ten minutes of being jailed, Oliver was released on $24 bond, her story ended. "When I left, they were still singing."[82]

On November 16, Hall spoke on behalf of the demonstrators at the FH board meeting, as reported in the meeting minutes of the board of directors:

> *Fellowshippers in Jail*: Prathia Hall, attractive and eloquent member of our College-Agers, gave a most moving recital of the sit-in protest on the Governor Richie Highway leading to Annapolis, State Capitol of Maryland. Like [the demonstrations along] Route 40, African diplomats, as well as Negro Americans, have suffered humiliation and even arrest when they protested discrimination in restaurants. Nineteen of our College-Agers, well trained in non-violent protests and fired by Dr. King's mission here, took part in the demonstration. Nine voluntarily went to jail remaining from Saturday through Monday, four refusing to take bail remain in the Anne Arundel County Prison. Two, already noted, have served fourteen days. Their cheerful, courteous, helpful behavior has won sheriff, jailors and police. Their continued presence in the jail has hurt the conscience of the whole community, beginning with the Governor. Citizens, white and colored in Annapolis, have come to call and stayed to learn about the deep convictions and happy self-giving of our young people. She reminded us that this is Joyce's 22nd birthday. A telegram to the prisoners was approved by the Board. All legal proceedings are being handled by Leon Higginbotham, Esquire, whose praise for the conduct and appearance of our students is very warm. A question period concluded the meeting, with thanks to Prathia Hall, whose words had moved many of our members to tears.[83]

On November 20, the eight arrested, including Hall, opted to wage a hunger strike.[84] The jailers were perturbed that the young women would not post bail because they wanted to remain in order to paint the cell where they were staying in the spirit of nonviolence and reconciliation. Having received permission from Sheriff Joseph W. Alton, they chose a light green.[85] A newspaper photograph showed the women smiling from their jail cell window.[86]

Hall remained in jail a total of two weeks, long after the paint was dry. Her mother called Marjorie Penney, concerned that Prathia was missing too many of her Temple classes and eager for Penney's assistance in Prathia's release. Penney's response did little to reassure: "You know, Mrs. Hall, your daughter is a very stubborn woman. And she has made a decision, and she's taking a stand, and she doesn't want bail posted for her. You'll have a hard time convincing her that she should be in class."[87]

Hall and several other students came to trial in mid-December for the November 11 demonstrations in Annapolis. A. Leon Higginbotham Jr. (Philadelphia NAACP) and Juanita Jackson Mitchell (Baltimore NAACP) represented the students in Anne Arundel County Circuit Court, arguing the unconstitutionality of their arrests. Chief Judge Benjamin Michaelson insisted on hearing evidence before issuing his decision. When the defendants requested a jury trial, Higginbotham questioned each juror about their views of "whites associating with Negroes" and "prejudice against the students because they were from out of state," since objections to both had escalated local bias against the demonstrators. The exclusively male, white jury deliberated less than fifteen minutes before convicting them in December 1961 for trespassing. Higginbotham immediately announced plans for appeal, and Judge Michaelson released the demonstrators on $50 dollars bond.[88] Eventually, the appeal was dismissed with the passage of civil rights legislation in 1964 and 1965, which negated the validity of the arrest.

At some point either that year or the next, Hall and Barrett were among student activists arrested on the Eastern Shore by state police at a chain fast-food restaurant along Route 40. Police released those arrested the next morning. Barrett suspected that the restaurant had demonstrators arrested to quickly remove them from the premises, then dropped charges the next day to avoid the hassle of prosecuting. As was true with many civil rights arrests and trials, there is no known legal record of the case.[89]

"I had been born to struggle"

Even as Hall knew deep within her that she was called to join the Civil Rights Movement, and once the completion of her college education gave her the opportunity to go, she agonized about disobeying her father's last directive to stay away from the danger of the movement. Rev. Leon Sullivan, a major Philadelphia religious leader and director of the Opportunities Industrialization Center, located around the corner from Hall's family home, counseled her that she could best honor her father's memory by faithfully obeying God's call, even if that meant going south. Sullivan told her, "Prathia, you've got to remember that your father died that you might live." She later reflected, "I didn't understand that at the time and I didn't want to understand it.... I wanted to tell Leon Sullivan a few things I wouldn't have been allowed to say."[90]

Rev. Hall was, as Prathia describes him, "a race man." Their home was often filled with conversations on racial advancement and the ideas of well-known speakers such as Howard Thurman and Adam Clayton Powell. His teachings on racial pride, the African American connection with African heritage, and the integration of religion and politics shaped her understanding of racial and theological identity. From her father, Prathia first came to understand what she later called Freedom Faith. Rev. Hall taught his daughter that God intended all human beings to be free and equips and assists them as they work for freedom. For Rev. Hall, this specifically meant that slavery and Jim Crow segregation were contrary to God's will, and that God was on the side of those opposing these systems of political and economic oppression. In contrast to the traditional Western separation of religion and politics, Prathia was mentored by her father's celebration of the black church tradition, "in harmony with the African worldview," which "understood them to be profoundly integrated.... Faith and freedom were woven together in the fabric of life."[91]

The cumulative influence of her father, the Greensboro sit-ins, her experience with nonviolent demonstrations through FH, and Sullivan's counsel empowered Hall to make her decision to throw in with the movement: "I couldn't help myself. This was the moment. Greensboro was the signal. It was 1960. That's what you're supposed to be doing. It was a part of that knowing, knowing God as I knew myself. And knowing that I had been born to struggle. And that this was everything that I believed in. That it was God's work. That it was God's Movement, and that I had to go." The Civil Rights Movement was a natural, necessary manifestation of her faith, both push and pull: "I think the reality of the problem was a pulling force.... We were taught that it was our job to make a difference.... But then there is a driving force also, and I think that faith is 'I feel God's fist in my back.' I don't have a choice, I have to do that."[92]

In spite of the dangers that lay ahead in the South, she felt destined for the movement. Her experiences growing up in North Philadelphia, attending predominantly white schools, learning nonviolent demonstration through FH, and the tutelage of her father steeped her in the philosophical, theological, and practical realities of social justice activism and uniquely equipped her for the movement. She later reflected: "I was convinced that [the movement] was God's work and also my sacred calling, and so I went south."[93]

CHAPTER 2

"LIVING IN THE FACE OF DEATH"

"Together, hub and spokes drove the wheel"

Building on her father's formational mentoring, FH had offered Hall her first organizational experience with practicing Freedom Faith. FH's eventual relationship with SNCC presented Hall with even greater opportunities for living out the tenets of Freedom Faith. A brief history of SNCC and its role in the Albany movement before Hall joined SNCC in 1962 will set the stage for Hall's journey to the South, where she quickly became one of the top leaders in Albany.

The Student Nonviolent Coordinating Committee (SNCC), founded Easter weekend in 1960 at Shaw University in Raleigh, North Carolina, organized voter registration and nonviolent direct action in conjunction with local activists and organizations. Though Martin Luther King Jr. also spoke at the Raleigh meeting, Rev. James Lawson had the students' ears.[1] That weekend Lawson—the first black divinity student at Vanderbilt University in Nashville, Tennessee, where he was later denied graduation because of his activism—also drafted the purpose statement of SNCC,

25

rooted in Judeo-Christian nonviolence, social justice, love, and redemption.[2] SNCC affirmed the importance and potential of everyone in the struggle for justice. Headquartered in Atlanta, SNCC initially had delegates from several Deep South and East Coast states.[3]

The difference between Martin Luther King Jr.'s Southern Christian Leadership Conference (SCLC), which typically led short-term campaigns, and SNCC, whose workers moved into communities for long-term voter registration drives, was commonly described as "SCLC mobilized, but SNCC organized." SCLC worked within existing structures, whereas SNCC operated via democratic leadership. SNCC cooperated with SCLC demonstrations, but many SNCC personnel resented King's sense of authority over local movement leaders and volunteers, assigning him nicknames such as Da Lawd. SNCC also resented the attention white media gave to King's work rather than to the hundreds of local volunteers who made the movement a national success. Ella Baker was an ideal SCLC mentor for SNCC because she refused to tolerate inflated self-importance, undemocratic processes, and hierarchy; when SCLC suggested SNCC be a "youth wing" of SCLC, Baker walked out of the meeting.[4] King enjoyed the enthusiasm of the young workers in SNCC and regularly contributed financially to the group as well as encouraged them spiritually.

When SNCC first organized, one of its primary strategies was voter registration in the so-called Black Belt: rural counties, formerly plantation lands, where black citizens outnumbered whites, and where most congressional representatives had great power from long tenures in office. (In 1960, there were three black members of Congress, all in the House of Representatives.) If black people could vote senior congressional representatives out of office, they could very quickly change the dynamic of Congress and its committees.[5]

What came to be known as the Albany movement coordinated voter registration and freedom schools in several rural counties across Southwest Georgia. SNCC field secretaries canvassed door-to-door asking black people to register to vote, which involved the legal process of going to the county office as well as localized intimidation tactics designed to prohibit successful voter registration. The largest city in Southwest Georgia was Albany, the seat of Dougherty County. Most black citizens worked as sharecroppers on land owned and economically benefitting white people. According to a SNCC survey of black residents in Terrell County, the average black family earned less than one-fourth of the average white household income in the county, and less than one-fifth of the national household income. Twenty-five percent of black adults had less than a sixth-grade education. In 1960, black people comprised 64.4 percent of the population of Terrell County yet represented only 0.04 percent of voters.[6] Forty percent of Albany's population of 56,000 were black, residing in a part of town known as Harlem. The key to Albany was its centrality to several surrounding counties, where black people outnumbered whites three times or more. Sherrod compared the Albany project to Ezekiel's wheel within a wheel, from the biblical book of the prophet Ezekiel. Albany was the center, organizing work in surrounding counties: "Together, hub and spokes drove the wheel."[7]

Three Freedom Riders arrived in Albany in October 1961 to begin SNCC's project there. Charles Sherrod led SNCC's work in Albany, working closely with Cordell Reagon and Charlie Jones. Historian Ray Arsenault argued that wherever the Freedom Riders landed in late summer and early fall of 1961, they spread the spirit of nonviolence, kindling local black support for civil rights efforts and creating "an interlocking chain of movement centers" throughout the South. At the same time, some locals avoided them, fearful of white retaliation for supporting SNCC's work. Sherrod recognized this fear and developed a strategy: "Many of the ministers were afraid to let us use their churches, afraid that their churches would be bombed, that their homes would be stoned. There was fear in the air, and if we were to progress we knew that we must cut through that fear. We thought and we thought... and the students were the answer."[8] Sherrod recruited students from Albany State University (ASU) to join them.

The Albany movement officially formed on November 17, 1961, as a cooperative effort among the local Baptist Ministers' Alliance, Federated Women's Clubs, Lincoln Heights Improvement Association, NAACP Youth Council, SNCC, ASU students, and other local supporters, including several Albany gang members. The early leaders of the Albany movement included President Dr. William G. Anderson, an osteopathic physician; Vice President Slater King, a realtor; and Legal Counselors Mario Page, a retired railroad worker, and C. B. King, an attorney.[9]

In particular, the King family, no relation to Rev. Dr. Martin Luther King, and the Harris family of Albany played significant roles in supporting the movement. Rev. Isaiah Harris, a local pastor, and his family often housed civil rights workers, and his church was a major hub of the Albany movement.[10] Not only were both of these families community leaders, but they regularly spent time encouraging SNCC workers to persist in their work, offering a ministry of presence and solidarity throughout the movement. Hall described the King family women as "phenomenal." Their loving support created a safe haven for the students: "The spirit of struggle was continuously strengthened and invigorated in all of us whenever we visited Mama King, mother and wisdom-bearer for the community, and especially for those of us far from home and the counselor of our own mothers and mamas and grandmothers."[11]

The Albany movement became the first massive black "uprising" since Montgomery in 1955. As Howard Zinn assessed, "it represented a permanent turn from the lunch counter and the bus terminal to the streets, from hit-and-run attacks by students and professional civil rights workers to populist rebellion by lower-class Negroes." Most importantly, the Albany movement spotlighted the reluctance of the federal government "to protect constitutional rights in the Deep South," as demonstrated through the mass arrests and the repeated failure of the government to intervene to protect civil rights workers from discrimination or even physical harm.[12]

With a sit-in to test the November 1961 Interstate Commerce Commission ruling against segregated public transportation, several SNCC workers and ASU students were arrested on November 22 and held over the Thanksgiving holiday, which bolstered community support.[13] More than seven hundred were arrested the following week in various demonstrations against the December 10 arrests of twelve students sitting in at the Central of Georgia Railroad terminal in Albany.[14] Forty black ASU students were suspended or expelled from the university in December 1961 for participation in antisegregation demonstrations, while zero white University of Georgia students were punished for participating in resistance activities in the same period. Attorney C. B. King represented the students.

Albany movement leaders offered to end demonstrations in exchange for desegregation of the bus station and release of those arrested, but Albany city leaders refused. The Albany movement continued demonstrations and boycotts, and arrests continued.[15] Approximately 150 National Guardsmen, ordered by Georgia governor Ernest Vandiver, and twenty state highway patrol officers were on duty to prevent retaliatory violence, particularly after reports that Slater King had been beaten in jail and that Charles Sherrod had been "brutally beaten" at a Terrell County prison farm.[16]

Martin Luther King Jr. was invited to speak at a December 15, 1961, Albany movement mass meeting, where he addressed fifteen hundred people in three services at two churches. King insisted that protests remain nonviolent.[17] City leaders refused negotiations with any of the civil rights leaders in Albany, and continued demonstrations led to massive arrests: 749 since December 10 (less than one week), a national record for people willingly arrested for civil rights protests.[18] SCLC wanted to assume leadership of the Albany movement, which deeply troubled SNCC.[19] SCLC, SNCC, and local civil rights leaders from Albany disagreed about strategy, which was the first time conflict between civil rights groups had "been aired in public."[20]

By the end of January 1962, the Albany movement implemented a boycott of city buses and white-owned businesses.[21] In early February, SNCC filed for an injunction against officials of the City of Dawson and Terrell County for interfering with voter registration attempts.[22] Although President John F. Kennedy issued a statement in support of civil rights and federal enforcement of civil rights laws later that year, Albany law enforcement circumvented such initiatives by arresting demonstrators "fast, quietly, and on non-racial charges," revealing flaws in the Department of Justice's "overvalue [of] public order."[23]

Police harassed and assaulted voter registration workers in the streets and in jail, but SNCC continued canvassing for voter registration throughout Albany, even expanding into nearby Lee and Terrell Counties. SNCC recruited teachers for freedom schools, to prepare people to successfully pass voter registration exams. SNCC also networked with community leaders for canvassing and mass meetings, seeking new potential registered voters as well as additional support for the Albany movement in spite of injunctions against demonstrations in Albany.[24]

Albany police chief Laurie Pritchett used a violent outbreak on July 24, 1962, in the Harlem neighborhood of Albany to promote his accusation that racial tension in Georgia was exclusively the fault of "Negroes" and, sarcastically, their "nonviolent rocks." King declared July 25 a day of penance. While raising awareness of police brutality toward civil rights workers, King announced that if nonviolence was not restored, SCLC would leave Albany.[25]

Table 1. Voter Registration in Daugherty, Sumter, Terrell, and Lee Counties, 1963

Voter Registration Demographic	Daugherty	Sumter	Terrell	Lee
Population total	75,680	24,652	12,742	6,204
African American Population (% of total)	27,245 (36%)	13,016 (52.8%)	8,206 (64.4%)	3,890 (62.7%)
Eligible African American Registered (% of African Americans)	2,850 (10.4%)	501 (3.8%)	51 (0.06%)	49 (1.3%)
Median Family Income—All	$4,401	$2,950	$2,057	$2,434
Median Family Income—Nonwhite	$2,430	$1,598	$1,313	$1,648
Median Grade Level Completed—All	10.5	8.4	7.6	6.9
Median Grade Level Completed—Nonwhite	5.9	5.0	4.5	4.0

Source: "Survey: Field Work, Spring 1963," SNCC Papers, reel 10.

By late August, with few marchers still available and little hope for federal intervention, demonstrations waned. SCLC left Albany, but SNCC persevered. Albany's white city leaders remained unwilling to negotiate with civil rights workers and persisted in arresting demonstrators, deploying the language of maintaining peace and public order to justify its actions.

"We spent long hours on those porches"

In the spring of 1962, while still a student at Temple, Prathia Hall told her mother that she wanted to join SNCC's work in the South. Ruby begged her daughter to get a "real job," to be a teacher. Finally, she relented: "Well, since you must go, God go with you. God keep you as you go." Prathia realized how difficult her work in the South would be for her mother: "I will always be grateful to her for that because she understood that it wasn't a choice, that I had to go."[26]

Hall went to a SNCC conference in April 1962 at the Interdenominational Theological Center in Atlanta. She vividly remembered seeing Ella Baker, Julian Bond, Ruby Doris Smith, and Bill Strickland. Hall reflected: "[The conference] was a powerful learning experience for me. I was tremendously inspired, went home really fired up knowing that I would be back just as soon as I could manage it."[27] As Hall moved into her senior year of college, she began coursework at Conwell School of Theology, then affiliated with Temple, "and struggled for the discipline to finish college before going south to join the movement in full time service."[28] Having finished her coursework at Temple, in late August 1962 Hall moved to Georgia. A Temple colleague whose family was also traveling south agreed to drive her, and she "just showed up" at SNCC's Atlanta office, unannounced.[29]

The first person Hall met was Julian Bond, head of SNCC communications. He arranged for her to stay at his mother's house for her first week. Hall appreciated Julia Bond, "a kind and gracious woman who seemed utterly unperturbed by the prospect of a stranger as a houseguest." Hall also met James Forman, Ruby Doris Smith, and other SNCC leaders. She had the opportunity to learn about SNCC's origins, operations, and current projects in which she might become involved. Hall remembered that "Jim and Ruby Doris were serious and sobering in their recitation of the facts of the SNCC experiences and their forthright exploration of the dangers, discomforts, and difficulties of work in the field. Yet their excitement and pride were as clearly evident as their courage and commitment."[30]

Charles Sherrod was also in Atlanta, organizing volunteers for SNCC's Albany project.[31] In Hall's second week in Atlanta, Sherrod recruited her to work on that project with him and Charlie Jones, both seminary graduates. Hall's transition from Philadelphia to Atlanta to Albany was seamless because, as she said, moving from one space to another was "all very natural" for her. She did not feel a "great moment of decision" regarding where to go and which projects to join but instead knew "it was in me." Hall delighted in working with ministers, but she continued to wrestle with her own calling: "I said very little about my own theological journey, however, since I was trying desperately to escape or evade the call to ministry."[32]

That summer of 1962, Hall found camaraderie among the SNCC staff in Southwest Georgia since many were also college students from the North recruited by Sherrod and Jones. Describing them in draft materials for a book about the project, Hall revealed the depth of her knowledge of her colleagues: "exuberant and intelligent Peggy Dammond from Boston; intense, creative and cerebral Kathleen Conwell from New York; quietly thoughtful Faith Holsaert from Brooklyn, who arrived in September; loquacious and determined Ralph Allen and his friend from Trinity College, Hartford, Jack Chatfield, the one with a passion for inquiry."[33]

By summer 1963, the circa two dozen SNCC Albany staff included a variety of student workers, students from ASU, young people from Albany, and college students from the North, both black and white. The 1961 Freedom Rides were biracial, which local people met with intensified violent resistance. Sherrod believed that if the beloved community—the Roycian concept amplified and popularized by Martin Luther King Jr.—would be racially reconciled, then SNCC should model this integration no matter the danger: "We can only do this if they see white and black working together, side by side, the white man no more and no less than his black brother, but human beings together."[34] Beyond theology, Sherrod had a specific, ingenious motivation for integrating SNCC. If white college students came south, they would bring their parents' financial support and national media attention with them, making voter registration a form of direct action.[35] Hall agreed: "As far as I was concerned, voter registration was direct action.... On the field, it was the same struggle."[36]

SNCC's Albany office was in a modest three-bedroom apartment at 504 South Madison Street, which multitasked as Albany movement headquarters and housing for a few SNCC workers.[37] Hall described the Albany freedom house as "not much of anything... sparsely furnished... people sleeping everywhere."[38] Male staff shared a "musty fold-out couch" in the living room, and female staff slept on a bed and cot in the back bedroom.[39] The modest and close quarters fostered collegiality among the workers, as Pete DeLissovoy affirmed. Giles Grocery donated canned food to the movement so that they would not boycott his store, and Sherrod would rip the labels off of the cans, "otherwise everybody'd eat the lasagna up first and all, all that's left is the string beans!" They never had a lot of food, but they always had enough.[40]

SNCC field secretaries, also known as field-workers, received "subsistence" income, anywhere from $15 to $40 per week; the members of the Southwest Georgia team each received $10 per week, $9.64 after deductions, and sometimes nothing at all.⁴¹ Many weeks, in order to buy food, SNCC workers earned money by "washing cars, dishes, floors, and windows, cutting grass, or any other chore around the house."⁴² When donated cars failed, a recurring problem in Southwest Georgia, SNCCers walked or rode mules.⁴³

The Albany movement prioritized voter registration over direct action, though they organized both. As Hall explained, the rationale behind this refocusing was based on local conditions: "We soon discovered that [lunch counter desegregation] was not where it was at. Then we went into the Black Belt with voter registration. The people there couldn't eat at lunch counters because they were only making twenty-three cents an hour. That was where it was at."⁴⁴

In going door-to-door to talk with local people about registering to vote, field secretaries built trust by acknowledging the physical, social, and economic consequences for attempting to register: "We'd sit sometimes and rock on the porch for hours. Our intention was to finally convince a person to go and register. But we'd sit and listen." Some houses sent the students away, their residents "paralyzed by fear," though "always gracious." Others wanted to know about the SNCC workers and their family backgrounds. Hall found that the local people eventually welcomed SNCC workers, based on earned trust: "After several visits, the fearful and the skeptical usually allowed us to come in or to sit on their porches and visit. The topic of the imminent danger soon made its way into the conversation. They told us of people who had 'just come up missing' or had been found floating in the river after some minor assertion of personhood or an infraction such as trying to register to vote."⁴⁵ She felt at ease engaging southerners in conversation because she "knew the church upside down" due to her heavily churched upbringing. About visiting people in their homes, she said "it was very easy for me to function very normally."⁴⁶

Hall also observed that SNCC workers "greatly respected that these people had been there all the time, and they weren't waiting for us to come in and save them." Long before SNCC "ever thought about coming south . . . they had been coping with the system themselves, by themselves, without a movement." The local people had weathered and survived the Jim Crow system for years. By the time that SNCC, which some communities called the "freedom people," arrived, "some people in that community had been waiting . . .

they were ready."[47] She appreciated the "two-way educational exchange" of voter registration canvassing:

> We spent long hours on those porches. It took a long time. You didn't just walk up to somebody and convince them to register to vote and take their life in their hands. And so you talk to a person sometimes two weeks before ... the time was right even to broach the subject. But during that time, we had the information about political empowerment, voter registration, literacy.... They had the wisdom of the ages. And that's what we received. And this was especially true in my experience in Southwest Georgia, and I'm so glad that I really had that before getting involved in the cities.[48]

As SNCC workers sat on porches "learning from these people who worked from sun up to sun down ... who suffered poverty and bigotry and brutality and never let it break them," Hall saw the student activists as the "primary beneficiaries of the process, and that we were privileged to be there."[49]

Those who feared voter registration, or even association with SNCC workers, understood the "entrenched white supremacy backed up by violence" that ruled Southwest Georgia.[50] Since whites controlled most employment, housing, and utilities infrastructure, attempting to register to vote almost always catalyzed intimidation tactics, ranging anywhere from threatened or actual job or property loss, significantly higher utility bills, to physical harm. Depending on the municipality, voting officials could unilaterally and subjectively charge exorbitant poll taxes on black people, require them to pass difficult exams in U.S. history, or draw out the process by requiring a two-week waiting period between registration and eligibility to vote, in the meantime printing in the local newspaper the names of all who registered to vote. Many prospective black voters lost their jobs or suffered destruction of their personal property and homes by merely attempting to register to vote, so asking a black person to register to vote was tantamount to asking them to risk everything. SNCC workers, too, took their lives in their hands to live interracially and promote civil rights.[51]

To circumvent these intimidation tactics, SNCC implemented freedom schools to help potential voters pass voter registration exams. Since sharecroppers had to meet daily quotas before they could go home, many SNCC workers worked alongside sharecroppers to meet their quotas so they could attend evening freedom school meetings.

"A woman who could absolutely magnetize a mass meeting"

When Hall arrived in Albany in late summer 1962, the Albany movement was "in full swing."[52] She and Sherrod were instantly kindred spirits. They frequently discussed the work of theologians like Martin Buber and Paul Tillich.[53] Their shared commitments to social justice, education, and Christian leadership helped them form a strong bond, which Sherrod described as "closer than boy and girl friend." Carolyn Daniels recalled a special connection between the two: "Sherrod was a minister. And the two of them could communicate, you know. So they would always be ... doing their little thing." For his part, Sherrod described Hall's contribution in Albany: "She was a beautiful person, in more than one way. She was smart. She could write. She was tactical."[54]

Hall and Sherrod keyed into the pastoral nature of SNCC's work, particularly its long-term strategy: "It was a life process ... it was important that the first thing was that we lived with the people. This is one of the primary distinguishing factors between SNCC and SCLC. This is the difference between mobilizing and organizing. And the kind of organizing that we had to do ... is that we lived with the people." Through canvassing, SNCC workers discovered the educational and practical needs of black communities, cooperating with community organizations and leaders to try to meet those needs.[55]

The respect that secular black leaders and SNCC workers had for the faith of local communities impressed Hall: "Everyone was impacted by the faith that the people had. Their courage was so much a product of that faith, and what makes people able to face death as a fact of life." Seeing the oppressive conditions that black people had long endured drew civil rights workers not only into an aspect of respect but "even [gave them] a sense of participation. ... After all, they were facing death, and drew from the deep well of strength and struggle that was already present in the people." The religious vitality of local communities "enriched" the entire community and sustained workers in the midst of potentially life-threatening opposition.[56]

Although Sherrod was the leader of SNCC's work in Southwest Georgia, Hall played a vital role. When Sherrod was out of town, which was not infrequent by 1963, Hall served as leader. Sherrod trusted her implicitly in that role, later reflecting that "I can think of nobody who didn't respect Prathia

Hall."[57] Whereas some of the staff occasionally experienced tension with Sherrod, Hall enjoyed good relations and wide esteem with staff.[58] When SNCC veteran Sheila Michaels mentioned Hall's reputation as a coleader with Sherrod, Hall modestly replied: "Really? I didn't think that. I didn't know that."[59] Similarly, at Ella Baker's funeral, a male SNCC colleague told Hall, "We would have followed you anywhere you told us to go. That's how we respected you." Hall's laughing response was "had I only known!"[60] Her significance was well-documented, however, as her name often appeared above or alongside Sherrod's in SNCC correspondence.[61] Indeed, historian Vincent Harding lists Prathia Hall with Bob Moses, Charles Sherrod, and Bob Zellner as leaders of the modern Civil Rights Movement who inspired and empowered thousands to realize their capability to change the world.[62]

Hall earned wide recognition for her preaching abilities. Even when she was a young twentysomething in the movement, Hall's peers quickly identified her uncharacteristically mature preaching abilities and spiritual leadership. Valuing those skills, Sherrod frequently selected her to speak on behalf of the Southwest Georgia project and for fund-raising. He described her ability: "She spoke well. She went to talk with people well. She recruited other students to work with us very well. She did everything well. She was a great speaker. [Although] Little known to the world, she would awe Martin Luther King Jr. down there in Southwest Georgia she spoke so well."[63]

Many of Hall's SNCC colleagues who were not religious nonetheless felt spiritual stirrings around her; something about her oration and demeanor invited them into the presence of God. Faith Holsaert, from a nominally Jewish family, was "blown away" by Hall's preaching, which she found to be "of a caliber and intensity and seriousness comparable" to major movement speakers like Martin Luther King. While transcribing one of Hall's taped sermons from Birmingham, SNCC secretary Judy Richardson was moved to tears: "She was so powerful, even from this little tape recorder, that I started crying.... The tears started just dripping down my face.... It's an image that I will always have.... And I am not churched, so for Prathia to get to me meant a whole lot." She further described Hall as "a woman who could absolutely magnetize a mass meeting.... Such a command of the language."[64]

Even before Hall realized or responded to her own religious calling, others in her sphere saw it. Peggy Dammond Preacely recognized Hall as a pastor in the movement because of her spiritual leadership of her SNCC teammates, who in essence "were a part of her early ministry." Sherrod heartily agreed with the assessment that Hall was "already a minister. She knew more Scripture than I did." Richardson agreed that Hall had both beautiful oratory and an ability to clearly convey her pastoral vision. Childhood friend Joyce Barrett described her as a "very powerful speaker to say the least." SNCC historian Wesley Hogan described Hall as "one of the movement's most powerful young preachers" and counted her with Lawson, King, and Sherrod as leaders of the black church in the 1960s.[65]

To Holsaert, Hall's preaching was paradigm shifting: "[Sherrod] selected a female staff member, Prathia Hall, the daughter of a minister, to preach at the Albany movement's first anniversary program, a night when Dr. King spoke from the same pulpit. I was bowled over by Prathia—I had not imaged a young woman my age could possess such oratorical power."[66]

Martha Prescod Norman Noonan described Hall's sermons as "filled with humor, and at the same time, they had a depth, an unusual depth of meaning. ... It was amazing that someone that young had that level of poise and confidence and competence all together." Sherrod recalled that Hall often prayed extemporaneously at mass meetings: "She prayed a lot at meetings. Long prayers." Whenever Penny Patch would remember Hall, she would see her as "talking in a mass meeting, or saying a closing prayer." Preacely recalled another well-known feature of Hall's prayers at meetings: "Prathia would pray, and pray, and pray. And we would tease her that her name was, you know, *Prayer*-thia Hall."[67]

Mary King was particularly taken by Hall's preaching, the pacing of her words, her imagery, and her "grasp of words and their emotive power." She recalled SNCC's respect for Hall's preaching: "In SNCC, we were not interested in hierarchies, but in authenticity. So Prathia was completely accepted. And whenever she would rise to speak, everybody gave her rapt attention. She was a riveting speaker. And nobody ever would talk, whisper, or cough while she was talking. She had such a strong, powerful presence."[68]

Bob Zellner recognized Hall's commitment to Christian nonviolence and the social gospel early in the movement. He argued that her spiritual maturity gave her rapport with Martin Luther King and other ministers in the movement: "[King] was actually captivated in some ways by Prathia, because she was a woman with a voice, a woman with great power and presence. And he couldn't help but be admiring of her ability as a communicator, even as a preacher." Zellner believed that King "learned a great deal from Prathia" in developing his preaching abilities, even though she was more than a decade younger than he.[69] Wyatt Tee Walker believed King connected with Hall because of her maturity and wisdom.[70]

Hall "was like a female Dr. King, because she had such a prayerful and statuesque way of standing and being," commented Preacely. "She had a calmness about her, but she also had a fire. And when she spoke, you listened, because she had a wonderful speaking voice." Elaborating on Hall's remarkable presence, Preacely noted: "It didn't seem like anything really frightened her. It was as if she was coming from kind of an inner guidance and an inner light, and as if her spiritual house was in order."[71]

Given that Hall and Martin Luther King Jr. knew each other through Fellowship House in Philadelphia and shared similar theological and philosophical convictions about the movement, there is little surprise that King recognized Hall's giftedness as an orator and movement leader. King and Hall grew up in Atlanta and Philadelphia, respectively, as the children of preachers, and educated in predominantly white schools. They both participated in debate competitions sponsored by the Elks and Masons. They were trained for the Civil Rights Movement in similar ways by Marjorie Penney and other leaders of Fellowship House. Hall sensed her calling to ministry as a young girl but resisted a life of ministry because of the guaranteed adversity for a woman in ministry, whereas King embraced his future as a minister even as he struggled with his own faith.

Hall and King interacted on numerous occasions through the Albany project, including the first anniversary celebration in 1962, for which they were both speakers, and the 1962 prayer vigil following the church burnings in Southwest Georgia. They continued to share speaking platforms as long as Hall was in the movement.

Hall also became very close with Martin Luther King Sr., known as Daddy King, who "became a substitute father, a sustaining force in the struggle." Hall later shared the story of having lunch at the King home after worship at Ebenezer: "I remember so well one day we went to worship at his church and he invited us all back to his home for the day. He was a tough leader, a no nonsense person. I was very close to him."[72]

In most issues of its *Student Voice* newsletter, SNCC solicited financial support from civil rights sympathizers. The solicitation in the March 3, 1964, issue featured a full-page photograph of Prathia Hall standing behind a pulpit, addressing a mass meeting. The photograph, taken by SNCC photographer Danny Lyon, vividly conveyed Hall's oratorical power and the respect her SNCC colleagues had for her leadership and wisdom.[73]

When years later Holsaert and Betty Garman Robinson shared with Hall their impressions of her preaching, she responded with surprise because she did not perceive herself as conducting herself any differently in large venues than she did in her own home. Hall realized that she "had more access to the speakers' platform than others because that was [her] home territory[,] but for them it was alien territory. It was very different." Northern students in the movement, white and black, found the pulpit intimidating, but even Hall, who had grown up with the church one floor below the family's living quarters, acknowledged that for many blacks, even those with "church backgrounds, . . . their religion was much more distant from the church so they would not have ventured there quite so easily as I did." Hall laughed when asked whether she was nervous speaking before a crowd: "Oh, Lord, I'd been doing that since I was three!"[74]

Holsaert found Hall to be "extremely generous" and noted that she never felt any racial barriers in friendship between them. Holsaert also appreciated Hall's commitment to and interest in taking them to church every Sunday and guiding them in the mores of southern culture: "We should wear hose . . . and iron your clothes for Sunday church, et cetera. . . . In a way, she functioned like an older sister for me."[75] Larry Rubin, who previously met Hall through Fellowship House in Philadelphia, appreciated that "she was able to communicate with local people very, very well" and noted the authenticity with which she made nonviolence a principle for life.[76] He also mentioned how remarkable her "dignity" was for her age.[77] Many of her colleagues noted her maternal nature, even though she was the same age as they were.[78] Richardson agreed that Hall "seemed much more adult than some of us were." Rubin added: "She was rather formal in the way she conducted herself . . . old-fashioned, polite." Joyce Barrett's perception was less about Hall's behavior than about her inherent character: "She had a dignity that most people don't have. I think she was born with dignity." Her reassuring confidence made them feel safe, according to Preacely: "Prathia had that kind of prayerful way about her that you could just kind of get under her wing."[79]

SNCC cofounder Julian Bond—later a twenty-year Georgia member of

Congress and chair of the NAACP—described Hall as "more formal" and "more deliberate" than other SNCC students. He found her thoughtfulness and wisdom remarkable and characterized her as "a young Ella Baker." Hall saw herself in Ella Baker as well, although extremely modest in making this comparison. She admired Baker's leadership and courage: "I was a wandering pilgrim trying to find my identity . . . I would find myself in her." Mary King also compared Hall to Baker because of Hall's "paying close attention to what community people felt, attuned to unarticulated yearning," working with people where they were, and paying attention to what they wanted and needed.[80]

Hall's welcoming presence awed Chuck McDew: "She didn't make people feel that they were talking to a minister. She was not at all prudish." Her ability to overcome social barriers impressed him: "Prathia could match you with somebody . . . and would make you friends forever." He further explained: "These people here, and people in Georgia, would not see Prathia as being other than another good sister who was a hard worker . . . that we're all sitting at the same table."[81]

Rep. John Lewis fondly reflected on Hall. "Sometimes you would see her in a meeting, during a discussion. It seemed like she would just sit in there, not saying anything, but taking it all in, just absorbing; and sometimes in a prayerful mood." Recalling Hall's participation in SNCC executive meetings, Lewis shared: "She didn't speak a great deal, like some people. . . . She didn't just run her mouth. When she spoke out or spoke up, she had something to say. And people would listen to her." He also remembered her dramatic flair for captivating storytelling. Recalling how others saw Hall, he reported that "she was known for her commitment, her dedication, her stick-to-it-ness; for hanging in there, for never giving up or giving in." He was struck by the example Hall set for others: "[she] did not speak ill will or have bad feeling toward a fellow human being." Lewis noted her sincere modesty: "she was known for not just trying to be on the scene—be there for when the cameras were around—but [for] going into places where you didn't see a camera." Lewis saw her "without a doubt, as a leader; that she was a leader in her own right."[82]

Sherrod also admired Hall's oral abilities. "She could sing. And she could use the King's English, and get her way. She's a great speaker. . . . She wasn't just a great speaker in a mass meeting. She was a great speaker in our meetings as well. When she was getting her point—wanted to make her point, if what we needed to do or what we needed not to do, she was also great at doing that."[83]

Hall's excellence in communication and leadership wasn't the only thing to set her apart from her SNCC peers. Betty Garman Robinson said, "I was always... inspired by her presence.... She had a presence that was beyond the ordinary.... I don't know what the best word would be, but a very steady, strong, passionate, inspiring presence." Don Harris agreed that Hall had an "extraordinary presence" of "dignity" and that she had a "sense of elegance and grace" that was "very, very clear." Peggy Dammond Preacely described her as "so in charge of herself, and more assured than the rest of us."[84]

"We have not only broken the sex line, we have broken the color line"

One of the most influential aspects of Hall's leadership was her assistance in training new SNCC volunteers. She was raised in the North by parents from the South, black but educated in predominantly white schools, and familiar with the black Baptist tradition. Even though they had relocated to Philadelphia, her parents raised her according to the black, Baptist, southern culture in which they had been raised, alongside a justice-conscious, unveiled understanding of systemic racism and classism. Because of her unique background, she approached southerners respectfully rather than disdainfully. She could educate northern white college students and nonreligious or non-Christian volunteers about the nuances and idiosyncrasies of southern black culture, etiquette, and propriety to aid them in forming relationships with local people. She stressed the importance of behaving according to southern social mores, particularly details such as wearing stockings and gloves, attending church every Sunday morning, speaking politely, and finding a healthy balance between embodying the integration of the beloved community without needlessly causing a revolution against southern sensibilities. Hall understood the complexities of white northerners living in the rural, black South and wanted to ensure everyone's safety. Her tremendous insight as a northerner raised by southerners uniquely equipped her to train new student workers to survive in the rural South: "Northern people who were never told that they couldn't go anywhere, couldn't do anything, to the bathroom they wanted to or the drinking fountain or the restaurant, were not used to any restrictions. And we were in an extraordinarily dangerous world. We were in a brutally dangerous world where especially the fact that we were racially mixed was dynamite. And I did not find those kinds of restrictions irritating."[85]

Larry Rubin described the practical and historical complications of northern students doing civil rights work in the South: "We had trouble understanding each other's accents, but more than that, there was always a problem of built-in resentment and built-in feelings of differences between us—those of us from the North and the local people in the South—and that was true of black Northerners as well." Preacely, a fair-skinned black student from New York, appreciated Hall's guidance and realized the importance of modeling a new community characterized by racial equality: "We've been singing long enough about 'black and white together.' We have to practice it, live it, and as we do we make real a certain kind of dream."[86] Both saw Hall as an example of overcoming those divides.

Because Sherrod knew he was inviting attack registering voters in rural Georgia, he demanded moral excellence from his team: "They live by a strict personal discipline. No drinking. No behavior that could even give the appearance of anything but strict morality." According to an Albany press release, "Snicks" were "not allowed to smoke, drink, swear or date." Females had to wear dresses, and "low necklines [were] forbidden." SNCC workers were expected to observe the mores of the communities in which they worked, to the extent that even the nonreligious were expected to "keep the Sabbath" and attend church services. For safety reasons, no one was ever permitted to travel alone.[87]

Interracial teams were particularly careful about avoiding black males and white females sleeping under the same roof because of the physical danger this posed for black males. Faith Holsaert, a Jewish New Yorker by way of Haiti who joined the movement in mid-September 1962, recalled Sherrod's explicit "lynch prevention code," which meant she, a white female, was never to do anything to endanger black males or herself by giving even a hint of "fraternization." A SNCC field report acknowledged the significant danger to all of the workers with bringing Faith Holsaert into Terrell County: "Due to the fact that we now for the first time, we have a white woman in the county, we are in a very tense state of being. We are concerned with what the community's reaction will be, both white and black."[88]

When SNCC workers would inquire about Sherrod's strict rules, Sherrod responded, "I was trying to keep you alive." Hall defended these strict rules as essential: "We have not only broken the sex line we have broken the color line. And because of this we must live up to the highest moral standards of the community."[89] Hall was instrumental in helping northern and nonreligious SNCC workers understand and navigate southern, black, rural culture.

Sherrod initially operated via a "loving protection" of women by men, which did not work practically when women were some of SNCC's best volunteers. Hall described the revision of Sherrod's "loving protection": "It didn't work because the other thing is that when everybody was wounded, then whoever could get up first was the one who had to get up first and move, and that was just a reality." Hall later said: "Sherrod was a very strong personality. I thought that many of us were pretty strong, too, among the women. And of course Sherrod was very sheltering and of course I dealt with a sheltering daddy all my life. So I wasn't about to now be bothered by Sherrod, which is some of the jokes now that people tell about him."[90]

Some women in SNCC were upset by Sherrod's strict curfews and other rules for their conduct, to the extent that some joked that jail was "the same as being in the project down there." Hall remembered these restrictions but considered them "more as safety issues." During daylight hours, SNCC workers could travel in mixed groups, but Hall warned about nighttime: "You didn't want to be caught out there when the sun went down. And of course as we traveled in the cars, we traveled very carefully. And sometimes if you were a mixed group, the color of the driver determined who could sit up in the car if we were passed by somebody, and the others had to get down to avoid being stopped."[91]

White women in particular felt restricted by SNCC's rules, but according to Hall, "there was no way not to because the very color of your skin and living with these black people and the whole gender thing and the whole white Southern fixation on white womanhood and living with black men and all of those kinds of things placed on you restrictions of the movement." Holsaert did not observe sexism within SNCC but did feel that the limitations on her as a white woman were different from those put on black women, particularly Hall: "Prathia had a male role and skills that I certainly didn't have [laughter], and so she had the greater freedom of movement." Connie Curry,

Mary King, Dottie Zellner, and other white leaders similarly understood SNCC to be a black freedom movement in which they were welcome guests. White SNCC workers demonstrated their deference for black leadership by cooperating with the organization rather than trying to reform it.[92]

When interviewed in the early 1990s, Hall recalled tension between some of the white and black women, particularly around black men dating white women. "On a moral level," Hall affirmed that people can romantically partner with whomever they choose as long as it is by mutual assent. As a black woman, however, she saw the potential threat to the survival of the race when black men partnered with white women. Though the women of SNCC were generally on positive terms with each other, "those conflicts [regarding interracial dating relationships] still existed and created a kind of ambivalence." Complicating the situation was the fact that white women's beauty standards stood as normative for all women, so that "the whole tortuous thing that black women go through regarding their physical image suffers terribly when black men choose white women."[93]

When asked if Hall ever faced gender discrimination in SNCC, Holsaert responded: "I think that she was so self-assured, at least on the surface, that I don't think anyone in SNCC would have dared to try to cut off her opportunities.... She really flourished partly because she was so confident."[94] Although Hall did acknowledge seeing "tremendous sexism, chauvinism and even some misogyny among SNCC men," she said that "even as a religious woman, I would never have had the freedom in SCLC that I had in SNCC. The difference in SNCC was that we could talk about it." She continued: "I don't believe that any men in SNCC ever disrespected me because of my gender. I never had the sense that I was not taken seriously."[95] However, when SNCC sought to appoint a dedicated fund-raiser, to travel and raise support for SNCC across the country and Hall was initially suggested as a strong candidate for the position, "[Jim] Forman mentioned that [a] male would be better since [the] job involved living virtually out of a suitcase."[96] By and large, however, "women felt themselves to be an important and integral part of SNCC," rather than restricted to purely supportive roles.[97]

Women found opportunities for leadership and service, according to Holsaert, because SNCC "treated [women] more democratically and in a more egalitarian fashion than anywhere else in culture at that time." Martha Prescod Norman Noonan remembered a general understanding "that there would be women in front of the press, women giving talks, women deciding strategy, philosophy.... We grew up in the era of Daisy Bates, Rosa Parks... so it's sort of like you could be all that you could be."[98]

Black women understood their racial and gender vulnerabilities, and they understood that attaining dignity, equality, and an end to sexual oppression, brutality, and terrorism were important aspects of their fight against segregation. Bernice Johnson Reagon joined the movement precisely because of this awareness: "If you were a girl, some really bad things could happen to you—and often there was not one thing you could do about it.... So, uncovered, without shelter, with every ounce of strength I had, and all my heart and soul, I joined this Movement for FREEDOM!" Though she did not count herself as part of the women's movement until the 1970s, her civil rights activism in Albany planted a seed that helped her realize that "this [oppression hierarchy] doesn't have to be a given. There might just be another way to be Black and female in this universe."[99]

Prathia Hall believed that black women had an easier time adjusting to life in southern black communities for two reasons. First, "there is a sense in which our social incubator in the Black community trained and nurtured Black women to do whatever was necessary," whereas white women "came out of that whole pedestalization and trivialization of women that the southern power establishment imposed on them." Second, she also noted that even black workers from the North would likely have had family connections in the South, making them welcome and comfortable in the communities in which SNCC was working.[100]

Reflecting later in her life on the sexism in the movement, Hall described the "complicitous... partnership" that black women had with men. On the one hand, male dominance in leadership and interactions with the press were sexist. On the other hand, "women often went along with that, feeling that it was important to our community that Black males be seen as competent, standing up and giving strong leadership. I don't think, at the same time, that women felt that taking that posture was depriving them or taking anything away from them.... At that time, there was an attitude of partnership." Hall contextualized this within the long history of black women's support for black men's leadership as part of racial uplift: "There has been an attitude of support for black male leadership by very, very strong, assertive black women" to counter "the ways in which black men have been demeaned, because there were no places in which black men could give leadership with dignity except those places which were controlled by the black community ... the black church and the black movement organization."[101]

Rep. John Lewis lamented that the movement did not sufficiently look inward to recognize and correct its own discrimination against women's leadership: "Prathia, if she had been a man and not a woman, people would know much more about her.... She would have been much more visible—not just within SNCC, but in the whole movement and in America."[102]

Hall was also a leader in preparing SNCC volunteers to adapt to the psychological realities of working in the "overlay of terror and violence" in the rural South, living with the reality that "at any moment and at any time, someone could come and kill you.... If a car was heard too late at night, everybody just froze, because we didn't know whether that was friend or foe." The potentially life-threatening circumstances in which they lived naturally led to intense fear. Hall explained: "Fear was part of the survival kit. The challenge was to use fear as a signal to exercise caution while refusing to allow fear to paralyze you."[103] She taught the volunteers to understand their fear:

> Fear was the most sane and intelligent response in a system like this. Our response was, we lived with the fear, we came to understand it and then our job was to work with it and to help people not to be afraid to learn how to keep fear from paralyzing you and to take necessary action in spite of fear and that was a slow process. We worked in the fields sometimes, we sat on porches, listening and talking before the subject of voter registration was mentioned. In that process, we were learning together how to allow the yearning for freedom which was lived so deeply, so profoundly within the being of the people to not only surface but to surround and transform the fear.[104]

Another obstacle for northern students who stayed in host homes was the reality of rural poverty: outhouses instead of indoor bathrooms, no air-conditioning in the Georgia summer heat, and new types of cuisine. As Preacely recalled, "they shot a squirrel for breakfast or skinned [sic] a chicken."[105] Hall described the rural poverty of Southwest Georgia:

> When I compare it with the slums of the cities, it seems that here, even the poverty seems primitive. The big city slums are a complicated, mechanized, industrial ugliness, woven in an intricate pattern which has a thread

around many men. But here the shacks are low and makeshift—not the leftover houses of the wealthy or the middle class, but the shabby heirlooms which were built shabbily and have been passed on from slave to slave, from generation to generation. The shacks are low, the food simple, the work back-breaking, the poverty degrading. When you look up at the beautiful pure sky above, your glance has to come a long way down to see the unadulterated ugliness of the system on the ground.[106]

One memorable incident struck Peter DeLissovoy about Hall's leadership and respect within the Southwest Georgia community. On his second day in Southwest Georgia, the new recruits returned to their host home to find all of their belongings stolen. The group asked Hall and Sherrod what to do. Hall immediately walked up to James Daniel, an Albany gang leader, who had become a major supporter of SNCC's work in Southwest Georgia, and demanded, "James, get those things back." As DeLissovoy recalls, "Within three hours James Daniel had located the bunch of thieves in the Ritz movie theater with all these goods, watches, sleeping bags, everything. And they were [brought] right back. Everything: typewriters, every possession was returned the same day."[107]

Hall noted the adjustment between her Philadelphia community and SNCC:

> The new community was really strange because we were black and white. We were Northern and Southern.... We had come from different places, different spaces. Some of us were very religious in our motivations. Others were very political.... But, we had a common goal, and we had a common commitment. And I think that's what kept us together. And we had a common task, which was to stay alive today.... Your differences begin to pale in the face of a need to stay alive... And we could not stay alive without depending on each other.... Just the nuances of being black and white and living together in the same houses, or walking down the street together would so enrage the local whites that we could be shot down just like that.... So we were living together and working together because of what we believed. And that took precedence over our differences.[108]

As Hall trained student volunteers to operate within southern culture, she also taught them how to relate to the locals and to each other and to understand the multilayered, systemic oppression of black people.

Mass meetings gathered civil rights workers and members of the black community to discuss their work, confess their fears, coordinate plans, call themselves to organized action, and sing freedom songs, the bread and butter of the movement.[109] Hall described the meetings as "pure power," and later reflected: "I had never in my life been so profoundly moved as I was by the mass meetings that were the central rallying points of the Movement. . . . It was impossible to stand as a spectator outside the circle of this communion." She appreciated the "rhythm of the feet, and the clapping of the hands from the old prayer meeting tradition . . . the lined hymn tradition."[110] They reenergized people to persist, helping them to overcome their fear of white retaliation. Charlie Cobb noted that "as much as the movement was about challenging white supremacy . . . the movement was also about challenging black people within the black community" to take a stand for themselves.[111] This communion kept Hall going in later days and months:

> Every mass meeting was a prayer meeting and every statement and every report was a testimony. So whether you called yourself religious or not, it was about the struggle of the powers of life against the powers of death, and that's religion. And when we would walk up to the churches, coming to the meetings, the people would already be there and the church would be rocking with "A Charge to Keep I Have." The last verse of that old, old hymn is: To serve this present age / My calling to fulfill. / Oh may it all my powers engage / To do my Master's will.[112]

The communion of freedom singing connected her with the others gathered there as well as with her family and the black church as a whole: "I'd heard those songs before . . . in the piney woods setting of the churches of my mother's heritage in Nelson County, Virginia . . . as they were repeated by the daughters and sons of the American Southland in the churches of Philadelphia and other Northern cities." Singing them in a mass meeting deepened Hall's understanding of what was happening: "Somehow, in this place, Southwest Georgia, with hostile police ringing the exterior of the church, [freedom songs] were neither repetitious nor in any way imitative of the familiar; they were worship which contained within the reality of its expression, a power which affirmed life and defied death." Singing freedom songs was prayer and proclamation that "fashioned fear into faith, cringing into courage, suffering into survival, despair into defiance, and pain into protest."

Hall time and again turned to freedom songs for strength for the rest of her life.[113]

Through days of voter registration, canvassing on foot, waiting in line at the county courthouse, being crammed into filthy jail cells without water or food, helping sharecroppers meet daily quotas so they could attend mass meetings, and the ever-present fear that at any moment death could come, Hall described: "The prayer meeting song is a testimony about what has already come, happened in one's faith and what will happen in the future. . . . My back is against the wall and I am right now in need of help!! One calls up that help by affirming that it is already there." Hall explained: "When fear was so real and so powerful we could taste it, we would sing those songs. And that we were bound together. There was a connection. That was where the community was." When jailers demanded they stop singing, civil rights workers knew their message was getting across: "We knew we were being heard, and we would just sing louder and longer."[114]

Freedom songs breathed life and hope into darkness and despair: "The survival kit of oppression includes humor, faith, and music. We couldn't live if we couldn't laugh, we would not have lived if we didn't believe, and we couldn't have done any of that without the music."[115] Mass meetings began with an hour or more of congregational freedom singing:

> Music was a lifeline, a source, a well from which we could draw, a source of courage and strength in the face of eminent danger. With these forces of death with their guns loaded and sometimes drawn, surrounding you and taking down your name or license plate number, to be able then to sing and the relationship between the songs of the movement and the songs of the church is of one fabric, that's a continuous thread. What the Freedom Singers and various movement projects did was simply add to the words, develop the subtle variations in the melodies, were almost a living expression of what we're living right now. In the movement rallies there would be some slight variation from the old prayer meetings that . . . has a different phrasing of the melody, those pregnant pauses, those are underlying, underscoring, it's almost like you're gulping for breath in the face of fear. . . . What do you do when you are so surrounded by this powerful force of death? You sing life.[116]

"Because the mass meetings were a place of reinforcement for us," Hall explained, "they were under constant surveillance." Phone lines were tapped, and local law enforcement often lurked outside the meetings, recording the names of those in attendance, barging in on meetings, and making threats. Hall recognized the intimidation tactics but persisted: "It would be insanely dishonest to claim that we were unafraid.... The challenge was to use fear as a signal to exercise caution while refusing to allow fear to paralyze you."[117]

One of the most significant contributions of the Albany movement to the larger Civil Rights Movement was music. Cordell Reagon brought songs from the Nashville student movement and Freedom Rides to Albany, where he organized the SNCC Freedom Singers: ASU students Rutha Harris and Bernice Johnson, SNCC field secretary Chico's brother Chuck Neblett, and himself. The quartet toured the country spreading the music of the movement. Guy Carawan, a folk singer associated with SNCC, produced *Freedom in the Air: A Documentary on Albany, Georgia 1961–1962*, an album that sold for $4.00 as a fund-raiser for SNCC field-workers in Albany, eventually raising enough to support SNCC workers across the South. James Forman described the album as, "an excellent way for people from other areas to hear for themselves, in on-the-spot recordings, what the excitement and dignity of the Albany Movement sounded like."[118]

"Terrible Terrell"

Hall demonstrated Freedom Faith as she moved into Terrell County. Although in the summer of 1962 SNCC workers occasionally returned to Albany for mass meetings or other resources, they conducted the bulk of their work in Terrell and Lee Counties. In particular, Terrible Terrell, also nicknamed Tombstone Territory, was notorious for civil rights infringements and was the first entity to be prosecuted for voting violations under the Civil Rights Act of 1957, which prohibited intimidation and similar tactics used against black voters.

Hall and several other students stayed in Carolyn Daniels's home in Dawson, the Terrell county seat. Daniels operated a beauty salon attached to her home, and her son Roy studied at Dawson's segregated high school. Hall admired Daniels's dedication to the movement, the way she "participated with fierce commitment in the long discussions and activities of the project." Hall later reflected on the danger Daniels incurred by hosting the SNCC workers. Although her income was uncommonly independent of "direct white control," intimidation tactics left her livelihood exceptionally vulnerable. Nevertheless, Daniels made her home into a "Freedom House," with "wall to wall people." Hall recalled the "perpetual disarray and elevated noise level of a house full of students waging philosophical debates, serious strategy sessions, and general, youthful clowning [that] did not seem to disturb her at all."[119]

Those staying with Daniels received $30 total monthly for host home expenses, which Hall could stretch to feed the entire group for the full month. Daniels compared Hall to Jesus feeding the multitude with the five fish and two loaves. "Sherrod always had to have his gallon of milk. And the milk was always there.... Sherrod even asked me one day... 'How did we manage it?' Said, 'You kept a car and we ate.'" Daniels described Hall's knack: "That's just the way Prathia was.... Whatever needed to be done, she would try to do it. ... She was just a leader. She was just a spiritual person. You could just feel it, you know, whenever she was involved, because that's the way she was." Daniels also noted that Hall ensured the group said grace at every meal and that Hall always conducted herself with a propriety that was never pretentious. She carried white gloves in her purse and seemed to many of her SNCC colleagues to be "more proper, as more feminine, as more dignified than the rest of us."[120]

Very soon after arriving in Dawson, she experienced the local police scare tactics firsthand. Police raided a mass meeting at Mount Olive Baptist Church on the night of July 25, the second police raid on a mass meeting in two weeks. Sherrod led the meeting, and Ralph Allen, Penny Patch, Charlie Jones, and Hall were in attendance. Allen brought two women planning to register to vote. As they walked to the church, the number of vehicles present surprised Allen until he realized that "about twenty local white citizens" were there to harass the attendees and disrupt the meeting.[121] As Sherrod led the singing of "Pass Me Not, O Gentle Savior," *New York Times* reporter Claude Sitton heard a dozen cars pull up to the church.

The police outside spoke loudly and called out the license plate numbers of cars parked outside the church—implying that those attending would be subject to future harassment such as fabricated vehicle citations, inflated utility bills, losing their jobs, damage to their property, or physical harm. Hall and others continued their meeting, in spite of their fear. Thirteen "hat-wearing, cigarette-smoking, tobacco-chewing" police officers burst through the door;

they "tried to intimidate the cool, poised bespectacled Sherrod, who refused to be stampeded."[122] Sherrod simply continued: "If God be for us, who can be against us. We are counted as sheep for the slaughter." Sherrod prayed aloud for peaceful relationships between black and white and for courage to persist in the struggle. He even prayed for the sheriff by name, that God would "free the sheriff from chains of hate and racism."[123]

As those gathered for the mass meeting began to sing "We Are Climbing Jacob's Ladder," Deputy R. M. Dunaway beat his flashlight against his palm in the back of the room. Lucius Holloway, a Terrell County voter registration leader, addressed Dunaway: "Everybody is welcome. This is a voter registration meeting." Terrell County Sheriff Z. T. Mathews ordered Dunaway to take the names of those attending the mass meeting, telling a reporter: "You know, Cap, there's nothing like fear to keep niggers in line."[124]

Hall stood firm: "We sang our freedom songs with defiant and prayerful fervor." As the congregation began to hum "We Shall Overcome," police withdrew from the church. About the attendees, Sitton reported: "Their voices had a strident note as though they were building up their courage to go out into the night, where the whites waited." As the mass meeting dismissed, Hall and others walked into a swarm of local police officers standing outside, leveling threats of terror at them.[125]

Hall later reflected candidly on the realities of fear in the midst of terror:

> We've talked a lot about coming face to face with death, and I think sometimes for young people that's very hard to imagine. But we did it, we had to do it every day. That meant that if you were driving down the road and a car came up behind you, if the car stayed behind you, you were terrified that you were going to be shot from behind, and if the car passed you, you hit the floor, which put you in a pretty difficult position if you were the driver. Nobody here has ever said they were not afraid. In fact, anybody who came into that situation and wasn't afraid, we didn't want anything to do with.[126]

As Hall worked in Lee County with Penny Patch, Kathleen Conwell, Peggy Dammond, and Joan Maxwell, police used intimidation tactics against the women, including threatening to harm them or harm those who helped them, stopping them without cause, and threatening to bomb the homes where they were staying.[127]

A formal public education structure for black children in Lee County existed only since 1956, prior to which they were educated at churches and vacant houses.[128] Hall and other SNCC workers recruited families to file a school desegregation lawsuit, but with the constant threat of white intimidation tactics, they found less interest in pursuing legal action than anticipated.[129]

Deputy Marshall D. E. Short of Sasser arrested Roy Daniel (also known as Roychester Patterson), Hall, Ralph Allen, and Willie Paul Berrien for speeding on August 30, 1962. Short fired two shots in the air while pulling over the vehicle. Patterson challenged the speeding charge since he was only driving 30 miles per hour, to which Short retorted, "You think you can do anything you damn well please."[130]

Hall showed tremendous courage and prophetic spirit in the midst of this police brutality. She "answered him by looking him in the eye—which was something that was forbidden, for black people to look white people in the eye—and said to him, we're talking to people about registration and you have no right to stop us." She described his reaction: "He became just enraged. Changed colors, began literally foaming at the mouth, . . . cursed me in, with names I had, some I had never heard before or since." She later elaborated that after Short repeatedly shouted "Shut up!," he was "trembling with rage and calling me a long-haired yellow bitch, he pulled a gun and began firing at the ground around our feet."[131]

After emptying his gun, Short arrested all of them and held them at "this filthy little vermin-infested hole which passed for the Sasser jail. . . . It was about three times the size of an outhouse and smelled as bad." The group was segregated in their cells by race, not gender.[132]

In that moment by the side of the road, Hall did not fear the shooting, her arrest, or being in jail. She feared "that perhaps no friendly person had seen us, and that we might be held there, and then taken out in the middle of the night, and done away with." As Deputy Short fired at her feet, Hall felt numb, which she later recognized as "a gift from God."

> If I had moved one muscle, I would have given him the excuse he wanted to raise the gun point blank and fire. . . . I was numb. . . . I believe my numbness was a gift from God that saved my life. . . . And that I didn't move, I know that I was held because there were other times when we had to operate out of fear. . . . Fear could be a very positive thing. Because for instance, fear would

make you not do something stupid, you know. But in that particular incident, I wasn't operating out of fear, I wasn't operating. I was just there. By the grace of God. I was glad to stand in that vermin infested hole because I was alive. But I came very close to not being alive.[133]

Hall and her fellow SNCC workers survived.[134]

Learning that the Albany movement planned several voter registration attempts for September 4, 1962, a group of three thousand Klansmen and sympathizers held a meeting in a pasture seven miles outside of Albany the evening before.[135] After the 8:00 a.m. mass meeting on September 4, Prathia Hall and three other SNCC field-workers—a white male and female and Roy Daniel—began their work of canvassing.

As the four SNCC workers left the home of Lehman Davis, who had recently registered to vote, they "saw a great cloud of dust, a pickup truck barreling down the road." Deputy Short backed into a dirt road near the house, stopped the group, and shouted at them: "So, you're back, I'm going to hang something on you." Short harassed Allen about his vehicle registration and license plates.[136]

Short demanded that the workers pile into Ralph Allen's vehicle and leave town. Allen drove the vehicle outside city limits and turned right on a dirt road, at which point Short pulled up alongside the truck, demanded they exit the vehicle, and pulled a gun on them. He repeatedly shouted "Get!" while firing shots in the direction of their vehicle as they drove away from the scene. Hall recounted that "[Short] chased three of us out of town by firing gunshots at our car and threatening to fill us full of lead and put us all in the cemetery." Short followed the vehicle all the way to Dawson, threatening to shoot them when they stopped to use the telephone. As they reached the edge of town, Short shouted from his car window, "Get out and stay out" and fired a warning shot into the ground.[137]

Hall's discernment of Short helped her survive his brutality against them: "That was another one of those moments when you look death in the face and you also look at the enemy, which is that evil, and the victim who is the bearer of that evil, in the face, and it takes care of the fear problem."[138]

On September 5, 1962, the next day, Hall gathered with other SNCC workers at the Harris family house in Albany to welcome new recruit Jack Chatfield. They piled into "a little teeny Nash Rambler," which they filled with loud laughter, "a kind of defiant act in the middle of a tense city that had been shaken by a mass movement." After stopping at a gas station, Hall asked the group to confirm their plans for the next day as they continued to Dawson, around ten or eleven at night.[139]

The SNCC crew staying with Carolyn Daniels settled in for the night. Jack Chatfield was enjoying a late night snack in the kitchen, while others were already asleep. Hall described the quiet roar of a car motor: "As it slowed in front of the house, there was a hail of gunfire." Shots riddled Daniels' house. Chatfield never forgot the sounds: "They were so loud that I thought someone had thrown a firecracker, a cherry bomb, right into the midst of us and [it had] exploded."[140]

SNCC trained workers with precautions for moments like these. They had learned to sleep on pallets on the floor to dodge nightrider shotgun attacks, often aimed at the level of a person lying in a bed. Hall had also been trained to hit the floor at the sound of gunfire.[141] That night, "when the shooting started, they all tried to hide": Roy behind the refrigerator, Sherrod under a piece of furniture, Chatfield under a window, and Hall and Daniels on the floor in a back bedroom. "Quietly and breathlessly we waited until several minutes after the car drove off."[142] Sherrod called roll to ensure everyone survived the shooting. Prathia Hall and Chris Allen suffered minor bullet graze injuries, but Jack Chatfield had been shot twice in the arm.[143]

Afraid that the night riders might return, Sherrod turned off the lights and insisted that everyone stay down. Hall recounted the shooting: "We hit the floor as we had been trained to do, while a blast of shotgun pellets was sprayed into the house. After the car drove off, we waited several minutes and then called to each other to learn if anyone had been hit. We were all alive, thank God. But this had been a very close call." She said: "We were crawling around on the floor for quite a while after that not knowing if they were coming back."[144]

After nearly forty-five minutes, Sherrod moved toward the phone. Knowing he could not trust the Georgia or local police, the Georgia Bureau of Investigation, or the FBI to protect them, he called *New York Times* reporter Claude Sitton, a southerner with a reputation for fair coverage of the movement, at midnight, and gave him the story. Indeed, Sitton published a thorough report of the night's events, including the history of police harassment of demonstrators. Sitton described Daniels's house as "a four-room dwelling of concrete blocks, faced with red bricks and topped by asphalt shingles" with "ten neat holes punched through the front door screen by blasts of buckshot." The house was three blocks down a dirt road from where the pavement ended—the demarcation between the white and black parts of town.[145]

Hall's and Allen's minor injuries could be easily treated at home. Chatfield's gunshot wounds required medical attention. Chris Allen and Ralph Allen drove Chatfield—these were the three whites staying with Daniels—into Albany: "The idea was that if there were just three white guys, we wouldn't attract any attention." As they passed a gas station, "a car screeched out" toward them aggressively, and a police car stopped them and loaded them all into the SWAT car, arrested them, and took them to the hospital in Dawson. "Why they didn't want us to go into Albany, I'm not sure, but they didn't." The doctor slammed the hospital room door open and asked Chatfield, "What are you doing sleeping with niggers?"[146]

Police received a call about the shooting just after midnight. Dawson police chief W. B. Cherry reported that officers found the home empty when they arrived but did see evidence of "shotgun blasts." Cherry's version of the story similarly erased police harassment of the workers at the gas station earlier that evening, instead claiming police helped them because their car had broken down.[147]

Over the phone the night of the shooting, Hall told Sitton that "it's fear that slams the doors in our faces[,] and hope that makes those same people whisper about us and get down on their knees and pray for us." In that conversation, Hall described her father's teaching about racial justice and the family's decision to move from Virginia to Philadelphia in the 1920s: "I feel that he left the South to somehow redeem me. And now it's my job to come back and redeem somebody else." She hoped that their work in the South would create space for black people to flourish in the South: "The sweat and blood of these people is in the very soil of this land."[148]

The Sasser arrests, police threats, and house shootings were all reported to the FBI and the federal Department of Justice. Within the larger investigation of Southwest Georgia racial violence, detectives followed leads on the vehicles allegedly seen after the shootings as well as bullets recovered from the scene. Each investigation, however, returned the same results: no suspects and no evidence of police brutality or civil rights infringement.

The shooting did not deter Daniels or any of the SNCC workers. Hall knew such danger was a constant possibility but did not dwell on the incident: "We had been warned in orientation sessions not to go into the field unless we were prepared to die. That night any and all romantic thoughts about our freedom adventure dissolved as we came face-to-face with the real and present possibility of death." Chatfield later joked: "I was inclined to stay up late and read in the kitchen, which would seem to be crazy because that's where I was shot, so you would have thought I would have gotten out of the kitchen after that, but I didn't. Nobody did, actually." Daniels revealed their resolve: "We kept going, kept in the streets, kept taking people to register, kept getting people to vote."[149]

They did keep going, and Daniels continued to be a primary target for white supremacists because of her enthusiastic advocacy for civil rights. Daniels joined the movement after Sheriff Z. T. Mathews assaulted her son in 1961; she was outraged that although she was a homeowner, business owner, and taxpayer, neither she nor her family had legal protection. She was the first Dawson resident to open her home to SNCC students, sheltering as many as nine SNCC workers at a time, including Charles Sherrod, Prathia Hall, Jack Chatfield, John Churchville, Ralph Allen, and Chris Allen. She led a freedom school, and she often escorted voter applicants to the courthouse. On December 8, 1963, nightriders again attacked her home. As gunshots came through her bedroom window, she rolled under her bed. A bomb thrown through the window rolled under the bed next to her, but "somehow the bomb did not go off."[150] Daniels' neighbor's house was struck by over a hundred bullets. The only gun in Dawson capable of such a shooting was a 50-caliber machine gun, belonging to Sheriff Z. T. Mathews.[151] No doctor would treat Daniels's bullet wound; she was instructed to clean the wound with alcohol and go home. By the time Daniels returned home, the bomb had destroyed her house.[152]

Even after her house was twice the victim of nightrider attacks, Daniels continued her work in Southwest Georgia.[153] Hall said that, by 1965, the number "frequent[ing] her beauty shop and talk[ing] openly with her about voting and matters of civil rights" had increased, demonstrating her influence in the community.[154] Daniels adored Hall, and SNCC workers often noted in their field reports that she "misses Prathia," who was working with the Selma project by fall 1963.[155] Hall described Daniels as a mother figure. Discussing the 1962 shooting into Daniels's home, Hall said, "It did not move her. It did not unnerve her." Hall was aware of the personal difficulties Daniels faced that made her sacrifices for the movement even more inspiring: "She was a single mother struggling to make it, but she was steel, she was strength for all of us, and she took all of us, with our Technicolor selves and our strange ways and some Northern and some Southern and all of that, and she wasn't that many years older than many of us, but she mothered us."[156]

"You know these white people will burn our church down"

Because of the real and present danger facing those who supported the Civil Rights Movement, SNCC often struggled to find churches willing to host mass meetings. Daniels's church, Atoc AME Church in Dawson, was too frightened of retaliation to allow Daniels or the SNCC workers to meet there: "You know these white people will burn our church down."[157]

Hall reflected on the frustration of local churches and local people refusing to help SNCC: "We had to translate, we had to interpret that; it was a rational fear speaking. The courage was beyond reason, beyond the level of the rational! The courage to go down to the courthouse or the courage to open the doors and say let's have the meeting here was a courage that transcended reason."[158]

This "courage that transcended reason" was Freedom Faith. Hall came to understand the profound demonstration of faith that churches made by cooperating with SNCC workers: "Churches were burned down, sometimes two or three in a night. For a congregation to open their doors and say, 'you may meet here,' was again as profound a test of the Freedom Faith as ever there could be. It's almost quite miraculous that there was always at least one church that would say, come."[159] In the summer of 1962, four black churches in Terrell and Lee Counties, all associated with the movement in some way, were burned by white supremacists.

On August 17, two days after the burning of Shady Grove Baptist Church in Leesburg, SNCC workers from Terrell and Lee counties gathered at the home of Mrs. Raines to assess the psychological damage of the burning on the community. At the meeting, workers emphasized their plan to recruit the community to work together to reconstruct the church and found the people steadfast in their commitment to the movement. They also discussed personnel availability, including Hall's, and that she would remain in Terrell County. Conwell noted one "good result" of the church burnings was the necessity of rotating where meetings were held, which drew new people from the various congregations into the mass meetings.[160]

Two Southwest Georgia churches, Mount Olive Baptist Church (Sasser) and Mount Mary Baptist Church (Chickasawatchee), were burned the night of September 9, both wooden, located five miles apart, and torched within one hour of each other. A member of Mount Olive who awoke at 2:00 a.m. to the blaze told reporters that "I didn't sleep a wink after that. I was too scared." Hall received word via telephone that Mount Olive was ablaze: "We dressed quickly and made our way to the church. There were no firefighters. The church had already burned to the ground." They wept together at the sight.[161] Hall reflected:

> As we stood there, more people gathered, members and friends of the church. We held hands together and sang and prayed. As we stood there watching the remains of Mt. Olive, Mr. Southwell of the Georgia Bureau of Investigation arrived. I extended my hand and said, "I'm Prathia Hall." He looked at me and said, "Don't you know better than to stick your hand out there like that to speak to me?" I said, "Don't human beings speak to each other that way?" He walked away saying, "Well it ain't the way I live."[162]

The next day, SNCC workers received a phone call that Martin Luther King Jr. intended to come to Albany to attend a prayer vigil over the ashes of Mount Olive Baptist Church in Sasser. Sitton was also at the vigil and wrote a moving article for the *New York Times* about the ceremony. "As the sun sets across the cotton fields, some fifty Negroes and two whites met at Mount Olive for a 'prayer vigil.' Joining hands, they sang softly, 'We Shall Overcome.' A wisp of smoke rose from the ashes of the church. . . . The whites in the automobiles that shuttled slowly past looked on and said nothing."[163]

After the song, Hall led the group in prayer, as Larry Rubin later recalled: "'Lord, help us keep our heads up,' Miss Hall said, her voice breaking. 'Help us, Lord, as Mount Olive, Shady Grove, and Mount Mary Churches rise again out of the ashes. Lord, we're going to be free. We want to be free so our children won't have to grow up with their heads bowed."[164] According to oral tradition, throughout the prayer, Hall repeated the phrase "I have a dream," each time followed by a specific vision for racial equality and justice.[165] Recognizing the power her words held, Sitton quoted a substantial portion of Hall's prayer in his article about the event. Sitton did not include any text from King's remarks at the same vigil, nor did Sitton customarily quote prayers.

Larry Rubin vividly remembered her speaking at this event: "She was really quite a powerful speaker. I remember being awestruck."[166]

Hall recalled that, after the service, King sought and received her permission to use the phrase "I have a dream" in his own preaching. Hall was a fairly private person in general and in no way an attention seeker. She did not boast about her connection to King, though, later in life, when friends asked her about her role in "I have a dream," she did acknowledge that King initially heard the phrase from her. She added the caveat that she was not responsible for King's subsequent use of the phrase because she feared people might use her assertion to discredit King's significance.[167] The fact that King asked Hall if he could borrow the phrase "I have a dream" spoke volumes of his respect for her, affirming her as a preaching peer.

The burning did not deter SNCC, but SNCC's resilience did not deter segregationists either. At an open-air voter registration meeting on September 13, Terrell County's civil rights volunteers decided to raise a tent as a temporary meeting place until the churches could be rebuilt. A church in Valdosta had been burned over the summer, and the September 17 burning of I Hope Baptist Church in Terrell County was the fifth church burned in Southwest Georgia in the summer of 1962.[168] Between 1961 and 1963, forty-one black churches in the South were torched.[169]

Even though mass meetings were often held at Mount Olive Baptist Church and a minister and deacon of Mount Mary Baptist Church had been supporting the voter registration drive, Sheriff Mathews told newspaper reporters that the burnings had nothing to do with voter registration. He claimed that area whites were "not too much disturbed" about black voter registration but did resent "outside agitators," a common phrase used against nonlocal civil rights workers. He also cited white disapproval of interracial cohabitation of the SNCC workers, drawing on the long-held white assumption that black men posed a sexual threat to white women.[170]

Prathia Hall answered Mathews's claims with bold confidence: "We may have had visits from white girls at our headquarters . . . but none are staying here. The fires are the latest harassment. We've been getting the works." Hall told reporters about her recent encounter with Deputy Short and her arrest for speeding on August 30 as examples of police intimidation tactics against SNCC.[171]

SNCC chairman Charles McDew demanded that President John F. Kennedy "halt the Nazi-style reign of terror in Southwest Georgia."[172] SNCC leader James Forman appealed to Attorney General Robert Kennedy to "restore law and order" and promised that SNCC would organize efforts to rebuild the burned churches.[173] President Kennedy responded to the events in Southwest Georgia: "To shoot... two young people who were involved in an effort to register people, to burn churches as a reprisal... I consider both cowardly as well as outrageous." SNCC workers demanded strong governmental action against civil rights violations in Southwest Georgia but were rewarded with only sound bites lacking tactical support.[174] Sheriff Mathews cited the federal court order as evidence of racial voter registration discrimination being a settled issue. Clearly federal intervention was insufficient at best. Jackie Robinson, Nelson Rockefeller, Reinhold Niebuhr, Harry Belafonte, and other celebrities rallied behind SNCC's fund-raising efforts in Southwest Georgia. Nearby religious organizations contributed money to rebuild the damaged homes and churches.[175]

Jackie Robinson, the first black player in major league baseball, visited the church ruins and spoke at an Albany movement dinner. Robinson grew up near a plantation in Cairo, Georgia, owned by the Sasser family, after which the town had been named. He initiated a fund-raising effort to raise $35,000 to help rebuild the churches. The combined funds raised by multiple secular and religious organizations, including the Fund for Rehabilitation of Burned Churches ("an Albany Negro organization"), exceeded the goal, pulling in approximately $60,000. Monks at the nearby Trappist monastery in Conyers, Georgia, offered to produce stained glass windows for the churches.[176]

In November 1962, the Southern Regional Council, a multiracial organization, charged Kennedy with "no acknowledgement of a Federal duty to protect Federal rights, the rights of speech and peaceable assembly and equal protection of the laws." Howard Zinn criticized the FBI, which, though its agents took dozens of interviews that confirmed "clear violations by local police of constitutional rights with undisputed evidence of beatings by sheriffs and deputy sheriffs," had failed to take any action.[177]

Despite the obstacles and very real physical danger, Hall persisted in the freedom movement. Her experiences during her first two months in Southwest Georgia deeply shaped her understanding of Freedom Faith and her sense of divine calling to work for racial justice with SNCC.

CHAPTER 3
"IN JAIL FOR A JUST CAUSE"

"She was in the North speaking at a rally"

In the fall of 1962, after the shootings and church burnings, Hall returned to Philadelphia for a series of speaking engagements. SNCC executive secretary James Forman often asked her to speak at northern SNCC fund-raiser events, and numerous organizations invited her to speak as well: "A lot of time when something pivotal happened in the South [she] was in the North speaking at a rally."[1]

Hall's first engagement was the SNCC Emancipation Celebration at Tindley Temple United Methodist Church, where the Freedom Singers also appeared.[2] Hall spearheaded SNCC's work in Philadelphia, organized through Fellowship House. A spectator described her message at the celebration: "Her account was very simple and deeply moving."[3] The Jewish Labor Committee also made a generous financial commitment—a car, $1,000, and several supply drives—to the Southwest Georgia project during Hall's campaigning in fall 1962.[4]

Marjorie Penney appreciatively reflected on Hall's frequent connection with Fellowship House through northern speaking engagements: "Some of our young people who had gone South with Dr. King to work on the whole voting registration thing came back and spoke of the bravery of the black people.... The intensity of the self-giving of many of these young people ... in cities like Albany, Georgia; Americus, Georgia; Cleveland, Mississippi; Jacksonville, Mississippi; Florida towns; name it, and somebody from the Fellowship House was in there for a long or short time."[5]

On September 21, 1962, Hall spoke on a late-night broadcast of radio station WHAT 1340 in Philadelphia. Around 11:48 p.m., the Hall family telephone rang. Hall's sister Betty answered the phone. An unidentified caller asked for Mrs. Hall and then said to Betty: "You damn niggers need to mind your own business. I am going to do like the people in Terrell County and do some shooting tonight." Betty hung up the phone, but the caller phoned again, repeatedly threatening to shoot the Halls in their home.[6]

Federal authorities instructed Ruby Hall to alert the Philadelphia police since the matter would fall under local jurisdiction. Detective Charles Graham of the Philadelphia Police Department investigated the calls but had no leads. A memo from "Director, FBI" dated September 24, 1962, instructed the Philadelphia Police Department to keep the FBI and its Atlanta branch, which handled the investigation of Southwest Georgia racial violence, apprised of the investigation.[7]

Hall realized the burden that her activism placed on her family, who received hate mail and harassing phone calls frequently, as did the families of many SNCC workers. She described her mother as a "trooper lady, warrior lady" and her "number one supporter." Hall's mother "worried all the time, wanted me to come home." Hall was aware that "family conspired on various occasions to try to get this one or that one to try to persuade me to come home, which irritated me no end at the time, but once you become a parent, you certainly understand."[8] Hall's FH colleague Joyce Barrett sensed the pressure Hall faced from her family to return to North Philadelphia, but Hall's extreme modesty and privacy about her personal life precluded the two from discussing these issues.[9]

The Albany movement invited James Forman to speak in November 1962 on behalf of SNCC at the first anniversary celebration of the founding of the Albany group. Unable to attend, Forman asked Sherrod to speak in his place, but movement leaders requested that Forman find someone from out of town. Sherrod asked Hall, who along with Martin Luther King Jr. and many other leading civil rights activists accepted the invitation.[10] She returned to Philadelphia after the event to continue fund-raising.

"Her dignified dress might offend Sasser farmers"

In January 1963, U.S. Attorney Floyd M. Buford of the Department of Justice (DOJ) filed suit against Deputy Marshal Short for six counts of civil rights violations against Hall, William Berrien, and Ralph Allen from late August 1962, to which Short pled not guilty.[11] Short's pretrial remarks alleged that he stopped the SNCC workers' vehicle because of its out-of-state plates and incorrect parking position, that he asked them to leave town because "Negro citizens in Sasser" had complained about SNCC workers threatening those who would not register, and that he offered to escort them out of town "for their safety and protection."[12]

Assistant Attorney General Burke Marshall supervised the investigation leading up to Short's trial, which the FBI lumped in with its larger investigation of civil rights violations in Lee and Terrell Counties, including the torching of four black churches and the unlawful arrests and violence against civil rights supporters—not to mention the other incidents that the Albany movement had reported to the FBI, including the beatings of pregnant Mrs. Slater King (which caused a miscarriage), Bill Hansen, and C. B. King. Investigators delayed pressing charges against Short, however, until his involvement in the church burnings and other shootings could be ascertained.[13]

The DOJ investigation uncovered that William Challis noticed the civil rights workers fixing a flat tire as he passed them in his blue 1962 Ford Galaxie. Upon seeing the workers, Challis returned to town to demand their arrest. Deputy Short arrested them and brought them to the Methodist church. To investigators, Sasser, Georgia, town marshal W. T. Adams "specifically denied talking with anyone who was driving a 1962 blue Ford Galaxie. He specifically denied hearing anyone say 'lock them up.'"[14]

During the January 1963 federal grand jury trial in Americus, DOJ lawyers insisted that black people in the courtroom be identified as "colored folk" rather than "Negro" and enforced segregated seating.[15] DOJ lawyers requested that the SNCC workers, particularly the three witnesses in the trial, behave according to southern mores during the trial. They were asked to refrain from interracial gathering, though Daniels and Ralph Allen allegedly embraced in the hallway outside the courtroom. DOJ lawyers "would not allow one young Negro woman field secretary, Prathia Hall, to wear a hat in the courtroom" because "her dignified dress might offend Sasser farmers," giving "the impression that she was an 'uppity nigger.'" Hall described the scene: "I was called as a witness for the prosecution. I dressed as I had been taught was appropriate for a court appearance. I wore a business suit, hat, and gloves. As I waited to testify, I was approached by one of the Justice Department attorneys and asked to remove my hat, because the local whites were offended by the presence of a black woman dressed in such professional attire."[16]

Hall, Berrien, and Allen testified, recounting the events in which Short fired gunshots at their vehicle and at them, as well as arresting them on fabricated charges. Short claimed that he stopped them for speeding, then brought them peaceably into his office, and that the arrested workers ran into the jail cell together, implying that they wanted to have sex, a common accusation by segregationists against civil rights workers. Short's defense cast the northern students as outside agitators, further strengthening segregationist animosity toward Hall and the other students. He alleged that he ran the SNCC workers out of town for their own protection from angry whites.

In spite of obvious falsehoods in Short's testimony, including the speed capabilities of his 1953 pickup truck and his reasons for stopping them, DOJ officials did not challenge Short's testimony. Short's lawyer made, as SNCC students recorded in a field report, "slanderous remarks about the morals of SNCC," particularly concerning "the language and behavior of Miss Hall." When on the witness stand, Hall could not bring herself to repeat what Short had said to her. Judge James Robert Elliot allowed her to "state that Mr. Short had been abusive."[17] Hall explained that she was instructing Edith Page and Catherine Mallory in preparation to register to vote, and she accused Sasser officials of running the SNCC team out of town to prevent the successful completion of their voter registration work.[18] Larry Rubin recounted that during the trial, Hall laughed, which to him "was just an example of her courage . . . the way she held up when she was arrested." He was impressed that "she didn't allow herself to be intimidated." He found her reaction particularly powerful since the sheriffs were unaccustomed to such reactions from black people or women.[19]

After twenty minutes of deliberation on January 25, 1963, a twelve-man all-white jury acquitted Short of all charges.[20] Rubin overheard jurors saying to each other that they would not convict "a man who stood for segregation."[21]

After Short's acquittal, Hall and eleven other SNCC workers gathered in an old farmhouse to pray. Holsaert remembered their prayer: "Oh Lord, give us the power and wealth to be vessels of jubilee and truth in an unjust and untrue society." Howard Zinn characterized the antagonistic climate in which civil rights workers faced the so-called justice system: "The only federal prosecution in Albany during the attorney generalship of Robert Kennedy was *against* civil rights workers who had picketed a segregationist grocer," referring to the charges against Joni Rabinowitz in 1963.[22]

"It's good to be back home"

SNCC's work in Southwest Georgia continued in the face of ongoing difficulties. The project now included eleven field secretaries—Prathia Hall, Jack Chatfield, Carver (Chico) Neblett, John Churchville, Joyce Barrett, Don Harris, Ralph Allen, Eddie Brown, Faith Holsaert, Alfonzo Hubbard, and Joni Rabinowitz—who rotated from Albany to surrounding counties. Four lived at the Albany office, two at Koinonia Farm in Americus, and the rest with host homes in the rural counties.[23] SNCC expanded to Sumter County in November and December 1962.[24]

Americus, the county seat of Sumter County, was a trading and manufacturing town of just over 13,000 people. Approximately 52.65 percent of Sumter County's population was black but represented only 1.01 percent of registered voters. In 1942, Clarence Jordan and his wife, Florence, established Koinonia Farm, a biracial community eight miles southwest of Americus. Koinonia offered resources and support to SNCC, including local contacts, help distributing information, and meeting space.[25] Many whites blamed Jordan for inciting racial unrest in the community, and nightriders frequently attacked the farm. For over a decade, Americus merchants boycotted the farm in an attempt to bankrupt the venture.[26]

When Hall returned to voter registration work in Southwest Georgia on February 23, 1963, she brought childhood friend Joyce Barrett with her. Fellowship House director Marjorie Penney, Aura Yores, and Claire Maier—who went to the 1960 founding meeting of SNCC—drove Hall and Barrett to Albany.[27] Hall phoned Holsaert at the Albany office to let her know that she would be arriving with one black and two white women. The phone line was evidently bugged because immediately following, Marion King reported that local radio stations were announcing two new white women joining SNCC.[28] Sherrod distributed area SNCC workers in various locations to make room for the visitors, who arrived around 1:30 a.m.[29] Of her return to Southwest Georgia, Hall wrote: "It's good to be back home."[30]

The next day, February 24, at Koinonia Farms, the Southwest Georgia team met with the FH visitors amid what Hall remembered as a beautiful morning: "The sun spread its refreshing light and warmth on my first day back in S. W. Georgia."[31] Penney, Yores, and Maier offered moral support and suggestions for effectively working with people for social change, and they donated some needed supplies as well as assistance with odds and ends around the SNCC office.[32]

Penney, Yores, and Maier left Albany on February 25 after an evening mass meeting. The meeting was "run in real SNCC fashion," with each county reporting on its progress. Hall described the people as "almost transfixed in admiration" of each other's reports. She appreciated the multiple oral testimonies because "this kind of witness increases intercounty unity and at the same time gives form and backbone to the emerging leadership in the counties."[33] Penney, Yores, and Maier reported to FH on their return: "Fourteen young people are working in the counties—teaching sharecroppers to register and vote. The living conditions of these brave young people is appalling. Joyce remains in the student office in Albany; Prathia is back in Terrell County where she was wounded last fall! We feel that both girls are taking our places. One happy fact is that the Knit Goods Workers Union have purchased a good used car for the students."[34]

While in the North, Hall wrestled with the verdict of the Short trial. She felt "despair," but on returning to Southwest Georgia, she realized that "the people in the counties looked on it as a measure of hope" because Short's trial was "the first time a white in this area had even been questioned and brought to trial for an injustice to a Negro."[35] The biggest surprise awaiting Hall was the progress made in Sumter County, "the delight of my heart." In her field report accounting her late February activity at Koinonia, Hall lavished praise on the high mass meeting attendance and consistent voter registration attempts in Americus:

> People sit in the meetings with their heads high as they sing and talk about freedom. Even a *teacher* was present and offered his services in our new

night school project.... Can you imagine a real live teacher? We are on our way. Mr. Weston—fire, articulate and militant—told the people "don't you go down to that court house with your head down, scratching when you don't itch. Stand up! And speak up!" Already they are talking about economic security and establishing a savings and loan association. Yes, Sumter may prove to be the salt of our movement.[36]

Hall returned to Daniels's house with Faith Holsaert, who dubbed them a "triumvirate of female workers." As the only white worker staying with Daniels, Holsaert was "always with Prathia or Carolyn."[37] Hall spent the remainder of February 1963 there. Terrell County mass meetings were well attended—"a tent full"—and Hall noticed "a new spirit of progressiveness" among the people. She felt that "warm arms of friendship and shared suffering welcomed me into the family."[38] Hall canvassed for voter registration with some high school students and Albany's Rev. Samuel Wells, whom she greatly admired. She also assisted in the SNCC office as much as she could while battling the flu.[39]

Hall's field reports described a "snatching" technique of approaching people in the street in front of city hall and taking them to register to vote on the spot. She found the method to be "extremely good." She appreciated its confrontational aspect: "Since people were frightened—like the woman who pushed me away as she ducked into a store to avoid giving me her name which I asked her for when she hastily told me she had been registered for years. I don't know, some I believe, and some I don't." The approach was particularly effective with people who were open to registering or were on the fence: "As a group we found 15 who more than anything else, needed an invitation."[40]

On Sunday, March 3, Hall and Holsaert were still suffering from the flu, so after helping make copies for the Albany night school and driving Barrett and Eddie Browne to Albany churches to distribute the fliers, the two went back to bed to rest. Hall's letter to SNCC, drafted the next day, began with an eloquent, prophetic statement: "There's a throbbing all over me, a never ending ache back and forth across me. It is cold pain frozen within my soul by the suffering of the years and add to this my plight—I stand within the center of a razor blade, high walls of stainless steel around me—boxed. The ugly face of Segregation hovers over me ... but this is the beginning."[41]

The next day, Sherrod met with the team preparing to move into Terrell

County—Hall, Holsaert, and Neblett—primarily about practical safety in the rural counties. They decided to remain within one block of Carolyn Daniels's home in Dawson, and to take Eddie Brown with them if they decided to leave the block, as a witness.[42]

At a March 4 mass meeting, Slater King, Charles Sherrod, Marian Page, and Rev. Pamela June Anderson reinforced the importance of maintaining the boycott of segregationist businesses, particularly given the proximity of the Easter holiday. Hall was unsettled by the meeting, confused by the crowd's quiet agreement instead of its usual "clap at everything" response to Sherrod's exhortations. Both Sherrod and Slater King expressed disappointment with the "lethargy" of the people in Albany regarding the movement.[43] Gathered, the crowd listened to President Kennedy's forty-minute radio address on the occasion of the fiftieth anniversary of the Department of Labor, which disappointed Hall: "He oaked the salve of irrelevancies on the people's conscience." She lamented that he did not use his "good-natured charm" in "ways in which he could really serve."[44] After the meeting, Hall, Barrett, Holsaert, and a few other SNCC volunteers spent time with C. B. King.[45]

Around 1:00 a.m., Hall left with Holsaert and two other SNCC volunteers for Terrell County.[46] This particular move into Terrell County was important because of Faith Holsaert. Moving white men into black neighborhoods in Terrell was a significant step, made easier by the "affectionately open personality" of Ralph Allen. Holsaert's transfer to Terrell, however, created "havoc for the white community" because she was a white female. She understood the risks and liabilities and agreed to "be extremely careful in an attempt to avoid violence." Holsaert stayed several nights at Daniels's house but never officially lived there because of the certain danger such news would bring.[47] During the first week of Holsaert's residency, she and Hall canvassed close to where she was staying, for safety: "You see, we are trying to gauge the climate in the community in an attempt to control a potentially explosive situation. If there is violence we would like to feel that we have done all we could to prevent it—everything short of dishonest compromise that is."[48] They recruited several high school students to keep them informed of what the community was saying about SNCC.[49]

Examples from Hall's Albany field reports provide an impression of the workers' specific interactions with the locals. Hall invested several visits with a Mrs. Holloway, who supported the movement but would not register, nor would she allow others in her household to register from fear that the men would lose their jobs. Hall did most of the talking, offering many good reasons for Holloway to at least come to a meeting, which Holloway agreed to do if SNCC could provide a ride. The perpetual issues with SNCC not having reliable cars often limited them.[50]

In yet another report, although Hall was well acquainted with Mrs. Bell's daughter, Peggy, Hall described Mrs. Bell herself as "A STRANGE BREED." Bell allowed SNCC to visit her and her daughter but made clear that neither she nor Peggy would register to vote. Mrs. Bell later became extremely supportive of the Albany night school. Peggy, around nineteen years of age, had a small child and could not register because of her mother's threats to kick her out of the house "if she had anything to do with it," rooted in Bell's fear of segregationist retaliation. On March 6, Hall met with Bell privately while Holsaert and Chico Neblett met with Peggy in another room of the house. Hall recognized that Bell was observing them just as they were getting to know her. Bell's reasons for not registering gave way to new excuses, which Hall viewed as evidence that Bell might be losing her "firmness" against involvement. As they left her home, Mrs. Bell "went to the yard to chop wood." Neblett helped her for thirty minutes, but she still told Holsaert and Hall that she could not attend the mass meeting because she had too much ironing to do. "Faith and I just didn't have the time to do her ironing for her. Maybe next time we will, if we think it will work."[51]

The Sumter County team drove Holsaert and Hall to the mass meeting in Terrell County that evening. A large number of high school students hoped to attend, but SNCC's difficulty securing working cars prevented their transportation. Hall took notes during the meeting, and Holsaert sketched people from the meeting, something she had wanted to do but could not because she was usually taking notes.[52]

On Thursday, March 7, 1963, the Albany City Commission voted six to one to desegregate Albany and reopen the Carnegie library—which had been closed for seven months to avoid demonstrations. Albany movement and SNCC leaders were "overjoyed" at the decision, not realizing its emptiness as a scheme to further insulate Albany from federal civil rights prosecutors.[53]

The ordinance only meant that the city would no longer enforce segregation, leaving the decision of integration to individual citizens and business owners. The library immediately removed all chairs to prevent integrated seating. Police asked demonstrators to leave restaurants, libraries, and movie theaters. The city later privatized all three swimming pools. Claude Sitton reported: "[Police Chief Pritchett] sitting in his newly renovated office flanked by the flags of the United States and the old Confederacy, glanced up from his glass-topped desk and grinned. 'You look around and see if anything's integrated, and if it is, call me will you?'" Pritchett worked around civil rights laws. Though he had arrested 1,500 demonstrators since November 1961, he always did so with nonracial charges, such as parading without a permit, obstructing traffic, or loitering. He laughingly claimed to enforce the law "without regard to race, creed or color." Pritchett also promoted himself as protecting local black people who opposed the movement.[54]

News of Albany's integration did not immediately reach Hall, hard at work canvassing for voter registration throughout Terrell County. On the afternoon of the ruling, Hall visited Mrs. Brown, Mrs. Bell's sister, who had convinced herself that she might contract various diseases if she attended a mass meeting. Hall suggested to Mrs. Bell that sometimes going to church can help a person feel better when they are sick, but Bell responded with another story of someone who became terminally ill from attending a meeting. Hall noted: "It's amazing what forms fear will take. Maybe one day we can write a report just on the many ways fear comes out once it has been digested. Such a report might give us some insight into dealing with and remolding fear into courage." Brown asked Hall about the rebuilding of Mount Olive Baptist Church, burned in the summer of 1962, and Hall said she believed this was coming soon. Hall noted in her field report that the church's rebuilding would mark a "turning point" in their work in that area, which Hall suspected explained city leaders taking such great lengths to interfere with these efforts.[55]

After visiting Mrs. Brown, Hall and Holsaert met John Churchville and Larry Rubin, who were to drive them to the Sumter County meeting. As they stopped at a fuel station in Dawson, a police car also stopped at the station and followed them to Carolyn Daniels's home, where Hall and Holsaert were staying. The car continued to follow Rubin and Churchville "with their bright lights on to the edge of town."[56]

The incident scared Hall. The next morning, after Hall saw a white man with a raised tool approaching the window, she "let out a terrific scream and went leaping like a mountain goat into the bedroom." Holsaert flattened herself against the wall, and Neblett assured them both that the man worked for the electric company and was only inspecting the meter. Hall explained that when she saw him "she hadn't waited around to ask questions," not realizing that he had come to disconnect their power due to an unpaid bill.[57]

Later that day, Hall and Holsaert canvassed a young student from Carver High School who seemed drawn to them as a "mother-sister combination," which this student craved after her parents' separation. Hall and Holsaert asked her about police brutality against black people in her neighborhood on the weekends, and the girl confirmed that this happened regularly, even to her father. As Hall and Holsaert visited Mrs. Toliver, who was open to registering but could not attend mass meetings because of her young children, Hall rocked one of the babies to sleep. Hall and Holsaert offered to stay with the babies so Toliver could attend the meeting. Next, they visited Mrs. Hightower, a seamstress, who offered to take Mrs. Toliver with her to the next meeting.[58]

On the evening of March 8, Hall and Holsaert went to Albany for a staff meeting and party. The two were reassigned to Dorchester, and Neblett would stay in Albany. Holsaert expressed frustration at the amount of investment required to make inroads in the rural communities and the interruption in these relationships caused by transfers to other areas.[59] On Saturday, March 9, Hall and Holsaert worked on field reports and cleaned house. They were worried about growing tension in Albany and were glad to attend the mass meeting that evening where they learned of progress with voter registration canvassing.[60]

On Sunday, March 10, because of a malfunctioning vehicle and the danger of walking, those staying with Daniels were unable to attend worship. They were, however, able to attend an evening meeting, where they observed police interrogating Sherrod, trying to trap him on "contributing charges" to the demonstrators arrested the previous day.[61]

As the activists met, a loud knock on the door announced the arrival of several Mississippi SNCC leaders: "We didn't even say hello, we just sat back and sang for about half an hour." Hall and several others left for Dorchester after the meeting to attend an interorganizational workshop hosted by the Fellowship of Reconciliation on nonviolence, relationship between the organizations, and strategy, joining with other civil rights leaders such as James Lawson, Bayard Rustin, and Martin Luther King. Hall spoke as the SNCC representative for Southwest Georgia and emphasized the importance of leadership from within the local community. Those at the interorganizational workshop also discussed ways to encourage community economic efforts. When the meeting ended on March 13, Hall, Holsaert, and Neblett returned to Carolyn Daniels's home in Dawson.[62]

Daniels spent two weeks in Florida for a job, which led many in the community to suspect that "Mrs. Daniels has run away from it all." The three workers staying in Daniels's home were flooded with calls from people in the community wanting more information.[63] When Daniels returned home on March 16, her shop was crowded with people who wanted their hair styled for the weekend, so Hall and Holsaert used the opportunity to recruit voter registrants.[64]

On Monday, March 18, Hall and Holsaert visited Mrs. Perry, Daniels's next-door neighbor, who was, in Hall's words, "sort of the everybody's maiden aunt type." Holsaert noted: "Mrs. Perry does appreciate the niceties of life, and Prathia and I can nicety her right into registering, I think."[65] They next visited Mrs. Sanders, an older woman restricted to her home while caring for ill parents. Sanders forbade her granddaughter Mary from participating because of the danger.[66] Cases like Sanders led Hall and Holsaert to suggest SNCC organize itinerant freedom school tutors offering education to those unable to come in the evenings. They recognized the power of education and its appeal in the rural counties.[67]

Later that day, Hall and Holsaert visited Mattie Mae Jackson, a former client of Daniels, who "just hadn't had time" to have her hair done since the shooting at Daniels's home. She avoided eye contact with Hall and Holsaert, sneaking glances at them occasionally. They encouraged her to see the opportunity for her to be part of changing the system that she feared, but as they were talking, she sat on her bed, "trying to shrink into as little space as possible, trying to exist as little as possible." Hall and Holsaert continued canvassing on Tuesday, March 19, even as they noticed two white boys on bicycles watching them and white-driven cars often passing Daniels's house.

For a March 20 all-day staff meeting in Terrell County, Hall and Holsaert prepared a report of their activity and recommendations based on their canvassing experiences. They suggested creating responsibilities and leadership opportunities for some of the high school students. Holsaert reported: "Prathia has stated very well the present situation in Dawson as far as our opposition is concerned. That is that the frenzy there is high, but that the authority has subjected itself to a new discipline, and that when these two elements are brought together, we will have real trouble."[68]

After the meeting, Hall, Holsaert, Larry Rubin, and John O'Neal canvassed to promote the mass meeting in Terrell that evening. Though Terrell meetings typically averaged fifteen to twenty-five people, there was standing room only in that evening's tent meeting. A carload of young men in their twenties arrived, one of whom had turned to alcohol to muster the courage to attend. SNCC celebrated the age diversity of those in attendance, each of whom could "penetrate another level of the community." Hall and Joyce Barrett were in Philadelphia from March 21 to 28 because of a death in Barrett's family. While there they spoke to several union groups, promoting SNCC's work and recruiting northern support.[69]

In late March, Hall was back in Terrell County with Faith Holsaert and Chico Neblett.[70] Neblett commented that he, Hall, and Holsaert worked "well as a team even under all the restrictions." The three frequently discussed strategy and ways to foster better group relations within SNCC.[71] The entire Southwest Georgia team traveled to Sasser, in Terrell County, every Wednesday for tent meetings.[72] Their work must have been fruitful because Chatfield heard over the radio in early April 1963 that Terrell County had formed a Terrell County White Improvement Association, "organized for the sole purpose of figuring out and dealing with integration groups in this racially-disturbed corner of the free world."[73]

In mid-April 1963, Sherrod implemented his idea of revolving staff among the counties, which was widely unpopular with SNCC's staff. Under the new plan, workers traveled between counties for meetings and to help each other as needed.[74] All field staff from Southwest Georgia met in Albany on May 14 and decided to focus their efforts exclusively on making Albany an "open city." In the meeting, SNCC staff agreed that success in Albany would directly benefit not just Dougherty County but the other counties, as well.

After their conversation, SNCC workers actively recruited at area schools for additional volunteers willing to be arrested in the inevitable backlash against their intensified efforts in Albany. Meetings and marches continued the next day as well. At Terrell County's mass meeting, Hall and Holsaert reported that Terrell County was "carrying on fine without them" and that the meeting was well attended: "a full tent without the Albany kids to swell the numbers." Terrell County was best equipped to self-manage due to the rebuilding of the churches burned in summer 1962. Sumter County boasted high registration numbers. Lee County, however, had several willing canvassers, but SNCC workers struggled there without transportation or strong local leadership.[75]

Barrett wrote a letter about SNCC's decision to focus on Albany to Fellowship House on May 14, addressed to "Family":

> We've just decided to go all *out* ourselves and raise hell.... Sherrod has said I'll be one of the first ones to go to jail—which may mean today or tomorrow. If I go, I'll probably stay a while. Do whatever you can for publicity for us, especially if Prathia or I are involved (she may lead a night march).
>
> We're sitting on a powder keg down here. The Birmingham riots are being felt across the nation. Students fighting in Knoxville, Nashville, sitting-in in Raleigh. Some kids shot at the police last night here—and threw bottles. We have no choice but to *move* now. I love you all.[76]

Upon receipt of Barrett's letter, Marjorie Penney shared at a Fellowship House meeting: "The girls expected they would be arrested very soon as activities get hotter in Albany. They had little money available at the time of their last letter." A board member motioned to send $100 to Hall and Barrett from the board, which was "overwhelmingly approved."[77]

Within the first week of this aggressive new recruitment campaign in Albany, May 14 to May 21, ten civil rights workers were arrested. Hall and Barret, along with Joni Rabinowitz, William Anderson, and Slater King, were arrested on the morning of May 21 for distributing leaflets outside the Dougherty County Courthouse, urging black citizens to vote against a $7.9 million bond to fund construction of new city facilities. When voters inquired whether the new facilities would be integrated, city leaders gave only vague answers or changed the subject.[78]

The "Big Push" in Albany struggled, however, to find brave people willing to be arrested. The Interfaith Ministerial Alliance, a group of ministers from area churches, met to coordinate efforts and marches, but "the real problem behind the whole meeting was that none of the folk there outside of SNCC were prepared to go to jail."[79] Workers continued nurturing the mass meetings out in the counties and pressing for increased voter registrations.

In June 1963, the Southwest Georgia Project nearly halted when twenty-two of its twenty-six staff were arrested within one week in a police attempt to deter SNCC's daily demonstrations.[80] Arrests began June 20, and by June

22, more than 140 demonstrators had been arrested: "They were picked up singly and in twos and threes, during marches, while canvassing, or as they entered a local church to attend a mass meeting." Police "slapped and manhandled" women, and white integrationists were jailed with other whites, who physically assaulted them for what they saw as betraying their race.[81]

When Cathy Cade's father, William Cade, came to Albany in June 1963 after his daughter's arrest, he went to the SNCC headquarters. He described his interactions with Hall and Barrett: "I was introduced to Joyce Barrett, Prathia Hall, and the rest. Joyce was a young white girl very pretty, delicate face and good figure. Prathia was a young colored girl about 20–25 with a good mind and very commanding presence—somewhat masculine in her authority, I should say." Once Sherrod arrived, the four conversed about the project and Cade's status. Her father recalled that "during the next two hours of conversation interrupted by the phone ringing every 5 minutes, Joyce and Prathia constantly said to Sherrod, Don't you think this is right and he always agreed. It was apparent that the two girls were running the show." The next day, Cade attended a mass meeting at Arcadia Church at 8:00 p.m., led by Hall: "Prathia Hall started the meeting with a reading from the bible about the torture and martyrdom of the Christians according to Paul. Prathia is an excellent preacher with a beautiful contralto voice. She led several freedom songs and also introduced me as the father of Cathy who was one of the girls in jail."[82]

During the month of June, Chief Pritchett moved twenty-two imprisoned SNCC workers to Lee County. The remaining students, including Hall, hid in the SNCC offices "to avoid wholesale arrests by the Albany police on charges ranging from 'distributing leaflets without a permit' to 'investigation of suspicion of vagrancy.'" A phone call alerted the students to move to the home of SNCC supporter Aurelia Noble, with no suggestion for how to get there. The group disguised themselves in dark coats and smeared soot on their faces, hiding under the cover of night. They escaped through a back door into absolute darkness, hiding from police cars whose lights were casing the SNCC office and nearby alleys. When a dog barked at their presence, its owners turned on backyard lights, and the group froze in an alley for almost an hour until the lights were turned off.[83]

Arriving at the safe house, the SNCC students were "offered sanctuary" at Albany's Beulah Missionary Baptist Church. Rev. Samuel Wells and schoolteacher McCree Harris drove the students (the white students lying down across the seats) to Beulah. The males slept "in a room on one side of the church with the deacons, females on the other side with the deaconesses." After one of the students from the North played "jazzy blues piano," Beulah "evicted" the students. They hid in Shiloh Church for eight days. Joann Christian Mants's father, James Christian, and her cousin, Monroe Gaines, guarded the back door of the church, "under a spotlight, with their guns across their laps" to protect the workers from the Klan, which had been "circling" the church after dark.[84]

Hall and childhood friend Joyce Barrett spoke to SNCC reporters: "We are afraid here. We are afraid that this community may explode."[85] Demonstrations—met with police intimidation, arrests, and brutality—were the only way to communicate with city leaders or draw national attention to racial injustice in the South. Chief Pritchett stayed "one jump ahead" of SNCC's plans, however, since SNCC lacked sufficient funds to post bail for everyone arrested; some remained in jail "long past their time."[86] Without masses of people to support the core two hundred Albany volunteers, demonstrations did not reach the potential Sherrod hoped they would.[87]

As Ralph Allen described, "factually and tangibly, nothing was accomplished except the destruction of the impact of much of Sherrod's idealism. . . . This is not to say that Sherrod's theories about the people are not true, but rather to say that they must be taken along with an honest assessment of their context, i.e., tyranny of Pritchett, and his rather studied policies of suppression." Allen was a young, black volunteer who worked with Don Harris in Sumter County after working in Dawson with Sherrod, with whom he had significant differences of opinion concerning strategy. Certainly not all SNCC workers in Southwest Georgia held such strong views against Sherrod or his tactics. Allen even suggested that Sherrod relinquish his administrative duties to someone better skilled in this area, and instead focus his time on vision and planning.[88]

Prathia Hall shared Sherrod's idealism, speaking often of the inherent good in people, with faith that justice would win the day. After returning to Southwest Georgia from Atlanta on July 12, Allen found "Prathia on cloud 6 1/2 telling me from up there" that their next demonstration—a prayer meeting at a church near the pool, followed by a series of demonstrations, pickets, and boycotts across the city—on July 13 "was the day." Hall helped plan the demonstration, optimistic that local volunteers could be recruited.[89]

Mass demonstrations like the multisite event planned for July 13 required hundreds of volunteers, which SNCC had not had in Southwest Georgia since early 1962. SNCC's executive secretary James Forman recognized Hall's ability to lead a large movement and later selected her to lead the Selma, Alabama, project in fall 1963.

SNCC's July 13 mass demonstration plan did not go as planned. When police thwarted the planned attempt to integrate the pool, Randy Battle, Phil Davis, and Pete DeLissovoy began running toward the pool: "We turned around—and when we started running, we hit that fence and were over that fence and in that pool in a second. And we swam on 'cross that pool to where the ladder came up and then we went out that back gate."[90] As they ran, a collie chased them, accelerating their getaway from the police. They ran to Arcadia Church and hid up a tree in the churchyard. As the water dripped from their clothes and shoes, three deacons noticed them and sheltered them inside the church building. Battle described white reaction to what some referred to as the Great Pool Jump:

> Look here, though, the funny part of it, the best part of it all, when we hit that water in the pool, when they looked over there and saw "them niggers" in that pool, goddam it them white folks and kids went straight up in the air, they didn't climb out, they went straight up in the air and *flew* over to the sides—I mean that's what it seemed like to me. I bet you in half a minute there wasn't nobody in the pool but the three of us. And they started screaming and hollering, "Niggas! Niggas!" Them white folks hit the air like *dolphins*, you know, right up in the air they flew."[91]

In the afternoon of July 13, Hall, Holsaert, Barrett, and Ralph Allen met with C. B. King to discuss concerns regarding relations between staff members. At a staff meeting the following day, several themes emerged. Taking stock of the situation in Albany, namely the lack of new local volunteers, the Southwest Georgia SNCC team transitioned from mass demonstrations toward radical, small demonstrations with a higher probability of victory, such as the Great Pool Jump. Leaders who pushed for this change did so based on their belief that "Albany could no longer bear the burden of the movement without some kind of victory." By focusing their limited resources on "smaller, more specific goals," they believed that "a series of victories may rebuild the power of the Albany movement." One of their first implementations of this approach was to delegate research projects to discover potential sites for focused efforts.[92]

The interracial nature of the Southwest Georgia project remained a sore spot even for some within SNCC and the Albany movement. While Sherrod, Hall, and Forman remained committed to integration as necessary, others expressed subtler resentment at the increasing number of whites in SNCC. For example, at the end of the July 14 Albany meeting, Hall returned from Atlanta with news that two new students, both white, would, in Ralph Allen's words, "descend from the heavens above to bestow their 'creativity' upon us." Allen believed that the growing number of whites in Southwest Georgia aggravated white Albany, resulted in more frequent and more expensive arrests, and enabled "a detached melancholy" spectator-mentality in Albany's black community.[93]

Throughout the summer of 1963, the Southwest Georgia Project continued to absorb new workers, and, with the Albany Big Push plan gathering workers from rural areas, the population of SNCC workers in Albany swelled to an all-time high. The SNCC house became overcrowded with people, causing inconvenient and dangerous situations for the workers, which Allen explained in a field report:

> Actually, you take all the problems raised above in connection with the detrimental effects which whites have had upon the people of Albany, and you add to that the number ten,—ten or so people who aren't self-sufficient and who have to be told when it's time to eat and where, have to be kicked out of the Big house at night so Prathia can get to sleep, ten people who have to be closely watched because they aren't sensitive enough to know what they are doing in the eyes of the community, don't know that they should be afraid of being seen alone with a black chick, or that they should be afraid and wary of certain types of social intercourse."[94]

Certainly an interracial team was more difficult for Sherrod and Hall to lead than an all-black team would have been. Hall played a key role in educating northern whites in the culture of the rural black South, particularly the necessity of leaving the comforts of the SNCC house in order to do voter registration canvassing and of developing sensitivity to the behaviors that could endanger SNCC workers and local volunteers.[95]

After mass arrests throughout the summer, including that of several dozen teenage girls held in the Leesburg Stockades for several weeks without clean water or basic amenities in August 1963, the DOJ intervened by convening a federal grand jury in Macon, the first ever to examine civil rights in Southwest

Georgia. The whole affair, however, functioned as a trial against civil rights workers for demonstrations at a white-owned grocery store in April 1962.[96] Great Pool Jump coconspirator Joni Rabinowitz was convicted of perjury for denying her presence at the demonstration, despite the testimony of multiple witnesses that Joyce Barrett was present at the grocery store, not Rabinowitz—who was likely targeted because her father, Victor Rabinowitz, represented Fidel Castro in U.S. trials concerning the U.S. embargo on Cuba.[97] Five other Albany civil rights workers were charged with perjury associated with the case. Demonstrations erupted in Americus after the verdict, and police started shooting into the crowd as they sang freedom songs, trampling and attacking demonstrators with cattle prods and other weapons.[98] Police brutality in Americus escalated, and four civil rights workers were charged with insurrection, facing the death penalty. Don Harris, Ralph Allen, John Perdew, and Zev Aelony were held for several weeks under these charges before they were released in November 1964.

By the fall of 1963, the "solid movement people in Albany" were tired. Police had mastered the art of mass arrests, and the city had instituted discriminatory policies to interfere with voter registration and integration.[99] By the end of 1963, however, SNCC workers in cooperation with local civil rights workers had raised the number of registered black voters in Terrell from fifty-one in 1960 to 140 (a 270% increase). The statistics remained harrowing, however, as registered black voters in Terrell County still numbered less than 5 percent.[100]

Just as SNCC made inroads in Albany by late 1963 and early 1964, police harassment of movement activists continued in the rural counties.[101] In spring 1964, Albany attorney C. B. King announced his candidacy for Congress for the Second District, which included Dougherty, Baker, Randolph, Terrell, and Worth Counties. SNCC's Southwest Georgia Project expansion covered nearly every county of the Second District, which sparked exponential growth in voter registrations.[102]

> "We've got to get Prathia out of jail today.
> We need her, man."

A slave market before the Civil War, Selma, Alabama, later became a military hub for the Confederate army, a well-known center for lynching until the 1950s, and the birthplace of the White Citizens Council. The black

Table 2. Voter Registration in Dallas and Wilcox Counties, 1962 or early 1963

Voter Registration Demographic	Dallas	Wilcox
Population Total	56,667	18,739
Black Population (% of total)	32,697 (57.7%)	9,894 (52.8%)
Eligible Registered (% of Black population)	130 (0.9%)	0 (0%)
Median Family Income—All	$2,846	$1,550
Median Family Income—Nonwhite	$1,393	$1,031
Median Grade Level Completed—All	8.7	6.7
Median Grade Level Completed—Nonwhite	5.8*	5.5

Source: SNCC, "SNCC Work in Central Alabama," undated, SNCC Papers, reel 10.
* 78 percent of the illiterate population was African American.

population of Selma, the seat of Dallas County, numbered nearly 60 percent by 1961, yet less than 1 percent of those black citizens were registered to vote, compared to 64 percent of eligible white voters. Adjoining Wilcox and Lowndes Counties had never registered a single black voter even though in each county 78 percent of the population was black. The U.S. Department of Justice filed suit to enjoin intimidation tactics against black voter registration, but by late 1963, the suit still had not come to trial.[103]

SNCC explored the possibility of working in Selma in 1962 but initially decided that a project there would be too difficult. When Bernard Lafayette visited Atlanta in 1962 during a break from study at American Baptist Theological Seminary in Nashville, he asked Jim Forman about starting a SNCC project. Forman was hesitant but gave Lafayette the go-ahead to lead Selma.

The Selma project faced several unique challenges. Due to exceptionally high black illiteracy rates there, literacy was a major element of the Selma freedom campaign. Freedom schools educated people in reading, writing, and U.S. history and politics so that they could successfully pass voter registration exams; this also indirectly helped people qualify for better jobs. These efforts struck a nerve since economic disparity motivated white opposition to the enfranchisement of black citizens. Fifty-two percent of families in Dallas County earned less than $3,000 annually, or less than $54 per week, whereas 6 percent of families earned $10,000 or more annually. The president of one of the largest manufacturing businesses in Selma was also president of the White Citizens Council. Other council members held strategic positions in banks and city government and regularly used their power to force other white business owners to participate in and contribute financially to the council as well as to Governor Wallace. The council ran ads with taglines such as "Ask Yourself This Important Question: What have I personally done to *Maintain Segregation*?"[104] Whites in Selma also published *Sex and Selma: The True Selma Story*, which made explicit accusations of sex, exploitation, and greed against civil rights workers.[105]

When SNCC began working in Selma in February 1963, few in the community supported its work, and churches refused to host mass meetings. SNCC workers were regularly followed, beaten, fired at, and unfairly sentenced, as were local volunteers who supported voter registration.[106] Police did nothing to protect the civil rights workers or local sympathizers from segregationist violence, even after a September 1963 Fifth Circuit Court of Appeals ruling against Dallas County for racial discrimination and intimidation tactics.[107] Lafayette was attacked and frequently targeted for arrest. Between September 15 and October 2, 1963, more than three hundred were arrested in Selma because of voter registration work. School attendance dropped from 1,500 to 480 in the week of September 15 alone.[108]

In a 1998 reflection on the movement, Hall described the danger for civil rights workers in Selma: "There was tremendous risk involved in taking freedom's stand. Selma—the atmosphere—the air was pregnant with the smell, the sound, the taste, the sight, the puss, the pain, the heat of brutal violence. But the vision, the fire, the hope, the thrust, the hunger of freedom was so much more powerful."[109]

Even though the federal government filed suit against the arrests, Sheriff Jim Clark maintained authority in Selma, and armed police regularly used intimidation tactics. When Forman came to Selma in May 1963 to speak at a mass meeting, Sheriff Clark's officers surrounded Tabernacle Baptist

Church during the meeting, making a scene about recording license tag numbers. Those gathered remained in the building until 1:00 a.m. until they felt safe to exit.[110] Sheriff Clark attended every mass meeting "with his gun on his hip and frequently, an electric cattle prodder in hand," retaining some three hundred militia in army fatigues and helmets to oppose civil rights and union activism. At a September 1963 meeting, Rev. B. L. Tucker hid in First Baptist Church to avoid a warrant. Sheriff Clark entered the church without regard for the prayers or singing of the more than three hundred people gathered there, grabbed Rev. Tucker by the neck from the pulpit during a prayer, and pulled him to the car.[111] Sheriff Clark ordered dozens of state patrolmen to Selma to surround the First Baptist Church, where mass meetings were being held. Once Selma's jail filled, Sheriff Clark sent the arrested to Camp Selma and Camp Camden, which were state prison road labor camps.[112] Just before his September 24, 1963, arrest, SNCC staff worker Worth Long reported: "Selma is in a state of siege. Everywhere you look you can see state patrolmen or members of the special posse brandishing clubs and cattle prods."[113]

In summer 1963, Bernard and Colia Lafayette took a leave of absence from SNCC's Selma project to test integration in Chicago for the American Friends Service Committee (AFSC). Forman did not hesitate to name Prathia Hall the new leader of the Selma project. She showed excellent leadership in Southwest Georgia, and Forman was confident in her ability to manage Selma.[114] Hall modestly described her appointment:

> Jim Forman and I (and I don't even know why I was asked to go, but Jim asked me) went to Selma. It was an extremely dangerous time. I remember the first mass meeting and how the church had been ringed by the sheriff on horseback and carrying those huge carbines and rifles and Al Lingo and the Alabama State troopers surrounding the church.... In the week ... which followed ... all of the men who had been involved in the project were in jail and at that moment I became the project director.... Need determined how people were utilized.[115]

Hall recognized key local leadership that was indispensable to the success of SNCC's work in Selma. Similar to Southwest Georgia, one of the strengths of voter registration canvassing in Selma was its outreach to young people. SNCC built on the existing gang structure of Selma to harness the influence of these organized young people with canvassing and freedom schools: "With the help of these students and a group of interested adults, the entire town of Selma has almost been canvassed for the first time."[116] Additionally, Hall recognized the importance of the Boynton family, and particularly Amelia Boynton, as a pillar of the Selma project: "In my experience she was the leader of the local movement. There were men and others who were leaders, but it seemed to me that she was clearly respected as a peer among them. And she certainly was by the SNCC people." Amelia Boynton opened her home and office to SNCC workers. Bernard Lafayette worked out of Sam Boynton's office, frequently visiting Boynton during his illness. The first mass meeting in Selma occurred shortly after Sam Boynton's death and may have been a way for mourners to convert their grief into productive activism.[117]

In October 1963, after five civil rights workers were convicted in the Dallas County Court for the September 25 demonstrations, SNCC waged a mass voter registration day, bringing hundreds to the county courthouse to register to vote on October 7. Selma project leaders held mass meetings every night in anticipation of Freedom Day, and several high-profile leaders, among them Jim Forman and comedian Dick Gregory, came to Selma to support their work. Whereas Gregory's speech was more politically charged and biting, Forman's remarks were practical. He instructed those present to look through the phone book for black citizens—"You'll know who's Negro, because they won't have Mr. or Mrs. in front of their names!"—to call about coming downtown on Freedom Day. He delegated each letter of the alphabet among the crowd.[118]

The evening before Freedom Day, Hall and other SNCC workers gathered at Amelia Boynton's house awaiting the arrival of author and SNCC supporter James Baldwin. They fellowshipped in Boynton's kitchen, Forman continuing to address the group even as he scrambled eggs in a frying pan. When Baldwin arrived with his brother, David, the group waited to hear what he would say, but he wanted to hear their plans. Forman spoke first, and then the entire room was buzzing with conversation and debate.[119]

Aside from being present at Boynton's the evening before Freedom Day, October 7, 1963, Hall hid in the days prior to Freedom Day, expecting arrest. Howard Zinn, who was present on Freedom Day, was impressed by Hall when he spoke with her at Boynton's:

> I wondered if Patti [sic] Hall would show up at the courthouse. She was a field secretary for SNCC, a pleasant, very intelligent young woman from

Philadelphia, with a reputation for fervent oratory at mass meetings. She had gained her experience in the movement the preceding year in Terrae [*sic*: Terrell] County, Georgia. Now she was directing the voter registration campaign in Selma. She'd been absent from the mass meeting Saturday night: word was out that a warrant had been issued for her arrest. Yesterday, Sunday, I had spoken to her at Mrs. Boynton's house and was going to interview her at length, but we delayed it so she could get some rest.[120]

Knowing that only thirty or forty of the people in line would have the opportunity to register to vote given the intentionally prohibitive registration process, nearly three hundred gathered at the courthouse in demonstration for voting rights. Sheriff Clark harassed those in line and denied them access to food or water brought by supporters while they waited, nor would he allow them to reclaim their place if they left the line for refreshments or relief.[121] Just before noon, Forman informed some in the line that Sheriff Clark and two deputies had just arrested Hall at Mrs. Boynton's house. Clark returned to the courthouse to gloat over the arrest, calling Hall "his catch." Clark began arresting many of those gathered for "unlawful assembly."[122] Just after noon, Forman walked to the Boynton home to use the phone to alert the Atlanta SNCC office of the arrests, grabbing six SNCC workers on the way, insisting they come with him because the project could not afford for them to be arrested as well. When J. L. Chestnut, the first black attorney in Selma, arrived at the Boynton home, Forman told him: "We've got to get Prathia out of jail *today*. We need her, man."[123]

Fourteen civil rights workers, including Hall, were arrested during the October 7 Freedom Day. Hall was scheduled for a November 14 trial for picketing and contributing to the delinquency of a minor, but the trial was delayed until December after the Georgia Justice Department attorney refused to appear.[124] On February 17, 1964, all fourteen were convicted for violating city ordinances—unlawful assembly and provocation—and fined $300 each. Hall may have also been part of a group of twenty-six arrested in Wilcox County on December 7 regarding alleged discrimination against those who applied to register to vote there.[125]

The Dallas County Voters League and SNCC maintained momentum for voter registration through the mid-1960s. As SNCC's team helped potential voters pass the exams, Alabama issued a state law requiring that voter registration exam questions be changed monthly.[126] The KKK and White Citizens Council held considerable power in Dallas County and continued to harass those in the movement, particularly its leaders and activists who had come to Alabama from out of state.[127] SNCC applied for additional Voter Education Project funds for its expanding work in Alabama.[128]

"Willing to walk face to face with the forces of death in the struggle for life"

Hall described her work in the rural South as the best education she ever received: "I had been to school, I had been to college before I went south, and I've been to school a lot of years since. But the most important lessons that I ever learned, I learned in those rural counties from people who could not read or write their names." The most important part of her work was "talking and listening, teaching and being taught, singing and praying, and offering a helpful presence to women and men, young and old, who acted on the belief deep in their hearts that they *would* overcome some day."[129]

Hall often described this as "mutual educational exchange." SNCC workers had information about how to vote, and the local people "had learned the system and how to stay alive in the system morally, mentally, and spiritually—how to live in an oppressively crushing system without being crushed." She met people who had supported their families on less-than-subsistence wages earned by back-breaking labor and had weathered discrimination, threats, and violence with "strength and nobility." Women like Daniels inspired Hall, "just knowing that they had endured this treacherous brutality for generations, and yet it had not killed their spirit. They were not crushed, they were not victims. They were survivors. They were overcomers."[130] Elsewhere she said:

> The primary lesson I received from those black sages was that of faith for living in life-threatening circumstances. It was a faith first made manifest by our slave fore-parents who defied the teachings of the slaveocracy. ... Those profoundly spiritual women and men developed their own moral critique of the slaveholders' oppressive brand of religion and expressed the slaves' absolute conviction that slavery was contrary to the will of God and that God definitely intended them to be free. These sons and daughters of those enslaved ancestors continued to hold on to that freedom-faith. The freedom-faith fired and fueled the fight.[131]

Hall's father inculcated the theological understanding that God meant all people to be free, that "freedom and faith were woven together in the fabric of life," and that "service to people was service to Christ." In Albany, she contextualized her understanding of Freedom Faith as facing one's fears with courage and confidence that the God who led her there would bring her home. Hall's extended incarcerations added rich hues to her theology of suffering for freedom: "You can never appreciate the peace, the solace, the quiet appalling silence. You read about it in the Bible. But you can't appreciate it unless you've been in jail. Been in jail for a just cause. There is such a purging of the soul that you feel as though you have been relieved of all of your sins. The burdens of the world have been taken off of you."[132]

When someone persevered with courage in spite of their fear, Hall viewed that "as profoundly religious as saying a prayer or doing any kind of religious discipline." The person who trusted God to assist them in their pursuit of freedom in spite of their fears was "now willing to walk face to face with the forces of death in the struggle for life."[133] Hall praised the courage and resilience of generations of black people who survived the brutality of slavery and Jim Crow because of their faith in God: "How had they done that? They had done that because each generation had passed on to the next generation this thing that I call Freedom Faith." Echoing Frederick Douglass's "something" inside of him that was "a religious awakening, a sense of greater destiny, and a deep yearning for his own freedom" and the "something within" of Adam Clayton Powell that gave him the "power to speak" truth to power and "tremendous stability and security" of his purpose, Hall shared this internal certainty of God's call to work for liberation for all people, even knowing the risks of such action.[134] This same Freedom Faith that sustained generations of black people would continue to sustain them as they opposed Jim Crow: "It may cost my job, it may cost my life, but I want to be free, and I want my children to be free. So I'm going down to the courthouse, and I'm going to sign my name. And I'm going to trust God to take me there, and I'm going to trust God to bring me back. That's courage. That's faith. That's Freedom Faith."[135]

Hall's time in Georgia refined her understanding of Freedom Faith from romanticized ideas of braving evil for the sake of good to a more spiritual understanding of faith capable of facing death for the sake of life: "There's the courage that's lived when one *lays down one's life* for a cause, and there is that other courage that is lived when one *lives one's life* for a cause" (original emphasis). She called "living in the face of death . . . the most powerful expression of freedom-faith." Hand in hand with the black sages of Southwest Georgia, Prathia Hall "walked face-to-face with the forces of death in the struggle for life."[136]

CHAPTER 4
"EQUALITY NOW"

"Welcome to Atlanta, a segregated city"

Based on Hall's leadership in Southwest Georgia and Selma, SNCC invited her to Atlanta in late 1963 to help with a growing demonstration campaign there. She quickly became "the Student Nonviolent Coordinating Committee's chief of the Atlanta campaign."[1] During one of SNCC's meetings, Hall made the following statement in her address to local civil rights activists and leaders: "Negroes must also bear the blame for the desecration of humanity that is segregation. For we have been silent much too long. We've been preoccupied with telling our city power structure not what it needs to know, but what it wants to hear. We are here today because we can no longer bear the shame of our guilt, because delay means compromising our dignity ... we are here today to serve notice on the city of Atlanta and the state of Georgia. We are tired of segregation and we want equality now."[2] Hall and the others in Atlanta were prepared to pay the cost of asking for equality now. Twenty-one SNCC workers, including Hall, landed in Atlanta jails over Christmas 1963.

The U.S. State Department invited Kenya's minister for home

affairs, Oginga Odinga, to visit the United Nations in New York to celebrate his new position, and SNCC had arranged for time with him while he was in Atlanta. On the weekend of December 21 and 22, Hall was among two dozen SNCC workers gathered at the Peachtree Manor hotel to meet with Minister Odinga. "Freedom songs of both countries had been exchanged, and the students escorted Mr. Odinga to his car amid goodbyes of 'Uhuru.'"[3] After the meeting, the students went to a Toddle House restaurant to eat but were denied entrance, in plain sight of Odinga. Presidents Kennedy and Johnson had both made strident efforts to befriend leaders of newly independent African nations to prevent their potential alliance with Russia, but racial segregation in the United States proved a sore spot in these negotiations, of which Odinga's trip to Atlanta was a prime example.[4]

On Monday, December 23, Prathia Hall, Roberta Yancey, Lillian Gregory (wife of comedian Dick Gregory), and a group of other SNCC workers returned to the Toddle House on Peachtree Street. When the restaurant refused to serve them coffee, they sat-in at the counter. Seventeen were arrested on the spot, and according to the *Tri-State Defender* (Memphis, Tenn.), state attorneys waited on the scene.

The next morning, Christmas Eve 1963, Hall, Gregory, and Yancey were arrested. "Misses Hall and Yancey, who refused to cooperate with police as did most protestors arrested at the eating place, were dragged and carried to a paddy wagon. Mrs. Gregory, who is expecting a child in April, 1964, walked." Hall, Gregory, and Yancey held stock in Dobbs House Inc., which owned the Toddle House chain, and made national headlines—"Stockholders Accused of Trespassing," "New Civil Rights Tactic—Buying Stock," and "New Type of Woman in Civil Rights Work"—for being arrested on their own property, held at $100 bail.[5] The three were held in solitary confinement at what was known as Big Rock jail in Atlanta.[6]

The Executive Committee of SNCC sent Atlanta mayor Ivan Allen a heated telegram concerning the arrests: "We hold you totally responsible for any harm that comes to the three prisoners who are now in the Fulton County Jail, Miss Prathia Hall, Miss Roberta Yancey, and Mrs. Lillian Gregory." The telegram urged Allen to pass an ordinance for full integration of public facilities in Atlanta.[7] In a later telegram, SNCC appealed to Allen's desire to present Atlanta as a modern city in its correspondence, contrasting Atlanta's "liberal image" with throwing demonstrators in jail on charges of trespassing.⁸ SNCC also telegrammed Attorney General Robert Kennedy in protest of the arrests.⁹

Also on Christmas Eve 1963, SNCC workers staged demonstrations at Allen's home and office with signs reading, "Black is Not a Vice or Segregation a Virtue; Atlanta's Image is a Fraud" and at the airport with welcome posters: "Welcome to Atlanta, a Segregated City." On Sunday, December 29, SNCC workers repeated their demonstrations at Allen's home, singing freedom songs, demanding a public accommodations integration law, and protesting the unsanitary conditions that Yancey, Gregory, and Hall faced behind bars, where they were held until January 2.¹⁰

Attorney Howard Moore represented the three in their municipal court hearing for their Christmas Eve arrests. The Atlanta manager for Toddle House Corporation, Harold D. Furrow, testified in court that "the three were creating a disturbance." Though bail was set at $100 each, they opted to remain in jail.¹¹

After ten days, Hall, Yancey, and Gregory were released from jail. Four days later, on January 6, 1964, SNCC announced that John Lewis and the Dobbs House management had reached a satisfactory agreement following demonstrations that closed twelve of its locations and resulted in the arrest of twenty-four demonstrators.¹² January 1964 marked an "all-out drive to make Atlanta an 'open city,'" and SNCC took actions that were "more provocative than any civil rights campaign the city had ever witnessed."¹³ Nearly two hundred were arrested for civil rights demonstrations within the month, however, and over three hundred had been arrested since December.¹⁴

On January 11, immediately after a meeting of the Atlanta Summit Leadership Conference, a coalition of national and local civil rights groups, John Lewis, Wyatt Tee Walker, Martin Luther King Jr., Prathia Hall, state NAACP field secretary Leon Cox, six SCLC workers, and Gary Robinson were arrested during a sit-in at the segregated Heart of Atlanta Motel.¹⁵ After her release from jail, Hall returned to Albany for demonstrations at that city's Toddle House restaurant. On January 15, she, Eddie Brown, Slater King, Joyce Barrett, and two others asked to see the manager of the Albany Toddle House when they were asked to leave. After the manager "called (or pretended to call)" the police, the group dispersed. The next day, Hall, King, and Richard Morris met with a "boss man from Toddle House," who expressed willingness to integrate for the sake of his business. The man asked for fifteen days to make his decision and to allow his employees time to adapt.[16]

SNCC's repeated demonstrations led to the successful integration of more than fifteen Dobbs Houses and Toddle Houses in Georgia and some locations in Florida, Texas, and Tennessee as well. Toddle House refused to press charges against the twenty-four civil rights workers arrested.[17] Both black and white organizations on all sides of the segregation debate struggled with the demonstrations.[18] Conflict even ensued between various civil rights organizations regarding strategy, particularly the stark contrast in demonstration approaches between the more conservative NAACP and SCLC versus the more assertive SNCC.

On January 23, 1964, SNCC issued a news release naming Prathia Hall as the leader of SNCC's project in Atlanta. The announcement read: "Miss Prathia Hall, 23, from Philadelphia, Pa., will direct SNCC efforts in Atlanta. Miss Hall has worked for SNCC for over a year, and has been active in voter registration work and direct action in Albany, Ga. and surrounding counties, Selma, Ala. and Greenwood, Miss. She is a 1962 graduate of Temple University and studied political science and religion."[19]

On January 28, 1964, SNCC again directed demonstrations at Mayor Allen: "Demonstrations began with a march of about 75 Negroes and a few whites on city hall. The group sang 'freedom songs' for about an hour, then trooped upstairs to the office of Mayor Ivan Allen Jr. They waited outside the mayor's office while he conferred with Prathia Hall, one of their leaders," asking her for a thirty-day moratorium on protests. In the meeting, Hall read the following statement: "Despite its 'liberal' reputation, Atlanta is still a segregated city. Businessmen are permitted complete discretion whether or not they will perpetuate the continuous insult of segregation and discrimination."[20]

Many public businesses announced desegregation in summer 1963 but had since resegregated.[21] Forman wrote to President Johnson about the Atlanta demonstrations, insisting that Johnson's administration press for desegregation of public facilities. An assistant to the president responded to Forman that Johnson's administration was prepared to advocate strongly for desegregation but anticipated heavy pushback.[22]

Hall and Forman represented SNCC, at Allen's invitation, at a January 29 meeting between white and black leaders in Atlanta, held at the Butler Street YMCA. Allen called the meeting to address "a racial dispute that has resulted in picketing, mass arrests, and scattered incidents of violence during the past four days." Hall and Forman offered to grant Allen's request for a thirty-day cessation of all demonstrations in exchange for the release of all jailed demonstrators, but Allen declined.[23] In spite of Allen's claims of supporting integration, historian Stephen Tuck suggests that Allen was more trying to avoid negative publicity of racial discrimination, which was a nonconfrontational form of white resistance.[24]

The SNCC Executive Committee, of which Hall was a member, issued a strongly worded statement supporting continued demonstrations, such as those in which Hall had been arrested: "Negroes across the country . . . one hundred years after the Emancipation Proclamation, find themselves half slave in the South and half free in the North. . . . As long as injustice and racial discrimination exist in this country, demonstrations will continue."[25]

"She belongs to me, 'hide, hair, and talon'"

A battle quickly ensued between federal officials and Georgia state courts over jurisdiction concerning civil rights cases. Demonstrators were at the mercy of Atlanta's Fulton County Superior Court judge Durwood T. Pye, notorious for excessive bail amounts and harsh sentences. He "insisted upon approving all bonds himself," and the Georgia Supreme Court had mandated that he reduce his bonds numerous times.[26]

Judge Pye required appeal bonds be posted with "unencumbered property located in Fulton County," refusing to accept cash payments. Both criteria specifically limited bail release for civil rights demonstrators. He fined the Atlanta branch of the NAACP $25,000 for refusing to release financial records. He obtained indictments against 101 civil rights demonstrators in Atlanta, dating back to 1961, claiming that Georgia's antitrespass law was "flouted, defied and violated." Even for defendants who had been previously freed on bonds of $300 or $500, Pye often "acted on [his] own motion" to raise bail to $3,000 or more.[27] Pye served as head of the Georgia Education Committee, an openly pro-segregation organization. As a judge, he was known as "a scholarly white-supremacist," opposed to "the mongrelization of the races." He was also known for giving maximum sentences to white civil rights workers.[28]

Though Pye could have tried all of those arrested on January 11 at the

Heart of Atlanta Motel together, he insisted on trying them individually and required that all thirteen attend each of the thirteen trials. Joyce Barrett described the tactic as "trying to tie us up" from participating in or organizing further demonstrations during the time it took to get through all the trials.[29] Prathia Hall was to be the second defendant tried. After the first student's trial, the group's lawyers found precedent to remove local cases to the federal court. The U.S. District Court filed a petition on February 17 for seventeen of the at least twenty sit-in cases to be moved to federal jurisdiction.[30]

The federal jurisdiction tactic angered Pye, as reported in *Time*: "The Federal-state showdown began when Judge Pye refused to surrender jurisdiction of SNCC worker Prathia Hall, who was held for 14 days under $4,500 bail."[31] Hall anticipated Judge Pye sentencing her to the maximum extent allowed: six months in jail, one year in the county work camp, and a $1,000 fine. Although she appeared in all of her calls to court, the trial court delayed proceedings for irrelevant reasons. Hall's lawyers claimed in court proceedings that she was being subjected to "cruel and inhuman punishment" by the Northern District of Georgia "by virtue of the fact that she is not actually being detained and held in the custody of the Sheriff of Fulton County, Georgia, on excessive, unnecessary, and unreasonably high bail pending trial upon an indictment charging a misdemeanor violation," which was in itself an unconstitutional act of racism. U.S. District Judge Boyd Sloan, in Gainesville, Georgia, issued a second temporary restraining order against the state court trying Hall on March 19, 1964.[32]

Judge Pye insisted he had rightful jurisdiction over Hall, that she belonged to him, "hide, hair, and talon."[33] He affirmed the January 28, 1964, indictment of Hall by the Grand Jury of Fulton County, claiming legal right to detain her until she posted bond: "This Court declines to surrender jurisdiction.... Under no circumstances whatsoever is the Sheriff to deliver her to the United States Marshal."[34]

On March 20, Hall and other defendants filed a motion in U.S. District Court appealing for Sloan's help on the basis that they would not receive a fair trial in Fulton County because of Pye's history of excessive bonds and sentences for civil rights cases. Sloan issued a restraining order against the Fulton County solicitor, sheriff, and any others working under Pye's orders to take action against any existing civil rights defendants. Hall was already in custody, however.[35]

Judge Sloan demanded to assume Hall's case after a brief hearing where he determined that she was being illegally held for not posting bond. He censured the county court for not allowing Hall to sign her own bond even though she was not a property owner, reducing the bond amount, or proceeding with the hearing of her case. Sloan charged Fulton Superior Court with violating title 26, section 3005 of the Georgia Code. He issued an injunction prohibiting Pye and the county prosecutor from trying or prosecuting Hall. "Armed with a writ of habeas corpus, U.S. marshals whisked her out of her cell and freed her on $1,000 bond" around 1:30 p.m. on March 24. Sheriff T. Ralph Grimes did not impede federal marshals from taking Hall, though Pye's court filed a motion to remand the case back to Fulton County the same day.[36]

Sloan ordered Hall to be held by federal commissioners and issued a temporary restraining order against Fulton County officials until she could post bail. Pye erupted when Hall failed to appear for her misdemeanor trial on March 23. Because she had been "taken from him by the United States court and . . . was no longer in his custody," there was no way for the court to enforce the trial.[37] The Associated Press quoted Hall on her release: "It feels very good to be out."[38] The case progressed through various stages of appeal between Fulton County and the State of Georgia and was not fully dismissed until April 2, 1968.[39]

In total, federal court orders prevented the trials of fifty-eight civil rights defendants by removing them from Fulton County jails.[40] Pye reluctantly recessed Hall's case and told reporters that "the United States government, which has taken the defendant (Miss Hall) away, should bring her back. When that is done—if it is ever done—the trial will resume."[41] Pye quickly scheduled trials for forty-two more defendants, all of whom were also removed from his jurisdiction, and a March 25 court order enjoined Sheriff Grimes, Judge Pye, and anyone taking orders from either of them, from taking action against any civil rights petitioners.[42]

The showdown between federal and state courts, initiated by Hall's case, was rare. The U.S. Code allowed a defendant to petition for removal of their case from state to federal court "if his civil rights are nullified by the state's legal apparatus." Although the violation of civil rights were difficult to prove, and federal courts were hesitant to accept such appeals, the swarm of civil rights cases in Georgia in 1962 and 1963 and Pye's racist reputation aided the successful appeal to the Fifth Circuit Court of Appeals. Pye unsuccessfully counterappealed to the U.S. Supreme Court against federal seizure of civil rights cases from his jurisdiction.[43]

"A new type of woman in civil rights work"

While Hall was held under Judge Pye's orders, a *Washington Post* article on the organizational prowess of women in the movement, "New Type of Woman in Civil Rights Work," recognized Hall's significance: "The Student Nonviolent Coordinating Committee's Prathia Hall, 23, a Philadelphian, presently is in jail for violating Georgia's anti-trespass law by trying to register at the Heart of Atlanta Motel. Miss Hall, who has been arrested a dozen times, is a tall, stately woman who sees the whole civil rights movement as 'one human being's treatment of another.' She often speaks of the 'sense of dignity and nobility' Negroes in the rural south have acquired through voter registration campaigns."[44]

In many ways, Hall's work built bridges between South and North to support civil rights work. Not only did Hall's southern family background help her train northern students for work in the South, but her fund-raising and speaking tours brought the emotional and financial support of northern churches (and denominational bodies) to civil rights work in the South. She was a civil rights warrior.

Dr. Anna Arnold Hedgeman—a co-organizer of the March on Washington for Jobs and Justice, coordinator of special events for the Commission of Religion and Race of the National Council of Churches in South Dakota and Nebraska, an advisor for the contents of the 1964 Civil Rights Bill, and later a cofounder of the National Organization for Women—heard Hall speak on multiple occasions during Hall's tour of the Dakotas and Nebraska. On one such occasion, Hedgeman admired that Hall arrived to the speaking engagement directly from a demonstration picket line and "reported with unbelievable calm" that "I have come tonight not to entertain you, but to trouble you." Hall then described in graphic detail how black people and civil rights workers were "kicked, beaten, spat upon for the sin of working for participation in democracy." Hedgeman was so moved that she shaped her recommendations for updates to civil rights legislations based on Hall's message: "Remembering that day and listening to Prathia made it absolutely necessary that my report on the need for help on legislation relate itself adequately to the story she had just presented to us." Hall had formed such significant relationships through her speaking tours that when news of her 1964 Atlanta arrest reached the Midwest, executive directors of state councils and conventions began networking to organize help for her and others with her.[45]

"Just being their real selves"

In 1964, Harry Belafonte financed a trip to Africa for select SNCC workers. Belafonte wanted to demonstrate that SNCC was part of a worldwide movement for freedom, as well as provide a much-needed respite for key leaders after the disappointing 1964 Democratic National Convention in Atlantic City, where delegates of the Mississippi Freedom Democratic Party, both black and white, were denied representation. SNCC executive secretary Forman had been intentionally connecting SNCC's work in the United States with freedom initiatives worldwide and promoted SNCC's trip to Africa in the context of the African independence movement.[46] SNCC invited James Forman, Ivanhoe Donaldson, Courtland Cox, John Lewis, Fannie Lou Hamer, Unita Blackwell, Ruby Doris Smith Robinson, and Prathia Hall to participate in the trip, each being identified as the top four male and female leaders of SNCC.

The team made a two-week visit to the Republic of Guinea, September 12 to October 5, as guests of President Sékou Touré. While in Guinea, SNCC's travelers met with the National Revolutionary Council as well as with President Touré three times. John Lewis and Don Harris remained in Africa for several additional days, traveling to Liberia, Ghana, Kenya, Ethiopia, and Egypt, during which time they met with a number of political officials, political activists, newspaper reporters, and Malcolm X, as well as attended the Zambian Independence Ceremonies.[47]

One of the most formative experiences of the trip for Hall was seeing black people with self-determination. As she witnessed luxurious living accommodations designed, managed, and occupied by black people, as well as the lowering of the British flag and the raising of the new Zambian flag, for the first time, Hall saw black people in authority, proud of their culture.[48] Hamer similarly noted the power and beauty of African people, and African women acting naturally and freely, "just being their real selves and not having to pretend to be somebody else."[49] The domination of white norms had long caused black people to see themselves as inferior, but witnessing black people running their own country, holding every possible job, and doing so without apology displaced black shame with black pride. This experience clearly exposed the entrenched injustices of white dominance, reinforcing SNCC leaders' commitment to the global freedom struggle that would allow all black people to hold their heads high.

Hall's connection to Africa persisted long after the trip, evidenced by her inclusion in a group of SNCC workers who stayed abreast of news from South Africa, particularly of the mutual benefit of the U.S. Civil Rights Movement and South African self-determination to each other. Indeed, Hall remained informed of news of the South African freedom movement well past her involvement with SNCC.[50] She received selectively addressed memos concerning potential SNCC projects in Africa. For example, an August 17, 1965, memo from Don Harris, drafted on hearing that South Africa was developing a nuclear reactor, was addressed to "Prathia, Ruby [Doris Smith Robinson], John [Lewis], and Jim [Forman]."[51]

"One of the most moving speakers I have heard in my life"

Hall's rising leadership only strengthened her renown as a speaker. After the shooting at Carolyn Daniels's Dawson home in September 1962, Hall spent the fall of 1962 fund-raising for SNCC throughout the Northeast. Her first engagement was a rally at Tindley Temple Methodist Church in Philadelphia, where she shared the podium with Albany's Dr. Anderson. After Hall spoke for the Women's International League for Peace and Freedom in December 1962, Naomi Bernstein, the program chair "felt particularly moved to help SNCC in some way partly because [she] was so impressed with the courage and strength of Praethia [sic] and her co-workers.... Praethia is a very eloquent and sincere young lady." Bernstein sent Hall a copy of her letter to Jim Forman "so that she will know what listening to her for a half-hour meant to us and others like us."[52] Jerry and Naomi Bernstein requested that Hall speak at a September 7, 1963, rally in Philadelphia to begin an AFSC group there, and Hall shared important Philadelphia activist connections with the Bernsteins to assist their work.[53]

Fund-raising and student activism picked up significantly in Philadelphia, particularly through the joint efforts between SNCC, Philadelphia's AFSC, and Fellowship House and Farm. Hall's speaking and connections laid a strong foundation for establishing this work.[54]

Hall spoke at the 1963 Methodist Conference on Human Relations in Chicago, which she found particularly meaningful and "well worth the time taken from the work to be done in the field down here." Dr. King also spoke at this meeting, held August 27, the night before the March on Washington. Hall watched the march on television from her Chicago hotel room.[55]

By fall 1963, Hall was on a nationwide speaking tour for SNCC.[56] Her speaking engagements included the 1963 Lutheran Student Association national conference in Lake Geneva, Wisconsin; the National Federation of Catholic College Students in Minneapolis; the September 1963 Baptist Student Ministry General Assembly of the American Baptist Assembly; and the September 5-11, 1963, National Student Christian Federation at Chicago Theological Seminary. After speaking at the October 1963 National Council of the Churches of Christ in South Dakota and Nebraska, Dr. Anna Arnold Hedgeman, the organization's coordinator of special events, wrote to Forman: "It was my privilege to hear Prathia Hall in Nebraska and she is one of the most moving speakers I have heard in my life."[57] Hall also spoke for the North Iowa Conference of the Methodist Church's "Race Dialogue Seminars" in November 1963, addressing social aspects of racial tension. Hall was the keynote speaker at the Kansas Baptist Student Movement's state convention in December 1963. Earlier that month, she spoke for St. Benedict's College in Minnesota about her experiences in Albany, Georgia. Often religious leaders who heard her speak would invite her to speak at their next rally, such as happened with the pastor of First Methodist Sheldon, Iowa, who wrote to her to ask her to speak at their district rally in 1964: "We did like your spirit and know you are bearing a witness that many of us are unable to do.[58]

Hall continued speaking at gatherings of the Friends of SNCC, a network of SNCC supporters, across the North during the spring and summer of 1964, raising financial resources for SNCC's work in the South. These rallies mobilized northern sympathizers to become politically involved in support of civil rights legislation. She also spoke at club meetings, such as the Mason City District Woman's Society of Christian Service meeting in Osage, Iowa, April 7, 1964.[59] On August 9, 1964, Hall was the final speaker at an ecumenical memorial service for slain SNCC workers Andrew Goodman, James Chaney, and Mickey Schwerner, hosted by the Philadelphia Friends of SNCC at St. Thomas Episcopal Church in Philadelphia.[60]

The Bernsteins of Philadelphia were so captivated with Hall's speaking abilities that they frequently requested her as a speaker. Naomi Bernstein, part of a large Reformed Jewish Congregation in Philadelphia, requested that Hall speak at their annual Social Action Sisterhood Meeting, held March 1, 1965. Hilda Wilson, of Philadelphia Friends of SNCC, inquired: "The woman who contacted me had heard about Praethia [sic] Hall and wondered if she might be available. I think Prathia would be ideal for this kind of group." The meeting organizer hoped to give the five hundred women in attendance specific ways to assist civil rights work in the South: "Because of the strength this group *could* give if they wanted to, I feel, as I said before, Prathia would be most ideal."[61] Hall was deeply involved in SNCC's Selma project at the time, as well as speaking engagements at a number of colleges and community organizations, but Betty Garman, northern coordinator for SNCC, affirmed that the meeting would be worth Hall's time if Hall was available.[62]

Specific requests for Hall to speak were only one source of her speaking engagements; James Forman and Julian Bond often recommended Hall to speak in their places. When Vincent Harding asked Julian Bond to appear at his February 29, 1964, Student Conference on Religion and Race, Bond responded, "I think Prathia Hall would make a better presentation. I will be there, however, if I can prevail upon her to appear in my stead, I would prefer it." A civil rights organizer in Manhattan, Kansas, began her letter to SNCC: "Prathia Hall was in Manhattan this Fall and that will be a never-to-be-forgotten evening."[63]

The Commission on Ecumenical Mission and Relations of the United Presbyterian Church in the USA hosted an orientation for "Christian leaders from this and other countries who have shared the experience of social upheaval in our time." The meeting focused on the theological issues of the Civil Rights Movement in the United States (held at the International Theological Center in Atlanta, May 7–9, 1964). The commission, which enjoyed a strong relationship with SNCC, initially asked Forman to help with planning and had written to Hall specifically to invite her to be part of the conversation, requesting her "theological insights" from the Movement. Forman was in England during the conference, and Hall assumed his place in planning and speaking for the event.[64]

Prathia Hall's exemplary leadership and dependable character were widely recognized within SNCC. By March 1964, Hall was elected to SNCC's Executive Committee.[65] Hall's leadership, particularly her grasp of the complexities of civil rights activism, was so well respected that SNCC asked her to train volunteers in its 1964 Mississippi Freedom Summer. She recognized the potential for increased awareness and support possible with a large influx of white volunteers, a key strategy utilized in Southwest Georgia. Hall felt prepared to advance this strategy into Mississippi Freedom Summer.

Hall's unique background as a black person from the North, educated in predominantly white schools, with southern relatives, gave her the insight and vocabulary for guiding northern white college students in navigating southern black culture. She could translate between northern, southern, white, black, urban, and rural culture, making her indispensable to SNCC's work. Hall trained the college students who volunteered for Mississippi Freedom Summer, headed by Robert Moses. Beginning June 21, 1964, at Western College in Oxford, Ohio, Hall prepared nearly a thousand volunteers for voter registration canvassing and Freedom Schools in a two-week training orientation, sponsored by the National Council of Churches.[66]

Whereas white students who joined SNCC in the early 1960s could eventually earn positions of responsibility within SNCC, the nature of Freedom Summer did not as easily render itself to inclusive leadership. White volunteers for SNCC "did not have this period of incubation, of sensitization" because they were "oriented in a hurry." Many of these students "had never had to 'take low' for anything ... never had to not speak their mind ... never had to not do whatever they felt like doing." Because white students worked within black communities, their actions "immediately put everybody's lives at risk," which is why Hall and other SNCC leaders gave Freedom Summer volunteers more restrictions than was typical for SNCC.[67]

On June 10, 1964, approximately two dozen SNCC staff met to discuss the Mississippi summer project, an aggressive voter registration drive throughout the state. When conversation steered toward Bob Moses's collaborative relationship with the Council of Federated Organizations (COFO) for the Mississippi project, Moses's loyalty to SNCC and its priorities came into question. Hall challenged the group: "There are undercurrents not far below the surface that should instead be discussed at this meeting, such as violence and nonviolence, black and white tensions, and Jim Forman's role." Mary King was amazed at Hall's ability to capture and redirect the discussion to productive avenues. She praised Hall's leadership in this meeting: "[Moses and COFO] was not what Prathia Hall, strong, proud, and always a moving speaker, wanted to talk about."[68]

The pressing conversation regarded the real and present danger facing civil rights workers in Mississippi, intensified by the aggressive nature of their voter registration campaign. Hall knew that their proposed project would result in volunteer deaths, that they would be organizing a project certain to have casualties, and this forced the question of what made a project truly nonviolent: "What is happening now is that for the first time we as a staff are coming to grips with the fact that this may be *it*. . . . I don't have a martyr complex; I'm fighting because I want to live. Living in this system has not been life for me. But, I can't take someone else's life knowingly. We must decide what is life and what is defense of it." According to Mary King, every eye in the room was on Hall, waiting to hear her next words. She continued: "Willie [Peacock] said he was concerned for the people around the office who might die. But at the same time you shoot a person breaking in to plant a bomb, you might shoot someone who broke in because of hunger. I thought we were going to Mississippi because people have been getting killed there for years and no one cared. I thought we were going there to say to the world that if any of us dies, it was not a redneck who shot us but the whole society that had killed us."[69]

Particularly since some of those working with SNCC in Greenwood, Mississippi, were carrying firearms, Hall recognized the need to reiterate their nonviolent strategy, even in tense short-term experiences, as part of their long-term mission: "We are fighting here because we want life to be worth living." Hall was not afraid to die and continued that they would persist even if someone had to "bring our blood to the White House door."[70] King grasped Hall's meaning: "Prathia was making us confront the probability that there would be deaths as a result of the Mississippi Summer Project." This was the first time in preparation for that event that the SNCC staff had considered their responsibility for one another and the likelihood that they or the new students they were recruiting might die.[71]

At the November 1964 SNCC meeting, Hall again demonstrated sage leadership. Various factions within the leadership argued concerning the organization's purpose, strategy, and future direction. While others drowned in the minutia, Hall articulated the importance of conversation toward constructive changes for SNCC: "Maybe the past hang-up meetings lead to this serious meeting. Now we're at least arguing that we have disagreements and that we have a lot to learn. Things were really happening in the workshops, and this is a good sign as to where the retreat is going." Hall hoped that SNCC would continue to be the "outside force to get other outside forces to bring about change" and that SNCC should "make it so uncomfortable for the power structure, that it has to deal with the problems." She also suggested that since direct action functioned as a component of other strategies and not in isolation, each strategy should discuss incorporation of direct action campaigns within their projects.[72]

Between late 1964 and early 1965, Jim Forman named Hall as the Atlanta office manager: "She should be considered as the person in charge when you want to solve a problem through Atlanta." Ruby Doris Smith Robinson worked directly under Hall as personnel officer. Forman's health suffered, and Hall and Robinson relieved pressure from him so he could rest.[73] During this time, Hall also performed clerical duties as needed, such as making calls on the WATS line (a precursor of flat-rate long-distance calling, which SNCC used as its primary communication with workers in the field).[74]

Hall's exemplary leadership and dependable character were recognized beyond SNCC. An October 18, 1965, memo from Bayard Rustin of the A. Philip Randolph Institute included Hall's name on a selective list of leaders: John Morsell, A. Philip Randolph, Dorothy Height, Norman Hill, Whitney Young, Prathia Hall, Walter Fauntroy, and James Farmer. The memo summarized a mid-October meeting in preparation for the White House "To Fulfill These Rights" conference, scheduled for spring 1966.

"A bloody mess"

As in Southwest Georgia, much of SNCC's work in Alabama was helping the local people overcome their fear. Voter registration work in Alabama was dangerous, and Sheriff Jim Clark relentlessly pursued civil rights activists in Selma. He spied on mass meetings, taking names and car tag numbers. Segregationists targeted movement leaders, and those who attempted to register to vote were often physically assaulted by police.[75] SNCC expanded its work, undeterred, and Selma officials continued mass arrests of demonstrators, often with harassment, brutality, and injunctions banning any kind of demonstration, including lining up to register to vote, "in and around" the courthouse in Selma.[76]

Malcolm X visited Selma in early February 1965 to support the movement there. In one of his final speeches, he said: "If white people realize what the alternative is, perhaps they would be more willing to listen to Dr. King." X referenced rising militarism within the movement and the potential for retributive violence should white authorities in Selma continue assaulting black citizens. Two weeks after leaving Selma, X was assassinated in New York City on February 21, 1965.

As Hall led a February 4, 1965, meeting in Marion, Alabama, she reported that two hundred parents were arrested the day before, protesting against the previous day's arrest of over seven hundred children. Hall lamented the jail conditions: four hundred detainees in a bare fifty-by-sixteen-foot space, without a working toilet, heat, beds, blankets, or access to water or medicine, even for the pregnant women among the parents arrested.[77]

The escalation of violence—and more than three thousand arrests—in Selma in February 1965 inspired SCLC to orchestrate a nationally advertised march. SCLC planned a fifty-mile march from Selma to Montgomery to demonstrate for racial equality. When SCLC announced their plan, SNCC elected not to participate. Betty Garman Robinson recalled a SNCC staff meeting, held the night before the march: "I remember the Alabama staff saying, We have to march with the people, even if SNCC is not going to take a position in favor of this march.... If we've been working with the people and the people are going, we are going to stand with the people, and we're going to be a part."[78] Immediately following the meeting, John Lewis and John Love departed for Selma.

King initially hesitated over the march on learning that Governor George Wallace planned to use any means necessary to prevent their success. He wanted to delay the march. Hosea Williams, one of his aids in SCLC, and SNCC's John Lewis agreed to lead the march.[79]

On Sunday, March 7, 1965, at 3:00 p.m., two thousand marchers started out from Brown Chapel AME Church in Selma on their walk to Montgomery. As they reached the Edmund Pettus Bridge over the Alabama River in Selma around 4:00 p.m., they saw that Sheriff Clark had blockaded the bridge with armed state troopers. Clark demanded they desist their march, but the marchers continued to the bridge. With the call of "Troopers advance," Clark unleashed his officers on the marchers, who huddled together for protection and prayer under the assault. Horseback officers trampled them and blinded them with tear gas.[80] Even as marchers ran from the scene, "troopers and posse men, mounted and unmounted, went after them."[81] Police waged war against the marchers for more than two straight hours, no holds barred.

Seeking refuge after the attack, between two thousand and three thousand wounded marchers returned to Brown Chapel. Volunteers treated minor injuries and offered spiritual and emotional support to survivors of police brutality. Grass-roots resistance to nonviolence had already been escalating, and leaders of SCLC and SNCC needed to prevent retaliatory violence demonstrations, which would surely be met by even more intensified white violence against Selma's black community.

When SNCC received word about the attack at the Edmund Pettus Bridge, its leaders were still meeting in Atlanta. Harry Belafonte quickly chartered a plane to transport key leaders to Selma later that day. Working at the national office in Atlanta that organized the flight, Judy Richardson realized that SNCC was sending only men and told Forman, "we need to get Prathia there." Alongside Forman and four other SNCC leaders, Hall traveled to Selma to assist with the aftermath of Bloody Sunday; she never forgot Richardson's sisterhood in getting her on that plane.[82]

The memory of arriving in Selma on March 7 haunted Hall: "When we got there, it was a bloody mess. The church was a bloody mess. People were bleeding and in pain."[83] Hearing the people talk about being "ready" for the next police attack, two SCLC staff members started singing, "I love everybody in my heart, I love Jim Clark in my heart, I love the state troopers in my heart." Seeing blank stares from the people and fearing potential violent retribution against the white community, one SCLC staff member demanded that everyone sing "I love Jim Clark" and mean the words in their hearts, or they wouldn't see Jesus when they died.

To Hall, this was "spiritual extortion." She continued, "These were people who had lived their whole lives with only the hope of seeing Jesus when they die.... That particular incident was an abuse of the people's faith." Even in nonviolence, Hall believed there had to be "a place for the expression of legitimate rage." She understood that SCLC was loath to see demonstrators resort to violence, but she also understood that "at that time they were too brutalized to become violent. They had been beat. They had been really beat."[84]

Following Bloody Sunday, Hall was among the SNCC leadership who strategized SNCC's next steps in Selma. Across the South, by 1965, SNCC prioritized voter registration over direct action demonstrations. Particularly with the momentum built by the Mississippi Freedom Summer, the Mississippi Freedom Democratic Party, C. B. King's candidacy in Southwest Georgia, and Bloody Sunday, SNCC ramped up its efforts to register as many black voters as possible.[85]

Having returned to Southwest Georgia following the aftermath of Selma's Bloody Sunday, Hall was arrested with Barrett and many others in May 1965, organizing with the other interned protesters a fast to protest their arrest. In a letter to FH on their eighth day in jail and the second day of their fast, Barrett reported on the effect Hall's strength of faith held for all of the activists in jail: "Prathia and the gang have just finished singing 'Near the Cross'—and it seems very fitting. Today I don't feel very idealistic.... I guess my faith needs strengthening." Barrett described their cell mate, a prostitute and drug addict who, after overdosing on smuggled pills, was given a shot at the hospital and returned to the cell, where she convulsed in withdrawal for hours. Just as Barrett and Hall had laid down for the night, the addict hung herself using a blanket; Barrett and Hall could not loosen the blanket, but a guard did eventually pull the victim down. The days turned to weeks in jail without food or anything other than fitful sleep, but Hall and Barrett never lost their "nonviolent curl."[86]

For a brief period during summer 1965, Hall also helped with AFSC school desegregation efforts in Georgia and Mississippi for federal agencies. In July, 1965, Hall traveled to Houston, Wheeler, and Telfair Counties in Middle Georgia. School systems employed a multitude of intimidation tactics to prevent black students from integrating white schools, such as strictly limiting when students could register and publishing the names of those who registered. Local police did little to protect families of black registrants from white reprisal, which had the effect of limiting black registration at white schools.[87]

Hall networked between local ministers, NAACP leaders, and national organizations. She spoke at meetings, educated the community on procedures for school desegregation, and organized lists of black families interested in registering their children for white schools. A growing number of students transferred from the black school in Perry to white schools in Warner Robins, but after her three-day visit, Hall felt that she "had just gathered enough information to put in two or three more days at full steam with very good results." Hall recommended an "intensive campaign" for school desegregation in Warner Robins to Connie Curry, who returned to Houston County later in June 1965. From the list of contacts that Hall had gathered, Curry was able to help fourteen students apply for transfer. The students who applied were denied, and AFSC field representatives helped these students appeal through the court system.[88]

Jean Fairfax, the AFSC's lead for southern programs, specifically requested Hall to report on Sunflower County, Mississippi. Hall knew about the Carter family, the only family to sign the freedom of choice forms for school integration, for which someone had shot into their home on August 16, 1965. While the shooting caused no injuries, other SNCC workers warned Hall not to venture into the Carters' hometown of Drew in Sunflower County unless she was prepared for arrest. Hall reported to Jean Fairfax: "A Mr. Jones who lives on a plantation near the Carter family came into Ruleville to talk to me. He talked about the fear that kept people from transferring their children. He said that many families discussed the matter when the forms were first sent out. They were afraid of reprisals. The shooting incident had ruled out the choice completely." Fairfax immediately called Assistant Attorney General for Civil Rights John Doar, who contacted the FBI about investigating desegregation in Drew public schools.[89]

Between the events of early 1965—the assassination of Malcolm X, the murder of Rev. James Reeb in Selma, and Bloody Sunday—and the consistent emotional and physical violence toward activists at the hands of law enforcement and community leaders throughout the duration of the movement, many who practiced nonviolence questioned their resolve. As leaders like SNCC's Stokely Carmichael promoted Black Power, and as black communities continued to suffer terrible costs for their involvement in the movement, commitment to nonviolence waned.

SNCC moved toward Black Nationalism, eventually expelling all of its white personnel. Hall found herself in stark disagreement with the organization, as did many others. She believed nonviolence and interracial cooperation were the necessary means *and* ends of the movement. Everything in her religious and intellectual background nurtured her in interracial, intercultural, and ecumenical cooperation for social justice. While Hall supported the success of black men, the post–Waveland retreat "Black macho rhetoric" of SNCC disturbed her as a woman.[90] She did not support the expulsion of whites from SNCC, nor did she support the marginalization of women from leadership roles, further complicated by the Feminist Manifesto, written by white SNCC workers Mary King and Casey Hayden, inspired by second-wave feminism.[91] For Hall, the Civil Rights Movement was about "one human being's treatment of another," advocating for the right of every human being to be treated with a "sense of dignity and nobility."[92] The rise of Black Power, the marginalization of women from leadership, the white focus of second-wave feminism, and the increasing physical toll of repeated trauma compounded into a complicated, profound grief.

Distressed about the direction SNCC was going and exhausted by years of trying to live out her Freedom Faith in the face of white anger and violence, Prathia Hall returned to Philadelphia in 1965, reuniting with her long-term boyfriend, Ralph Wynn, whom she had met there before she joined the movement.[93] She and Ralph had become engaged by fall 1962, but remained on-again and off-again while Hall worked in the South. During and prior to their long engagement, Hall wrestled with the idea of marriage on two levels. As a strong and industrious woman, she worried that marriage might impede her future, limiting her career and personal potential. She also worried about Ralph himself, since he was more conservative than she on several issues.[94]

In 1997, Hall told Ella Baker's biographer that in the early 1960s she had sought counsel from her mentor about the realities of marriage for strong women:

> I was trying to deal with whether or not to marry.... I kind of thought that I probably wouldn't marry. I had been engaged and then broke the engagement. And then later we kind of reconciled and I ended up married. But during that time I talked to Miss Baker and that was when she just shared a little bit of her experiences about being married and about how men had difficulty being able to accept strong women. And how difficult it was. At the same time, she would never tell me what to do, she just said what her experience was and the choice was mine.[95]

These conversations with Baker gave Hall a sense of solidarity: "It was the gift of talking to a woman who really understood my struggle, one that I didn't have to explain myself to." Reflecting on the importance of those conversations, Hall said, "The more I talked to her, the more I understood myself." Hall had always felt "different" from even close members of her family, but in Baker, Hall found "a kind of daughterhood." Baker "understood the being different and how passionately committed I was. It was in every fiber of my being, it wasn't something that I was just down there doing. It was my identity."[96]

Having rejected the new militancy that was incompatible with her Freedom Faith, Hall married Ralph almost immediately after returning to Philadelphia. Fellow SNCCer Constancia Dinky Romily was Hall's maid of honor. Ralph's job required that the couple move to New York, where Hall worked for SNCC's New York office. After the birth of their daughter, Simone, Hall worked for the National Council of Negro Women on Project Womanpower, which attracted "a number of the SNCC women." Hall also worked with the AFSC. Among the few speaking engagements she accepted was the Mississippi Freedom Labor Unions and Their Effect on the Southern Economic System on October 28, 1965, at the Loeb Student Center of New York University Friends of SNCC.[97]

Generally, Hall embraced a season of rest after the movement, which she later compared to Vietnam veterans returning to the States, often needing years before they could talk about what happened: "We have a name for it now, post-traumatic stress syndrome. You had been through a war." Not only was each activist processing their emotional experiences of living in the nightmare, but many, across racial lines, faced continual intense personal pressure from unsupportive, invalidating family members. Hall believed that these compounded stressors required recovery time after the movement, and in some cases, caused premature deaths, incited hasty and unhealthy marriages, and delayed the ability of activists to write about their experiences.[98] Having left the battleground of the South as SNCC transitioned from its nonviolent stance closer to militancy, Hall was determined to find a way to practice her Freedom Faith. This eventually led her into pastoral ministry, where she could continue to promote interracial and ecumenical partnerships for human rights and justice.

CHAPTER 5
"BLACK, PREACHER, BAPTIST, WOMAN"

"I was running nowhere but into the hand of God"

As a child, Prathia Hall dreamed of mission work in Africa, but the injustices in her own country drew her into domestic activism. She entered Temple University in 1958 as a pre-law student but later reflected that "a disquieting consciousness of call to ministry produced an ambivalence regarding career choice and preparation." In 1962, before her work with SNCC in the South, Hall briefly enrolled at Conwell School of Theology in Philadelphia: "Concern regarding the bias within my denomination against women in the ministry and, as I now understand, my own lack of sufficient spiritual maturity to handle that bias, prompted me to withdraw." During her SNCC years, Hall explored her competing desires to attend law school and seminary. She feared the difficulties of life as a female Baptist pastor, but even alternative pursuits as noble as civil rights law could not shake her sense of call to ministry.[1]

After leaving SNCC, Hall served in a number of community organizations. From 1966 to 1967, she was a field representative for Project Womanpower, an organization that recruited and trained local women to participate in social action programs such as daycare, black heritage education, and nutrition. From 1967 to 1968, she served that organization as assistant director, coordinating its field staff and training in New York.[2]

In 1969, Hall transitioned into the National Council of Negro Women (NCNW), originally serving as a program specialist, developing, coordinating, and assessing programs, as well as applying for grant funding. In 1971, Hall became director of the NCNW's Training Institute in New York.[3]

From 1975 until 1979, Hall directed the Hempstead Community Action Program, a delegate agency of the Economic Opportunity Commission of Nassau County, New York, which offered Head Start, community revitalization, drug abuse and prevention programs, youth development programs, and other neighborhood services. She was directly responsible for coordinating all of the organization's programs as well as managing its administration.[4] Throughout the 1970s, Hall also consulted for the College for Human Services and the Philadelphia Council for Community Advancement. She was active in the Board of Education of the Union Free School District and the Roosevelt (NY) Economic Opportunity Council.[5]

Hall remained a strong supporter and engaged member of community activist groups for the rest of her life, including efforts to promote education, public health, adoption within communities, and inclusivity regardless of race, class, gender, or sexual orientation.

With a decade and a half of experience leading community organizations, Hall still could not shake her sense of calling to preaching. She described her wrestling: "The agonizing over my true vocation was diminished but not eliminated, as I worked in the South from 1962 to 1966 and thereafter in the human services/community development field in New York." In 1976, she endured "a period of intellectual and spiritual restlessness" that prompted her return to school, this time with certainty of her call to ministry. Her "decision was accompanied by a deep sense of repentance for the years of reluctance" to accept her call. Dr. H. J. Trapp, pastor of Thankful Baptist Church in Philadelphia, supervised Hall's ordination process, completed in November 1977.[6]

In the initial vote concerning Hall's ordination, the motion passed. A group of men not present at the first vote attended the subsequent meeting and "called for the question again because they had very strong feelings." In the second vote, the motion reached a tie, which resulted in tabling the motion "in the interest of unity." The moderator of the area association of black Baptist churches, Trapp, was a close friend of Hall's father, and counseled her throughout the process. He created a new council of clergymen from the association certain to approve Hall's ordination. She was licensed as a Baptist preacher in the spring of 1977. Trapp entreated the committee not to delay her full ordination because she "was more ready for ministry than the usual candidate who comes along."[7]

Though Hall initially resisted her call to ministry because she knew how difficult the road would be for her as a Baptist woman, she confided in a ministerial colleague at the time that "the call to ministry reached the point it could no longer be ignored," that she must "either preach or die."[8] The only source of doubt concerning her call had always been her gender: "Had I been born male, I would never have questioned that."[9]

At the 1992 Hampton Ministers' Conference, Hall shared the significance of seeing women ably performing in ministry and academic work, which "eventually broke [her] away from [her] old conformity to the restrictions placed on women." Though she had been ministering for years under other job titles, her eyes were newly opened to her giftedness for preaching: "I never wanted to admit I was preaching but time after time, when I spoke, miracles would take place—God did bless." She offered two examples. During a male pastor's sermon, Hall was invited to speak from the floor and was so moving that the pastor "sensed that it would be utter nonsense for him to intervene." She gave the invitation to respond to the sermon that morning, and "*four* adult men and one young lady came forward—three of the men and the lady for Baptism—one of the men having been a Catholic all of his life." Second, speaking in a garage in California, eleven people made decisions for faith, including nine for baptism. "The pastor, God bless him, with tears in his eyes proclaimed things about my ministry that up to that time I had not the nerve to even *think* for myself."[10]

Hall later talked with homiletician Donna Allen about being called into the ministry:

> I feel that preaching is a claim of God by which we are possessed. We talk about and use the language of "my call," but it is not our call. God has chosen us. This is a vocation by which I was not even pursued but I was possessed. What I finally realized about my own call was that, all that time I thought I was running from God, God was holding me while I ran. I was running no-

where but into the hand of God. God was using all my experiences to prepare me for ministry.... I have known since my childhood that my life was not my own to pick and choose what I wanted to do.[11]

Hall entered Mercer School of Theology in New York in 1977, experiencing "a new sense of being 'at home' in a field of study" that she described as her "first love."[12] Returning to school was a "joyous, almost therapeutic balance" for her life. In 1979, still residing in New York with her husband, Ralph, Hall commuted to Princeton Theological Seminary, in Princeton, New Jersey, to earn her master of divinity degree.[13]

Also beginning in 1979, Hall commuted from New York to Philadelphia every Sunday to pastor Mount Sharon Baptist Church, which her father had founded.[14] In fact, her church membership remained with Mount Sharon her entire life. She officially became a member through baptism on her profession of faith in 1951. While living in New York, Hall and her family were involved with Faith Baptist Church of Hempstead and Memorial Presbyterian Church of Roosevelt, but she never officially joined. Between both congregations, Hall wore many hats: pianist, youth group coordinator, Sunday school teacher, Bible school coordinator, lay speaker, and minister.[15] For at least the first four years of her pastoral tenure at Mount Sharon, Hall was not paid a salary for her work. In the early 1980s, Mount Sharon relocated to Broad Street in hopes of growing its membership. Hall asked that the property on West Girard Avenue be given to the pastor in lieu of salary, and to prevent white gentrification of North Philadelphia.

Hall gravitated toward urban pastoral ministry, meeting "the personal and social needs of persons through the liberating gospel of Jesus Christ."[16] In a later reflection on Mount Sharon, founded as a mission church to meet the spiritual needs of children and youth of North Philadelphia, Hall realized that at the beginning of her pastorate, the church was "a small, bruised congregation, suffering from the wounds of recent conflict and separation and manifesting a crisis of identity in its tenacious hold upon a romanticized image of the past and confusion regarding how it should move forward." Her "primary task as pastor" was guiding Mount Sharon "toward utilization of the strengths of the past as foundation and resource for meeting the challenges of the present." Individually and collectively, the church bore the brunt of the "poverty and deprivation" of the neighborhood, and Hall understood her call "to minister to people who hurt the most and receive the least." Rather than relying on clinical pastoral care skills, Hall believed the most important balm for her congregation was "a liberation-modeled ministry," rooted in the historical tradition of the black church.[17]

Though confident in her calling to Mount Sharon, Hall often struggled with the demands of the work. In an early draft of her "The World In Whose Hands?" sermon she shared some of the difficulties of pastoring a mission-oriented church in North Philadelphia. "There is nothing glamorous about the assignment.... There are days, I tell you, when the neighborhood children to whom we minister are running through the place, when twelve can quite authentically simulate an army demolition crew, when I truly believe they may any minute bring the building down." At times, the children brought "the lesson that the street has taught them" into discussion during bible study or choir practice—"that's the lesson to fight over anything or nothing"— and Hall felt the weight of her assignment. "There are days when I find myself in that little place on Girard Avenue literally tearing out my hair, and I look up the Lord of the Church and say, 'Lord, I know you told Peter to feed your sheep, but are you sure this is our assignment? These sheep?' ... And the voice of the Lord of the Church resounds clearly in my consciousness, so clearly I may not be able to sleep that night, 'Feed these sheep: I have left them in your hands.'"[18]

In her community, Hall participated in several organizations focused on investing in the lives of young people in her community and around the world: the Philadelphia chapter of the Association for the Study of African American Life and History, Black Leadership Women, Clergy Concerned about South Africa, and One Church/One Child.[19] She also regularly engaged with her local elected officials. She and other ministers collaborated to oppose House Bill 2044, which sought to limit government assistance to poor people.[20] The legislature passed the bill on October 7, 1980, without addressing the latent classism, racism, and sexism in HB 2044, which Hall fought with a correspondence campaign and testimony before the Senate Public Health and Welfare Committee.[21]

Hall remained firmly Baptist even as she studied at Princeton, a Presbyterian seminary unaffiliated with Princeton University. She appreciated that her "practical religious involvement" had been ecumenical. Rather than denominational affiliation, she prioritized theological education in a school that openly affirmed women in ministry in word. Hall believed that studying "in such an enlightened environment" would grant her "the intellectual and spiritual freedom to confront the real issues which are critical to the Church of Christ in our time."[22]

Hall completed her master of divinity degree in May 1982, while still commuting from New York, coming away with three awards for scholastic and preaching excellence. She applied to the master of theology program at Princeton because her MDiv coursework inspired "a serious desire for further study," particularly of the black "faith tradition related to the contemporary struggle for liberation and wholeness," in anticipation of later doctoral study.[23] By fall 1983, Hall began her doctoral studies in religion and society at Princeton Theological Seminary, overlapping the completion of her master of theology in 1984.[24]

In 1982, Hall became the first female member ever inducted into the Baptist Minister Conference of Philadelphia and Vicinity.[25] In an interview with *Ebony*'s Joy Bennett Kinnon, Hall reflected on her experiences of being the first female Baptist pastor in Philadelphia:

> Every spring there is a great revival in [Philadelphia]. . . . The church is at least half full of preachers. For a few years, I attended that revival desiring to find medicine for my own needy soul. . . . The revivalist came out and thanked God for . . . the presence of all the brother preachers; and, then invited all the brother preachers to stand. Sitting in the pew, I was immediately confronted with a crisis of identity. Which do I own, my call or my gender? Do I sit and deny this call, this claim of God on my life decreed by God before I was formed in the womb? Do I sit and now again, another time add to my own history of shame, for the years I tried to do everything else but answer this call? Or do I stand and deny my gender? A preacher I am, a brother I am not. I finally resolved the violent conflict by standing. Because, when I stood I stood as I am. I stood in the total authenticity of my being—black, preacher, Baptist, woman. For the same God who made me a preacher is the same God who made me a woman. And I am convinced that God was not confused on either count.[26]

"I do not know what else I can be asked to give"

During the early years of her doctoral program, Hall was in the thick of a highly contested divorce from Ralph Wynn, with whom she had two children, Simone and DuBois. Ralph did not support her return for doctoral education, which catalyzed within her a process of awakening, recognizing the years of her husband's lack of support and his abusive behavior toward her and their children. Ralph was verbally, emotionally, and physically abusive toward Hall, which she documented dating back to the 1970s, intensifying in the 1970s and early 1980s. Two weeks before Hall's ordination in 1977, Ralph beat her so badly she required hospitalization.[27] Hall took great offense at Ralph's behavior toward their children: confiscating money DuBois earned from his paper route, treating Simone like a "slave" to housework and chastising her weight, and sneaking out at night, poorly hidden from the children, with no explanation.[28]

Attempting to save the marriage, Hall wrote letters to Ralph, defending her desire for further education as part of fulfilling her call to ministry. In one letter, stained with tears, Hall recounted her faith that if God had called her to this work, God would provide for their financial concerns and heal their marriage as they worked together in obedience to God. As she mailed these letters to her lawyer as documentation, she asked that they not be sent back because, as she explained to a lawyer she consulted early on, "it is a painful reminder of how I have allowed myself to be humiliated, demeaned, and toyed with [over] the years knowing that I was married to a seriously disturbed man and yet foolishly believed that if I loved enough, understood enough and gave enough he would change." This awakening led her to one conclusion: "I have no more to give. This situation has seriously threatened my physical health, has me on the brink of emotional breakdown, and is seriously hurting my children." She further explained: "We cannot live with the hatred Ralph evidences for us any longer. I must have a divorce now. For many years I stayed in this situation trying to spare my children a broken home. The home is broken and they are suffering. Divorce is the only responsible action."[29]

Hall wrote to Louise Robichaud, her lawyer in 1986: "I take full responsibility for the fact that I lived with Ralph for 19 years and took his abuse and deceptions, but in July of 1984 I began action to change that situation. I changed the locks on my apartment and in September 1984, I filed for divorce."[30] Ralph's unwillingness to support Hall's career, though she had supported his at great cost to herself, transformed into contempt and resentment toward her and their children. She refused to report Wynn's abuse because she was afraid that "any scandal or domestic problems would be used against [her] at a time when there was considerable hostility to the ordination of women to ministry."[31] Ultimately, pursuing her call cost her marriage and her ability to speak her whole truth.

Ralph purposefully delayed the divorce process through noncompliance with court orders during their separation, including failure to provide consistent child support and to supply required documentation.[32] Ralph's financial irresponsibility in the divorce caused severe hardship for Hall, including extended legal battles, significant up-front costs for her children's care, and prolonged exposure to Ralph's cruelty. Ralph also interfered with the sale of their home in Roosevelt, confounding interactions with the IRS and potential buyers. Hall finally won relief from the court for the sale of the home, in 2002.[33]

Hall agonized over the injustice of the justice system in her case: "Ralph is treated there as if he is a reasonable, decent, honest, hardworking, self-sacrificing man. And my statements regarding the way he has been with his family are ignored."[34] In July 1985, Hall wrote to Judge Bernard Rudd of the Superior Court of New Jersey about his admonitions to her during the proceedings:

> I filed for divorce after twenty years of a very abusive marriage. As per the advice of the counsel the allegations listed in the complaint were stated with *extreme* restraint. The allegations in the defendant's counterclaim were not only totally false but were in themselves examples of extreme cruelty. For twenty years, I have been bombarded by his accusations charging me with exactly the behavior he is carrying out. It is very difficult, your Honor, in that context to be lectured about "giving" and letting go of the hostility for the sake of the children. I have been in intense psychotherapy for the past sixteen months because for eighteen years I tried to do exactly that. Believing that I must keep the family together at all cost, I suffered to protect the children, my husband's reputation and our public image of a stable, happy home. From the outside we looked *very* good. The price of silence was severe emotional damage to myself and my daughter, now nineteen years of age. It was not until my then twelve-year-old son overheard me pleading with his father for money to pay bills and receiving mockery and threats in return said to me, "Mommy, this is not fair to you. You deserve better than this," and "I know daddy is wrong and it is hurting us to live like this," that I visited a lawyer and signed a complaint. I take the marriage vows very seri-

ously. During these twenty years, I have *given* my life, my love, my labor, my health, identity and very nearly my sanity. I do not know what else I can be asked to give.[35]

Even Hall's children, who loved their father, recognized that their father was not acting fairly in the divorce, as Hall related:

> The day that Ralph left for a business trip in a limousine, leaving us in the house with no electricity, no telephone service, and consequently no food is the day he lost the respect of his children.... They still love both of their parents but I do not believe they were simply trying to please me when they adamantly stated that they did not want their father to have joint custody.... If the children should find themselves alone with their father and he goes into one of his violent rages and assaults them, they should not feel trapped by custody into feeling that he has valid authority over them at that point.[36]

Hall feared that Ralph's anger exposed the children to physical danger. In July 1984, while the family was still living together, Ralph and the children were joking, and then "Ralph suddenly became insanely angry and began brutally beating DuBois for no reason." Hall and her daughter Simone dissipated the tension, but the incident gave Hall and her children significant concern about Ralph's temper and his potential to physically harm them.[37]

In 1983–84, the first year of Hall's doctoral study, she also suffered medical complications, her mother became critically ill, and a close family member died suddenly. "The traumatic and cumulative impact of these events" created significant obstacles to her first years of study.[38] Her PhD advisors had no hesitations concerning Hall's aptitude to complete her work, but several expressed concern about Hall's ability to focus on doctoral work given her pastoral ministry, social activism, and family pressures.

"She is destined for a certain greatness"

When Hall returned to the doctoral program at the Princeton seminary in 1985, she found studying to be "not only exciting learning but good personal therapy." Particularly as she encountered coursework on social justice, she resonated deeply with her academic work: "I was able to freely engage in dialogue with my colleagues and to raise my own questions."[39]

Dialogue was not always as free as Hall had hoped, however. As she progressed deeper her PhD studies, she felt more keenly the isolation of being a black woman in the program:

> I cannot speak for black women Ph.D. or Th.D. candidates in any general way. The program at Princeton seminary is essentially the same for all students with some provision for the students' individual interest. The only other black woman Ph.D. candidate at PTS [Princeton Theological Seminary] and I often commiserate about the particular pressures which we experience as doctoral students. They include the sense of carrying with you the entire African American population at all times; the fear that any failure on our part will reflect badly upon the race in an institution which has graduated less than one handful of black Ph.D.'s; the loneliness experienced in seminar discussions when our questions have not been addressed and colleagues act utterly dismayed when we insist upon bringing into the conversation the experience and reflections of black people's historical context and that of black women specifically.... During the period of my residence I have found my presence itself to be unique. There have been no other black Americans, male or female, in any of my classes and usually not more than three women.[40]

Rather than allow herself to be mired in dismay at the isolation she felt, Hall reflected on the silver lining of her opportunity to build bridges and open eyes: "Students have often commented that my presentations have often served to clarify the issues for them." She also found that her "special insights as a black woman have functioned to make unnecessarily abstract conversations more concrete."[41]

With her children also facing racism at their schools, Hall helped found the African American Awareness Club Parent Support Group. This tiny group of three parents lobbied the West Windsor–Plainsboro school district to recognize and eradicate racism from its schools. Their written statement explained racism, listed numerous incidences of racism by white students (and teachers) against black students (and teachers), and called for decisive leadership by the administration against racism.[42]

On September 10, 1986, Hall suffered severe injuries when a tractor trailer collided with her car, demolishing its entire left side and totaling it. The accident left Hall with multiple herniated lumbar and cervical discs, ordinarily treated through surgery, but in Hall's case was treated through physical therapy alone for unknown reasons. Her pain often "incapacitated" her for five to ten days, sometimes requiring hospitalization.[43] Hall submitted incomplete comprehensive exams, due to severe pain.[44] She petitioned for a leave of absence from her doctoral program in spring 1988.[45] Several of her professors formally expressed their concern about her commitment to her PhD program, some even describing her as having "fugitive status" and having a history of being "the kind of student who needs considerable prodding and initiative on the part of the faculty to keep the work on track."[46]

Albeit slowly, Hall persisted in the program. Having completed her coursework, with only her dissertation remaining, in 1989 she moved to Ohio to join the faculty of United Theological Seminary (UTS) outside of Dayton, where she remained until 1998.[47] Leonard Sweet and Daryl Ward were primarily responsible for recruiting Hall to the United Methodist UTS, where she taught courses in ethics, African American studies, and women's studies: Introduction to Christian Ethics, Womanist Ethics, African and African American Women in Religion, the African American Religious Experience, Critical Issues in Black Theology, and Women in the African American Religious Tradition.[48]

Hall gravitated toward UTS's concern for black church ministry as part of the universal church, rather than an "exotic area of interest."[49] Throughout her career, she was actively involved in the Association for the Study of African American Life and History, the Association of Black Seminarians at Princeton, Congress of National Black Churches, and many others. She believed that the theological foundations of the black church could facilitate the healing and redemption of the global church, in freedom and liberation.

UTS permitted Hall to teach Tuesdays through Thursdays, with the remaining time and summers on leave to complete her dissertation.[50] When she won the 1993–94 Fund for Theological Education Dissertation Grant, she negotiated to teach only one day per week during the fall 1993 semester and teach one course in spring 1994 so she could focus on her dissertation.[51] Also in 1993, Hall became the first woman to preach from UTS's chapel.

The Interdenominational Christian Fellowship Union honored Hall for her preaching in 1993.[52] UTS President Daryl Ward offered warm congratulations for this honor on behalf of UTS: "I know of no one more deserving. United Theological Seminary is proud to have you as part of our team. We spend too much time honoring people who do silly things. We honor people who catch balls, bounce balls, throw balls, and hit balls.... If a TV camera could be 'Holy Ghost Literate,' we would be calling you "Air-Wynn" by now!... I choose you as my mentor in preaching, my model in Christian compassion, and my mark in Godly living."[53] Jeremiah Wright similarly praised Hall's leadership in preaching: "You have set the standard of excellence in preaching, in pastoral care, in love, and in counseling. Seminarians across this nation... are all indebted to you for your fine work, your brilliant mind, your spirit-filled life, and your inspired preaching."[54] A tribute by a fellow woman in ministry celebrated all that Hall had accomplished: "I cannot imagine what this journey would be for you if you were male, with your gifts for preaching, witnessing, church building, teaching, administration, community organization, singing the hymns of Zion.... Thanks be to God for you Prathia."[55] Other organizations and individuals who wrote tributes to Hall in the award program included the Church of God in Christ Commonwealth of Pennsylvania Jurisdiction, the City of Philadelphia City Council, the Philadelphia Baptist Association, Mount Sharon Baptist Church, and Hall's mother, Ruby.[56]

During her time at UTS, Hall also served as associate dean of spiritual and community life, associate dean of the Doctor of Ministry Program, dean of African American Studies, and director of the Harriet L. Miller Women's Center. She furthered the development of a curriculum to "prepare students for ministry in African American faith communities and effective, informed ministry across racial and cultural lines in the whole Church."[57] Through chapel, she facilitated deeper spiritual engagement within the community. She often officiated at services if she was not preaching in them, and she invited the UTS community to reconnect with meaningful liturgy and other spiritual formation practices, across denominational and other boundaries.

Hall crafted retreats on worship and race relations, and she initiated a concerted effort to recruit more black students to seminary education at UTS.[58] She also planned public worship for UTS's diverse population, which she did "with grace and good humor" and "without compromising principle."[59] Hall faithfully supported the school's commitment to its African American Ministries Program during the seminary's leadership and financial turmoil in the mid-1990s, including ensuring the continuation of scholarships, financial aid, academic support, mentoring programs, and access to doctoral programs.[60] She also participated in UTS's Faculty Study on Ecology, Theology, and Justice in 1994, in conjunction with an initiative of President Bill Clinton.[61]

Hall was a finalist for an associate dean for ministry studies at Harvard Divinity School, but ultimately was not selected for the position. Charles Adams, then pastor of Hartford Memorial Baptist Church in Detroit and ranking official of the Progressive National Baptist Convention, as well as one of her recommenders for that position, described her as "the best combination of scholarship and ministry that I have ever known. She is the best preacher I've ever known. She is the best pastor I've ever had."[62] The recommendation from her dissertation advisor, Peter Paris, emphasized Hall's integration of scholarship and ministry, excellent communication skills, and collegiality with coworkers and churches. "She has the capacity to relate meaningfully to people of all walks of life, including a wide breadth of diverse perspectives, philosophies, and theologies.... As a matter of fact, all who associate with her attest of the benefits they derive from that association and I am no exception."[63]

Preaching engagements, teaching, and research kept Hall on the road and in the air a great deal. According to Presttonia Brown: "She traveled incessantly. I mean, I've known her to come in on a Sunday morning or get in Saturday night, stay at a hotel, be at service at Mount Sharon, and be back on a plane or whatever going back to Dayton or to wherever she had to be on Monday morning." Explaining Hall's sense of calling, Brown continued: "She had it in her mind she needed to accomplish these things, and she had a lot to do in a little bit of time."[64] UTS student LaGretta Bjorn volunteered as a personal assistant to help Hall coordinate schedules and preaching contract negotiations.

While teaching at UTS, Hall remained firmly committed to completing her dissertation, but personal and pastoral demands on her time and energy competed with research. She applied for extensions on numerous occasions, and reviewing committees sent her strongly worded provisional extensions, insisting that she make progress in order to continue in the program and that she remain in regular communication with Princeton regarding her progress.[65] Her dissertation advisor strongly advocated for Hall to remain in the program: "I am willing, therefore, to be as helpful as I possibly can to her because I discern clearly (as those of you who know her also do) her multifaceted leadership talents and skills as preacher, pastor, teacher and role model for many.... In my judgment, she is destined for a certain greatness."[66]

Throughout her ministry career, Hall endured severe financial hardship. As a single mother and full-time graduate student with mounting legal and medical bills, Hall relied on preaching invitations and student loans for additional income. She also grieved that her work demands and physical limitations interfered with time she wanted to spend with her children. She studied creative techniques for parenting with the financial and time resources of a single parent.[67] Even once she had secured a full-time income at UTS, Hall juggled the expenses of her son's tuition at Morehouse College and care for her mother and other family members.

On March 6, 1992, Hall's daughter, Simone, died at the age of twenty-five. She had long suffered with health and emotional struggles, including an unplanned pregnancy with long-time family friend Henri McMillian, which resulted in the birth of Michael McMillian on April 30, 1989. During labor, Simone suffered a cranial bleed that resulted in physical complications that troubled her for the remainder of her life. She lived in Philadelphia with her maternal grandmother, Ruby Hall, relying on the help of aunts and other family members to care for her son.[68]

Simone, however, had been strong willed and "fiercely loyal" to her friends, as Henri observed: "If someone needed help, she was there for them."[69] Hall wrote a moving tribute to Simone for the funeral, which lovingly remembered Simone's unique personality, virtuosity in the arts, and independent spirit. Hall also recalled her difficulty in accepting Simone's choice to raise her son despite her health challenges, celebrating Simone's maternal bond with Michael McMillian and promising to raise him as Simone had intended.[70] Nearly ten years later, Hall reflected on Simone's death: "It is an awesome question to learn to live in a space without the physical presence of the child of your own body and one who had been in your life for twenty-five years, but I am learning by living the question. . . . Faith makes it barely bearable."[71]

This exceptionally difficult loss delayed the submission of Hall's dissertation proposal by almost a full year.[72] The delay in progress weighed heavily on Hall, who had administrative as well as teaching responsibilities at UTS on top of a full preaching schedule. After she preached at Tuskegee University in October 1992, Tuskegee's dean of chapel, Edward Wheeler, wrote Hall a personal letter of gratitude with strong encouragement that she prioritize her dissertation. The two, who had been faculty colleagues at UTS before Wheeler's 1991 move to Tuskegee, likely discussed this during her visit.

Wheeler told Hall: "I hope you are *making* the time necessary for you to get your writing done. I know you are on the go. Some of that is the preacher in you that does not know how to say 'No' and some is attributable to economic necessity. I know something about both from a personal perspective." Encouraging her not to get lost in the moment, Wheeler continued: "The work does not disappear. You must do it or it will not get done.... Complete the dissertation and life *will* become much sweeter and you will have more time and energy to do what you enjoy doing (End of Sermon)."[73]

Though the Princeton seminary approved her dissertation proposal in November 1992, Hall continued to file for extensions. When UTS applied pressure on Hall to complete her dissertation, some of the faculty stepped in to cover her course load so she would have more time to devote to writing.[74]

To justify her delayed progress, Hall's therapist, Dr. Leonette Vanderhost, summarized Hall's care since September 1992:

> Rev. Wynn has struggled to continue to work at the Seminary without interruptions caused by her physical state and has been at least partially successful. However, she has been unable to combine work with finishing her degree requirements. She has also been unable to do all that is physically required to lessen the pain, including exercise and following a strict diet. This is partially due to her attempts to meet her work requirements, which involve time and energy constraints. She is also, however, depleted by her feelings of despair and depression caused not only by the death of her young daughter but, also, by the death of her closest friend.[75]

Hall proposed various study leaves throughout 1992 and 1993 in order to make progress on her dissertation. UTS initially structured Hall's position to allow generous time for completing her dissertation, with the expectation that Hall would solely focus on her doctoral work during this time. Dean Newell Wert actually stipulated in a memorandum of understanding that Hall should "confer" with him "before accepting any public engagements (preaching, lecturing, etc.) and that "these should be held to a minimum."[76] This was difficult, as Hall relied on preaching engagements for supplemental income and personal fulfillment.

Hall secured a Forum for Theological Education grant, and UTS president Leonard Sweet generously offered to underwrite half of an eight-month study leave. Traditionally, such a study leave would have been unpaid, but UTS granted Hall half of her salary, even with secured additional grants.

Sweet did emphasize to her, however, that UTS had given her tremendous latitude and understanding: "I especially appreciated your note's sensitivity to the ways in which United has been extraordinarily generous and understanding about your divided commitments, both with your continuing pastoring of the church back in Philadelphia and with the special arrangements and back-up coverage to allow the course of your Ph.D. work to continue apace. We would like to continue that tradition of investment in you without deleterious damage to the programs of the seminary."[77]

As early as October 1993, Hall's work at UTS came under close scrutiny, particularly her directorship of the Women's Center.[78] Hall's application for an ethics position at UTS prompted Provost Maxine Beach to confront Hall about upholding her responsibilities at UTS: "You have been hired to do a job at United that many feel has not been done.... I am seriously concerned about the administration of much that falls within your realm. I realize that you are working away on the dissertation—but also on other commitments in your life (speaking, preaching, etc.), but you do have responsibilities here that must be cared for. If you are not going to do it, then you need to let me know." Many faculty members perceived Hall's administrative abilities as lacking: "Often I hear that the Women's Center 'used to do that' or 'that is what Prathia is supposed to be doing.'" Beach described alums as "mourning the loss of the Women's Center" and even having said that "when [the college] hired Prathia we gained a public figure and lost a Women's Center."[79] Hall felt that "quotes from persons who are to [her] anonymous seem to be accepted as accurate statements creating a negative file regarding [her] work at United."[80]

Beach also criticized Hall's demeanor, specifically her "lack of joy and the heavy spirit." Intending to encourage, Beach suggested that Hall might be in the "wrong job": "Your great contribution to the African American Church and to women is to be honored and celebrated. I rejoice in your preaching and feel my desire for moving on set loose each time I hear you. Therefore, what feels like the burden of your life here is hard to watch. As a woman to woman, I wish for you joy!" Ultimately, however, Beach was preparing Hall for bad news: "As Provost of United, my responsibility is to make needed changes and to celebrate the goodness of this place.... At this time I will have trouble recommending that you continue on in that position."[81]

To facilitate Hall's ongoing role at UTS, Beach and Hall cohosted a dessert conversation meeting at Beach's home on at least five occasions in spring

1994.⁸² In May 1994, Hall received a memo from Provost Beach that the seminary was eliminating her position and dividing up her responsibilities to committees. UTS offered Hall a one-year contract to work in the doctoral studies office, which Hall accepted.⁸³

Hall's June response to Beach's memo conveyed her frustration that the validity of her position was discussed without her having the opportunity to give input. She submitted a defense of her position, including her loyalty to the seminary:

> The issue of time and loyalty was mentioned several times in your memoranda. . . . That the issue of time could be considered an issue of loyalty shocks me, since I am aware of the enormous amount of effort and financial resources I have committed over the past five years to *being* at and with United. It is certainly not logical or usual for one to accept employment which requires weekly or biweekly commuting over a distance of nearly six hundred miles. Approximately twenty to thirty percent of my salary has been used for transportation expenses. That counts, in my life and understanding, as extraordinary loyalty and commitment. I have made this sacrifice and declined offers of positions much closer to home, because of my belief in the vision of United articulated to me and for a time experienced by me.⁸⁴

Hall felt that "the very facts" that once drew UTS to her were being used "as evidence of lack of commitment and service." Though frequently away for speaking engagements, she argued that her work helped to put UTS "out there." She pastored Mount Sharon while working at UTS, a precedent established by many other professors who pastored congregations, although perhaps not in other states. Hall responded to grievances against her still incomplete dissertation with explanation of her financial responsibilities of putting a son through college, the partial leave for research that did not include a reduction in responsibilities, and her medical complications. To complaints that she had failed to fulfill her job description, she argued that she had followed Leonard Sweet and Daryl Ward's request to focus on the most critical aspects first: "Women's Center, worship and faculty presentations." She noted that, while she was held responsible for the administration of chapel, the shared leadership of the chapel presented challenges. Hall defended her pattern of "working carefully and diligently to be faithful to United Methodist worship patterns while honoring the diversity of traditions represented" at UTS. Reconciliation and unity required "some conflict and some suffering," Hall argued, as well as "the collective will to do it."[85]

Perhaps the most alarming development in Hall's work at UTS was the poor performance review of her faculty role. She described her ongoing review procedures with her supervisors and faculty peer groups, as well as her full disclosure of her community and personal obligations, and expressed surprise that the present grievances had not been mentioned in any of those forums. She wrote to Maxine Beach, "I think you can then see how startled I was by your memoranda which judged me on the basis of conversations which neither the Vice President for Academic Affairs to whom I reported nor my faculty peers ever had with me."[86]

Though Hall was transitioning into a new role in doctoral studies, she hoped that by responding to UTS's grievances against her, she could facilitate "constructive and helpful" dialogue as the school moved toward becoming "the UTS community we have declared and therefore willed ourselves to be."[87] Hall transitioned from a temporary one-year position in doctoral studies to the role of associate dean of the DMin program, which included a temporary appointment as dean of African American ministries during Daryl Ward's sabbatical.

Hall was permitted to assume the position without a terminal degree with the stipulation that she finish her degree by 1996, even though she continued to face difficulties in her relationship with the seminary's administration. J. T. Roberson was very pleased with Hall's work, which he said "far exceeded what [he] would expect from an associate dean in this office," but Provost Beach maintained reservations about the quality of Hall's work.[88] Hall also requested things such as housing, a faculty appointment, and a salary increase, which Beach denied.[89] As of August 1995, Hall reported directly to J. T. Roberson, which Provost Beach believed would better hold Hall accountable to completion of her assigned tasks.[90]

Hall received extensions from both Princeton Theological Seminary and UTS to complete her dissertation, and she was awarded financial assistance for a period of leave through the Davis-Putter Scholarship Fund.[91] From 1995 to 1996, Hall served on the Ford Foundation's Rights and Social Justice Program as a domestic consultant for the African American Church Advisory Committee.[92] On February 9, 1997, at the consecration of Rev. Dr.

Repsie M. Warren, Hall received the Humanitarian Service Award from the Third Senatorial District of the Pennsylvania State Senate and the Society for Helping Church, honored for her "benevolence to Society Church and the community."[93]

Hall submitted her first three dissertation chapters in April 1996 and her final chapter in November 1996. Her dissertation, "The Religious Consciousness of African American Baptist Women," analyzes the constructive work, moral leadership, and ministry of mission of the Women's Convention Auxiliary (WC, now referred to as the Women's Auxiliary) of the National Baptist Convention, USA (NBCUSA), from 1916 to 1961, picking up the history where Evelyn Brooks Higginbotham left off in *Righteous Discontent* (1994).[94] Hall examines the dilemma of the WC having independent space yet being subordinate to the male leadership of the NBCUSA: "It was a predicament of often competing and conflicting loyalties to Christ, Church, denominational leadership, family, race, women, and self in which loyalty to others could result in disloyalty to self."[95] As a concrete example of this dilemma, Hall focused on the Nannie Helen Burroughs presidency of the WC and the battle for control of Burrough's National Training School for Women and Girls in Washington, D.C. (now the Nannie Helen Burroughs School), utilizing a womanist social-ethical methodology, or "consciousness of the multidimensional oppressions which impact black women's social reality, with special attention to the primary forces of racism, sexism, and classism." Acknowledging what scholar Kimberlé Crenshaw labels "intersectionality," Hall's womanist methodology understood that "each dimension is complex, systemic, dynamic, and cumulative, creating a multiplier effect of racism times sexism times classism in black women's experience."[96]

Between 1994 and 1996, Hall suffered more personal and medical tragedies. A second car accident, in February 1994, exacerbated her previous back injuries, and what appears to have been adult-onset diabetes led to severe vision impairments and hospitalization. Debilitating back pain occasionally confined Hall to bed. She would leave her apartment door unlocked in case she needed to call in help, and some of her UTS students made a habit of visiting to check on her. LaGretta Bjorn recalled one such visit in which Hall initially said she was OK, but when Bjorn lingered a while, Hall confessed her need of help; she could not even get out of bed to get herself a glass of water. In 1996, Hall's brother Berkeley succumbed to substance abuse and addiction.[97]

During the 1996-97 academic year, UTS conducted a national search for a reworking of Hall's position into a tenure-track faculty position—professor of Christian ethics and dean of African American studies. Hall was a finalist. In a letter to Cheryl Townsend Gilkes, she expressed her frustration that some at UTS did not fully understand the importance of her integrated relationship with both church and academia, and her particular hope to use her standing in the black church "to advance opportunities for women." She also mentioned that her students were "very hungry for [her] civil rights experience."[98]

Due largely to a campaign by Hall and Daryl Ward, nearly thirty black church leaders from across the country, among them Samuel Dewitt Proctor, Henry and Ella Mitchell, Jacquelyn Grant, Pamela June Anderson, Daryl Ward, and Otis Moss Jr., wrote letters of support for Hall's application to UTS. Their letters emphasized Hall's careful bridging of the church and academia and her significance as a black woman preacher and scholar.[99]

The recommendation from Otis Moss Jr., then pastor of Cleveland's Olivet Institutional Baptist Church, conveyed the general consensus about Hall's giftedness: "Dr. Wynn has a distinguished record as a leader in the Civil Rights movement, the African American church, the African American community at local, national and global levels.... [She] has combined the pastor-scholar teacher-leader commitment in an admirable way."[100] Molly Longstreth, research associate professor at University of Arkansas Fayetteville, observed that "she is one of the few faculty at United who remind one without words, but instantly, of the presence of the Holy Spirit. Prathia works, preaches and teaches with her very presence."[101]

Samuel Dewitt Proctor, a former pastor of Abyssinian Baptist Church in Harlem, submitted a handwritten letter in support of Hall. His secretary was not available, but because he considered the letter "urgent," he drafted it himself:

> In the light of my long association with Prathia Hall-Wynn at United, and my familiarity with her work in the cause of the enhancement of the quality of life for all persons and the African-American community in particular, and because I know of her superior training and gifts in Christ's ministry and her dedication to high quality theological education, I am eager to attest to those qualifications for her as a candidate for Professor of Chris-

tian Ethics and Dean of African American Ministries at United. Such an appointment would be applauded wildly.[102]

The search "concluded without an appointment" due to concern about the future of the African American ministries program at UTS. Hall retained her interim title of dean of African American ministries, but remained a lecturer rather than a professor.[103] The dean position was eliminated June 30, 1997. Hall was allowed to use the title for one year, during which UTS granted Hall a study leave "for continued research and writing following the completion of a Ph.D. program."[104] Per the agreement made with UTS on completion of her services, Hall could remain in her on-campus apartment for half of her leave time, and UTS forgave most of Hall's financial debt to the seminary. UTS had purchased her house, complicated by Ralph's failure to pay his monthly responsibility to UTS for his portion of the home, in addition to extending her benefits for the full academic year. Though Hall requested that UTS serve as a positive reference for Hall, UTS's lawyer encouraged them to only verify dates of employment. Both parties agreed not to damage the other's reputation.[105]

In spite of these setbacks at UTS, Hall passed her dissertation oral defense unanimously, completing her Princeton PhD in spring 1997. Henri McMillian, one of many family members in attendance at Hall's defense, described the event as "one of the most amazing things" he had ever seen: "Eight professors drilled her from 10am until 1:30pm, and again for another hour in the evening. They tried to beat her down, warred her until they couldn't take it anymore." According to McMillian, they announced her successful completion of the defense by saying, "Dr. Wynn, have a nice day."[106] Hall's son DuBois, grandson Michael, mother Ruby, and LaGretta Bjorn also attended Hall's graduation.

Hall never learned to type or use the computer, so she relied on Bjorn, who had since graduated from UTS but continued to assist Hall, to type her dissertation and coordinate her preaching engagements. Bjorn's pastoral ministry and scholarship was deeply informed by her work for Hall, as she told her mentor some months after Hall completed the PhD:

> Thank you for being such a good and caring friend. Some things that make me happy that you are my friend: You have been someone with whom I could always be my "real" self and know that I would not be judged; every-

one needs someone like that in their life, at least for a while. By your example you have taught me how to be a better pastor, a better person, and to be a lot less judgmental. By letting me help with your dissertation you have reminded me of my elementary school grammar lessons (most of which I have forgotten) like the fact that sentences should never begin with "however." You don't treat me differently because I am "smart." When I do really dumb stuff you graciously forget about it long before I can.[107]

By the time of Hall's graduation, Bjorn and Hall had become so close that Bjorn's son, Akil, called Hall "Aunt Prathia," and both attended Hall's mother's ninetieth birthday party, in Philadelphia. Ruby Hall was particularly grateful for Bjorn's help, in every sense.[108] In gratitude for Bjorn's assistance, Hall took the two of them on a trip to Barbados.

Hall was also spending as much time as she could with her grandson, Michael, whose mother, Simone, died before his second birthday. Grandmother and grandson enjoyed extended visits together during the summer. Hall took him to London, Africa, and many other places. They had an "extremely special relationship."[109]

Hall applied for faculty positions and visiting scholar positions, including the Scholars-in-Residence program at the Schomburg Center for Research in Black Culture for the 1998–99 academic year, but did not secure a visiting scholar position until 1999. During the 1999–2000 academic year, Hall was a visiting scholar in the Womanist Scholars Program in the Department of American Baptist women at the Interdenominational Theological Center (ITC). She hoped to further her research of black women and their leadership within Baptist life. While at ITC, she taught a course on womanist ethics and the African American church.

In 2000, Prathia Hall earned the Martin Luther King Jr. Chair of Ethics at Boston University in the School of Theology, a dream appointment for her in many ways. She moved to a luxury apartment within walking distance of campus. She had sufficient resources to generously support civil rights and social justice organizations, as well as to fly her son DuBois and grandson Michael from Philadelphia to Boston to visit her.[110]

Hall's dissertation research deeply influenced her ministry and later academic work. One might wonder if Hall noticed the similarity between her research narrative and her own life, namely the rhythm of progress followed by setback. The WC's struggle against domination by the NBCUSA in response to its success recalls the same pattern of Hall's rise in the civil rights movement, her influence on landmark victories like the Civil Rights Act of 1964 and the Voting Rights Act of 1965, and her influence on greater opportunities for women in ministry, meshed with significant personal struggles and adversity including abuse, divorce, health issues, and discrimination. "As society increasingly acknowledged the rights of women, Hall found her voice as a great womanist preacher and thinker and simultaneously found a black Baptist denomination far more reluctant to treat her as an equal."[111] Doing this work within this context cultivated a deeper understanding of Freedom Faith, which sought liberation for all peoples and criticized any form of bigotry within black churches.

CHAPTER 6

"I'M 5'6", BUT I SHOULD HAVE BEEN TALLER"

"The black church is strangely quiet"

Freedom Faith was the steady, theological undercurrent of Hall's activism and ministry. Freedom Faith, "the absolute, positive, without a trace of doubt, conviction that God intends this people to be free," emerged from "an understanding of God as deliverer, of Jesus Christ as liberator, and of the Spirit as power."[1] Drawing from black church history and heritage, Hall challenged black churches to recognize and then act as if their future depended on continuing the legacy of Freedom Faith:

> The pilgrimage of the sons and daughters of Africa on North American soil has been long and tedious. The terrain has been more rough than smooth and the road more crooked than straight. The mountains have seemed unclimbable and the valleys have constituted a "low ground of sorrow." Yet there has been a spirit and a strength which has moved from deep within the souls of African Americans which has kept them sane amid incredible adversity.... Somehow, Black people have possessed a spirit and have found a strength which has enabled them to press forward, even while the winds of

deprivation, adversity, and fear were driving them backward.... Freedom-Faith has been the continuity-factor from generation to generation. It functioned for the fugitives, the rebels, and the abolitionists, just as it had for the first generation of believers.[2]

Hall understood the black church as the mediator of the struggles of black people "for survival and freedom." Black Christianity did not adopt the religion of slave masters but rather represented "an absolute contradiction of the Christianity of the slave masters." "Such a faith does not dissect the religious from the political nor in some cases, the sacred from the secular."[3] Black Christians answered the moral challenge of slavery by organizing themselves into an invisible institution with space for free worship. The birth of the black church catalyzed the birth of the freedom struggle of black people through "twin striving."[4] Without the freedom struggle there would be no church, and without the church there would be no freedom struggle.[5] In other words, "liberation is so profound that we are consequently freed and empowered to struggle against those external determinants which oppress all children of God."[6]

Hall's research, broadly speaking, addressed moral crises facing black churches, including racism, economic disparity, sexism, and a declining sense of purpose, which she insisted black churches respond to as the mediator of the struggles of its people for survival and freedom. Black heritage nurtured hope by reminding black people of their "capacity for survival and struggle" as well as of their obligation "to survive and to struggle." Hall challenged black churches: "We will betray the inheritance and abort the future if we do not face and overcome the challenges of the present."[7]

Hall was concerned with intrachurch dynamics that could undermine its mission: the migration of middle- and upper-class black people away from historically black neighborhoods and churches, the decreased role of the church as a central organizing point of black communities, and the idolization or imitation of white patriarchy.[8] Yet in the face of these contemporary struggles, "the Black Church is strangely quiet," and "generally uncritical of the American Society in matters other than race."[9] "African Americans survived three and a half centuries of slavery and one hundred twenty years of racist oppression" because black churches have been the centers of their communities, adapting to the changing needs and struggles of black people.[10] In agreement with Peter Paris's prophetic principle of criticism, Hall argued that the church "cannot limit that principle of equality to race and remain true to itself." When the church ceased to mediate the struggles of its people, it ceased to be the church.[11]

"We are being our African selves"

Hall recognized patterns of "retrogression" in black churches since the 1970s. Historically, black churches moved toward freedom motivated by its faith, but in the twentieth century black churches regressed toward hierarchy motivated by greed for power.[12] For black churches to continue their historical identity in light of their current "crisis of the struggle for community survival in which black men and black women find themselves separated" due to the convergence of racism and sexism, then the church must respond to the moral crisis of gender as mightily as it had historically responded to the moral crisis of race, with Freedom Faith as the backbone. The church had to recognize that "the struggle will not move forward without the contributions of black women."[13]

> Any serious movement toward transformation and liberation must involve analysis of the dynamics of rac/sexism as it impacts not only the lives of black women, but the struggle of black people for freedom and justice. I believe that an understanding of how racism and sexism converge in a cumulative impact of devastating proportions upon a community in crisis will help to explode the myths which fuel the bitterness that keeps black men and women from functioning as partners in the struggle for mutual liberation.[14]

The struggle against slavery required a shared commitment of men and women to labor together as partners: "Look at Harriet Tubman and Sojourner Truth and Frederick Douglass working and struggling together. Now I doubt very seriously that any of the brothers who were among those slaves led to freedom by Harriet Tubman had a problem with the leadership of women." Gender hierarchy was not a historic value of black churches: "In their time a woman's interest in herself was not automatically interpreted as hostile to men and their progress, at least not by Black people." Hall reflected on the continuity of this idea in her formation: "It runs deep in my own upbringing—articulated most strongly by my father."[15]

As a keynote speaker to the sorority sisters of Delta Sigma Theta, Hall situated strong womanhood within the black church tradition: "We are the products of a system of social and political organization wherein strong women did not equate to weak men. Women in many places served as religious and political leaders. . . . We are inheritors of sacred and societal traditions in which women served as priest, chief, and even warrior queen." Hall celebrated this legacy as "good news," because "when we are doing whatever it takes to struggle for the survival and progress of our family and our people, we are not being domineering, castrating matriarchs. We are being our African selves. We are who we are—all over the diaspora." Black sororities, like Delta Sigma Theta, stood in the legacy of black clubwomen's work, "lifting as we climb."[16]

In later expansion of her doctoral research on the Women's Convention Auxiliary (WC) to the NBCUSA, Hall argued that when the women of the WC, or any women's organization within a denomination, sacrificed their own liberation for denominational loyalty, they compromised the integrity of the entire black church, because they tolerated the oppression of black women for the sake of restoring black men. Perpetuating gender oppression and ignoring the moral crisis of gender distorted the church's identity. In so doing, the church ceased to mediate the struggles of its people for freedom and liberation.[17]

The women of the WC built a multifaceted organization of education, missions, social service, and local church and community engagement that, Hall argued, better served the needs of the church than did the NBCUSA. The WC focused more on moral leadership than on celebrating their own accomplishments and found a myriad of ways to operate in spite of the multiple consciousness of oppression stacked against them, including the misogynistic oversight of the NBCUSA.

Black Baptist women have often been at a moral crossroads, torn between obedience to God's call for their lives and the mandates of their churches. Hall recognized that "the faith of the African American church sometimes inspired accommodationist strategies and at other times protest or resistance or rebellion."[18] She further wondered why the women of the WC would accept second-class citizenship rather than speak up for their identity as created in the image of God and as fully equal. The women of the WC, Hall believed, found disobedience costly, beyond what they could shoulder. In the dilemma between identity and unity, the WC chose unity.[19]

When the WC silently complied with the 1939 Williams Mandate—which explicitly named the history of the WC as "an auxiliary of and a subsidiary body to" the NBCUSA, rather than an independent entity—choosing denominational loyalty at the cost of self-sacrifice, Hall argued, they compromised their integrity and their moral leadership. Ultimately Hall blamed the NBCUSA rather than the WC for this injustice, asserting that with its treatment of the WC, the NBCUSA turned its back on its "history, identity, and integrity through misogyny, autocracy, and greed." By silencing the WC, the NBCUSA had in effect silenced the voices of all black people and lost its credibility as a church.[20]

Writing to childhood friend Jeremiah Wright in 1996, Hall contextualized her sense of purpose for her research on the WC with her connection to African ancestry. Her father often talked with her about Africa, which she first visited in 1964 with SNCC. Her later visit to Africa with her mother, son, and grandson deepened her connection with the long history of her people: "I tell you, standing in the slave dungeons, I could hear the voices of the ancestors and I understood my assignment in a brand new way." As a scholar, Hall savored the "wonderful privilege to be a channel for the voices and spirits of the ancestors." She understood that this was also her purpose in writing her dissertation: "The incentive has not really been a Ph.D. for me. It has always been the opportunity to tell these sisters' story."[21]

Hall's visits to Africa influenced her research profoundly. She often cited Guinean president Sékou Touré, whom she met in 1964: "The measure of a society's progress and development is the way it treats women." She added that a society should also be judged by the way it treats children, condemning modern U.S. society for its "exploitation" of children and disregard for children's innocence. Hall frequently named patriarchy pervasive within black churches, which according to Touré's metric, countered any so-called progress from adequately ministering to women and children.[22]

Particularly in Hall's earlier work, she emphasized the detrimental influence of white patriarchal hierarchy, particularly white myths about black sexual identity, in distorting black self-identity: "When black men and black women internalize the myths about black males and black females, psychological rationalizations surface which immobilize both." White oppression infiltrated black family life through black imitation of white societal norms, which "stem[s] directly from the society's conspiracy to destroy black men and in the process black women and black families."[23] Hall continued:

> The scars are deep and go back to the damnable helplessness which gripped black men as they watched their wives, daughters, mothers and sisters raped by white men in slavery and since.... We have always known that our men were extremely vulnerable in a hostile society. A look at the present day prison population lets us know that this is still the case. But worse than the killing and the raping, the oppressor has implemented his strategy of oppression in such a way as to breed suspicion and resentment between us. No people can successfully struggle for liberation if they cannot live and work together in mutual trust, partnership, and cooperation. When we fall victim to the lies that have been planted among us, about us, in order to destroy us, we cooperate in the perpetuation of our oppression.[24]

Hall argued that white society had convinced black men of the lie that "black women are freer than black men and have somehow been favored in the structure of the society." By pitting black men against black women, white society undermined the stability of black families and black churches. But in order for the church to be the mediator of the struggles of black people, the church must expose white lies: "This is absurd indeed. Not only is the status of the black women lowest because they function in a racist, sexist society as the slaves of slaves, but the oppressor has, in fact, set into a motion a pattern in which white men brutalize black men and black men come home and brutalize black women. The pattern must be stopped. And the Church must provide leadership in reversing the cycle of destruction."[25]

Even with awareness of the historical reasons why black churches elevate men's leadership—toleration of sexism for the sake of greater racial advances—Hall believed that excluding women from leadership had taught women to be silent and to accept "that child care and the kitchen were essentially our jobs." Hall continued: "The psychology of this oppression is that (women) are taught to not have confidence. Many black men and women have bought into this by believing that (women) can be missionaries and evangelists but not pastors." Behind this double consciousness, women have created new identities for themselves to accommodate sexism: "She has internalized the pathology. She has internalized the hatred in the same way that many have internalized the racist hatred and feel better when Whites are in power."[26]

Hall made explicit the significance of this connection: "Brothers, you need to understand what the fallout is. Seventy to 80% of your church members are women, and stuff you carelessly say bruises and batters. Many women are being battered from the pulpit for their faithfulness to the church." This prejudice "tacitly signaled to young people that violence against women is okay." Preaching gender hierarchy dangerously established theological foundations that pitted black men against black women: "Wife-battering has been tolerated in many places including the church because of a belief that it is a man's right and responsibility to *rule* his house by whatever means necessary. The life of Eden's exiles has indeed been miserable." Elsewhere, Hall laid bare the universality of spousal abuse, across barriers of "race and class and creed," including the fact that "the abusers may be ... neighbors, members, or even leaders of our congregations." She lamented the countless times that battered wives sought guidance from their churches, "only to be told to return to the abusing husband and work harder to be prettier, a better wife and to not make him angry."[27]

In a quest to better understand what attitudes within black churches created so-called spiritually mandated abuse of women, Hall called black churches to "honestly face the contributing role that much church teaching on domestic relations has played in tolerating and even perpetuating abuse within families, alienation between men and women in the workplace, and confusion regarding gender roles in the society at large." When the church perpetrated the "theological scandal" of sexism, the church condoned domestic violence and blessed the deterioration of black families.[28]

The Bible, Hall argued, overturned sexism: "Domination and conflict, inferiority and superiority, sexism and bigotry may be the marks of old creation but they do not belong to those who claim the grace and redemption of Jesus Christ.... Men and women have a new way of being married—a new way of being a family which does not dominate or scapegoat but rather achieves partnership." This new way of relating to each other must be at the center of the church's ministry to families and the church's understanding of human identity "if we are to equip our families and our young people in particular to face together the challenges of the struggle for the survival and liberation of our people."[29]

Black male complicity with white patriarchal structures threatened black churches and families: "Black religious leadership would do well to reflect upon the absurdity—and dangerous absurdity at that—of allowing the same theological establishment which rationalized, condoned and/or tolerated racial oppression to interpret for it the biblical witness regarding gender.... How can conservative religious leaders such as the moral majority group be trusted to define for black people what a black family is and how it should relate?" Hall believed much of the destabilization of black families, particularly the growing enmity between black men and black women, emerged from "the desire on the part of some blacks to have black families look and act like white families or at least as white families are believed to look and act." Challenging the church and its leaders to draw from the rich theological, psychological, and historical heritage of black people rather than from the dominant culture, Hall continued: "Transformation and liberation can only occur when the crucial institutions of communal life are allowed to function free of definitions and distortions imposed by the oppressive culture."[30]

Hall labeled this desire to be like one's oppressors a form of idolatry. When black leaders enforced white norms, they elevated "the biases, the bigotry of the culture to the level of deity." In continuity with a line she often incorporated in her preaching, Hall explained: "Just as racism deifies whiteness so sexism deifies maleness. Sexism exalts the genital fixations of a confused and oppressive society to the level of a theology and claims that this bigotry is ordained by God." The black church must mediate the struggles of its people for liberation and freedom, rejecting oppressive narratives in pursuit of freedom in its fullest form: spiritual, political, physical, and emotional.[31]

Hall echoed the assessment of Susan L. Taylor, Dorothy Height, Michele Wallace, and Paula Giddings that pitting black men and women against each other in sexist hierarchy was contrary and detrimental to black identity. She argued that mutual partnerships were the only way forward, rooted in cooperation with and mutual respect for each other. "Efforts of black Americans to adapt to the hierarchical mode of human interaction have distorted the communal virtues of the organicist heritage and have utterly fractured relations within black families and within the community.... The hope is to restore black women and men to partnership in the struggle for transformation and liberation. The fact is that our present and our destiny are irretrievably bound together. There is only one way forward—together."[32]

In order for black churches to mediate the struggles of black people, Hall insisted on the need for deeper awareness of the theological and exegetical fallacies that blessed sexism: "We call upon black theological and social analysis to clarify for us the contemporary crisis... undermined by the Church's historical and contemporary ambivalence toward women... so that the Black Church does not become a stumbling block to its own mission of salvation and liberation." She lamented that a church so wounded by racism could become an oppressor of its own people: "The scandal is even more outrageous when we, who have been the victims of the idolatry of racism and therefore, know first-hand how the racist act distorts the humanity of victim and perpetrator alike, stoop to practice the kindred idolatry of sexism there by inflicting upon the women *and* the men of our race, the dehumanizing crime of sexist bigotry."[33]

Hall engaged in extensive exegetical study of passages used to justify sexism, which she incorporated into a variety of papers, speeches, and sermons, ultimately concluding that the biblical text presents humanity as partners in care of the earth and human family. Hall argued that "careful examination of every biblical text commonly used to deny the equality and/or the ministry of women will liberate the church from misinterpretations which dishonor the character of God and humankind."[34]

Hall researched "male exegesis of scripture," particularly of Genesis 1, which she argued caused "the development of cultural norms which not only dehumanize women, but also see through an unholy, indeed, idolatrous exaltation of men." Explaining the severity of the problem, Hall continued: "these norms mitigate against the development of a just and ethical social order by functioning to absolutize the sinful cultural context and social order against which scripture was written." Whereas patriarchy in the text is the product of human sin, Hall argued that Jesus and Paul modeled a new society of "mutual submission and mutual service."[35]

Rather than women learning to play the "carnal power game of dominance and submission and characterize that as Christian," Hall insisted on acknowledgment of this capitulation to culture and on an ecclesial reorientation around the teachings of Christ: "Confession is not enough. Cleansing is required." Such cleansing involved the church confronting "its own complicity in the perversion of the message of the gospel regarding women, racial minorities, and the poor." A critical piece of the repentance and cleansing process for black churches, according to Hall, was the leadership of women in ministry. Though small in number, Hall believed that "the few who exist at present are strategically located to impact the Church at large." The church, and seminaries providing theological education, "must begin to take feminism seriously."[36]

Hall promoted feminism, aware of its complications. She identified feminism as primarily a "middle-class white women's struggle, insensitive to the problems of Black and poor women and to the potential economic threat it poses for Black men." She wanted to utilize resources from feminism to create an "appropriate methodology," native to black communities, which could address sexism, classism, racism, ageism, and other forms of antigospel prejudice.[37] Just as slaves created separate space to reflect on the meaning of scripture for black people, leaders in black churches needed space independent from white feminism to reflect on the meaning of scripture for black women and black communities. Hall worked with sister scholars in a variety of academic disciplines to cultivate this field, now known as womanism.

Acknowledging a complicated, yet essential, component of sexism in black churches, Hall offered an academic altar call, as it were, for liberation:

> Our liberation struggles can only move forward if we forthrightly attack all oppression, external and internal. An honest appraisal of our rhetoric and our conduct will reveal that many of our reasons for clinging to inappropriate attitudes about women and their place in church and society are neither theological nor sociological, they are emotional. Thankfully, the love of God and the blood of Jesus cleanses us of all unrighteousness, if we are willing. The love of God will free us of all of the scars and wounds to which we cling so closely. God will not honor our struggle against racial oppression if we persist in offending God with internal sex and class oppression. This hour of crisis is also our hour of opportunity.[38]

Writing at the "eve of the twenty-first century," Hall named the issues facing black churches as "a crisis of survival." In addition to white societal norms disrupting black families, classism threatened to further divide black communities from each other: "The nature of the crisis is complex and contains within it the confusing contradiction of significant and even exemplary progress on the part of some upper- and middle-class blacks and, at the same time, the tragedy of approximately thirty percent of our population stuck in the quicksand of underclass poverty and despair."[39]

The struggles of racism and sexism converged in black families, according to Hall. The growing gap between single black men and women—excluding married, incarcerated, and homosexual men, which left only one eligible black man for every five black women—posed a significant threat, as discussed in a 1985 *Ebony* article: "Most Black men are living responsible lives as parents and providers. . . . The achievements of Black men in arts and sciences, engineering, business, communications, government and sports are obvious and unassailable. . . . At the same time it should be remembered that most Black women are still confined to low-paying jobs at the bottom of the economic ladder." Hall's particular concern was for the growing marginalization of black women: "The bottom is getting larger. It is composed of women trying to raise children alone on salaries from the lowest paying jobs in the society, with the fewest available services and disappearing support systems."[40]

If the majority of black homes included a working mother, then "the survival of black families is dependent upon the incomes of black women." Hall continued, "As women are critical to the survival of the family, they are equally critical to the struggle for freedom." Marian Wright Edelman echoed this in a personal letter to Hall: "I am convinced that it will be women—especially mothers and grandmothers—who will have to remove the man-made mountains that deny our children their birthrights and the chance to reach their God-given potential. It is people of faith—especially women of faith—who must mobilize and insist on child protection and investment now."[41]

Hall addressed the sexist pressure for perfection, experienced by both black men and women. "Strong black men try to do it all, and they run their wives and families crazy trying to take care of them," ignoring routine and preventive medical care, afraid to show any sign of weakness or need for help, dying "too soon of a heart attack or cancer or stroke or effects of diabetes." Similarly, Hall claimed that "strong black women suffer from the superwoman syndrome," trying to be all things to all people in absolute perfection with no rest, dying "all too soon of depression and exhaustion." Hall argued that the only way to build "strong marriages, strong children, and strong people for the present age" was to "leave this paradigm behind."[42]

Critical analysis of sexism was essential for the future of black churches, Hall argued, because "sexism not only limits the development and progress of black women, it undermines and retards the development and progress of black people as a whole." Because of the historic role of black women in black communities as "the heart and soul of our struggle," Hall insisted that "the continued active, relentless commitment, participation, and yes, leadership of black women is critical." Moving forward must involve "full partnership between sisters and brothers united in struggle through Christ."[43]

"We are still in the wilderness!"

In October 1995, Hall received an invitation to colead the Congress of National Black Churches, Black Church Leadership Conference, specifically to write the call to black church leaders for why a conference titled "The Role of the Black Church in the Survival and Development of Our People with Dignity" was needed.[44] Hall offered a womanist challenge:

> The struggles of African American people for survival and liberation were born in and of the religious movements which became the African American churches. Consequently, our people's quest for survival, development, and dignity is not only intrinsically related to the heritage of the Black Church, it is a test of our faithfulness to the ministry of Jesus as declared in Luke 4:17–20 and also a measurement of our own authentic identity.
>
> Today, all around us the oppressed lambs are crying for the bread of freedom and dignity. Some of the cries come from the poor in the streets outside our churches. Some come from women captives within our churches. Others cry out that the sound of our prophetic proclamation will fearlessly confront the self-obsessed agenda of politicians and all those who wish to reverse the gains purchased with the blood of freedom's struggle. Do we hear the lambs a'crying? The command of the Shepherd is still: feed my sheep! We are therefore compelled to gather in the Black Church Leadership Conference, in obedience to the Shepherd, that we might gain our voice and more effectively feed the crying sheep.[45]

While some black church leaders argued that faith and politics should not mix, Hall insisted faith and politics *must* mix for two reasons. One, separation of church and state was never a luxury afforded to black people because they have never been free in either regard. Second, Hall described this question as a "coalescing between the prosperity religion and the old conservativism" that defended separation of church and state solely based on new upward mobility for those particular black people. She continued: "We can be as pious as the day is long. We can quote scriptures at computer pace.

We can bicycle through the Bible at breakneck speed, never touching down long enough or seriously enough to allow the Word to interrogate us." Such "tissue-thin, stubble-faith requires of us no ethical responsibility" for the black community that has enabled mobility, and, according to Hall, this behavior "leads to some strange and deadly attitudes in our struggle."[46]

Speaking to the political and social context of the post-Reagan United States, Hall warned black churches to remain alert: "There is no time to romanticize our blackness" because "the White House has a package for us that will explode like a letter bomb in our hands. And they will use folks who *look like us* to deliver it."[47]

Reflecting on the changes in her North Philadelphia neighborhood, Hall cherished its state in her childhood: "stately brick and brownstone row houses." The Reagan-era intensification of the wage gap between white and black Americans led to her neighborhood's 1990s condition: "a bombed-out war zone." She was most despaired by changes in the people under the ever-growing economic despair threatening urban black communities: "Those who had little money but a job and a treasury of plans, hopes and dreams—especially for their children—have been replaced by zombies. In fact, children, youth, and aged wander in dazed despair. Hope has been driven out and dreams have been replaced by the cynically elusive fantasy of hitting the lottery." Lamenting, Hall reflected: "Home looks like a rubbish heap and just as Israel wept at the memory of Zion, I weep when I remember home."[48]

Though most traditional civil rights organizations faced declining membership and financial struggles in the late twentieth century, Hall insisted that these organizations were still necessary for progress. She advocated for a transition to local organizations, where churches and local social agencies could focus on one-on-one relationships with the community. She also wanted to empower "everyday people to recognize that they are not powerless." Myrlie Evers-Williams, chairwoman of the NAACP, had similarly called for the NAACP to rediscover its "grass roots." Black heritage did not begin with slavery but was "as ancient as the human family." Black churches "are the inheritors of a rich and regal ancestry on African shores . . . of an African religious worldview which worshiped the supreme God, embraced a spirituality that understood the divine to be involved in and concerned about human beings and therefore present with them in their pilgrimage."[49]

Hall firmly credited the black church and her community for "preparing her for a PhD and the Hampton platform as soon as [she] could talk." She praised her mother, assisted by the church, for giving her "opportunities to speak and to think and to learn." She mentioned domestic workers who gave her "crumpled dollar bills" in proud support that she was going to college, telling her to "AIM High" and "Daughter, I'm praying for you."[50] Hall elsewhere elaborated on this story:

> Every time I want to make myself comfortable and let somebody else struggle for our freedom and our future, the memory of Fannie B. Holloway rises up to haunt me—a scrubwoman—domestic worker—a hard life. But when she saw me walking to school, my arms filled with books, she'd swell with pride, a great smile would break out on her face. She'd stand a little taller, and she'd call me to her and press a crumpled $1.00 bill into my hand and say, "Daughter, do good, I'm praying for you." And when I remember Fannie B. Holloway, I remember that twenty years after those school days when I became the pastor of Mt. Sharon Baptist Church, her homegoing service was the first over which I presided. And when I remember that, I remember that as I stood at her graveside and committed her worn and weary body to the ground, I promised God and Fannie B. Holloway's spirit that I would be there for somebody else's son and daughter, as she had been there for me.[51]

According to Hall: "If truth be told, that is what the church and the community did for most of us."[52]

Writing in 1994, just days after attending a civil rights activist symposium in which leaders lamented the failure of the 1964 Civil Rights Act to end racism in the United States, Hall noted that what had historically worked for black churches would not be sufficient for the "socially complex realities of the present era," in part because many black people who enjoyed economic gain have left the black church, claiming to have "made it on [their] own without the help of the Black church or the Black community."[53] Hall believed that successful black people had a responsibility to black churches and black communities:

> A community with arms wrapped around us, a community in which those that we would aspire to emulate were there with us sitting in church next to us, walking down the street before us, in the classroom with us, always encouraging us, challenging us, refusing to allow us to believe that we could not learn, that we could not be the persons we dared to be, as if any of us

made whatever it is we think we made without.... We stand today not just on the shoulders but on the graves of those who fought the fight of faith, those who waged the struggle, those who opened the doors so that all we had to do was walk in, those who went to jail, those who gave their very lives often in early death, who did it for the sake of our future.[54]

Hall continued that "the great irony is that the primary challenge to our Christian social responsibility is our success." Because some black people have been more successful, they have "begun to look at the poor the same way enemies of racial uplift and social justice do. We're tired of the struggle. We want to enjoy our justly deserved blessings." Hall also lamented that many remaining in the church have "abandoned" black people, prioritizing other-worldly divine rescue and personal morality over this-worldly activism and social justice. Pie-in-the-sky theology abused and neglected those who did not make it, "now left to their own devices to struggle and die in the quicksand of underclass poverty and devastation." Hall named such misplaced priorities as toxic for black churches: "We cannot afford the sedative of promised land illusion—we are *still* in the Wilderness!" Hall drew on black church heritage: "Our fathers and our mothers, with one foot slipping out of slavery, with pennies, not even nickels and dimes, built colleges and dared to call them universities, and then made them live up to the name. They built churches and institutions for us." Instead of inheriting those riches and compounding resources for future generations, Hall accused that many had "marched on off into buppy [*buppie*, combining *black* and *yuppie*] land and never looked back."[55]

Until the church had a faithful answer for its treatment of women and children, until the church had exhausted its opportunities to serve those in poverty and those who needed family support, its mission was incomplete. Speaking prophetically, Hall urged: "Remember that you have received so much more than any generation before you. You have been blessed with opportunities about which they could only have dreamed. And to whom much is given, from her is much required. We are the beneficiaries of the cumulative struggles of those who preceded us. Therefore, I urge you to face three areas of contemporary crisis which challenge our present and our future: 1) Underclass Poverty, 2) Sex, class, age, color isms, and 3) The youth crisis."[56]

Hall accused black churches of "sleeping on the job," of having made insignificant progress in mediating the struggles of its people for justice and freedom since the 1960s. She critiqued those who failed to instill black heritage into their children: "For some reason, we are the first generation to decide that we would spare them the painful memory of our suffering.... We did not want to pass on to our children the memories of our past. And so we stopped telling them the story." Such neglect, Hall believed, left young people unprepared for blatant racism they would face in college and as they attempted to establish themselves in the world.[57]

In a Vanderbilt Divinity School address, hosted by the Kelly Miller Smith Institute, Hall challenged black church leaders to revive and revision the meaning of black churches as a liberating force. The church was born of the freedom movement: "If the church had not fought for the freedom and survival of Black people, there would have been no black church." The church was born from black women: "Had there been no black women, there would have been no Black church, further, there would have been no Black Church Freedom Movement." Passing on the stories of black heritage means naming women as builders of the church: "They fought classism as fiercely as they fought racism and sexism. There would have been no foreign mission work or home mission work to speak of were it not for their love, their labor, and their dollars—raised often, literally one penny at a time." When black churches committed sexism, the church "abandoned its own prophetic principle of the equality of all human beings before God... surrendered its birthright in order to keep company with structures of socio-cultural oppression." Hall's message called black churches to transform into a fully liberating community, by telling the whole story.[58]

Throughout her career, Hall heralded black women as the mothers and midwives of the black church who had historically "mediated—by any means necessary, possible and/or impossible—the survival of the group" even when black churches failed to do so.[59] Black women's embodied and spoken proclamations of freedom reminded black children that the derogatory labels made by racist society are false and that they are "the sons and daughters of mothers and fathers of mothers and fathers of mothers and fathers who survived the hated Middle Passage, who made it through the devastation of slavery, who survived the insults and the abuse of segregation and Jim Crow, who not only survived but even today stand where they stand in spite of every attempt to destroy them." For black people, survival for freedom was a divine destiny:

"God still intends us to be free . . . And for our children . . . that liberation is their destiny."[60]

In a version of "Building between Heritage and Hope" delivered at Morehouse, Hall used lyrics from "Lift Every Voice," the African American National Anthem, to relay the "powerfully dialectical tension which those words contain . . . the strength, the rhythm, the joys, the tears, the pain, the problems, the incredible progress, the defiant determination and extraordinary faith of our ancestral stream." She admitted the myriad of emotions she experienced when she sang that song, how even her mother's tone-deaf singing could not detract from the power of the song, and how "we experience in the same moment the pregnant promise of our future." In spite of doubts and fears, "we shall seize this moment with all of its contradictions and forge from it a future for ourselves and our generations yet unborn."[61]

"Prophet's mantle"

Hall had a vision for black churches in her own right but saw herself as building on the work of figures like Nannie Helen Burroughs and Rev. Dr. Martin Luther King Jr., moving black churches toward a more holistic understanding of freedom and equality. She recognized the same injustices that Baptist clubwomen and civil rights leaders opposed, persisting in black churches in her day, and she saw herself as called to lead the charge. While she did not write about her own story in parallel with Burroughs as she did with King, she did position herself, and every woman serving faithfully in black churches, as the mantle bearers of Burroughs and all black clubwomen who made a way out of no way to provide for their communities. She could not sacrifice her call to ministry for the sake of racial unity, nor could she allow racial unity to blind black churches to sexism, classism, or any other oppressive force.

Hall often paralleled her sense of calling with King's: recognized as a teenager, resisted even while preparing for ministry, and bringing heavy consequences in its acceptance.[62] Similar to her own understanding of faithful prophetic ministry in the black church, "King's love of the church did not preclude his critique of the church . . . indeed love for and loyalty to the institutions of our membership and our upbringing *require* critique." Hall was a highly sought Martin Luther King Jr. Day speaker, and she frequently received letters from institutions after her speeches recounting the high demand for recordings of her speeches and of discussion groups and local organizations formed as a result of her speeches.[63]

In "In Search of a Society Where Freedom Rings and Justice Reigns: The Martin Luther King Model," Hall observed that King was "a very human person . . . as human as we are." In rare form, Hall elaborated on her relationship with King: "He loved to clown, tell jokes, dance, and play pool." Hall and King shared lively conversation: "I argued strategy and tactics with him vehemently along with my SNCC and SCLC comrades in the struggle." She was often a frequent guest in the King home: "I was invited by him to join the King family at home after church where SNCC worker Debbie Amis and I enjoyed a wonderful afternoon of enlightened conversation and a delicious soul food meal prepared by Mrs. King."[64]

King deserved respect, but Hall did not want to put him so high on a pedestal that today's generation felt unable to take up his work. Hall certainly admired King's life and sacrifice for freedom, but she acknowledged that he "made his fair share of mistakes." She noted his "comfortable middle-class life, which protected him to *some* extent from *some* of the abusive evils of racism and Jim Crow segregation," appreciating his decision to pick up the "prophet's mantle" (original emphasis). She described King's own feelings of inadequacy, and his frequent resort to prayer, particularly in times of need. Hall hoped that people would not get so distracted by King's dream that they forgot to join him in his struggle: "not his *dream* but his *struggle* to create a society where freedom rings and justice reigns" (original emphasis). The next generation had to continue in the struggle: "It is important for people of all ages, and especially young people to understand that you, too, can pick up the prophet's mantle and carry forward the struggle to create a society where freedom rings and justice reigns."[65]

In a 1992 baccalaureate address for Stanford University, Hall painted an honest picture of the state of the world: "We are passing to you with your diploma a planetary mess." Acknowledging that many young people did not want to take responsibility for social problems, Hall continued: "You are right. It is not fair that you are called to fix and to settle and to heal a planet and its people. But this is the fact. . . . And should you decide to opt out of the struggle and let the world go to hell in a handbasket, it will be suicide. For you, our only hope of a future, will go down with it." In order for peace and justice to work in tandem, "they meet and embrace first in our hearts," causing us to crave peace and justice everywhere: "That awesome, exquisite kiss within us causes us to settle for nothing less in our world. They become the content and the context of our existence. The quest for their actualization in our world ... establishes our priorities." After recounting her experience of police shooting at her feet in Georgia in 1963, she ended her remarks with the following challenge: "You alone will decide how you will respond to the challenges of your generation. Difficult as it is, you have before you the opportunity to proclaim and then dare to create a new way of being human."[66]

America, at the end of the twentieth century, was at best a "rhetorical democracy," failing to deliver its promises of freedom and justice. Hall exposed the overincarceration of black and brown men and the oppressive economic policies that threw money at jails and their white owners while neglecting inner-city schools and communities. She insisted that reparations were needed, but also that "the real challenge is to eliminate *all* poverty regardless of lines of race," since reparations ignored white poverty and exacerbated bitterness between white and nonwhite poor.[67]

Referencing the 2000 presidential election in which Gore won the popular vote but Bush won the electoral vote, Hall made systemic inequity plain: "We have a great rhetorical democracy. That is all we shall have if we fail to correct the gross electoral abuses exposed for all to see in this presidential election. We seek good relations with the government but the King Model teaches us that if we truly care about our institutions, we must honestly critique them and call them to the high ground of authentic democracy. Speculation about the likelihood or lack thereof of a recession cannot obscure the contradiction of such gross inequity in wealth, welfare, and well-being in our land." Hall understood the direct effect that systemic inequity had on children, particularly on black children. Upset by Bush's "coopting" of the Children's Defense Fund's slogan "No child left behind," she challenged community leaders to "help him to make the words reality in government policy" because "these words are not a slogan, they are our solemn oath and our sacred commitment."[68] Hall believed education must be a top priority to eradicating poverty and racial inequity.

While circumstances had improved somewhat since King's lifetime: "Freedom's victory and the reign of justice depend on called, challenged, and committed people who will honestly deliver the moral critique of freedom and justice to the nation and its powerbrokers. Who are those people? We are they!"[69] The historic legacy of black women, the Civil Rights Movement, and King's model of nonviolence empowered and demanded that everyone join in the struggle. For Hall, the only way to move forward was to offer up critique to injustice and oppression wherever they existed, even within the church.

CHAPTER 7
"THE LIVING GOD IS NOT A BIGOT"

"Keepers of the fire"

"It may be that in the present hour," Hall penned, "God is resolving the debate and setting aside the controversy, for it is an incontestable fact that the living Lord is choosing to lay claim upon the lives of an ever-increasing number of women and charging them to preach the gospel of Jesus Christ. And daily women are answering yes to that all-compelling call of God." She traced the inclusion of women proclaimers back to Jesus, who "welcomed women into his itinerant seminary," engaged women in "high-level theological discussion," praised women for their discipleship, and commissioned women to be the first preachers of the gospel.[1]

For many women preachers, and certainly for Hall, accepting the call to ministry came after years of internal struggle and avoidance, knowing the multifaceted cost of pursuing pastoral leadership. Black women often came into ministry later in life and at greater personal cost than other women faced.[2] An unjust consequence for black women in ministry was an above-average divorce rate, with divorces occurring most frequently because the women's husbands did not support their call to ministry. Certainly this was the case for Hall, as well as for many of the women she mentored.

Accepting the call, and shedding unsupportive relationships in order to do so, was in itself a baptism in the liberating gospel of Jesus: "When the 'yes' finally ushered from the center of their being, they knew that it had been there all the time and that before they were even formed in the womb they were called and anointed."[3]

Hall understood that only acceptance satisfied the call: "Like Jeremiah they learned that to refuse to preach is to experience a fire in one's bones that can be quenched by nothing less than faithful, obedient preaching." Nonetheless, acceptance came at a great cost: "These preachers, with their many thousand sister preachers across the church could not have imagined how rugged a road they were choosing when they answered yes to that call of Christ. They were faced with two choices: the living death of denial and disobedience or the rough path of rejection and pain. They chose obedience, a costly obedience.... The pulpit provides for them no safe haven from suffering." Speaking from her deep conviction that black churches must mediate the struggles of its people for freedom and liberation, Hall recognized that the prophetic cry in the wilderness that sustained black churches emanated from women preachers: "The great irony of this rough and risky relationship between women preachers and the churches is that without the radical obedience to Christ that characterizes the ministries of these faithful preachers, the 'isms' threaten to utterly extinguish the altar fire.... The church is therefore challenged to hear them or risk the removal of its lamp stand from the altar."[4]

In a later reflection on her calling, Hall wondered about previous generations of called women: "I look at my mother, who is 84, and I am convinced that my mother is as called to ministry as I am, but she came along at a time when women could not hear the call." Because of entrenched sexism within black churches, particularly, and cultural white patriarchy, generally, "there are so many sanctions in place that they can't hear the call." Given these circumstances, women have historically ministered as a wife or otherwise navigated the limiting conventions in order to seek out opportunities to serve.[5]

Hall knew too well that women in ministry fought for every inch of influence they dared to claim, understanding what the church lost by rejecting women's preaching. Even Jesus's disciples ignored the first proclamation of the gospel; they thought they knew Jesus, but they ignored the most important news about Jesus: "Perhaps if they would have received the report of the women, perhaps they would have known the Lord is risen. He is risen, indeed. Prejudice and pain left them broken, blinded, and ignorant. The report of the women disturbed them, but it could have delivered them. But, they were blinded by bigotry.... And my sisters and my brothers this was not to be the last time that the Gospel would be missed ... and many of us ... are still missing the Gospel, because God chooses a messenger who is woman."[6]

Though being a woman in ministry was costly and dangerous, Hall offered a womanist insistence for obedience to the call, to mediate the struggles of all people for freedom and liberation: "As keepers of the fire, women preachers are challenged to withstand the trial of sexism and to use that experience to help the church remove every 'ism,' every idolatry which threatens to extinguish the sacred flame."[7]

"Scripture can be used to liberate women"

A prophetic womanist hermeneutic must be rooted in the heritage of the black freedom struggle: "When we learn our past—that we have already come through—then we are empowered with respect to what we must go through to cure the social ills of the twenty-first century." Through her life experiences, academic work, and ministry, Hall realized the dilemma threatening black women: "It was a predicament of often competing and conflicting loyalties to Christ, Church, denominational leadership, family, race, women, and self in which loyalty to others could result in disloyalty to self." Her womanist social-ethical hermeneutic sought "consciousness of the multidimensional oppressions which impact black women's social reality, with special attention to the primary forces of racism, sexism, and classism." Further, she clarified that "each dimension is complex, systemic, dynamic, and cumulative, creating a multiplier effect of racism times sexism times classism in black women's experience."[8]

Hall merged her theological education with her own experiences as a woman in ministry, contextualizing her womanist identity, decrying oppressive forces of any kind, and advocating for all human beings as made in the image of God. The purpose of preaching was liberation: "For whatever it is that we who mount the sacred desk do when we come to the pulpit, if it is not good news to the poor, if it is not deliverance to the captives, if it is not sight to the blind, if it is not freedom to the oppressed, it may be sweet, it may be eloquent, it may even be deep, but it ain't preachin'."[9] Though preaching ministry sometimes pushed the proclaimer "to the cliff," such were the exact moments preaching should occur: "Wherever there is sickness, suffering, poverty, pain, captivity, oppression, sightlessness, sinfulness, there is the place for proclamation. There is the preaching place."[10]

Rooted in Freedom Faith, Hall's preaching illuminated the moral contradictions of the black church's perpetuation of oppression within itself. Donna Allen describes Hall's deep engagement with the text using womanist hermeneutics: "As Hall interrogates the Scripture, she explains how others have misinterpreted the text through superficial and gender-biased translations. She then reclaims the text by exploring with the audience what a more 'accurate' interpretation reveals. . . . Hall's rhetorical strategy demonstrates that just as Scripture has been used to oppress women, Scripture can be used to liberate women."[11]

The inclusivity of Hall's womanist hermeneutic, however, pursued the full liberation of all persons, regardless of race, gender, class, ability, age, or sexual orientation. The message of the gospel was both personal salvation and social justice. For Hall, bridging the two was critical for preaching:

> God leads us, and all our gifts and energy and skills that we develop to declare the Good News of God in people and in the social world. For me, both of those are critical. If it is only the personal, it is not the Gospel. If it is only the social, it is not the Gospel. But it must be an integrated personal and social order where God is at work for justice and righteousness and salvation. The Good News is Christ. The Good News is Christ—that which stands in stark contrast and graphic opposition to bad conditions and human lives and in the social order. The Good News is possibilities where there have been dead ends. The Good News is life where there is death. The Good News is the Word of life which opposes death.[12]

Hall brought authenticity to the pulpit, weaving scholarship, prophetic witness, and her experiences together in beautifully crafted poetic language. From the pulpit she boldly addressed death, domestic abuse, racism, financial difficulty, physical illness, disease, public policy, education, and sexism.

She intentionally spoke to the lived realities of her listeners, knowing that her sermons must connect with the daily economic, cultural, and family dynamics her congregation faced. Jeremiah Wright compares Hall favorably to other preachers: "Prathia was infinitely better trained than nine-tenths of them and had a ministry that was an authentic ministry with integrity. No whistles or buzzers and the B.S. and hype—all solid, all genuine."[13]

Having observed each of Hall's pastoral anniversaries with a banquet, Mount Sharon Baptist Church marked her tenth pastoral anniversary with an even more festive celebration. The *Philadelphia Inquirer* covered the March 1988 event, testifying to the importance of her ministry and community leadership: "Folk came from far and near. Black and white together." A reporter noted that this was "perhaps the largest delegation of male preachers of the Gospel to attend a banquet honoring a woman preacher."[14] In the keynote address, Rev. Dr. Charles Adams remarked: "She is the epitome of preaching excellence, spiritual depth, theological authenticity, and pastoral dedication. She is without peer in her competence and compassion as a pastor, a preacher, an exegete, theologian, and activist." Acknowledging the difficulties Hall faced because of her gender, Adams continued: "She is also consistently committed to her Christ baring the reproach of having to conduct her ministry against the bigoted disparagement of those who erroneously think that the Ministry of the Word of God is the private preserve of the male sect. She is climbing up the rugged mountain against narrowness, meanness, intolerance, evil and prejudice, and has succeeded in becoming stronger as a result of being challenged. No one can honestly hear her preach and not know that God has called her to deliver the Good News of Jesus Christ."[15]

A particular point of brilliance in Hall's preaching was continuity between her womanist hermeneutic and the black preaching tradition, making her radical message accessible to all and contiguous with the historic emphases of black churches. Michael Eric Dyson describes Hall's unique style as a womanist preacher:

> Hall's powerful preaching introduced me to the genius of black female homiletical artistry. She interwove biblical narratives with stories from her pioneering career as a civil rights activist. Hall topped off her sermons with rhetorical flourishes and stylistic gestures gleaned from her Baptist breth-

ren and refined in her feminist crucible. Her sermons also displayed a thrilling measure of tuneful speech, known colloquially as "the whoop" and more formally as "the changed sermon." As they say in such circles, she had "the learnin' and the burnin.'"[16]

Hall intentionally utilized techniques of the black preaching tradition—pauses, crescendos, syncopation, repetition, alliteration, and the whoop—so that her message of womanist justice resonated with that heritage "verbally, musically, harmonically," and particularly with its expression of "suffering and celebration," demonstrated in the following segment of her "Between the Wilderness and a Cliff" sermon:[17]

> So go, sisters, with healing hands. GO with serving hands. GO with blessing hands because they emanate from loving, healing, blessing hearts. Go in the wilderness and at the edge of the cliff. Prepare the way of the Lord. For every valley has been exalted and every mountain and hill has been brought low. Oh, the rough places have been made smooth and the crooked places and crooked people have been straightened out. And all flesh, all flesh, shall see it together, the poor and the powerful, the pitiful, all flesh. The oppressed, depressed, suppressed, repressed, all flesh, shall see it together for the mouth of the Lord has spoken it. Hallelujah to the lamb. Hallelujah, hallelujah, hallelujah, hallelujah. Oh, thanks be to God.[18]

She also occasionally followed the black homiletical pattern of preaching with references from Genesis to Revelation in one sermon, tracing God's action across the entire narrative of the biblical text from its first book to its last. In "Journey with Jesus," she practiced this type of preaching as she described the moment that two disciples on the Emmaus road recognized Jesus:

> Suddenly, they saw him. They knew him. They knew who he was. They knew where he'd come from. They knew suddenly. They saw him as he is: Judah's Shiloh, Jacob's star, Deborah's wisdom, Jeremiah's balm in Gilead, Esther's courage, Zerubbabel's signet ring, Ezekiel's wheel, Israel's highway to God, Rachel's comforter, Mary's Magnificat, Calvary's lamb, risen, risen, risen, risen, risen as he said. Oh, they saw him, and they knew him. The women were right. It was not gossip. It was gospel, the best news this sin-cursed world has ever heard. The Lord is risen.[19]

Hall preached a broad range of topics throughout her ministry career, yet her message always centered around the connection between faith and justice: "My womanist consciousness is so much a part of me that I bring it to the text. God has put this burden on me of justice—justice as an inclusive metaphor for preaching."[20] She offered fresh and provocative readings of biblical texts, focused on social justice and equality, rooted in her womanist convictions.

On the rare occasions that Hall mentioned her civil rights activism in a sermon, she most commonly referenced being shot at by Deputy Short in Sasser, Georgia. Her sermon on the hemorrhaging woman approaching Jesus secretly, for example, noted that this moment in Mark 5 reminded her of when the police officer was shooting at her feet; Hall emphasized the woman's awareness that "Jesus has the capacity to hear and to be touched by our suffering," which Hall believed inspired the woman's courage to touch Jesus in the crowd.[21]

The most prominent themes of her womanist hermeneutic are her explorations of women in the biblical text and of "chain removal." Hall recovered women's stories in the biblical text, advancing liberating exegeses of texts commonly used to oppress women. More broadly, chain removal signaled the need for the complete shedding of any remnant forms of oppression within the church in order for it to participate fully in the liberating gospel. Within these two themes, Hall consistently preached the need for working together as one human family to mediate the needs of the people for freedom and liberation. She invited her hearers to consider their experiences as part of a larger story of God's work in their lives and in the world around them, as Christians, as the black church, and as bearers of Freedom Faith.

"Sexism is a liar"

Though Hall preached a holistic liberation for all people, her sermons devoted considerable attention to proclaiming liberation for women. She primarily utilized two strategies in her womanist hermeneutic. First, she modeled the positive recovery of the stories of biblical women, centralizing those characters as models of faith. Second, she addressed misinformed understandings of biblical texts commonly used to oppress women, offering corrective exegesis in support of the liberation of all people and the full humanity and equality of women.

"BRAZEN ENOUGH TO TELL THEIR STORY"

Approaching the text with a hermeneutic of suspicion, Hall recovered women's stories from misogynistic interpretations, presenting new readings of these sisters of the text. She emphasized their lived realities, centering them in the narrative, and honoring them as faithful models of discipleship.

In "Encounters with Jesus from Dying to Life," Hall addressed the woman in Mark 5 who had menstruated every day for twelve years. Not only did she bring this woman to the forefront of the sermon, but she also expounded on this woman's lived reality as a theological necessity for faithful preaching of the text. This sermon also brought long-needed candor about women's health issues to the pulpit, honoring women and their bodies as holy. While recognizing that talking about menstruation might offend some, she nonetheless proceeded because "describing the issue of blood to my listeners, then the obvious would become profound":[22]

> Imagine this poor woman's condition—365 days of checking for stains, worrying about overflow, and planning what she would wear based on what was happening in her body. Twelve years times twelve months—that is 4,380 days of life dominated by bleeding. Twelve years during which time every day was that time of the month. We do not know the specific duration of each hemorrhage, but suffice it to say that the sister had no rest. Twelve months times twelve years of bloating. Twelve years times twelve months of cramps. Twelve years times twelve months of light-headed weakness. Twelve years times twelve months of fabricating adequate sanitary protection first-century style. Twelve years times twelve months of raging hormones. Twelve years times twelve months of suffering.[23]

Hall reminded her hearers that this woman not only had been taken advantage of by doctors for years, but that her condition isolated her from her community because of the cultural mores of the day: "This woman whose body and soul are bleeding is utterly isolated by her religious community."[24]

Hall defended the urgency of such sermonic honesty: "There are things in the Bible that women can explain in ways that men cannot. And that should be alright. Women in the congregation listen attentively to men preachers give football illustrations and boxing analogies. Surely men can listen and learn about what their wives and daughters go through." Faithful preaching necessitated candid truth about women's bodies: "Women weren't supposed to talk like that, but I had dared to be brazen enough to tell their story."[25]

In womanist tradition, Hall did not let the woman's medical condition define her. Because "she heard about Jesus," the woman took healing from Jesus by touching his clothes: "Courageously, oh yes, she trembled, but courage often trembles. She was afraid but that is when courage is called for. She knelt down before him and told him the whole story." Jesus paused on the road to engage compassionately with her, "reversing society's order of priority." Jesus healed her, affirmed her, and named her to his family, unafraid of her body. Contrary to the societal norms, her bleeding did not make him unclean, nor did Jesus's interaction with the woman worry Jairus, who was there on the road for his own desperate reason. Rather, Jesus commissioned the healed woman to be an ambassador of shalom in her community. "He grants her Shalom! Go in Peace! Be cured! Be healed! Be well! Be free! Let no one negate you! Let no one abuse you! Let no one demean you! Let no one degrade you! Let no one defraud you! I give you wellness and wholeness in your womanhood. And I give you peace. You are restored to your community."[26]

Hall examined how Jesus's response to this woman stood in opposition to the scorn and swindle that others subjected her to—doctors who had been taking her money for years while making her condition worse, and her community who rejected her as unclean. But Jesus "was neither queasy nor offended by the fountain of her blood," and his "healing fountain" reversed "her fountain of seemingly endless, painful, foul-smelling flow."[27] Instead of rebuking her for contaminating him or requiring her to be purified, Jesus "pauses to commend her faith and to grant her salvation and Shalom."[28]

Hall's exposition of the hemorrhaging woman who Jesus commissions to proclaim shalom echoes a similar call to liberating action within black churches. Just as Jesus reversed dying in the hemorrhaging woman, just as Jesus reversed death in Jairus's daughter, Jesus "turns around the social structures of death." To participate in Jesus's liberating work within black churches, Hall insisted: "Let us turn around police abuse, child abuse, brutality against women, and brutality against men ... homophobia and xenophobia ... sexism, classism, ageism, and colorism."[29]

Utilizing a similar womanist hermeneutic in "Crippled by a Spirit," elsewhere titled "Burden Bent," Hall emphasized the perspective of the bent-over woman, who had spent eighteen years looking at the ground: "This sister, bent, burdened, and having viewed only the ground for 18 years makes her way to the synagogue on the Sabbath day. Today, Jesus is at the synagogue." Though the synagogue was crowded, Jesus saw the woman, and proclaimed, "Woman, you are free from your ailment." Emphasizing a deeper meaning, Hall continued: "Remember, her ailment is the spirit of infirmity—the crippled body is the work of the crippling spirit and just as some healing occurs only through prayer and fasting, this one needs 'a laying on of hands.'" When the religious leaders rebuked Jesus for healing on the Sabbath, Hall emphasized that Jesus was not concerned with laws but with freedom: "You hypocrites. You free your cattle and donkeys on the Sabbath that they may roam free and drink water. And you dare resent my freeing this woman from the grip of Satan's crippling spirit? She is your sister, a daughter of Abraham. I have set her free from her burdened, bent over living." This passage reinforced Hall's belief that the church was to "heal and to help, to remove burdens and to bless."[30]

Hall's sermon on the bent-over woman also explored the metaphorical elements of the story, particularly racist and sexist lies: "We do know her cultural situation. A first century Palestinian woman in a culture which empowered crippling of women as scapegoats for sin and poverty, legally and culturally a slave." She continued: "We know about that crippling of Black Folk as non-persons, women as wanton wenches, men as sex crazed brutes, mindless, cannot learn." Hall celebrated that, for most of black history in the United States, black people refused to believe those lies about blackness, "but now??" "To be lied on is one thing. To believe the lie is another." She cautioned her hearers to discern and discard the lie: "We do not have to be what the culture says we are, nor become what the culture says we must become!" When Christ healed the woman, she sprang "up from self-pity, up from pain, up from self-inflicted crippling, up from self-perpetuated crippling, up from self-participation in crippling imposed by culture," so now likewise can everyone bent over from cultural oppression spring up because "there is nothing on your back."[31]

Likewise, in her sermon about the Samaritan woman at the well with Jesus, "When Jesus Tells Her Story," Hall highlighted an internalized oppression that led the other women drawing water to isolate this Samaritan woman: "There is this affliction—I call it the pathology of oppression—which tempts and seduces us to turn in on each other and make life harder for other sisters. It happens in situations of racial and class oppression. It happens in the church." Having been assaulted by "arguments of women's inferiority," some women oppress other women from "internalized self-hatred." Hall's sermon also relishes that, rather than condemning her domestic situation, Jesus "simply affirms the truth of her response" to his question. Hearing the truth about her own story was "her first sip of living water." After the woman asks if Jesus is a prophet, Jesus offers her another sip of living water by telling her the truth about God.[32]

Hall's sermon also emphasized Jesus's public affirmation of the woman: "talking about water and worship with a woman—a Samaritan woman, asking to drink from her Samaritan vessel. But more than all of that holding high level theological discussion about the true nature of God and right worship with the same Samaritan woman. And now more than that he reveals to her his Christocentric identity." To Hall this meant that sexism in the church had nothing in common with Jesus's ministry: "The Living God is Not a Bigot, and I hear God speaking to the Church. I am tired of false worship. I am tired of racial and gender and class bigotry. I am to be worshiped in spirit and in truth." The woman at the well clearly understood Jesus because "no longer is she hiding out. She is yelling. She is calling all the way to town—come see the man who told me my whole story." People believed this woman's proclamations, as Hall explained, because "[living water] fills us with the whole truth—the whole story—that we might worship God in spirit and in truth."[33]

Though "When the Hurts Do Not Heal" is not specifically about a female biblical character, Hall restored honor to Job's wife, rescuing her from condemnation as selfishly challenging Job's obedience to God. Her sermon explored Job's wife's suffering, loss, and relationship with God:

> We have been beating up Mrs. Job for as long as this story has been told. Perhaps we condemn her so vicariously because she reminds us so much of ourselves. But you won't mind, will you, if this preacher has a word to say for Sister Job? Let us walk a mile in Mrs. Job's shoes. Everything that Job lost, she lost. A woman had no property of her own. She had no identity of her own. She was the servant of her family—the servant of her husband. The sons and daughters, which Job lost, she lost. She bore those children. They were her children, too. She brought them into the world. She nursed them and nurtured them and guided them and now, grieved for them! Sister Job hurt. And is there any hurt more grievous—God knows, I know of what I

speak—standing by the bedside of a loved one in unrelieved pain? Watching and knowing the helplessness of your watching. Willing even to exchange places with them and knowing that even that is impossible. And how many of us on that same bed of affliction have said to God, "I have had enough God! Take my life and get it over with!"? I am simply suggesting that Sister Job did not regard God lightly. She knew that the living God would always vindicate the Holy Name. She took God very seriously. Sister Job was desperate because her hurt would not heal.[34]

As Hall recast texts from women's perspectives, she subtly wove elements of her own life story into her sermons. Though she held private her own suffering from domestic abuse, she frequently mentioned domestic violence in her sermons. In general, Hall's modesty and private personality restrained mention of the explicit circumstances of her personal suffering. Rather, she drew those experiences to convey the dynamics, feelings, and theological crises of suffering, such that a hearer who knew her story intimately or had survived something similar would immediately recognize her generalized self-disclosure.

"Between the Wilderness and the Cliff" addressed women's journeys of accepting God's call, facing opposition at church, at home, and within their own minds. Comparing Satan's dialogue with Jesus during the temptation in the wilderness to the experience of women in ministry, Hall imagined what Satan might say to tempt a woman in ministry to surrender her identity:

> Preacher, if you are really God's anointed woman, just let me name you, let me form you, let me get you to dance my tune, let me get you to jump at my command, let me get you to do my tricks. Preaching woman, let me tell you who you are, where you belong, when and where you can preach. You can make a pretty good reputation just doing Women's Days. You'll be alright. Just stay in a woman's place. Stay in the woman's slot. Stay in the female box. Because if you will surrender your identity to me, I won't have to worry about God getting the glory out of your ministry. I won't have to worry about you fulfilling the dangerous mission to which God has called you. Bow down to me and sabotage the divine project, prove who you are.[35]

Later in the same sermon, Hall urged women in ministry onward: "So, preachers, teachers, servants of God . . . don't you surrender your identity. Sister preacher, whether they believe you or not, you better know who you are."[36]

Hall also offered examples of her theological struggle in times of suffering. In "Journey with Jesus," as she described Cleopas and the other disciple traveling to Emmaus in grief, she asked her congregation: "Have you ever walked in their sandals, so preoccupied with your own pain, so preoccupied with your own misery, with your own burden, with your own cares that the Burden Bearer and the Heavy Load Sharer was actually in your presence but you could not see, and you did not know?"[37]

Perhaps the sermon in which Hall most powerfully disclosed her suffering is "When the Hurts Do Not Heal" on the story of Job: "Hurt hurts. Whether we've done it to ourselves as we sometimes do, whether mean and ungodly structures hurt us and deprive us, whether other human beings hurt us, when we hurt, we hurt. I found out, if you haven't, and if you haven't, I dare you to live, there are some heartaches in this world that the electrocardiogram doesn't know a thing about. There are some earthquakes that will rock your life, but no scientist can measure it on the Richter scale. Hurt hurts."[38] She echoed themes of God presently active with believers, saving people and systems: "Even if the pain does not leave you, I've learned that there is healing that transcends pain. Hurting is not the last word." Continuing with Christocentric womanism: "Look at him, coming all the way from heaven down, down, down, down, down to where the hurts do not heal. Look at him. He didn't stop there. He's still coming up, up, up, up as a root out of the dry grass. Look at him this morning. Healing in his voice, healing in his face, healing in his clothes. Look at him. Healing crippled men and crippled lives, turning funerals into celebrations, wretchedness into pleasantness, and grief into grace. Look at him."[39]

In "An Outrageous Assertion," Hall echoed her experiences of suffering, allowing for uncertainty in this life even as she keeps her faith in God:

> And now I say to you that I do not know what God has in store for me, but I do know that every time despairing, destroying, demeaning, defeating experiences in this tent threaten to overwhelm me, then the Spirit speaks to me and tells me that it is not me that is suffering. It is not me despairing. It's just this earthly tent, this earthly tent that houses me.... Sickness cannot destroy you. Sorrow cannot conquer you. Enemies cannot defeat you... I do not know about tomorrow. I don't know, it may bring me poverty, oh, but the one who feeds the sparrows, that's the one who stands by me. I don't know about tomorrow, my path may be through storm or flood, but I'm anchored,

yes, I'm anchored in my Jesus, and I'm washed in his blood. Many things about tomorrow, I don't seem to understand, oh, but I know who holds tomorrow, and I know he holds my hand. "For we know that if this earthly house we live in be destroyed, we have another building from God, a house not made with hands, eternal in the heavens." Thanks be to God. Hallelujah and amen.[40]

These examples lay bare the raw emotional dynamics and theological crises of suffering as only a survivor could proclaim. Though she did not specifically relate these examples to the trauma of losing her father, living and working in the face of death in the Civil Rights Movement, domestic abuse, her difficult divorce, her physical injuries and limitations, or losing her daughter, Hall spoke powerfully about her lived experience of reconciling suffering with faith and of unconquerable hope.

In a rare instance of explicitly addressing her suffering, Hall's experience of losing her daughter heavily influenced the way her sermon on the hemorrhaging woman depicted the frantic father seeking Jesus. Hall explained: "Can you identify with him [Jairus]? I certainly can and on a very personal level. I buried a daughter, so I deeply feel his pain. It was essential to describe the urgency of time, and thus I describe him as stepping all over Jesus' toes and thinking, 'Come on Jesus, hurry! Can you get to my house now?'"[41]

Hall's sermonic attention to the stories of women, both in the biblical text and those in the pews, restored women and their experiences to primary importance within churches and faithful prophetic proclamation. She placed female characters in the forefront of her sermons. She emphasized the positive roles of women in the text, beyond wife and mother. By honoring women and considering them with dignity, Hall proclaimed that women's bodies are normative, women's experiences are valid sources of theological revelation, and the liberating gospel requires gender justice.

"BEYOND EDEN"

In addition to reevaluating women's stories, Hall's womanist hermeneutic also challenged misogynistic interpretations of texts historically used to oppress women. She offered a womanist corrective exegesis in support of the liberation of all people and the full humanity and equality of women.

Hall confronted black churches concerning where the freedom struggle should have continued but fell short: "When it comes to gender, we have used all the rhetoric, illogic, and distortion possible to cling to gender based oppression." Sexism "is deadly to the church" because when black churches tolerate any form of "false barriers of oppression ... we sell out our freedom Church birthright, we distort our own ecclesial genetic code—We mess up our Black Christian D.N.A." Just as Judaizers in Galatia distorted the liberating truth of Christ, black churches that perpetuated oppression and blamed their bigotry on God also distorted the liberating truth of Christ.[42] "The Christian Church has no permission from its founder to perpetuate the scandal of sexism."[43]

Perpetrating oppression against any other group defied the historic purpose of black churches. Hall preached that if black churches were to become "that easy privatized personal property salvation we learned from certain white folks," then the liberating impulse of the church must be at work somewhere else, outside of the institutional black church. Naming the leadership of women as evidence of Christ setting the world right side up, Hall continued: "Until we seriously and prayerfully and humbly address the scandal of sexism in the church, we are in mortal danger ... of having our lampstands removed." In other words, Hall argued that God would remove God's favor for black churches if they perpetuated sexism. Hall entertained no excuses: "Whatever you are afraid of, it *is a critical* issue. God is serious—why do you think God is calling so many women into ministry?" Connecting racism and sexism, Hall continued: "Scholars and white theologians stand condemned for ignoring racism, so stand you condemned for tolerating sexism."[44]

Hall's "Beyond Eden" sermon, which she preached at revivals throughout her career, offered an intellectual, yet accessible, examination of human creation in which male and female were created in the image of God: "God created them together in harmony, in physicality, in beauty, in solidarity, and in equality."[45] God created "the *adam*," an "earth creature," out of which both male and female emerged; this rejected the common misinterpretation that males were created first, and that females are therefore derivative and inferior. Eve was not subject to Adam as his helpmeet; she was "like him," and their relationship created "unity, harmony, and correspondence."[46]

According to Hall, the original creation of humanity as "harmony, equality, and solidarity," only changed when "sin entered the picture." God's judgment, she clarified, was not a prescription of hierarchy, but a description of sin: "Sin separates. Sin alienates. Sin creates scapegoats."[47] She continued: "So when we come together to that part of the story that talks about thorns and thistles and blaming all that kind of stuff, God is not prescribing this behavior as some way for human beings to relate to each other.... The divine prescription is back there in 1:26 and 27, created together in the image of God."[48]

Gender hierarchy, then, was a product of sin. Hall repeated: "Sin is what sin does.... Sin destroys. Sin dominates. Sin has us not liking each other. Sin has us using each other. Sin has us abusing each other."[49] Banished from Eden, Hall compared Adam and Eve's new existence to life in the refugee camp. Human disobedience led to exile: "Human beings have been roaming the earth like refugees ever since. And life in the refugee camp has been miserable.... In our exiled existence, woman became the scapegoat for sin. She was reduced to the status of property." Connecting racism and sexism explicitly, Hall continued: "Indeed the laws to govern slaves were patterned after the laws which governed women. Relations which had been created in harmony and unity deteriorated into alienation, domination, and conflict."[50] She lined her sermon with repetition of the phrase "in the refugee camp, life became miserable." This bondage, or refugee camp, doctrine distorted humanity: "In the refugee camp, woman became a scapegoat for sin.... In the refugee camp, the rabbis taught little boys to pray every day, 'I thank God I was not born a woman.' In the refugee camp, woman became nothing but a childbearing piece of property ... owned by her father, sold to her husband, and passed on in death to the husband's elder brother."[51]

Hall used Mary's Magnificat to transition from bondage to liberation: "Thanks be to God, God did not abandon us in the refugee camp mess.... Somewhere around the borders of the camp, I hear a little country girl from Nazareth singing a brand new song."

Though redemption had come, however, refugee camp doctrine lingered among the people: "Many of us refuse to be rescued... Our girls have been led to believe that they got to go along to get along, that they're just pieces of meat, just flesh, just a body, and that's really all that counts. And our boys have been led to believe that they are birds and bees and butterflies just roaming from flower to flower to flower to flower." Hall clearly named the culprit: "In the refugee camp, we have arrived at a distorted understanding of personhood, and therefore a distortion of personality and relationality," and ultimately, distorted theology:

And so we have exalted the genital fixations of a sick and sinful culture to the level of a theology and then dare to blame that bigotry on God. The lie that sexism tells about women and the lie it tells about men, these are not the worse lies. The most bodacious lie that this demon tells is the lie that it tells on God. For you see we lift this reasoning to the level of a theology and claim that God said it, that God ordained it, and I feel tonight God's fist in my back saying, "Preacher, I'm tired of folk lying on me!" The living God is not a bigot.[52]

Hall rejected sexism outright: "Sexism is a liar. . . . Sisters, we know the lies that it tells on us. That we're not too bright, and you know we're kind of a divine afterthought and we're either the temptress and the whore or we're the Madonna and neither one is real." Living in bondage doctrine, in refugee camp doctrine, "flies in the face of our rescuer" because when Christians live according to the lie of sexism, they "behave as if Jesus Christ had never come."[53]

Sexism was a theological scandal that hurt everyone. Hall explicitly named the price that men pay for sexism: "It says that you are so weak and so insecure that you cannot deal with us as God created us. You cannot deal with our minds and our spirits and our gifts and our talents, so you've got to create little biological boxes that say, 'My biology is this way, and therefore I belong here, and I can do this, and I can do that, and your biology is that way and you belong here and you can do this.' Brothers, that's a lie!"[54] In "Partnership in Ministry," Hall expounded on the psychological and physiological consequences of sexism for men, from "the weight and the guilt of the shackles of sexism's hierarchy" to the pressure "to be right *all* the time . . . lead *all* the time . . . to be strong *all* the time." These sinful forces were deadly to men, as demonstrated in their heart rates, high blood pressure, and cancer rates.[55]

Sexism perpetrated oppression within black communities instead of equipping and empowering black communities to work for freedom and liberation for all people. Hall proclaimed: "It's tearing us apart. It has black men over in one corner, trying to survive against the odds in their own private hell, and black women and black children over here in another corner trying to survive against all kinds of odds in their own hell. We won't survive like that." Jesus the liberator has rescued the captives: "So thanks be to God for the rescue mission. God's got something better for us. God has a way for us to relate to each other that is not by our fist, not cutting each other up with our tongue, not putting each other down, not finger pointing, not scapegoating. . . . We can't go back to Eden. But thanks be to God, we can go beyond Eden." Though humanity had sinned against gender harmony, "thanks be to God, we are rescued from the refugee camp. We are new creation."[56]

Hall's womanist hermeneutic shone as she challenged men to stop competing against women: "God made you beautiful. God made you fine. God made you strong. And God did the same thing for us." As long as black churches believed that human relationship should be based on "the refugee camp theology of a curse in Genesis 3," the church could not "be ministers of reconciliation to broken families" or bear witness to Freedom Faith. She acknowledged the multitude of challenges to black men's power, but she insisted that "power derived from keeping other people down or out is a false power" and that black churches "sanction hierarchy by modeling hierarchy."[57]

Emphasizing inclusive community over oppressive hierarchy, Hall continued: "And God knows if ever there was a time when we needed each other, we need every man, every woman, every boy, every girl, every child, every senior, we need it all. We need to be shoulder to shoulder, arm in arm, hand in hand, working together to redeem our communities. Working together to rescue our children."[58]

When preaching New Testament texts, whether explicitly related to female characters or the general biblical witness, Hall repeatedly exhorted hearers to "watch Jesus" or "look closely at Jesus" for a fresh examination of Jesus's inclusive welcome to women among the disciples and the full life of the church. She believed Paul honestly struggled with overcoming his "pharisaic upbringing," demonstrated most clearly "when it came to dealing with women." She imagined that "sometimes he wished they would just 'shut up' and ask their husbands at home what they had been unable to hear from their position behind the curtain at the back of the Temple." Yet Paul's ministry demonstrated that "women should be able to pray or prophesy in church," even if he had particular ideas about their attire. "He falls into repetition of the rabbinic teaching about women as the glory of man and man as the glory of God . . . but is unable to finish his argument without admitting that . . . all things are from God."[59] Even so, Hall distinguished between Paul's personal preferences and God's revelation: "Paul did not save us. Our Redeemer is Jesus. If you want to know how to treat women, watch Jesus."[60]

For example, in "Encounters with Jesus from Dying to Life," amid exposition of women's health issues and resultant isolation from the community, Hall highlighted Jesus's anointing of this woman as a proclaimer of the gospel:

> Throughout these two thousand years we have been told what women can and cannot do based on what this or that person said. Rarely have those who set the rules consulted Jesus. When they have even bothered to glance in his direction, they argue that there can be no women pastors and priests because there were no women among the twelve disciples. Yet this argument is absurd; there were no Gentiles among the twelve either. By that reasoning, we would disqualify just about every male in the pulpit today. The real problem of these gatekeepers is that they have not watched Jesus closely enough. . . . Sisters, when gatekeepers claim that your gender disqualifies you from this role or that role, tell them to look at Jesus. Until they do, they do not have the whole story. . . . Brothers, you go tell the brothers, when Jesus stops by and reverses longstanding socially and ecclesially accepted ways of doing things, don't panic. Just believe. Jesus has blessings abundant for everybody."[61]

Later in the sermon, Hall translated Christ's inclusivity toward this woman as a Freedom Faith mandate to the church:

> Let us keep our eyes on Jesus, for he specializes in radical reversals. He not only repudiates physical and spiritual death, he turns around the social structures of death. Let us watch Jesus and turn our world right side up. Let us turn around police abuse, child abuse, brutality against women, and brutality against men. Turn around homophobia and xenophobia. Turn around sexism, classism, ageism, and colorism in the African American church and the African American community. Let us turn our world right side up.[62]

As part of her womanist hermeneutic, Hall challenged the church to embrace feminine language for God: "If we continue to ignore the maternal and feminine in Scripture then we have a distorted view of humanity. . . . Do you speak of the divine in male terms only because it's easier—you feel better and besides, it's risky to do otherwise." Regardless of emotional preferences for the familiar, Hall insisted that in order to be a liberating community, black churches must imagine God as feminine, and feminine as holy: "I must tell you—that this is not about our comfort level—I am just as uncomfortable as you are right now. But much is at stake. Our humanity and God's divinity have been misrepresented."[63] Hall raised these prophetic challenges in the 1980s, 1990s, and 2000s, putting her at the forefront not only of preaching about these issues within black churches but also within U.S. religion broadly. During her preaching ministry, liberation theology was a small subset of intellectual religion, but she brought it to the pulpit across the country, week after week, year after year, spanning races, denominations, and regions.

In her 1998 baccalaureate address at Vassar College—one of the historical Seven (white) Sisters but already coeducational by 1998—Hall spoke on Isaiah 44, emphasizing the students' parallel with Israel, emerging from "a time of trouble" at the same time as feeling "the possibilities for transformation." Hall introduced the divine feminine: "She does not grow faint or grow weary, God's understanding is unsearchable." With a disorienting reassurance, Hall continued: "Yes, you heard correctly. I said *she* in reference to God. A part of the strength for your journey should be the knowledge that the living God who does all that these verses promise can and must be mournfully and authentically imagined as our divine Mother and our divine Father." Explaining that the *Imago Dei* meant that male and female were both created in the image of God, she elucidated the significance of the divine feminine: "How we image God determines how we image people." Seeing our common humanity across social barriers was the first step to eradicating "dominance and hierarchy as if they are sanctioned by God." She praised the graduates' accomplishments and challenged them to see themselves in common with all of humanity: "Now it's your turn to join the struggles for social transformation, armed with your wonderful skills, information, and youthful energy." She promised their success "because the Lord is the everlasting God, the creator of the ends of the earth, She does not grow faint or weary."[64]

Hall's womanist hermeneutic recovered stories of biblical women from misogynistic readings. She centralized women's experiences in hermeneutical inquiry and honored women as faithful disciples. She offered a corrective exegesis to passages commonly misinterpreted as supporting gender hierarchy. Her womanist reinterpretation affirmed the liberation of all people and the full humanity and equality of women.

"Chain removal"

True Freedom Faith required the complete elimination of any extant oppression within the church. Hall labeled this process "chain removal," avowing the absolute incompatibility of oppression (injustice) with the liberating gospel of Christ. Ahead of her time, Hall decried racism, sexism, classism, ageism, xenophobia, and homophobia within black churches.

Exegesis, for Hall, must include consideration of whether the text was authored in a context of racism, sexism, or classism and its historic use to propagate oppression. To determine whether the text reflected God's will or human action in God's name, Hall's sermons engaged in "an interrogatory conversation with the congregation and the text":

> I walk around in the text. I cannot take a verse out of context. We come to the text with our baggage. We cannot become neutral—we bring our social location, concerns, and presuppositions to the text. We need to knowingly be up front about that. So we interrogate the text. Sometimes the text is absurd. I believe that the Word of God is in the text and is not imprisoned in the paper. It is in the text. And in the process, the prayerful preacher is assisted by the Holy Spirit in dialogue with the text. And if you question the text long enough, it will begin to interrogate you. Then this is the stuff that preaching is made of.[65]

Hall's "Captivity's Capture" sermon proclaimed that since Christ had captured captivity, the church was now tasked with removing the chains. After elaborating on the disproportionate incarceration rate of black men, the high rate of unwed pregnancy among black women, and the failure of older generations to faithfully convey the strength and accomplishments of black heritage, Hall challenged the church to take responsibility in spreading the liberating message of the gospel:

> You know we get lazy as Christians, and we want to have a good time in the church and then send the Lord in the streets. Send the Lord to the crack house. Send the Lord to the prison. No, that's why God saved you. No long-handled spoon. You've gotta get down and dirty. You've gotta get up close and personal. You've got to be heart to heart, hand to hand, life to life. People will know you love them because you are there with them. You are

present with them in their struggle. You are present with them as they are going through.... We have work to do, and our work is the work of chain removal.[66]

Hall continued that, when the church kept itself in chains with stratification, this task became impossible: "Now some of us cannot be about the work of chain removal for we are stepping over too many captives in the church. The church seems always to be plagued by some little cliques and some little crowds that want to hold folk down, want to keep people in their place and got little organized boxes in which you put folk." Any place where prejudice lingered, the church rejected Christ and Christ's work in the world: "And in some places it's racism. In some places, it's sexism. In some places, it's ageism. In some places, it's heterosexism. Yes, I said that. Anything, any -ism that we can divide to separate us from each other and try to keep people from being the very human beings that God intended them to be, we can't set captives free if we're clinging to captivity. Sometimes we don't want our own chains moved: 'Leave me alone! I like my mess. Leave me alone!'"[67]

In a sister version of the sermon, titled "Captivity Is a Lie," Hall expounded on captivity's capture, wondering why so many black people, especially black youth, still live in bondage. Hall explained: "Jesus Christ *has* captured captivity. But he has left to the church the task of chain-removal."[68] She urged the church:

> This is our challenge: living our ministries that remove chains from hearts, minds, spirits, and bodies, so that the oppressed may go free and set others free. Engagement with the biblical message compels the church do the work of removing these chains.... Captivity, no matter where and how viciously it asserts itself, is a fraud. It postures a power it does not possess. Jesus Christ has already been there. Captivity has been captured. For us, the church, there is only this task: to believe, and then turn to the work of removing the chains—chains that have already been broken. The victory has already been won.[69]

The liberating gospel "give[s] the basis for critiquing all forms of oppression—both inside and outside the church," and it also classified "sexism, classism, ageism, and other forms of bigotry" as sin. The transformative power of the gospel empowered black churches to "articulate a moral critique of racism and to develop as a foundation of their faith the prophetic principle of the equality of all human beings before God."[70]

In "Partnership in Ministry," Hall addressed Baptist denominational complicity with sexism as well as texts commonly used to oppress women. She criticized Southern Baptists for perpetuating the lie: "Some of those same Southern Baptists who told women to graciously submit—have sent bloody, bruised women with broken ribs back to their homes and told them be sweeter, be prettier, don't do anything to make him angry." Rejecting a patriarchal distortion of Ephesians 5 making wives submissive to husbands, Hall emphasized Ephesians 5:21, in which all Christians live in mutual submission to one another as an act of love. When churches used a "fragmentation of the scripture," they engaged in the same distorted logic used to "rationalize and baptize slavery."[71]

All scripture related to gender should be read in light of Genesis 1:27, according to Hall: "God created humankind, not m-a-n kind. Our maleness and our femaleness both reflect something of the nature of God."[72] Because of Galatians 3:28, believers are "transformed and transcended" to become "completely new" such that "biology becomes irrelevant... anthropology becomes irrelevant... sociology becomes irrelevant." Given this liberation that Christ has already enacted, Hall was troubled that churches were still mired in hierarchy and category: "Why then do we find ourselves 2000 years later still clinging to illegal, idolatrous boundaries of race, and gender, and class?" Because the black church formed to mediate the struggles of its people for freedom and liberation, its very existence proclaimed "there is no longer slave or free."[73]

According to Hall's exposition of John 17 in "The World in Whose Hands?," Jesus "prayed for the Church and left the world to us," meaning that the mission of the church was to care for the world. Specifically addressing foreign relations in the 1980s and domestic policy on race and poverty, Hall acknowledged palpable pain and fear of irrecoverable decline: "a world of poverty and pain in the midst of plenty ... a world where the homeless poor turn boulevards into bedrooms every night ... a world where domestic violence has turned homes into battle grounds and every eighteen seconds a woman is being assaulted in her home by the man with whom she lives, husband, lover or friend." Reminding the church of its responsibilities, she remained firm that "the world, all of it, all of it: the parts we like, the parts we don't like, all of it" were in the hands of the church. Christ's presence with the church empowered the church to proclaim "life eternal" to a dying world. Otherworldly theology of escape was insufficient because God wanted freedom and liberation for everyone, now.[74]

"Preaching a Liberating Word to a Dying World" addressed the oppressive forces pastors face within themselves. The liberating preacher must be a liberated preacher, Hall preached, coming "to terms with his/her own baggage: personal, emotional, social, political issues which impede liberation." Such baggage "blocks the Word" until managed. Hall argued that preachers, especially those "who have been or are being oppressed—Blacks, women," must imitate Christ's kenosis, acknowledging their humanity, brokenness, and pain, so that they can find liberation and healing for effective proclamation.[75]

Liberating preaching speaks "closely, specifically to the dying," by naming the chains that bind, even those within the church: "race, sex, class, even homophobia." Criticizing preachers who oppress their hearers, Hall continued: "So watch the jokes you tell. Who do they include? A laugh at whose expense? The illustrations often absolutely contradict the purpose of the preaching." Preaching the liberating gospel could not commingle with oppressive behaviors: "The Black Church is in trouble. Our DNA is mutant with distorted strains. So we cannot preach an exclusive liberation that contradicts and undermines the whole project.... When we imitate oppressors rather than Christ, we invalidate our whole ministry."[76]

Particularly addressing the public personas adopted by certain black male preachers, Hall criticized tendencies within black churches to have "more big I's and little you's." She challenged that "the slave/free polarity in Galatians" should have also communicated to black churches "the idolatry of class in Church and Society." Black churches could not claim to be witnesses of Jesus with trite acts like "Jesus saves" buttons or saying "Jesus loves you and so do I" but rather must model Christ's liberating love and "preach, teach, practice, and model our Christian equality."[77]

Exemplifying her womanist hermeneutic of liberation, Hall's "Delivery for the Captives" sermon, which in many ways resembled "Between the Wilderness and the Cliff," addressed the church's response to incarcerated black men. She reported being "frightened even threatened" by the topic, recounting an incident where an intruder burglarized her mother's home, as well as a particularly profane incident of vandalism at her church. She explained:

"In a desperate society, everything is fair game."[78] Hall did not limit her prophetic proclamation to interpersonal acts of violence:

> When I am preaching to American, angry white folk, and airplanes are being hijacked and people are being blown up and hostages are being taken in the Middle East, I believe God wants me to tell white folk that they must remember that the deeds of the people they call terrorists are the product of a long series of unhealed hurts, that they must *ask* what did we do in Iran with the Shah of Iran that makes these people act this way now? And you asked me to preach about Black Men in Prison. The Church's Response. Do you see my dilemma?"[79]

Jesus's quotation from Isaiah 61, which is recorded in Luke 4, gripped Hall: "I was thrown from the preacher's dilemma into the preacher's agenda." Any talk of delivery for the captives must center around the liberating message of the gospel: "anointed to preach, sent to heal, sent to proclaim and to set at liberty them that are bruised."[80] Because black churches should mediate the struggles of its people for freedom and liberation, Hall insisted that preaching cannot stop at "cute, catchy slogan" Christianity, but must decry oppressive forces, working for the people's liberation: "The criterion by which preaching is judged is *right* here—if it is not good news to the poor, healing to the hurting, deliverance to the captives, sight to the blind, liberty to the bruised, and if it is not a *right now* timetable, it ain't preaching!! ... What can be any better news to the poor than you don't have to take it. God does not ordain your poverty."[81]

Not limiting "captives" to only incarcerated black men, Hall expanded her discourse to those who had violated the law, the unjustly accused, the elderly who are "captive in their own houses," perpetrators and victims of police brutality against black people, "those hungry, helpless, homeless, stealing bread," and merciless oppressors. She offered examples of young people blinded by their circumstances of suffering and wealthy people who blind themselves to the societal consequences of their actions. Hall echoed:

> Jesus Christ, anointed by the Spirit of the Lord has come all the way from heaven down-down-down-down, to our captivity, down to our cursed shackles, down to our shackled minds that tell us "we have to take it, shut up and give up—you can't do any better; down to the midst of our struggle—you,

that's right.... Jesus took captivity captive and caused death to die and after shaking death of out death, got up from the grave with power—all power—the power we need to give sight to the blind, the power we need to preach good news to the poor, the power we need to proclaim deliverance for the captives."[82]

Dissuading hearers from lingering in proclamation without action, Hall specified "the proclamation he announces ... is not just the *saying* agenda, it is the acting agenda, and it is doable."[83] Acknowledging the complexity of this task, she continued, preaching just as much to herself as to her hearers:

It will not be easy to confront fear and anger and grief with the action agenda of Jesus. But we *can* do it.... We must do it—our saying and our doing must be deliverance to the captives. Sometimes I look at those to whom we minister at Mt. Sharon in Philadelphia and those about them who are breaking and entering and destroying and I confess I look to my Lord and whisper, Lord, I know you told Peter to feed your sheep, but Lord, these sheep? Lord, even Peter didn't have to deal with these sheep. And my Lord, the Lord of the Church, the Shepherd of the sheep, speaks back to me saying, "Preacher, these sheep!"[84]

For Hall, the ultimate criteria on which the church would be judged was its mediation of the struggles of its people: "When I was hungry, did you feed me? When I was thirsty, did you give me drink? When I was an outsider, did you welcome me? When I was naked, did you clothe me? When I was sick, did you visit me? WHEN I WAS IN PRISON, DID YOU VISIT ME?"[85] The purpose of preaching was liberation.

In "A Letter to the Churches in Tough Times," Hall compared black churches to the early church in persecution. As those Christians cried out to God for help, she imagined God commending them: *I know* your works, your toil and your patient endurance ... *I know* you are enduring patiently and bearing up for my name's sake, and you have not grown weary ... I do not know what the Lord of the church would say to the contemporary church, but to that late first century church, the Lord said, 'I know'" (original emphasis).[86]

Comfort in struggle abruptly shifted in Hall's sermon to a womanist call for inclusivity: "You have a love problem. I know that you say you love everybody, but I don't know what you are talking about. Who is everybody?" She criticized lifeless liturgy, shallow gestures of charity, passive lay engagement, and purposeless churches: "You have soup kitchens, but serve the bread of contempt because love is no longer the main ingredient. Your church's program is an institution maintenance operation instead of the movement of Jesus Christ setting the world right side up."[87] Black churches could not stop at comforting themselves in struggle but must model a new way of being human, of loving others, in which everyone is honored as equally made in the image of God.

Hall's "Between the Wilderness and a Cliff" sermon addressed why the church sometimes ignored the liberating gospel. As Jesus read from the Isaiah scroll, announcing his ministry, the congregation turned on him. Hall explained: "But how did they hear him? They should have heard him gladly. Wouldn't you think? They were poor. They were blind. They were captive. He brought good news. It sounded mighty good. Mmm, Joseph's boy sure can tell it." But Jesus's good news was not heard as such because, according to Hall, the gospel always involved a radical reversal of the kingdom of this world: "Remember that good news to some is always bad news to somebody else. Good news to the poor is bad news to the rich who keep the poor, poor. Deliverance to the captive is judgment to those who hold them captive. Sight to the blind is disaster to those who exploit their blindness."[88]

The church in chains, however, surrendered its identity as children of God, according to Hall: "And surrendered identity is worse than stolen identity, when we lay it down. Ask Clarence Thomas and the pseudo-conservatives about it. They have checked their African American identity at the door to drink at the trough of oppressive power and have made a deal with Satan to destroy freedom's struggle and sabotage the divine project." As she often did, Hall emphasized black youths: "Parents, if we could only convince our children of who they are. Then they would know that they are too rare, too lovely, too precious in the sight of God and in our own sight... that they are our only hope of a future... that they are too valuable, too important, too irreplaceable to take their lives so lightly." The liberating gospel must remove the chains of oppressive lies.[89]

In, "The Proclaimer, the Proclaimed, and the Proclamation," a variant of "Between the Wilderness and a Cliff," Hall further explained the surrendered identity of black people who "lost their minds trying to prove to unbelievers that they are *just as good* as anybody else" (original emphasis). Black women "have destroyed their physical and mental health trying to prove in the workplace that they are just as good as men.... And, Lord have mercy, how many women ministers have faltered under the perpetual challenges to their identity as preachers of the gospel by a shamefully sexist church?"[90]

In "A Nightmare in Broad Daylight," Hall likened surrendered identity to living in chains, removable when the church remembers its identity as children of God: "So my sisters and my brothers, as you view this midnight, this nightmare in broad daylight, don't despair. Just remember who you are. Just remember whose you are. Just remember the battle has already been fought. The victory has already been won. Your job is chain removal." Transforming the nightmare would require everybody working together, modeling a new kind of humanity: "So take on every enemy. Take on death, sickness, and disease. Do battle. Make it hand to hand, heart to heart, shack to shack, tenement to tenement, and life to life.[91]

The liberating gospel required partnership, not hierarchy. Hall's "Broken by the Blessed" sermon emphasized Paul's message to the Corinthian church about stratification within the body: "You are consumed with silly factionalism as if Christ could be divided. You are observing and exalting class lines and barriers which have no place in the house of God. Some of you are feasting high on the cow or the lamb while others of you are starving." Worship should be an act of reconciliation and community: "You are not gathering to remember the broken body, the spilled blood of the Lord. You have turned the meal of sacred memory into a private party."[92] Hall crafted her own womanist translation of Paul's message:

> When we eat the bread without discerning, without seeing, without considering, without meditating upon, without judging our own conduct according to the profound meaning of the body, we once again break the body of our blessed Lord. And who does the breaking? We, who are the blessed, again, and again, and again break the body and bleed the Christ whenever we allow the bigotry and factionalism and sectarianism and denominationalism and classism and racism and sexism and ageism and any of all of the myriad ways we have found to separate, segment, stratify, distort, and destroy the body of Christ, we who are called by his name, preserved through his body, saved by his blood, and blessed by his life, death, and resurrection once again take the spikes and the hammer of the crucifiers, take the scourger's lash and in our own hands, break and break and break and break again and

again and again the sinless body of our Lord.... This is a critical challenge to the contemporary church. Our clubs, our cliques, our bondage doctrine, which rationalizes sexism and dares to blame that bigotry on God, does not just harm people. They again break and bruise and bleed the blessed body of our Lord.[93]

To faithfully live the gospel, Hall proclaimed that the church must work together, across every divide, to accomplish this new chainless, equilateral social order. The church best imitated the ministry of Christ by functioning as *one* body, proclaiming the gospel:

> When I hear folk talk about what women can't do and what men must do and where those folk out there belong, it grieves my heart. It saddens my spirit. It grieves my soul. They are breaking the Christ. When I hear them, my soul is bowed down. But oh thanks be to God, the Spirit of the Lord brings good news. The spirit of the Lord brings great news.... The steadfast love of the Lord never ceases. God's mercies never come to an end. They are new every morning. Our God is faithful. Our God is true. Our God is our strength. Our God is our capacity to change. Our God is love. Our God makes it possible for us to love. Our God does not send us to battle alone. Our God is our strong tower. Our God marches before us. Our God marches behind us. Our God marches with us. Our God works through us. Our God is a compassionate savior. We can pass the Christ test. We will pass the Christ test. Bigotry in the church shall fall. We shall be the people that God calls us to be. Hallelujah. Hallelujah. Hallelujah. Hallelujah. Hallelujah. Hallelujah. Hallelujah. Hallelujah.[94]

Speaking at the John F. Kennedy Library and Museum in 1998, Hall remarked that the only way for the church to truly embody the message of the gospel was to work together, cooperatively, across all divides: "There is tremendous work to be done. It cannot be done by any one group, as was the case in 1963—women and men across lines of race and class must catch the vision of a new America, must behold the flickering flame of freedom's faith and together *set* it to fire."[95]

In continuity with history and heritage, Hall celebrated the role of black women in the struggle. In her address at the 1998 National Coalition of 100 Black Women, she called black women to labor like the "women in the prayer bands of long ago," for as long as was necessary to save young black men from crime. "They need help in the chain removal process," and women should use their "ministries of preaching, teaching, and caring" to rescue a generation of young black males from social and moral ills, which Hall branded "a nightmare in broad daylight."[96]

Hall's womanist preaching expressed her Freedom Faith that even as believers faced oppression and suffering, God was faithfully present in their lives. Her "The Church under Construction" sermon offered an invigorating encouragement to the church as it removed the chains of oppressive lies:

> Christ is working in you. The project is his. The process is his. We are his. And Christ does not abandon churches under construction. Christ starts the work and keeps on working. In fact it is God working in us to will and do of God's good pleasure. . . . Now, look who we've got. We've got Jesus Christ, the visible expression of the invisible God. We've got Jesus Christ the anointed one, the risen one, the ascended one. Jesus Christ, the hope of earth and the joy of heaven, Jesus Christ, the same yesterday, today, and forever, Jesus Christ, Lord of the universe, Lord of the church, king of heaven, bishop of our souls, Jesus Christ, fairest of 10,000, rose of Sharon, lily of the valley, dayspring from on high, bright and morning star, working in us, working in you, great pastor, great people, great project, in progress, church under construction. . . . God does not do half-done work. The God who has begun a work in you will keep on working, will not stop working, until, not until the day of Jesus Christ.[97]

Such encouragement was not naive or otherworldly but firmly rooted in her belief that Freedom Faith meant God would empower and equip those who worked for justice and liberation. In "An Outrageous Assertion," Hall connected the realities of human suffering with the outrageous assertion of Paul in 2 Corinthians 5:1—"For we know that if this earthly house we live in is destroyed, we have another building from God, a house not made with hands, eternal in the heavens."

> When our grief is breaking our hearts and tears flow down our faces in defiance of our own will and it seems that we can neither speak nor bear the pain we are feeling, when the stress and strain of life has pushed us to the walls and our nerves are frayed, we are feeling hassled. Our heads hurt. And tension has made our bodies taut, and tied us up in tight little knots and we're

even too spaced out to read Scripture and bad news has distorted our ability to receive any news at all. And then from somewhere . . . this outrageous assertion. . . . What is it about this bold assertion that stops us in our grief, unties the knots of our anxious, stress-ridden nervous system, calms our most ferocious fears and wherein only moments ago we were sobbing in an uncontrollable manner, hurting with hurts so horrendous that they would not heal, and now, mysteriously, unexplainedly, we are not only calm, but we feel a shout coming on. Grief is transcended by grace, terror by triumph, and we have been changed instantaneously from victim to victor.[98]

Hall's womanism recognized the transformation from victim to victor, emphasizing the power of the gospel to save people and systems. Freedom Faith would prevail:

Pain and problem and trouble and sorrow and despair and defeat, tears, separation, grief, sickness, cancer, stroke, coronary failure, mental illness, dope addiction, street violence, domestic violence, wars and lost children are not the last word. Aging and arthritis, dying and burying are not the last word. . . . This knowledge, precious knowledge, calms our tears and fears, strengthens our resolve, even heals our affliction. This knowledge assures us that whatever it is that is depressing us: racism, sexism, economic oppression, dope addiction, nicotine, demeaning, dehumanizing relationships, our own weakness, our own hang ups, our own mess ups, our own faults, our own failures have no ultimate power over us. . . . The Spirit speaks to us saying, "Get up, dust off your clothes, you are not defeated unless you give up."[99]

Hall preached continuously for decades that black churches must not give up but must take up the mantle of the liberating gospel to remove the chains of oppression within itself and in the world. Freedom Faith meant working together for the liberation and freedom of all people. As Hall often did in her sermons, she interlaced the heritage of black churches with the hope of the gospel: "Christ the liberator is the Foundation, the center of our heritage. Now, when we look again we find that Christ is also our hope." Echoing her refrain to work on the building of the black church, Hall claimed the power of the gospel "in the face and against the battalions of the powers of death . . . marching through the streets and through our schools as if they are there by divine right. No way!!!" Hall's womanist hermeneutic found liberation and freedom in Christ: "We have a hope more powerful than death. We have hope—and that hope is Christ, the liberator, Christ the fellow sufferer, Christ who is grace in the wilderness and the Fire that extinguishes the Powers of Death." Black churches must continue their historical role as mediators of the struggles of the people: "Build, sisters and brothers, build! Build on your heritage and stand on your hope."[100]

CHAPTER 8

"THE BAPTIST CHURCH IS GOING TO HAVE TO DEAL WITH ME"

"I have to call it what it is"

Rooted in Freedom Faith, Hall's prophetic leadership pressed black churches to persist in their historic purpose of mediating the struggles of the people for freedom and liberation, specifically, uprooting oppressive forces within black churches and communities. Not only did she speak directly to these issues nationwide, but she also modeled inclusive ministry leadership and cultivated strategic organizational partnerships to enact her womanist vision of liberation.

A lifelong Baptist, Hall blamed black Baptist denominations and their leaders for historically and systemically oppressing those on the margins, particularly women, and insisted that any denomination perpetrating such injustices had turned its back on its people and the global community of faith.[1] She committed to remaining Baptist in order to speak prophetically as an insider against the church's prejudices. Explaining her conscious decision to remain Baptist, Hall told a reporter in 1997: "The Baptist church is going to have to deal with me. Some of us have to remain in the recalcitrant church. Everything we know about God is that the living God is not a bigot."[2]

Hall knew full well that staying Baptist meant she would be fighting deep-seated racism and sexism, without backing from the denomination. As a black woman in U.S. society, she described herself as "very well acquainted with powerlessness." She spelled it out: "As a Black Baptist Woman Preacher, I am therefore painfully aware of powerlessness!"[3]

The trauma of racism had historically overwhelmed concern for gender equity within black churches: "The pulpit has been the place where the black community has had strong male leadership . . . that could be independent in dealing with racial and economic issues within the community, because the pastor is paid by that congregation and has a certain freedom. It's also an issue because of the larger number of single-parent families and what it means to have a strong male image in the pulpit." Nevertheless, Hall recognized that this historical tendency had become an excuse to continue the exclusion of women from pulpits.[4] Flexing her Freedom Faith, she insisted that sexism within black churches could not repair the trauma of racism, but was rather part of the larger problem of oppression. She told a reporter, "Ministers have a responsibility to stand against racism, sexism, ageism—all the '-isms' that put people down. It's not a ministry if it doesn't liberate us."[5]

In a 1990 address, "Working on the Building," delivered at the B. Moses James Colloquium on African American Religion, Hall similarly argued that black church heritage cannot coexist with sexism: "We are the people who heard a distorted oppressive bondage doctrine from the slaveocracy and dared to fashion an independent hermeneutic. . . . Our interpretation led us to appropriate that understanding of scripture which proclaimed God to be a deliverer or those who strive in bondage. That the same people who adopted that independent interpretation of scripture regarding slavery or race would now buy into the lies of the distorters regarding gender is indeed heresy."[6]

If God was not a racist, neither could God be a sexist: "God is not a bigot." Citing Peter Paris's prophetic principle of the kinship of all people before God, Hall challenged: "How can it be that the God who does not respect persons in terms of their race, suddenly becomes such an oppressive respecter of persons regarding their gender?" Such thinking separates black men and women in segregated suffering, rather than bringing them together, "united for survival." Scapegoating black women combined complicity with destruction and oppression: "We buy into the arguments and accusations of the society which is destroying us. The accusations that Black women are advancing too much, are too educated, too strong, too this, too that, are really statements of hatred and vengeance against Black women for daring to continue to struggle for our survival."[7]

Addressing black church prioritization of the liberation of black men, which inevitably paired itself with the command for black women to "sit down and be quiet," Hall critiqued: "It sets Black men up." She continued: "Can Black men in 1990 liberate, rescue, all Black people by themselves? And when it becomes clear that they cannot, we will find that Black men have been set up as failures." Such "false ideology" wasted valuable resources and continued to neglect the real needs of black churches.

In the foreword to Elizabeth Bellinger's *A Costly Obedience*, Hall reflected on this Baptist bigotry:

> It is perhaps the most tragic contradiction of Christendom that the "isms" of race, gender, class, and the myriad forms of oppression that bigotry breeds have been allowed to invade and too often thrive in the household of faith. Further, it is indeed a theological and denominational scandal that among Baptists—that group of Christians who historically have held freedom of conscience and courage of religious conviction to be as sacred as believers baptism—women who confess that they have experienced the call of God to preach the Good News of the gospel of Jesus Christ are met with gross institutional opposition.[8]

Hall also believed that denominational leaders—Baptists and beyond—might allege that congregations were not ready for women in ministry when, in reality, those leaders were the ones not ready. She insisted that pulpit committee advisors, Baptist association and conference leaders, and denominational leaders needed to be intentional about helping qualified women find pulpits. Hall compared "the scandal of sexism" to "racism and classism as another idolatry." Referring to the Civil Rights Movement in a 1987 interview, Hall said: "In the 1970s the church woke up and confessed its sin of racism. There has to be a similar confession from males—black and white, Asian, Hispanic and Native American—about the sins of sex idolatry." In the same interview, when asked whether black Baptist men were bigots, Hall responded bluntly: "I have to call it what it is. This gender based exclusion is bigotry, and they blame it on God and say God ordained it. That is outrageous. The church has to be purged of that oppression."⁹

Inclusivity for women was insufficient. Hall's womanist vision sought the liberation of men from the oppression of sexism. She described the ways men surrendered their own identity within sexism:

> When brothers understand that sexism violates their integrity and their identity, then we all move closer to where God wants us to be in the gospel ministry. When brothers play according to the rules of the oppressive status quo, they accept and affirm the lie that sexism propagates.... The lie says that they are so weak, so pitiful, so pale, and so cold that they cannot handle women the way God made them. It also says that they cannot relate to women, live with women, work with women, and struggle with women, as sisters born of the same womb and united in the same struggle.¹⁰

Yearning for the freedom and liberation of all people, even men, Hall hoped that men would excel and "be [their] best selves," but that they would welcome sisters to blossom as well, and work together rather than against each other.¹¹

"She's excellent, if only she wore pants"

Mount Sharon Baptist Church historically affiliated with the NBCUSA and the Pennsylvania Baptist State Convention. In the 1980s, Hall transitioned Mount Sharon to dual affiliation with the Progressive National Baptist Convention (PNBC) and American Baptist Churches USA (ABCUSA) because of their commitment to social justice issues.

Hall was the first woman pastor to hold major committee responsibilities in the PNBC. Throughout her career, Hall served on a number of PNBC committees, including chairing the Program Committee for the PNBC for much of the 1990s and serving as PNBC delegate for the World Council of Churches in Zimbabwe in 1998.¹² PNBC President Charles Adams named Hall to the team that would dialogue with the Southern Baptist Alliance (now known as the Alliance of Baptists) about partnership between the two denominations.¹³ While completing her doctoral work and pastoring Mount Sharon Baptist Church, Hall was also a member of the Executive Committee of the PNBC.

In the early 1990s, the PNBC joined ecumenical efforts toward reconciliation with Cuba. La Fraternidad (Fellowship Baptist Convention in Cuba) requested that particular PNBC preachers attend their Annual Season of Revival in November 1991 but did not include any women. The PNBC interpreted this as a deliberate slight of Rev. Prathia Hall Wynn and Rev. Edith Kimbrough by the Cuban Department of Religion.[14] In reflecting on the failure of the Cuban Baptists to include women pastors, the PNBC also recognized its own failures in this regard: "The Progressive National Baptist Convention must 'clean its own house' before it begins to hold Cuban leadership accountable for a gender and racially inclusive Church. We too have structural constraints to implementing racially inclusive churches but we are far, far behind in incorporating women into decision-making. Few of our pastors preach or practice the prophetic nature of an inclusive church. Our leadership structures are abominably male dominated, and our patterns of distributing denominational resources are as discriminating against women as those of Cuba."[15]

In January 1992, at the request of Jualynne Dodson, ecumenical liaison for the PNBC, Hall traveled to Cuba for a "transforming initiative of peacemaking" with the Baptist Peace Fellowship of North America, under the auspices of the Center for Cuban Studies in New York City.[16] The Cuban pastors apologized to Hall in particular and invited her to attend the first ordination of the Cuban Baptist women that same month. Further, in a subsequent trip by Charles Adams scheduled for April 1992, the PNBC decided that at least two women pastors should participate with him "in order that we may begin practicing a gender inclusive Convention ministry."[17] Alliance of Baptists leaders Ken and Nancy Sehested, who assisted Dodson with the trip, sought Hall's encouragement for aspiring women pastors in Cuba.[18]

Although both of these trips brought various Baptist groups together in ecumenical and interracial partnership, they were also part of a larger strategy to develop a long-term partnership between the PNBC and Cuban pastors, and more broadly, to begin reconciliation between Cuba and the United States. As Hall prepared to join a U.S. delegation to Cuba in early 1992, she insisted that their group prepare a statement as the previous delegation had done. The statement promoted shared goals between the two groups, recorded the activities of the delegation, reflected on the strong African population in Cuba, and established their future commitment.[19] The PNBC similarly worked with the Methodist Church, which also was opposed to the ongoing U.S. trade embargo against Cuba.[20]

In 1994, Hall was the featured speaker on Freedom Night at the annual session of the PNBC in Memphis, Tennessee. She preached her "Captivity's Capture" sermon, though she had modified her traditional manuscript to fit this venue and to connect with fellow preachers. Hall decried the sexism of black churches as counter to their historical purpose of mediating the struggles of black people.[21] Similarly, the Progressive Oklahoma Baptist State Convention welcomed Hall as its preconvention seminar keynote speaker in May 1998 on the subject of "the Church in solidarity with women."[22]

At the 1999 NBCUSA annual convention, Hall was "vexed by the absence of even a single [female] candidate for president." She explained that until local churches called women as pastors, women would continue to be excluded from denominational leadership. Top NBCUSA leaders feared that female leadership might divide the convention and subject it to financial risk. Hall insisted that Mount Sharon Baptist Church remain a nonmember of the NBCUSA explicitly because of its failure to have women in top leadership positions.[23]

Hall was also prominent within the ABCUSA. Throughout the 1980s and 1990s, she was a chief ABCUSA strategist for greater racial and gender inclusivity, and she was part of the ABCUSA Women and Men in the Community of Faith. The ABCUSA pursued her in the early 1980s to serve as program manager for urban strategy development, which she declined.[24]

In 1987, Hall served on the Concern Committee for the ABCUSA, which recommended inclusive language strategies regarding race, gender, and social health issues like AIDS, as well as crafted recommendations to congregations about educating and empowering laity to advocate for environmental justice, public health, racial reconciliation on college campuses, and a peaceful end to South African apartheid.[25]

In June 1988, Hall joined a select group of clergywomen from across the country in a Racial/Ethnic Women in Ministry Conference hosted by the ABCUSA, in which racially and ethnically diverse women shared their experiences of serving in ministry. The delegation identified areas of inequity and systemic prejudice as well as strategized for immediate and long-term next steps toward racial and gender inclusivity, building on its 1986 meeting, "Patterns of Faith." In particular, the women lamented discrimination in hiring, devaluation of women's ordination, and lack of support networks. Some

Hispanic women found work in Anglo churches, but they reported a version of double consciousness, living in two worlds but homeless in both. Pacific Asian women wanted to preserve unique Asian ethnicities and languages in their ministries, to utilize their token ministry placement in order to make the system more inclusive, and to equip laity and male clergy for theological inclusivity. Black women lamented the exclusivity of placement structures, strove to create support networks for women in ministry, felt particular burden as caregivers in triplicate, wanted greater support for the whole family, and sensed that their voices were lost in white-male systems. Advocacy strategies across all groups included publicizing the work of women in ministry, ensuring women's presence and leadership at denominational and area ministry meetings, and facilitating conversations between men and women toward greater partnerships.[26]

The 1988 conference, held in Stony Point, Kentucky, created several documents of key concerns and issues for women in ministry, including education and reeducation, placement, visibility in the denomination, and strategies for actions and advocacy.[27] Hall and Rev. Kathryn Choy-Wong led a "Women of Color in the ABC" workshop, which prioritized cross-cultural conversations and strategizing. Rather than a panel of experts imparting wisdom to those in attendance, the pair's workshop honored the collective wisdom of the participants and expected that "expertise and insights as well as the agenda will come from the women participants themselves."[28]

Hall was again coleader for a similar workshop at the November 1988 ABCUSA Women in Ministry (ABWIM) Conference.[29] Posing the question "who will hear us?," this conference resolved that male pastors, youth, and laity should be better equipped intellectually and spiritually to reconcile racial and gender divides, to value all forms of ministry (and not discount women's service as less than "real ministry"), and to come together as one body. Placement systems—formal and informal—should be transparent and accessible, and women should cultivate their own informal systems for placement since formal placement favored men. The denomination itself should promote reconciling and inclusive efforts, beyond tokenism. Women in ministry should support one another, rather than territorially compete against one another.[30] ABCUSA, and Hall's leadership within it, pioneered work within Baptist life to be a truly interracial denomination able to "model a new humanity," no doubt seeing itself as part of King's Beloved Community.[31]

The National Council of Churches of Christ Women in Ministry Program was so pleased with the 1988 Racial/Ethnic Women in Ministry Conference that it offered to fund additional gatherings. ABWIM invited Hall to plan a 1989 Racial/Ethnic Women in Ministry Conference.[32] Hall was a regular presence in these conversations about racial and gender inclusivity in ministry, and often participated in or facilitated conversations like these at denominational meetings with the ABCUSA, as well as ABWIM, which invited Hall as keynote speaker for its 1988 annual convention.[33]

By late 1998, Hall was corresponding with the ABCUSA about candidacy for its 2000–2001 presidency.[34] Nominated but not selected, the experience opened Hall's eyes even wider to the demographics of denominational leadership.

In other ways, Hall helped facilitate healing in the "church under construction." In 1990, Robert Fisher, executive director of the Ohio Baptist Convention, contacted her to help him strategize attracting more Baptist seminarians to UTS and to think ahead about the possible move of Northern Seminary to Dayton.[35] The move would bring Northern into a stronger ABCUSA context, provide better educational opportunities for students, and lower some of the tangential costs of seminary for those students.

The Woman's Convention Auxiliary to the NBCUSA also welcomed Hall as their keynote speaker during the 1993 NBCUSA annual convention.[36] Hall was involved in similar types of organizing and gathering in the northeastern branches of the Women's Auxiliary of the National Baptist Convention.[37] She was part of a concerted effort to support the acceptance of women in ministry into the denomination, organizing with other clergywomen prior to the September 5, 1984, vote at the national convention in Washington, D.C.[38] She also led in worship meetings of National Baptist clergywomen.[39]

Addressing clergywomen's placements in a 1994 interview with Dorothy Schneider, Hall commented that episcopal polities placed women in a better position than congregational polities. Because first placements set the trajectory for career mobility, Hall directly critiqued men's advantage by receiving more desirable charges at higher rank from the beginning of their careers, establishing them for quick mobility and greater lifelong earnings. Women typically received "the worst charges"—small, underpaid positions at subordinate rank and sometimes multiple charges far from each other—which limited their futures. Hall exposed habitual ecclesial exploitation of women's gifts based on the understanding "they will be there forever, because there's no place else for them to go." Because women typically entered ministry as a second career, they brought tremendous "skills and talents" from their work experience. If women cannot find church placement, many start their own churches or ministries: "opening battered-women's shelters and doing a lot of street ministry, sometimes in very, very dangerous situations."[40]

One particular point of Hall's frustration with women's inferior placement was the fact that women consistently demonstrated higher capability than men. She understood that women typically graduated "at the top of their class, even going through extraordinary difficulties and carrying extraordinary responsibilities," amplified for black women who felt "pressure to be superwoman" because of their vast responsibilities. She elaborated that black women are often in "the sandwich generation," caring both for aging parents and for children, whereas white families often had external resources to assist with these responsibilities.[41]

Hall noted that often the biggest opponents to women in ministry were other women. She described this "pathology of oppression" as women's internalization of misogyny such that they cannot "be comfortable with things that women do unless they are things that women do with the approval of men." Rejecting the trite logic that women in ministry are trying to be men, Hall argued that female opponents to women in ministry actually hate themselves, specifically, and all women, generally.[42]

Though she pastored her father's church, Mount Sharon Baptist Church, in Philadelphia from 1978 until her death in 2002, Hall hoped for the opportunity to advance to a larger church. She applied for more prestigious pulpits, often at the invitation of that church's search committee, but she faced multitudinous sexism in her search process, ranging from microaggressions to outright misogyny. Even churches that had pursued her as a pastoral candidate ultimately called male preachers whom Hall considered "less competent, less qualified" than herself. More than once, search committees told her that "she's excellent, if only she wore pants," or that, if she were a man, she would have one of the most prestigious pulpits in the country.[43]

In spite of regularly drawing overflow crowds at Mount Sharon, "none of the acclaim has resulted in an invitation to serve as pastor from a major Baptist church. Hall has been passed over a time or two because Baptist lay leaders weren't 'ready' to be led by a woman." In her entire career, even after her 1997 recognition by *Ebony* as topping the list of "15 Greatest Black Women

Preachers," Hall never received a single offer to pastor another church. She felt that larger churches sought her candidacy to dispel rumors of sexism, with no real intention of calling her to their pulpits.[44] Hall lamented those experiences: "It is never easy being rejected because of your biology."[45]

"Bring that pastor to the point of confession"

Part of Hall's agenda of prophetic womanist ministry from within Baptist life was to model the kind of ecclesial citizenship necessary for a true renewal of black Baptist churches. Her public leadership extended well beyond Baptist life, offering examples of ecumenical, cooperative partnerships and innovative initiatives. In addition to receiving frequent invitations to speak or consult with various organizations—New York City Missions Society, Baptist Ministers Conference of Philadelphia and Vicinity, Black Seminarians, Black Advisory Council for the Eastern Baptist Theological Seminary, Black Theology Project, Black Leadership Women, Black Women in Ministry, New Jersey Council of Churches, Church Women United, Church of God in Christ Commonwealth of Pennsylvania Jurisdiction, Detroit East District of the United Methodist Church, Philadelphia Congress of the National Political Congress of Black Women, Atlanta Public Schools, and so on—Hall also earned a prominent speaking role in major conferences and institutes within the black church. She used this platform to decry sexism; support black seminarians, clergy, and women in ministry; and cultivate networks of support and advocacy for aspiring ministers and community activism.[46]

In June 1984, Hall addressed the Hampton Ministers' Conference regarding "women in ministry." She rejoiced that "whatever areas of discriminations are promoted by us humans, God ultimately intends to deal with all of us, without distinction." She offered biblical and historical examples of women's leadership, citing that "it's been going on in the black church for a long, long time." Rejecting human hierarchy, Hall continued: "God has never been a respecter of persons. . . . This is not just wishful thinking. This is the prophetic *word* of God!" (original emphasis). Visioning the future, Hall hoped for liberation in the church "because preachers who prophecy the will of God would see the church as a liberated family in which everybody is *used* of God: Ministers who would see the church as strengthened by the intelligence and insight and indeed by the graciousness of women" (original emphasis).[47]

Hall was invited to participate in the 1984 Racial Ethnic Women in Ministry Consultation of the National Council of the Churches of Christ.[48] She was also selected to participate in the World Council of Churches' International Consultation on Racism and Racial Justice in 1988. This group of thirty women and men from twenty-one countries on five continents gathered to strategize for racial justice and church engagement in global justice.[49]

Black Leadership Women, a Philadelphia organization in which Hall played a key part, advocated for equality of black women in leadership and the empowerment of aspiring black women to leadership. This group met regularly with black women leaders, key public officials, and others to address concerns with economic development, health, housing, employment, professional development, and the wage gap.[50]

The University of Virginia's Office of Afro-American Affairs and Department of Women's Studies cohosted a two-day symposium, held April 6–7, 1989, celebrating black women scholars—"And They Shall Rise: Afro-American Women Scholars in Religion"—at which Hall was a featured speaker alongside Kelly Brown, Jualynne Dodson, Cheryl Townsend Gilkes, Renita Weems, Clarice Martin, and Barbara King. Hall titled her presentation "Preaching as a Social and Political Phenomenon."[51]

She drew a standing ovation after her "Becoming Sisters and Brothers in the Same Struggle" address to more than two hundred black church leaders at the 1992 Hampton Ministers' Conference. She clearly linked racism and sexism as co-oppressors within black churches: "The same theological issues which we raise regarding racism are relevant and critical when it comes to sexism.... The contemporary alienation, which too often separates Black men and Black women into hostile camps heaping scorn and blame upon each other is not only devastating, it is suicidal." Hall traced the source of internal enmity between black men and women: "It is the product of a variety of... the materialism of the dominant culture which we are adopting and are, thereby, reducing others and ourselves from persons to things. But when this tragedy is tolerated, and, or, perpetuated, by the Church of Jesus Christ, it is homicidal and the blood is on our hands."[52]

Acknowledging the historic place of pastoral leadership in support of black manhood, Hall insisted that elevating black men over black women could not be part of the liberating mission of the church: "Nobody, nobody, wants and supports the recovery and leadership participation of Black men more than Black women. We are not the enemy. And as long as we are the scapegoats, the real enemies will never be confronted and subdued. Black men and Black women must not set each other up for an inevitable fall, by refusing to face the fact that either we will struggle together and survive together as partners, or we will perish apart as fools." Although sexism was being used as a biblical mandate, she called it out as an emotional instinct: "Although we talk most about theological and Biblical issues, the problem for many, many of us, male and female, has nothing really to do with the Bible or the Lord, in spite of what we say. The issue for many of us is emotional. Some of us have some shadows lurking in our hearts and minds that go back to a bad personal relationship. Others us of are still angry with our mothers over some issue we have not resolved. And for many, it just feels better to go along with the status quo." Whatever the reason, sexism could not be tolerated in the church, for "this is a matter of life and death . . . our survival as a people and the health and well-being of our personal and family lives."[53]

At the 1992 National Dialogue Conference of the Kelly Miller Smith Institute on African American Church Studies at Vanderbilt Divinity School, Hall joined a select team of seminary professors and pastors to address the question "What does it mean to be Black and Christian?" She played an integral role in crafting a document to guide national discussion on the topic, particularly the section addressing black theology as story.[54]

In her address at the October 1992 gathering, "The Challenge of True Kinship," Hall proclaimed that Black churches "defy God and curse Christ" when they practice sexism. She clearly established the mutual exclusivity of sexism and Christian discipleship: "You can't be a disciple of Jesus and harbor sexism in your heart."[55] Neither could black church leaders delay addressing sexism, "obstruct[ing] the progress of our own survival and liberation struggle." Black church leaders could no longer sidestep sexist oppression by dealing with other issues: "Do not pretend to care about our community-at-risk, if you are not going to deal with the whole problem of oppression, because we then compromise everything we say we stand for. We may fool ourselves, and we may fool a few people, but God is not deceived."[56]

Tradition no more excused sexism than racism. Whether excluding women from leadership or tolerating humor demeaning to women, any degree of sexism was sinful: "The extent to which one engages in sexism, or tolerates sexism, or fails to fight actively against sexism, or refuses to purge it from one's own heart, one's own soul, one's own mind, one's own life, and one's own ministry is the extent to which God is defied; and Christ is cursed and sabotaged by those who are the Divine project of human liberation.... It covers every aspect of life. We must understand that when the church distorts and oppresses women, it is not really about sisters. It is God who is being defied."[57]

Hall repeated a line she used often: "Sexism in the Church represents a theological scandal." Since God is no respecter of persons, "[exalting] the genital fixations and sexual distortions of the culture to the level of a false theology and [daring] to blame that bigotry on God" through sexism is a sin. As survivors of the trauma of racism, Hall could not understand why black churches would perpetrate the same oppression within itself: "The scandal is even more outrageous when we who have been the victims of the idolatry of racism, and know its abuse, stoop to practice the kindred idolatry of sexism."[58] Just like "the racist lie," sexism "distorts the humanity of victims and perpetrator alike ... thereby inflicting upon the women *and* the men of our race the dehumanizing crime of sexist bigotry."[59]

Turning to the present need for black men to advocate for black women to be fully included in pastoral leadership, Hall recounted the instance at the spring Philadelphia revival when the "brother-preachers" were asked to stand, and she experienced a crisis within herself of whether to stand in denial of her gender or sit in denial of her call. After that event, Hall relayed, Samuel DeWitt Proctor and Edward Wheeler "took up the issue." Grateful for their support, Hall described an unexpected moment of reconciliation: "God used Proctor and Wheeler to bring that pastor to the point of confession, so that he urged the three of us to come to his study, where he requested prayer and asked for help that he might do what he knows in his heart is right. It was a wonderful moment."[60]

Continuing the story, Hall shared that she later served on the doctoral committee of the same Philadelphia brother preacher. As a member of his doctoral committee, her ordination did not seem to bother him. As a fellow minister in the church, however, his actions suggested otherwise. Hall candidly expressed her outrage at this duplicity:

> Brethren, you cannot have it both ways. You cannot accept us and use us when we are useful, and then deny, degrade, and disregard us when our presence presents a challenge. Historically, our gifts and energies have

been welcomed only in narrow and constricted ways in the Black Church: the fund raising, the drudgery work of the church, and anything required to maintain the church. But these same gifts and energies have been prohibited, when and where there has existed the most remote possibility that these gifts and energies might disrupt the status quo of male power.... Power has to be questioned, analyzed, and challenged, whenever it is used to oppress rather than to liberate.[61]

Honest conversation between black women and men must address the problem of sexism: "real, pervasive, and destructive to our individual and collective existence."[62] When black men would tell her that they did not understand or remained insensitive to sexism, she boldly responded, "if you've experienced racism, then you have a framework for understanding sexism, so don't tell me you don't understand." Hall had grown weary of those who opposed racism but tolerated sexism: "It absolutely boggles my mind as well as grieves my spirit that brothers, with whom I have stood side by side in the struggle, brothers with whom I have bowed, knelt, prayed, worked, struggled, gone to jail, dodged bullets, and caught bullets, claim to be unable to make the transition from the critique of race-based oppression to the critique of gender and class-based oppression."[63]

Drawing on Jesus's temptation to surrender his identity in the desert, Hall offered a moving historical survey in which whites did everything possible to rob black identity from black people: "They called us: 'nigger,' 'winch,' 'buck,' 'slave,' but out there in the brush arbors, the wilderness, and the woods, the God of our ancestors, the God we had known on the other side of the waters met us and whispered words in our ears, and stirred a song in our souls.... We, like Jesus in the wilderness of temptation, would not surrender our identity." Jesus's temptation was parallel to the marginalization of women within black churches: "There are some among us who, like the so-called black conservatives, are willing to sell what they could not steal ... gleefully selling their African identity and their heritage of struggle ... in exchange for surrendered identity and sabotage of the Divine project of human liberation."[64]

Accepting misogyny within black churches, to Hall, resulted from surrendered identity, a clear mistake in creation theology. She preached: "We did not become men and women in order to become opponents. We became two for the sake of human harmony, solidarity, and progeny. Even when the one earth creature became two human beings, the most recognizable thing about them was not their delight of the differences ... [but] their sameness ... not a divine afterthought, but bone of my bone, flesh of my flesh, mind of my mind, spirit of my spirit, and one like me." The struggle against racism is inextricably bound with the struggle against sexism because humanity is "irretrievably bound together, anthropologically, sociologically, and theologically," such that all humanity is linked in a common struggle.[65]

Sensing discomfort from her hearers, Hall proclaimed womanist inclusion: "Brothers, I do not speak in this way to beat you up. You are too precious to me for that." She continued, "We cannot afford to go down from this conference still playing games." Near the end of her address, she stated plainly that "we will not overcome, if the present alienation between Black men and Black women prevails." Hall echoed Proctor: "the message of freedom cannot be communicated in the language of oppression."[66]

Casting her womanist vision of inclusion, Hall argued that issues of injustice could not be handled line-item but must be addressed completely: "If we do not go back to our places of practice and take on the whole multidimensional structure of oppression including issues of gender and class and homophobia, and all those other oppressions which we nurture, then we will have squandered the time and they money it took to bring us here." She later told reporters: "You know well that sexism is a demon that must be exorcised from our churches and first from our homes. . . . Gender-based oppression isn't a trivial inconvenience. It's human devastation."[67]

The Interdenominational Theological Center in Atlanta hosted a think tank on October 14, 1999, with the theme "The Future of Black Theology: Challenges of the New Millennium." Hall joined a select group of sixteen black scholars from across the country to spend the day brainstorming about the state of black theology, its evolution in the latter part of the twentieth century, its unresolved issues, challenges to black theology in the twenty-first century, and its future tasks to address those issues and challenges.[68]

Dorothy Height invited Hall to be a featured speaker for the National Council of Negro Women on December 4, 1999, in which Hall summoned her hearers to reenvision familiar biblical texts, particularly Genesis, with fresh eyes instead of "the perspective of patriarchal privilege." Drawing from her "Beyond Eden" sermon, Hall highlighted the "tension between men and women and especially Black men and women," calling her hearers to "turn *to* each other and not *on* each other." Beyond the refugee camp, Hall urged men and women to "work together as equal partners in the human project, co-workers in the rescue mission of our society," modeling the "New Creation, Divine Originals," because "only then shall we overcome."[69]

Reflecting as a womanist upon the 1995 Million Man March, Hall affirmed the progress of black men in asserting their own identity, acknowledging the double-edged sword of sexism within the black church since women have struggled to keep their sons safe, and black men have not been "allowed sufficient space for them to take personal responsibility for themselves."[70] Even so, no work of recovery could possibly succeed with misogyny:

> I must make it abundantly clear that while as a black woman I could understand and support the March of Men on October 16, the survival and liberation of our community requires the equal partnership of black men and black women in the family, in the church and in the community. There is no place in our forward-movement for misogyny too often demonstrated by some march organizers. The hatred of women, however dressed it may be in chivalrous garb, is absolutely destructive to women, men, and children. It must be totally purged from the hearts, minds, and practice of all who will function effectively in the continuing struggle for liberation.[71]

The involvement of the Conference of National Black Churches (CNBC) in the march greatly disturbed Hall. She challenged male leaders to imagine black women and their labor—opening doors, greeting, teaching Sunday School, ushering, singing in the choir, making bulletins, bringing family members, tithing, and organizing mission work—gone from churches: "If 80% of the Black Church stayed home, the doors would soon close and the institution would soon fold!" The CNBC could not be complicit with misogyny, ignoring the "missing and invisible 80%!" She listed a multitude of accomplishments by black women in science, education, politics, and business, as well as skills missing in black churches because black women were confined to pews. "We can no longer sit in silence . . . remain invisible . . . watch the blatant disregard of women." Calling the CNBC to repentance, Hall continued: "Racism is a sin we love to 'pounce' upon. Sexism is no less evil, divisive, or sinful. The time is now for atonement. And before atonement comes confession. Following atonement is repentance and reconciliation. The time is now!"[72]

In a 1997 newspaper interview after preaching a revival at Union Baptist Church in Swissvale, Pennsylvania, Hall blamed misinterpretation of the Genesis creation narrative as the source of "bondage doctrine" that blamed women for sin and licensed black men to treat women like property. She rejected male entitlement to "rule their house by any means necessary," including "fists, knives, and guns," which "creates havoc in the black community" and "destroys any basis for relationships to have harmony, passion and common goals."[73]

In addition to a rich platform of research, preaching, and public leadership, Hall modeled inclusive ministry. She advocated for women ministers, shared her pulpit, and cultivated networks to support women in ministry, both in theological education and in ministry placement.

A highly sought preacher, Hall itinerated across the country, including supply preaching, Women's Days, and consulting to promote women in ministry. One example, among many, of the latter, was Union Baptist Church in Philadelphia, who invited Hall in November 1984 to facilitate a discussion on women in ministry for its members, to help them move to an affirming viewpoint.[74] When Hall missed Sundays at Mount Sharon, she regularly invited other women to speak in its pulpit, giving her congregation exposure to numerous women in ministry, and giving other women in ministry opportunities to preach.

Tired of empty promises of eventual progress, Hall advocated for the full and immediate inclusion of black women in ministry. In order to be faithful witnesses to the liberating gospel of Jesus Christ, the church must be inclusive. Hall's convictions about advocating for women in ministry and against any kind of oppression stemmed from her own personal journey toward accepting her calling and rising out of racist and sexist circumstances. As a girl, the first woman Hall heard preach was Mary Watson Stewart of Detroit, about whom Hall reflected, "there was absolutely no mistaking she was a preacher." Even so, "even if they [women] were preachers, they weren't called preachers." In her own ministry, many churches asked Hall to preach from the floor rather than behind the pulpit, or only on a special Women's Day, because they would not accept a woman preacher on a regular Sunday. She insisted on speaking from the pulpit as a male would do, or she declined the invitation.

Hall recognized key differences between white women's and black women's experiences of gender equality in ministry. She explained to Barbara Ransby that whereas white women "dealt with... [a] sense of woman as inferior or as a lesser being or second sex," black women faced "a kind of duality... because of [the] racism we saw," particularly directed at black men, who were "prohibited from having a strong voice in anything but the church." Consequently, "there was a certain pride that Black women took in having strong, articulate Black men in positions of leadership." Herein rested black women's particular dilemma:

> Now the rub, I think here, is that the guys never realized how much of their leadership was by the permission of women. For instance, you'll find very few pictures of me [from the movement]. It's just not my personality. And then of course, who was doing the interviewing? Usually the white male press. Who did they think were the important people to interview? Just like you said, when they interviewed Miss Baker, it was to find out about King or someone else.... But what I am saying is that there was a kind of complicity among some Black women [to tolerate sexism for racial progress]. Not all Black women felt the same way.[75]

When *Ebony* invited Hall to nominate great women preachers for their first-ever Best Black Women Preachers in America awards, she used the opportunity to advocate for other sisters of the cloth.[76] In a letter to *Ebony*, Hall explained: "While I have had no difficulty identifying excellent women preachers, I believe that it is important to make the obvious observation that since the overwhelming number of preachers are men, we are selecting from a significantly smaller sample. Most of the women preachers have had fewer opportunities and a shorter period of time in which to develop their preaching skills. They are becoming great preachers." Looking to the future of the church, Hall added: "Thankfully there is a much larger cadre of women preachers of great ability entering the service of the church. They will be able to take their places with men as partners and co-laborers in the preaching ministry."[77]

Being a woman in ministry, according to Hall, required investment in the formation of aspiring women ministers. For example, Hall offered a workshop at the 1983 Black Women in Ministry symposium hosted by Princeton Theological Seminary.[78] She also was extremely involved in the Association of Black Seminarians at Princeton Theological Seminary during her education. Mount Sharon regularly ordained women, and Hall advocated with the Philadelphia Baptist Association for their ordinations to be recognized.[79] Hall was unanimously elected to the National Board of Advisors to the National Association of Black Seminarians (NABS) in October 1989 and was invited by Cain Hope Felder to meet with the executive committee in November 1991 in Dallas–Fort Worth to plan the 1992 meeting.[80] She often attended the regular meetings of the NABS and led workshops on the contemporary challenges to African American preachers and preaching ("Dare We Preach," 1990).[81] Hall was joined on the board by such scholars as Charles Adams, Delores Williams, and Peter Paris.[82] She was the keynote speaker at the African American Baptist Women's Consortium's Christian Women's Leadership Conference, "Preparing God's Women to Meet the Twenty-First Century," in October 1999 in Albuquerque, New Mexico.[83]

UTS described Hall as "an inspiration to our women students because she is a pioneer among African American Baptist women."[84] As director of the Harriett L. Miller Center for Women's Studies at UTS, she facilitated meaningful conversations about gender with her students and empowered them to lead their own conversations both in and beyond the classroom. She worked through formal and informal structures to recruit students to join her efforts, ranging from formal coursework and programs to the use of inclusive language in worship.[85] Strategically, Hall hoped to expand UTS's Women's Center to include male "friends of the Center" who could further the educational and supportive aims of the project. She also hoped to distribute the work among those involved, including an advisory board.[86]

In 1992, Hall organized, through the Women's Center, a viewing of *A Word in Edgewise* (1986), a film on the relationship between language and behavior, particularly language perpetration of gender bias.[87] After viewing the video with her staff and hosting a follow-up discussion, Hall drafted a memo to the president and dean of the seminary, as well as to several male professors, asking that the video be shown to all students. She explained: "It became apparent that the male faculty also needs the insight of the video tape. Their failure to take leadership and demonstrate principles of inclusion is limiting the ministry potential of students and faculty by their omission of women in significant parts of history." She offered specific examples, including "use of sexist language in chapel . . . extensive apology regarding omission of women's inclusion combined with marginal attention in the syllabus in the church history classes . . . [and] humiliating comments and ridicule offensive to class members regarding gays and lesbians in an ethics class." She arranged for the entire faculty to view the video and encouraged them to show it in their classes: "I do not consider this sufficient follow-up, but I do feel the need for further discussion among us to address our concerns in a clear and effective manner."[88]

When Hall led DMin seminars for UTS, she consistently used these opportunities to facilitate conversation about women in ministry. During a DMin seminar in 1989, Dean Samuel DeWitt Proctor and Hall coled a discussion on women in ministry and some nationally famous clergy who "diametrically opposed" women in ministry. Jeremiah Wright, a student at the time, recalled the conversation: "It was a brouhaha. It got to be ugly. . . . But Prathia stood her ground." Similarly in January 1995, Hall facilitated a DMin seminar titled "The Search for Integrity: The Challenge of Partnership," which brought together leading black clergy and scholars, including Cheryl Townsend Gilkes, Jeremiah Wright, Ella Mitchell, and Susan Brooks Thistlethwaite. To address inclusivity in the church "across barriers of race, gender, class, and physical challenge."[89]

In 2000, Hall participated in a similar discussion at Boston University, including female faculty and administrative staff. The conversation emphasized that women perceived men to hold all of the decision-making power and to hold themselves above the consequences for dismissing rules. The women also objected to male expectations that women be nurturers, rather than valuing that trait as fundamental to all decent humanity. The responsibility to be the primary caretakers for student needs placed undue burden on female faculty and staff. Those gathered also commented on the latent ageism within the university's sexism, both for students and faculty/staff.[90]

"A profound integration of the religious and the political"

In addition to Hall's prophetic leadership among black Baptists and black churches in general, she served as a consultant for racial and gender inclusivity. She also utilized her positions of leadership in community organizations to cultivate strategic partnerships that supported the liberating work of black churches in mediating the struggles of the people.

The Ohio Commission on African American Males and Ohio Department of Human Services invited Hall in 1994 to speak at "Mother to Son," a conference addressing single black mothers of sons, and inclusive of "young mothers, foster parents, divorced and separated mothers, 'left-behind' mothers, grandmothers who are now assuming responsibility for raising their grandchildren, as are others in our community who are raising boys alone." Her remarks, "Black Women: Agents for Change," targeted community organizers, community service providers, medical providers, teachers, criminal justice workers, and city leaders, equipping them with better understanding of the complex, historic, systemic issues involved with single black motherhood. She encouraged those present to work collaboratively with other organizations and community services on solutions to benefit their communities.[91]

Though Hall left SNCC in the 1960s, she and other SNCC alums intentionally stayed in communication with each other. Since the mid-1990s, SNCC alums have reinvigorated their collaboration and communication through an e-mail Listserv, crmvets.org, reunion conferences of major events in the movement, and the SNCC Legacy Project effort to safely archive SNCC records.

In April 1988, Hall joined her fellow SNCC veterans for a celebratory reunion at Trinity College in Hartford, Connecticut. She and others reflected on the movement, its history, its music, how historians and filmmakers portrayed what happened in the movement, and the next steps in the ongoing struggle for freedom. Panelists included Charles Sherrod, Diane Nash, James Forman, Bernice Johnson Reagon, and Howard Zinn.[92]

Through connection with Wyatt Tee Walker, Hall also came to be part of the Summit Conference on Apartheid, led by Dorothy Height, Marion Wright Edelman, and Desmond Tutu. She was invited to organize a Philadelphia-area Soweto Day in 1989.[93] She also shared information about economic boycotts against companies that supported apartheid in South Africa and was included as a clergyperson concerned about South Africa in the Pennsylvania Democratic State Committee's efforts to protest apartheid.[94]

Hall was among featured speakers at a 1994 symposium at Connecticut College, "Activism and Transformation: The Civil Rights Movement and The Civil Rights Act of 1964." Hall joined fellow SNCC veteran Lawrence Mamiya and others in "The Relationship of Religion and Social Activism in African American Communities" panel, specifically considering the historic challenges and relationships, as well as future organizing for civil rights domestically and abroad. Her focus was the relationship between faith and the freedom struggle in the Civil Rights Movement, both supportive and antagonistic, and the role of women in shaping religious activism.[95]

Hall joined Marion Barry, Julian Bond, John Lewis, and Bernice Johnson Reagon as keynote speakers at the seventieth birthday celebration of Jim Forman, held October 3, 1998, in Washington, D.C. Forman planned to publish a book with remarks made at the party, as well as letters by Representative John Lewis, Mayor Marion Barry, and President Bill Clinton. Hall and Sherrod, who shared a uniquely close bond during the movement, did not have regular opportunities to see each other. In 2001, Sherrod wrote a letter to Prathia saying that he wanted to be more intentional about staying in touch: "Let's keep ourselves hungry to hear from each other but let's stay fed!!"[96]

PBS broadcast in 2003 a documentary series on black spirituality, *This Far by Faith: African American Spiritual Journeys*, that had been in development since the late 1990s. The episode about the modern Civil Rights Movement featured Prathia Hall describing her awareness of racial prejudice, even as a small child, and her experiences of working with SNCC in Southwest Georgia. She explained the philosophy of nonviolence in the language of Freedom Faith. The episode ends with Hall preaching in Brown Chapel in Selma, where she tended to wounded marchers after Bloody Sunday 1965.[97]

Hall's bearing of the prophetic mantle through her academic work in intersectional oppressive forces and community solutions earned her several strategic appointments. In January 1995, Hall was invited to join the Ford Foundation's African American Church Program Advisory Committee, on which she served alongside Gardner Taylor, C. Eric Lincoln, Jeremiah Wright, and Michael Eric Dyson.[98] Hall was a natural fit for this committee given its focus on helping black clergy and churches provide social services for their communities.[99]

Hall was regularly involved in events with Marian Wright Edelman's Children's Defense Fund (CDF) and through her advisory board roles with groups like the Black Community Crusade for Children (BCCC), in support of social and community programs benefitting children and families.[100] She also partnered with the CDF and other organizations to oppose legislation that endangered black youths and black communities.[101] Such activism was a necessary manifestation of her Freedom Faith.

Hall also used her role as cochair of the Black Church Initiative committee of the BCCC to build partnership between the Congress of National Black Churches (CNBC) and the CDF.[102] Though Hall cochaired the Black Church Initiative committee with Otis Moss Jr., she was the BCCC's consultant for Black Church Outreach, tasked with creating a partnership between the CDF and the CNBC "and its member denominations for the promotion and implementation of African American Church programs for children." Because the CDF created a tremendous infrastructure for children and families, particularly those in poverty, and since many black pastors often approached political leaders concerned about those issues, Hall believed it would be critical to develop strategic partnerships between black church networks and the CDF, including initiatives like "Child Watch, Freedom Schools, Children's Sabbath, and One Church Ten Families."[103]

Hall recognized the potential of a partnership between the CDF's BCCC and black churches to address needs within black communities that resulted from urbanization, desegregation, and secularization. She noted: "The reality that results from these social dynamics constitutes a far more complex challenge to congregations which desire to keep faith with their historical roles in the formation, guidance, and development of African American children and their families." Bringing black churches into the work of the CDF, at every level from grassroots to national, inclusive of all sizes of churches and of women ministers and lay leaders, had the potential to "bolster the work of all involved to maximum impact, and to breathe new life into the Black Church." Drawing on her SNCC roots, Hall emphasized that these partnerships had to be "genuine partner relationships," where the expertise and resources of each entity would be respected and valued equally, and where all involved saw each other as allies.[104]

Hall diligently worked to schedule meetings between the various organizations in 1999, initially with a conversation at the former Alex Haley Farm in Tennessee and later at the CNBC annual meeting. She believed this would be a mutually formative and encouraging partnership for both groups.[105] Fred Lofton of the CNBC welcomed Hall's work, and invited Hall to present her ideas to the board of the CNBC. Her presentation won the Board's support, and she helped the CNBC consider how its programs like Project Spirit could partner with CDF programs. Via conference calls, Hall, Moss, and Lofton advanced these ideas into a strategic plan.[106]

Hall envisioned buy-in from key leadership as the first step, paving the way for expanded grassroots programming. Year 1 would focus on building buy-in as well as a leadership development event on nonviolence, inclusive of domestic violence. Year 2 would launch a Faith in Action Network of clergy committed to enacting social justice programming through their churches and communities.[107]

Hall's ideas for actualizing her vision involved intentional, strategic networking between black denominational leaders and structures, and important gatherings of black clergy. She knew who would be at which meeting and planned ways to collaborate, connect, and cooperate nationally and locally. She would give a keynote address at the 1999 CNBC conference. Because Moss, Lofton, and Hall were all in the PNBC, Hall also rallied the support of PNBC president C. Mackay Daniels in hopes of connecting the PNBC Women's Department with the CDF, even recommending that L. Henderson Bell lead a Freedom School seminar at the next PNBC annual meeting. She also hoped to take a similar "direct approach" with William Shaw, president of the NBCUSA. The 2000 Proctor Institute became the anchor of her strategy since many of the players would be there; she made suggestions for its program and recommended that invitations be extended to specific church leaders, including presiding leaders of major black denominations, leaders of black caucuses of nonblack denominations, presidents of women's departments, leaders of black women's organizations, leaders of youth departments and parachurch black youth organizations, and select seminarians.[108]

In Hall's featured address, "The Black Church and the African American Community in the Twenty-First Century," at the 1999 CNBC conference, she argued that the greatest asset of the black church and black communities was its heritage: "our faith understanding ... that our African ancestors brought with them, their conviction that all life is sacred." This theological heritage was "intensified by the suffering inflicted upon them during the Middle passage and the brutality of slavery," birthing a black church rooted in mediating the struggles of its people for freedom: "When we examine the embryonic stages of the Black Church and the Birth Canal through which it had to pass, we see that the Black Church came out of the womb fighting—fighting for its own existence and its own freedom. AND fighting for the survival and freedom of Black people. Were we to draw the genetic analogy, we would have to say that our genetic code, our DNA, is stamped 'Freedom Struggle.'"[109]

Black theological heritage honors the sacredness of life and "includes the belief that God cares about and is involved in the lives and struggles of human beings . . . a profound integration of the religious and the political." Just as the church's purpose is mediating the struggles of its people, its members must prioritize justice as the "expression of the righteousness of God and therefore a requirement for human conduct." Whether in brush arbors, sanctuaries, freedom schools, or education of children neglected by public schools, the black theological heritage has "declared that service to people is service to Christ."[110]

Based on the foundation that "freedom struggle is not just something we do, it is what we are," Hall laid out a "profound contemporary implication of this reality" for black churches in the twenty-first century:

> As we become more and more affluent, we are tempted to look, act, and become like other churches and other people. We may retain our distinctive worship style and yet relinquish our social-ethical responsibility and accountability. We can preach, shout, have a great time in the Lord and do nothing to eradicate poverty; nothing to save our children from destruction; nothing to hold government, companies, society at large, and ourselves accountable for how we treat the last of God's little ones; tolerate and even perpetuate bigotry, sexism, classism, colorism, ageism, heterosexism, and all the other deadly oppressions which destroy people and break the heart of God—within our own ranks. . . . The Truth is that when we abandon the freedom struggle for survival and liberation and perpetuate oppression within our own churches and communities, we turn our back on God. . . . God formed us to be God's prophetic witness on earth to the equality of all persons before God . . . We are to lead by example and teach the world what the Justice of God requires of human society.[111]

Hall called on those gathered at the CNBC's meeting to cooperate in fulfillment of the "divine mandate" to black churches to model justice and liberation. Promoting partnerships between the CNBC, the National Urban League, the United Negro College Fund, and the CDF, especially its BCCC,

Hall challenged leaders of all of those organizations to plan programs centering around the theological heritage of black churches and black communities. Driving her womanist vision home, Hall added that

> the Children's Defense Fund wants to support the important work of CNBC and its member denominations and affiliates; to offer the benefit of our extensive research and analysis of public policies which impact the welfare, protection, education, care, and development of children and their families; to share in programs which train child advocates and implement child advocacy ministries, and such programs as Freedom Schools, Child Watch, Children's Sabbath, and One Church—Ten Families in which juvenile court judges refer at risk youth to local churches, which then identify families in the congregation to mentor and support the youth and heal their family.[112]

Black churches must remember their historic engagement "in a process of communal nurture which required any responsible adult to encourage, correct, and protect not only their own children, but all the children," which Hall lovingly labeled "our informal adoption network": "We belong to the little ones outside our churches and they belong to us. What kind of impact do you think might be made upon the problem of teenage parenting if the churches were to begin to adopt teenaged fathers as well as mothers and their children and provide financial assistance, emotional support, instruction and guidance? Perhaps we could then begin to reverse the cycle of poverty and dependency." By collaborating, these organizations could build on the legacy of black heritage: keeping "faith with our sainted mothers and fathers who first built our African American churches," remaining "faithful to our God who has called us into being and brought us this far on our way," and continuing in the freedom struggle until all are truly free.[113]

Hall's brilliant leadership, preaching, and service led to numerous awards. In 1993, Hall was inducted into the Martin Luther King College of Preachers and Scholars at Morehouse College.[114] In 1997, she was named one of the top fifteen greatest African American women preachers in the United States by *Ebony* magazine. For Hall, the Ebony poll was a humbling honor that she hoped would elevate "credibility and visibility of all women preachers." She was the leading woman considered for its list of fifteen greatest black preachers, but did not "receive enough votes to crack the magic 15." *Ebony* added a black women preachers' category for that issue. Hall tied for first place with Rev. Carolyn Knight and Rev. Vashti McKenzie. Rev. Jeremiah Wright, of United Church of Christ in Chicago, told *Ebony* that Hall was "in a class of her own," and "lifts the gospel to new levels, lifting hearers simultaneously with an understanding of an awesome God that is unparalleled." Rev. Charles Adams, of Hartford Memorial Baptist Church in Detroit, told *Ebony*, "Better than anyone else in the pulpit today, she combines the best scholarship with keenly precise Biblical interpretation and passionately persuasive delivery."[115]

Hall's womanist vision of a liberating ministry, her denominational and organizational leadership, her cultivation of strategic partnerships, and her prophetic power in the pulpit unequivocally qualified her as a pillar of the black church. If she were male, she would have been a multiterm president of the PNBC and the ABCUSA, preacher in one of the nation's most prestigious pulpits, president of a seminary, or any other public leadership role she might have wanted. Though she remained limited in my many ways through her career, her influence in the black church issued a permanent challenge to mediate the struggles of the people and a resounding prophetic proclamation of Freedom Faith, that God equips and empowers those who work for freedom and liberation.

CHAPTER 9

"ONE OF THE FOUNDING MOTHERS OF THE NEW AMERICA"

After extensive testing, begun in 2000 while Hall was finishing her Visiting Womanist Scholars program at ITC, Hall was diagnosed in 2001 with aplastic anemia, at that time a life-threatening illness that required a bone marrow transplant for any hopes of survival. Bone marrow matches generally followed racial lines, and since black people tended to donate at much lower rates than other Americans, the likelihood of Hall finding a match was miniscule. Friends and family donated bone marrow, but none were a correct match. Even as she was dying, Hall used her condition to raise awareness of the difficulty black patients face finding bone marrow matches, urging black churches to recruit donors.[1]

Hall was often hospitalized for her illness, and a number of her friends helped her during this time. Her Boston University graduate assistant Echol Nix; childhood friend Presttonia Brown; friends Evelyn Brooks Higginbotham, Charles Adams, and Jeremiah Wright; and former UTS student LaGretta Bjorn assisted her greatly during her illness. They visited her in Boston often, managed her finances and appointments, ensured she had groceries and took her medications on schedule, and helped her stay connected with her family. Some days, Hall was quite herself, while on other days she was incoherent and suffering in pain.[2] Friends also hosted several fund-raising events to help offset her medical costs during treatment, such as a June 26, 2001, service at Philadelphia's Triumph Baptist Church—which Hall was too ill to attend.

Charles McDew, former director of SNCC, visited Hall in 2002 after learning of her hospitalization from SNCC alum Reggie Robinson, but neither realized the severity of her condition. McDew met two of Hall's academic friends, including Cheryl Townsend Gilkes, both professors at Colby College in Maine.[3] McDew was struck by Hall's ability to foster connection between friends from different periods of her life, how she could make everyone feel at home with her and with each other.[4]

DuBois decided to move his mother to Philadelphia in early August 2002.[5] Hall's health had been declining, but DuBois believed Hall would receive better care in Philadelphia than she would in Boston. Her mother and sisters believed she would improve once she was near family, but this was not the case. She died on August 12, 2002. Triumph Baptist Church in Philadelphia hosted Hall's funeral on August 20, and she was buried in Northwood Cemetery. Numerous ministry and SNCC friends took part in Hall's funeral.

In early 2003, friends and family held a memorial service for Hall for those who could not attend her funeral. This service launched a $500,000 fund-raising campaign to build a "worthwhile memorial" to Hall at Mount Sharon, which ultimately did not succeed. The idea emerged from Hall's own desire to build a memorial to her father.[6]

"One of our most gifted spiritual forces"

Hall insisted on the connection between Christian orthopraxis and liberating justice. Her Freedom Faith—the belief that God wants people to be free and equips and empowers those who work for freedom—was the central guiding principle of her life, activism, and ministry. Her powerful preaching, social justice activism, and bold opposition to sexism, classism, heterosexism, and other forms of injustice solidified her place among the greatest leaders of the black church. Not only did her transgressive ministry pave the way for a rising generation of black clergywomen, but her prophetic proclamation challenged black churches to carry their historic identity as bearers of Freedom Faith, according to her womanist vision of liberation for all people.

Hall was a role model and mentor for hundreds of young clergywomen. When Teresa Fry-Brown surveyed black clergywomen in 2008 concerning their primary female ministry mentors, Prathia Hall and two of her students were among the top five.[7] Of the fifteen women named in *Ebony*'s 1997 list of top black women preachers, eight were connected to Hall's work at UTS, particularly her leadership of their program for African American Studies and the Harriet L. Miller Center for Women in Ministry.

Rev. Dr. Susan Newman Moore, former executive director of Georgians for Children and current minister at Covenant Baptist United Church of Christ in Washington, D.C., described Hall as "the hub of the African American Women Clergy Network."[8]

Otis Moss III, successor to Jeremiah Wright at Trinity United Church of Christ in Chicago, wrote that Hall's "prophetic preaching and intellectual depth has been an inspiration to me and many other brothers and sisters of my generation." He praised Hall for serving as a role model to him "to demonstrate how to engage our academic institutions and religious community with care, critique, and love."[9]

Pamela June Anderson, pastor of Mayflower United Church of Christ in Detroit, wrote the following anecdote about the power of Hall's preaching: "As late as Monday night of this week, I received a call from the other side of the country from a seminarian who heard Dr. Hall at Tabernacle Baptist Church last month. The pastor was so convicted and convinced by Dr. Hall's presentation that he openly apologized to the women of his church for his sexist demeanor and, as I understand what followed, licensed four women in ministry students on the spot."[10]

Hall was the first woman that Rev. LaGretta Bjorn saw preach. Bjorn "could not believe the power and the presence that she has.... I was just mesmerized." When Bjorn began studying at UTS, Hall was the only African American female faculty at the seminary, so Bjorn and many others flocked to Hall: "She was somebody I wanted to teach me everything she knew." Hall was Bjorn's most influential preaching mentor, someone who embodied both social justice and the gospel in her preaching and her life.[11]

Fry-Brown recognized that Hall's calling to social justice and her calling to preach were fully intertwined, and that her activism came from a deep spirituality: "Her womanist sensibilities were most evident in the doing, her presence, her head up, eyes, fixed carriage even when her back ached, rather than talking. More praxis than mere discourse." Fry-Brown felt an instant connection with Hall as a spiritual mother and ministry mentor: "I was immediately struck by the measured warmth of her voice, the womanly gentleness of her pulpit presence even in the 'hoop' at the end, her big sister hand on top of my hand as she spoke connecting our souls, the way her eyes took in the entire person as if only the two of us were in conversation in the midst of many and her honesty in self disclosure, not as bragging but as Mother Wit. Her pastor's heart was ever present even when she was in pain or overburdened."[12]

Vanessa Ward, who copastored Omega Baptist Church in Dayton, Ohio, with her husband, Daryl, similarly reflected on Hall's influence and inspiration as a ministry mentor:

> I have to say that the late Rev. Prathia Hall-Wynn, a pastor and theologian who became a personal friend, meant so much to me. She spoke in Philadelphia when my husband, Daryl, was in seminary. I was in my 20s and I had never seen a woman stand in such strength and power. She spoke at a conference with mostly males present and her strong voice fighting for social justice commanded the room. She said that God called her to do this for the people and the community. I often quote her words, and try to follow in her steps. She was a phenomenal woman, graceful and gracious.[13]

Ward's husband, Daryl, offered similar praise:

> When I think of Prathia I think of grace in the midst of chaos. I think of the power and beauty of a rose. I think of dignity in the midst of agony. Prathia is a friend to all who love God and are willing to serve God. She challenges and she convicts and yet she has an incredible ability to console. I don't know another person like her. She has the innate ability and characteristics of a mother, yet she somehow embodies all of that in the image and person of a friend. She never imposes but yet she never walks away.[14]

In 2010, Jessica Davenport created a network for black clergywomen called Prathia's Daughters.[15] Women in ministry concerned with social justice connect through this online community to share testimonies, inspiration, and celebrations of their work. As Natasha Thimas notes, the Prathia's Daughters network "seeks to continue the historical legacy of Rev. Prathia and many other women in ministry whose social activism and concern for socio-political issues went hand-in-hand with their role in the church. They were women in ministry who saw the injustices and oppression in their communities and believed that God had something to say about it; women in ministry who knew that if a change was going to come in the church and in their communities, they would have to be the ones to bring it forth."[16]

Peter Paris, who supervised Hall's dissertation at Princeton, held Hall "in the highest esteem," admiring both her academic work and her service to the church:

> Prathia is not only well experienced in all levels of Baptist women's work but she has become a significant role model for numerous black women in ministry. She is undoubtedly one of our leading African American preachers, male or female. She is sought after as a guest preacher by all the leading pulpits in the country, has addressed many significant conventions and judicatories both within and without her own denomination. Yet, she is also a first rate scholar who has the capacity to integrate scholarship with a wholistic view of Christian ministry in a full and appreciative way. Prathia is consistently perceptive, courageous, pastoral and prophetic.[17]

Charles Adams, former president of the PNBC, named Hall "the best preacher in the United States, possessing proven ability to exegete, illustrate, celebrate and apply the scriptures healingly to the problems, pains and perplexities of the people who sit ready to hear a word from Yahweh." He also admired the way she united academic work, community activism, and church leadership: "She strikes a beautiful balance between addressing individual problems as well as the social-political-structural condition that helps to determine the quality of individual being and behaving." He marveled at the breadth of her pastoring and preaching abilities: "Many preachers can preach well, but not serve well as pastors. Pastor Wynn is a phenomenal, qualitative, sincere, loving pastor without sentimentality. Her touch is tender but firm. Her presence is healing but always professional. She is liberal without being loose. She is also conservative without being rigid. She is charismatic yet controlled, dignified yet spontaneously sensitive to the demands of the moment to which she deftly rises." On many occasions, Adams had turned to Hall for pastoral care for himself and his family, for she was the only person he trusted to do so:[18]

[She] is more than academic technician, moral diplomat and rhetorical genius. She is a genuine person, authentic humanitarian and loving pastor. She knows how to touch tenderly the hurts of human beings with Gilead's balm of understanding support. Her profound and intellectually responsible spirituality enable her to minister to the agonies of any community with healing in her words and love in her work. I know of no minister who so well balances competence with compassion, science with ethical sensitivity, truth with love. She is indeed the pastor's pastor; she is my pastor and sister in a shared commitment to the high ideals of universal justice, love and peace.[19]

After being named one of the top black women preachers by *Ebony* magazine, Hall received a letter from Noubeu Christensia in Douala, Cameroon, celebrating her international legacy: "Joy filled our hearts when we read about you in *Ebony*.... You are one of those who make Africa raise its shoulders high. We are very fortunate to have sisters like you to transform some of the stereotypical African images people have of us. You are vital to the collective pride of the black community."[20]

Hall's colleagues showered her with praise and noted the need to emphasize her contributions to the quest for justice and equality in recent U.S. history. Ed Wheeler, a faculty colleague, praised her prophetic yet pastoral voice: "You have celebrated the African American church even as you have held it accountable.... You dared expose the folly of the white church even as you invited it to see new possibilities." After her death, John Lewis expressed hope that Hall will be memorialized "as one of the founding mothers of the new America." Civil rights activist Wyatt Tee Walker said he wished he could "recommend her as a member, founding member of the National Hall of Fame for Human Rights." Preaching colleague Michael Eric Dyson described Hall as "one of our most gifted spiritual forces. God forbid that sexism blind us to her genius. May she rest in peace."[21]

Graduate school colleague Mariann Taylor Malone authored a profile of Hall as an assignment for Samuel DeWitt Proctor's Leadership in the Black Church course, which so touched Proctor that he gave Hall a confidential copy. Malone listed Hall's qualities that she wished to emulate: "educational accomplishment, physical stamina, a prophetic preaching style, a quiet spirit and quick smile, receptivity toward others, empathy for others, attentiveness to seminarians, commitment to the needs of black youth, commitment to incarcerated black males and females, a serious commitment to ministry, active participation in liberation theologies, leadership on behalf of women's concerns, successful ministry despite sexism and/or divorce."[22] Malone celebrated Hall as a role model for women in ministry and Hall's commitment to using her success to elevate other woman into pulpits and public leadership.

Lifelong friend Jeremiah Wright admired Hall as "one in a million," "a model that needs to be lifted up in every seminary of all races, for all seminarians of all races, so people can get a glimpse of what someone who has really said yes to ministry and who went to her grave living that ministry daily." He continued: "Instead of saying she's a female version, I would say Mahatma Gandhi is a male version of Prathia Hall Wynn."[23]

For Hall, the call to ministry was both "her glory and her burden."[24] She struggled for a great deal of her adolescence and early adulthood between her call to ministry and the harsh reality of being a clergywoman. She served on the front lines of the Civil Rights Movement, and she lived in ever-present danger as she witnessed and experienced suffering and unexplainable courage. Surrendered to her call, she faced immense personal obstacles as she pursued her education and career. She lost many loved ones, including the tragic deaths of her father, brother, and daughter. Her divorce was long, difficult, and expensive. Torn by both the call to preach and the need for additional income, Hall often accepted preaching engagements that severely taxed her time and energy. She worked full-time while in graduate school and was a single mother and pastor despite debilitating back pain from two major car accidents and diabetes. She preached all over the world and boldly spoke ahead of her time against sexism, racism, ageism, classism, materialism, and homophobia. She finished her education, raised two children and a grandchild, and mentored hundreds of black clergywomen through her ministry and teaching. Hall's sister Teresa Hall-Darden said, "She didn't give up easily. She was a valiant fighter. She ran into lots of barriers in her life, but it was justice that drove her."[25]

In a 1999 address at the Haley Farm, Hall offered a beautiful elaboration of Freedom Faith in response to questions about whether contemporary young people could "build a movement to transform the nation." Acknowledging the compounded oppressive forces targeting young black people, Hall acknowledged: "The world is on fire. Sit in any juvenile or family court and see our children burning up—burned out at 15, offered up as sacrifice on the altar of the nation's ignorance, arrogance, and negligence." She continued: "We notice that the way the expert fire fighters fight the raging forest fires is by building fire." Freedom Faith was that fire, already burning in the people:

> I say to you our daughters and sons, It is *in you*! Every time you behold the world as it is and dare to dream of what it must become that's the fire of freedom's faith. Every time you question jaded adults and tired leaders and say—It's a new day and I don't feel no ways tired—that's the fire of freedom's faith. And every time you grab hold of the United States of America and like Israel dare to wrestle and declare to it—We will not let you go until you bless us—*That* is freedom faith's fire. It is in you—It's in us.[26]

Hall's Freedom Faith inspired her to pursue justice from a young age through education, civil rights activism, community organizing, and ministry. Her preaching insisted that anyone who claimed the gospel must join in the work of liberation. Hall's womanism valued all people regardless of race, gender, or class and sought the equality and liberation of all people. She inspired hundreds of students and challenged them to continue the legacy of their Christian and black heritage in their ministries.

Hall's Freedom Faith—the belief that God wants everyone to be free and equips and empowers those who work for freedom—was the central idea of her womanist vision, communicated through her theology and preaching. As black churches continue their historical legacy of mediating the struggles of the people for freedom and liberation, and as all people of faith work together against oppression and injustice, Freedom Faith lives.

APPENDIX
Who Had the Dream? Prathia Hall and the "I Have a Dream" Speech

Led by A. Philip Randolph, civil rights leaders from six major civil rights organizations—SCLC, SNCC, CORE, NAACP, National Urban League, and the Brotherhood of Sleeping Car Porters—and other labor groups organized the March on Washington for Jobs and Justice, reluctantly permitted by President John F. Kennedy, which gathered over 250,000 people of different races and faiths at the Washington Mall. Since each organization coordinating the march contributed a speaker for the event, all speakers agreed to limit their remarks to five minutes each.

John Lewis spoke on behalf of SNCC, delivering his "Which Side Is the Government On?" address. Several march organizers pressured Lewis to modify his bold statements against the government, but Lewis and his SNCC constituents insisted on keeping the speech as originally worded. Prathia Hall, one of Lewis's speech advisors, was "a great help" to Lewis in refining early drafts of his original speech. Only after Randolph spoke privately with Lewis about the potential detriment radicalism might cause the movement did Lewis agree to soften the tone of his speech.[1]

Speaking from the steps of the Lincoln Memorial, Martin Luther King Jr. delivered his famous "I Have a Dream" speech at the March on Washington for Jobs and Justice, considered one of the most significant public speeches of the twentieth century.[2] However, King's sermon draft for the event did not include his "I Have a Dream" set piece. Gospel singer Mahalia Jackson, as King was nearing the end of his speech, shouted "Tell them about the dream, Martin."[3] King transitioned into his dream set piece extemporaneously, and news media broadcasted his speech nationally.

A number of women helped organize the August 1963 march on Washington but were omitted from its program. Dorothy Height, Ella Baker, Pauli Murray, and others were not invited to speak, though they exercised significant leadership and influence over the movement in the planning of the march itself. When women leaders asked that a woman speak during the march, organizers told them that they were already represented through the organizations involved and through singer Mahalia Jackson. Some of the women were deeply disturbed that their organizations did not rally behind them as SNCC had behind Lewis. Ultimately, most women prioritized the march over gender equity, but the gap between the movement's rhetoric of freedom and equality for all and its sexism became increasingly apparent.

Prathia Hall the dreamer

Prathia Hall received wide recognition for her preaching abilities from a young age. Even when she was a young twentysomething in the movement, Hall's peers quickly recognized her uncharacteristically mature preaching abilities and spiritual leadership. In interviews with Hall's movement colleagues about her preaching during the movement, more often than not the first thing interviewees mentioned was amazement at Hall's preaching, that she had a captivating "presence" about her and was a "powerful" speaker. She frequently spoke in mass meetings, and Charles Sherrod often selected Hall to speak on behalf of the Southwest Georgia Project, choosing her over himself, a seminary-degreed, ordained minister.

In late summer 1962, four churches in Southwest Georgia were torched; all were associated with the movement in some way. SNCC workers received word that King wanted to come to Albany to attend a prayer vigil at the ashes of Mount Olive Baptist Church in Sasser, Georgia. Jack Chatfield recalled arriving before King did, standing along the road from Sasser, and seeing King's driver, former Alabama student Bernard Lee, pull up to the site. Lee opened the door for King, and King made his way to the stage for a microphone check without greeting any of the students: "King said, '1-2-3-4.' [News cameras] shot him saying something about the church, and this took a very, very short time.... Prathia prayed.... He unhooked the microphones and was gone." Chatfield's recollection also conveyed the difficulties many of the student activists had with King: "They thought he had identified himself as a kind of Christ figure who had to immunize himself from attack," which is why many called him "Da Lawd" behind his back. While the students lived daily in the nightmare of the counties, King made short media appearances and left town.[4]

Claude Sitton was also at the vigil and wrote a moving article for the *New York Times* about the ceremony. "As the sun sets across the cotton fields, some fifty Negroes and two whites met at Mount Olive for a 'prayer vigil.' Joining hands, they sang softly, 'We Shall Overcome.' A wisp of smoke rose from the ashes of the church.... The whites in the automobiles that shuttled slowly past looked on and said nothing."[5]

After the song, Hall led the group in prayer: "'Lord, help us keep our heads up,' Miss Hall said, her voice breaking. 'Help us, Lord, as Mount Olive, Shady Grove, and Mount Mary Churches rise again out of the ashes. Lord, we're going to be free. We want to be free so our children won't have to grow up with their heads bowed."[6] According to oral tradition, throughout the prayer, Hall repeated the phrase "I have a dream," each time followed by a specific vision of racial equality and justice.[7] Though Sitton did not include the entire text of her prayer, he was obviously moved by the power of her words to record significant portions of what she said. Sitton did not include any text from King's remarks at the same vigil, nor did Sitton customarily quote prayers.[8] Larry Rubin vividly remembered her speaking at this event: "She was really quite a powerful speaker. I remember being awestruck."[9]

After the service, King sought and received Hall's permission to use the phrase "I have a dream" in his own preaching. Hall was a fairly private person in general and certainly not an attention seeker. She did not boast about her connection to King, though, later in life, when friends asked her about her role in "I have a dream," she confirmed that King adapted the phrase from her use. She was quick to say that King made the speech his own and did not plagiarize her.[10]

One important consideration in the origin of "I have a dream" is that black culture has historically differed from Western individualism in its prioritization of community. Bernice Johnson Reagon explained that the act of originating and saying something out loud would not make that phrase "yours" but rather would make it part of the community.[11] Major King scholars such as Clayborne Carson and Keith Miller have examined the larger ties between King's rhetoric and its roots in black history and folk culture. Both have placed King firmly in the black folk preaching tradition, in which drawing on the words of predecessors—called "voice merging"—was a legitimizing form of identifying oneself as a member of a community. Many of King's set pieces and memorable phrases are merged from black historical and folk sources such as oral tradition, preaching, and music, common for many preachers.[12] If King overheard a phrase, such as "I have a dream" from Hall, voiced in a communal setting, he would not have been expected to ask permission to use the phrase or to cite its source, just as he would not have been expected to cite the Amos and Isaiah passages he quoted in the same 1963 March on Washington speech.[13] That King sought Hall's permission to use "I have a dream" reveals his respect for her, affirming her as a preaching peer.

The word "dream" had long been used in black literature and hermeneutics to express the contrast between the U.S. ideal and the African American reality. Frederick Douglass: "I had dreams, horrid dreams of freedom through a sea of blood. But when I heard of the Anti-Slavery movement, light broke in my dark mind. Bloody visions fled away, and I saw the star of liberty peering above the horizon." W. E. B. Du Bois: "This is a wonderful world, which the founding fathers dreamed until their sons drowned it in the blood of slavery and devoured it in greed." Dr. Benjamin Mays of Morehouse College often challenged students "not to die with dreams unfulfilled—that the problem inhered in not dreaming at all." Dr. Kenneth Brown, commencement speaker at King's graduation from Morehouse, utilized dream language in his address: "If you can do one single thing towards a just, durable and creative peace you will have fulfilled your obligation to the world. . . . Your job for the next fifty years and mine for the next twenty will be to work towards world peace which is your dream and mine." King would no doubt have been familiar with the poetry of Langston Hughes: "Let America be the dream the dreamers dreamed." Howard Thurman: "[Jesus's] words were directed to the House of Israel, a minority within the Greco-Roman world, smarting under the loss of status, freedom, and autonomy, haunted by the dream of the restoration of a lost glory and a former greatness. . . . Deep from within [the then-established religious order] he projected a dream, the logic of which would give to all the needful security. There would be room for all, and no man would be a threat to his brother." Lillian Smith: "How many dead dreams will it take to destroy us all?"[14] Certainly "dream" is a biblical metaphor as well, through which God spoke to figures like Joseph, Daniel, and the prophets, and would have been extremely familiar language to any preacher, not just Hall and King.[15] Given how frequently King would have heard references to dream metaphors, it is certainly possible that his later speech was influenced by a wide range of sources to which he was exposed throughout his life.

While the language of "dream" was a long-held black theological tradition, a confession of a people struggling against oppression, Hall built on this foundation by offering a contextualized, dynamic proclamation of the dream at the Sasser prayer vigil in September 1962. The repetition of "dream" guided her listeners into reflection on what was and what could be, what had been promised and what had already been fulfilled, what God actually said and what people did in the name of God. Her use of the phrase was a prophetic proclamation of Freedom Faith, contextualizing the dream within the nightmare of SNCC's work in the South and inspiring King's "I Have a Dream" speech.

Martin Luther King Jr.'s "I Have a Dream" speech

King's manuscript for his speech at the March on Washington for Jobs and Justice, commonly referred to as his "I Have a Dream" speech, was originally drafted to last around five minutes and did not include the "I Have a Dream" section. His remarks merged several of his "set pieces," or "successful passages from his own sermons, sections from other preachers' works, anecdotes, Bible verses, lines from favorite poets," that he could string together to form a sermon.[16] In fact, the speech contained more constructed set pieces than original text. The delivered speech differed greatly from King's prepared manuscript, largely because on the spot he selected memorized set pieces that seemed appropriate to his point and to his particular audience. Early in the speech he modified the prepared speech only slightly, but by the end of the address he had abandoned his manuscript completely.[17]

The speech began with his "bad check" set piece, in which he compared the Emancipation Proclamation to a bad check, since black people were excluded from full equality or freedom in the United States.[18] King transitioned into the "urgency of now" set piece, at the end of which he made his first full-sentence addition to the manuscript: "Now is the time to make justice a reality for all of God's children."[19] King reiterated the importance of nonviolent demonstration: "Again and again we must rise to the majestic heights of meeting physical force with soul force."[20] He acknowledged that the freedoms of white and black Americans were "inextricably bound" and that as long as "the Negro is the victim of the unspeakable horrors of police brutality," the movement cannot stop, which he used to transition into his "we can never be satisfied" set piece.[21] King drifted from his manuscript, asking those gathered to return to their communities as activists, continuing the work of the movement. Modifying the "let us go back" set piece he previously omitted, King alternated the imperative for the hortatory: "Go back" instead of the planned "Let us go back."

After hearing Mahalia Jackson's interjection, King abandoned his manuscript altogether: "I say to you today, my friends, so even though we face the difficulties of today and tomorrow, I still have a dream." With each repetition of "I have a dream," King voiced hope of reconciliation, justice, and peace. King later reflected on his decision to insert the "I have a dream" set piece into his speech, without mentioning Jackson's prompt: "I started out reading the speech, and I read it down to a point, and just all of a sudden, I decided—the audience response was wonderful that day, you know—and all of a sudden this thing came to me that I have used—I'd used it many times before, that thing about 'I have a dream'—and I just felt that I wanted to use it here. I don't know why I hadn't thought about it before the speech."[22] "I have a dream" first appeared in King's speeches in November 1962.[23]

King first shared a dream that the United States would faithfully implement equality for all people, realizing the importance of connecting the values of the movement with American values and wanted to help white and black Americans understand the critical link between domestic freedom and international freedom.[24] King's dream set piece also drew on biblical language and familiar lyrics to spiritual music, connecting the movement with Christian orthopraxis.

The next line was of Georgia: "I have a dream that one day on the red hills of Georgia, the sons of former slaves and the sons of former slave-owners will be able to sit down together at the table of brotherhood."[25] In the two previous set pieces that referenced specific movement events, King began with Mississippi, no doubt recalling the June 12 assassination of Medgar Evers in his driveway in front of his family, just two months prior to the march on Washington. In the dream set piece, King mentioned Georgia first and Mississippi second. Perhaps this was coincidental. Perhaps King favored his home state. Or, perhaps King began with Georgia because he first heard "I have a dream" in Georgia, from Prathia Hall, locking the association between the two in his mind.

Another repetition device King utilized was "all of God's children." Quite possibly from Gandhi's name for the untouchables, *Harijans*, meaning "children of God," King used the phrase three times during the speech, emphasizing that all humans are children of God. First in the urgency of now set piece—"Now is the time to make justice a reality for all of God's children"—second at the end of the 'I have a dream' set piece—"This will be the day when all of God's children will be able to sing"—and in the final sentence of the speech—"We will be able to speed up that day when all of God's children, black men and white men, Jews and Gentiles, Protestants and Catholics, will be able to join hands and sing."[26] Prathia Hall's and King's theological predecessor, Howard Thurman, also frequently used the phrase "God's child," which often appeared in Hall's definition of Freedom Faith.[27] Perhaps Hall learned this phrase from King or from reading Gandhi firsthand. Perhaps this is a common phrase for preachers, connected to the biblical "children of Israel."

One of the most brilliant aspects of the speech was King's merging of social justice and economic justice. The March on Washington for Jobs and Justice was originally conceived as an economic protest, but the large influx of civil rights organizations shifted the focus to civil rights. King's rhetorical merging of social and economic justice in the culturally familiar language of the nation's founders, President Lincoln, and biblical prophecy, made a radical message highly accessible to his diverse audience.[28] The setting of the march that ended at the Lincoln Memorial and the connections King drew between the movement and Abraham Lincoln were intentional and powerfully effective.[29]

Who had the dream?

While King made "I have a dream" internationally famous, he first heard the phrase used in that particular way by Prathia Hall in Southwest Georgia. She adapted historic "dream" language, rooted in biblical tradition and the theology of black people oppressed in the U.S. South, offering a dynamic proclamation of the "dream" as a theological promise in the midst of the nightmares of racism and classism. Whether Hall's particular use of the phrase was the sole source of King's set piece is less relevant than the dynamic functioning of Hall's use of the phrase in inspiring King's set piece. Whether she was his only source or merely the spark that culminated years of influence, it was only after personally witnessing Hall's dream in Southwest Georgia that King started using the phrase in his preaching.

Though Hall's connection with the phrase had been a matter of rumor within civil rights activist circles for some time, Rev. James Bevel's public acknowledgment of Hall's origination of the phrase sparked investigation. Bevel, director of Nonviolent Education of the SCLC, explained that he and King traveled to Southwest Georgia to attend the prayer vigil at Mount Olive Baptist Church in Terrell County in September 1962. Most scholarly references to Hall's origination of the phrase point to Bevel's account of the event, including Richard Lischer's *The Word that Moved America*, Drew Hansen's *The Dream*, and Eric Sundquist's *King's Dream*.[30]

Lischer's monograph in 1995 relayed Bevel's account:

> In the service a young woman, a college student and member of SNCC, led the prayers of the community. She spoke with the conviction King had come to expect from the SNCC activists, but also with an innocence and idealism peculiar to the young. The students often spoke of their dream for black people in America, and, as she prayed, the young woman began to intone her own vision of the future with the phrase, "I have a dream." That evening, the whole church, including its most distinguished visitor, swayed to the phrase "I have a dream."[31]

Lischer confirmed Bevel's story through his own interview with Bevel. Lischer also interviewed Hall, and from this conversation he recollected, "While acknowledging that she used the 'dream' metaphor in her prayer, she, modestly, didn't claim to be the inspiration of King's speech."[32] Lischer seemed skeptical of Hall's modest denial, however, in his treatment of the influence of the prayer vigil on King. Specifically, because Hall denied being the inspiration for King's speech, Lischer included Bevel's account as a vignette but did not seriously consider Hall as the source of King's speech.

Hansen's 2003 monograph acknowledged Lischer's retelling of Bevel's account in an endnote but dismissed its credibility based on a lack of written evidence substantiating Hall's use of the phrase at the prayer vigil.[33] Sundquist also included Bevel's account in his 2009 study but only through a cursory mention rather than a serious investigation of Hall as the potential genesis of King's phrase: "As a young woman prayed, Bevel recalled, [Hall] began to intone, 'I have a dream,' and soon the whole congregation, King included, were swaying to its rhythm."[34]

Bob Zellner believed that Hall's modesty led her to deny involvement in coining the phrase when asked, even though she did originate the phrase.[35] Zellner elaborated:

> There was an un-credited inspiration that he had received, probably first by hearing Prathia do that "I have a dream" as a great part of sermons or messages that she delivered in Georgia. Because, you know, Dr. King was from Georgia, and sometimes those ringing phrases would be shared between ministers, and so forth. And I think that—what I understand from our folk understanding of that influence between Prathia and Dr. King, was that Dr. King actually asked her—we understood that he had actually asked her if he could borrow that, if he could use that. Since she had popularized it, in a sense, among us before it got to Dr. King."[36]

Rep. John Lewis, former executive secretary of SNCC and recognized as one of the Big Six leaders of the Civil Rights Movement, also suggested Hall as the source of "I have a dream." He shared: "As a matter of fact, it was Prathia, some people felt, that gave Dr. King the idea of the 'I Have a Dream' Speech. . . . Because she would talk about, 'I have a dream,' about 'over my head, I see such and such a thing; I see freedom.' And I've—some people in SCLC as well as the Student Nonviolent Coordinating Committee felt that maybe he got that idea from Hall."[37]

When questioned about "I have a dream," other interviewees either were uncertain or had not heard the theory of Hall's origination but found this plausible. Charles Sherrod attended the September 14, 1962, prayer vigil and remembered that Hall spoke at the meeting, though he did not recall hearing Hall say "I have a dream."[38] Sherrod did, however, recall being asked about her origination of the phrase on several occasions. Similarly, Judy Richardson, involved behind the scenes with the production of *Eyes on the Prize* (2006) and *This Far by Faith* (2003), did not remember SNCC rumors about Hall coining "I have a dream," but she did recall hearing researchers for those documentaries discuss Hall as the originator.[39]

Though Sherrod and Richardson gave neutral answers since they did not recall Hall originating the phrase, only one interviewee, Larry Rubin, answered the question with a negative answer. Rubin hesitated about Hall as the originator on several grounds. First, the movement developed a shared vocabulary of phrases, drawn from lyrics of spirituals, freedom songs, and biblical themes, which circulated widely. Rubin argued that no one would have thought of these phrases as their intellectual property, and certainly no one would have expected others to ask permission to adopt another person's phrase. Second, Rubin raised the issue of Bevel's lack of credibility, namely, his criminal record for sexual assaults. Third, Rubin argued that both Bevel and Zellner may have had personal issues with King and sought to promote Hall's origination in attempt to reduce King's significance. Fourth, Rubin mentioned the debate concerning the phrase "Black Power" between Stokely Carmichael and Willie Ricks, both of whom claimed to be the originator; according to Rubin, they started using the phrase around the same time, independently of each other. Rubin suggested perhaps the same dynamic existed between Hall and King, minus public debate. Ultimately positive in his recollection of Hall's preaching and relationship with King, Rubin noted that "it would be nice to think that she originated it."[40]

In 2011, Wake Forest University undergraduate student William Murphy found a speech by fifteen-year-old King with strikingly similar language to King's "bad check" set piece that begins the "I Have a Dream" address. A critical consideration is that the speech by adolescent King, titled "The Negro and the Constitution" (1944), closely resembled the "bad check" set piece but not the "dream" set piece. King wrote the speech for a high school Elks Society competition, which he won.[41] The speech drew heavily from the unfulfilled promises of the Emancipation Proclamation and the failure of the nation's founding values if black people continued to be excluded from freedom. Although he continued to develop this idea over time, the idea of his "bad check" set piece was clearly present in his 1944 "The Negro and the Constitution" address. Murphy's finding does not discount the argument for Hall as originating "I have a dream."

Charles Euchner's *Nobody Turn Me Around: A People's History of the 1963 March on Washington* (2010) also upholds Bevel's account of King overhearing Hall use the phrase "I have a dream" at the Sasser, Georgia, prayer vigil in September 1962. Euchner argues that King resonated with Hall's words because of the significance of dreams in his own spiritual pilgrimage. He cites King's kitchen vision during the Montgomery bus boycott in which God confirmed King's calling to persevere in the movement against racism. Euchner also cites King's affinity for drawing on Old Testament prophets in his preaching, which was typical in black preaching and was consistent with King's understanding of himself as a social justice prophet.[42]

Drew Hansen's *The Dream: Martin Luther King, Jr., and the Speech that Inspired a Nation* (2003), a homiletical study of King centered around the "I Have a Dream" speech, acknowledges the significance of Albany in the history of the phrase, which first appeared in King's set pieces in November 1962, after the Southwest Georgia church burnings that September. The earliest time "I have a dream" appeared in his writing was November 27, 1962, in King's speech in Rocky Mount, North Carolina. The first dream example King provided in that address was of Sumter County, Georgia, specifically to the church burnings, which lends significant credibility to the argument that "I have a dream" originated in Albany.[43]

Hansen presents two theories of Albany origination of "I have a dream." Dorothy Cotton, an SCLC staff member, remembered hearing a white SNCC volunteer, Kathleen Conwell, use the phrase in an Albany mass meeting: "I have a dream one day that my child can reach out and hold hands with your child ... and that it won't matter."[44] Cotton claimed that she told King about Conwell's speech during a ride to the airport the next day, after which King adopted the phrase. The alternate account claims that Hall used the phrase "I have a dream" repeatedly in her prayer at the September 14, 1962, prayer vigil at the site of Mount Olive Baptist Church in Sasser, which Hansen based on Richard Lischer's interview with James Bevel.[45]

Hansen interviewed Ralph Allen, Jack Chatfield, and Faith Holsaert about the use of "I have a dream" in Albany, which he argued lent "indirect support" to the phrase originating in Albany. The chronology of the September prayer vigil, Cotton's visit, and King's first known use of the phrase support Albany origination.[46]

Bevel's account of Hall's prayer failed at two places, according to Hansen. First, in interviews with SNCC's Southwest Georgia team, Hansen asked specifically about Bevel's claim. Chatfield did not remember Bevel's presence at the September 14 vigil, where he would have heard Hall's prayer. King's aide Wyatt Tee Walker did not remember hearing the phrase there at all, nor did he associate the phrase with Albany. Walker suggested that King could have used "I have a dream" prior to September 1962, perhaps in an unrecorded speech. Hansen also cited the "SNCC whisper line," a nickname for the high rates of gossip within SNCC's ranks, which would have been atwitter about the phrase coming from Albany had that been the case. Second, all of the Albany SNCC workers interviewed by Hansen denied any recollection that matched Cotton's account regarding Conwell.[47]

While Hansen does not completely reject Albany origination, he suggests that, even if King did initially hear the phrase there, he certainly customized the dream with his own language and flair. Hansen cited precedent of King using similar phrases, such as having a "vision," which King used as early as 1956, and which would have been familiar biblical language as well.[48]

Even though Hansen somewhat dismisses Hall's involvement, his work actually made great strides toward supporting the argument that King first heard the phrase from Hall. Hansen spoke with Hall in 2001 about the phrase, during which Hall began the interview with a carefully worded disclaimer, "making sure that [he] knew that if she did have a part in King's use of the phrase, she was 'greatly honored,' and that King 'did far more with it than [she] could have done.'"[49] Defending the borrowing of material common between preachers, Hall told Hansen: "I as much as anyone else would overhear and would also offer something that someone else would use." However, Hall does not remember hearing King use "I have a dream" before she used it in the prayer: "I remember saying 'I have a dream' in the prayer." She elegantly explained her inception of the phrase: "When there's a raging nightmare, you need a dream."[50] Because of the horrific violence she and others faced in Southwest Georgia, she knew that those gathered for prayer needed to hear a word of hope. She told them about her dream of "being free from the bullets and the burnings, being free to worship and free to learn."[51]

In her interview with Hansen, Hall did not deny that King heard the phrase from her. In fact, she acknowledged King as a preaching colleague and that they had appeared together at several preaching engagements, including one at a Methodist Church in Chicago on August 27, 1963, the night before the March on Washington for Jobs and Justice. Hall could not get to Washington in time for the march, so she watched on television from her Chicago hotel room.[52] She specifically said that she "didn't want to be a King clone," but noted that "I knew his lines and he knew a few of mine." Hall characterized their rhythm: "My work in the Northern fundraising was to tell my story, what the experience was. Tell them what happened when shotguns fired at us. So even when we were on the same platform, he had a sermon to preach and I had a story to tell." King's associate Wyatt Tee Walker teased Hall that she had been "preaching without a license for a long time." She said King paid her the "best compliment that anyone could be paid" when he said she was the one platform speaker he would prefer not to follow.[53]

Hall was an extremely private person and would not have been one to boast such a claim to fame. She barely admitted her involvement when asked bluntly by close friends, due to her modesty and high regard for King.[54] Hall's seminary student LaGretta Bjorn recalled a time when another professor at UTS was discussing the origin of the "I Have a Dream" speech while Hall was in the room: "It was almost embarrassment. She just sort of quietly walked out of the room."[55]

Hall's close friend Evelyn Brooks Higginbotham asked Hall about her involvement with the phrase.[56] Higginbotham said that Hall told her that she had first used the phrase, that King had sought her permission to use it, and that she admired how he adapted the phrase into his own preaching, that "he did far more with it than [she] ever could."[57] Martha Prescod Norman Noonan remained friends with Hall throughout their adult lives. When Noonan heard a rumor that "I have a dream" may have come from Hall, she asked Hall about the phrase herself. Noonan relayed that Hall remained extremely humble, but she did confirm that she had used the phrase at the prayer vigil and that King had asked her permission to use the phrase in his preaching. Noonan collaborated with Hall to include chapters from her about the Albany and Selma projects in a collection of memoirs by women in SNCC, *Hands on the Freedom Plow: Personal Accounts by Women in sncc* (2010). Hall's Albany chapter includes a biographical footnote authored by Noonan listing Hall as the originator of "I have a dream."[58]

Prathia's dream

"Dream" language was a foundation of black spiritual heritage, on which Hall built a dynamic proclamation of Freedom Faith, utilizing repetition and contrast between the dream and the nightmare. When asked, Hall never denied saying "I have a dream," nor did she deny that Martin Luther King Jr. heard the phrase from her. She admitted using the phrase, in King's presence, in a poetically sermonic way.[59] Hall specifically denied "credit for

King's subsequent use" of the phase, meaning she was discounting that King had used the phrase inappropriately.[60]

In light of this evidence, a case can be made for Prathia Hall as the source of King's "I Have a Dream" set piece. Hall was widely admired for her preaching, even as a college student, and she was frequently chosen to speak for SNCC at important events, often by King himself. At the prayer vigil for the torched church in Southwest Georgia, King first heard "I have a dream" from Hall's prayer and sought her permission to use the phrase in his own speaking. Having received the idea for the phrase as a repetition device for a sermon from Hall's use of the phrase in her prayer, King ultimately made the phrase his own by adding his examples and descriptors. Building on the theological heritage of black people, Prathia Hall had coined what became the most important phrase of one of the most important speeches of the twentieth century. The centrality of the Albany origination theory to Hansen's account of sources for "I have a dream," the chronological agreement of the prayer vigil in September 1962 and King's first recorded use of the phrase in November 1962, the preaching relationship between Hall and King, and the overwhelming recognition from SNCC workers and King that Hall was a powerful orator, corroborate Hall's origination of the phrase.

Beyond the historian's search to analyze the relationship between the sermonic rhetoric of Martin Luther King Jr. and Hall, her crafting of the phrase "I have a dream" is important to understanding Hall's own identity. When Hall spoke the words "I have a dream" in her prayer, she was proclaiming Freedom Faith, that the God who had nourished the Civil Rights Movement would remain faithful even in suffering and loss as they continued in the struggle for freedom. The realities of racial violence—shootings, bombings, beatings, and burnings—all around her contextualized her father's teachings, and she transformed the "dream" language of black communities into a vision of freedom for all people, Freedom Faith in the struggle for justice.

NOTES

Preface

1. Drawing on a variety of sources, I utilize recordings and transcripts of interviews Hall gave to others before her death. I have also gathered numerous news articles, two memoir chapters written by Hall before her death describing her work in Albany and Selma, audio recordings and transcripts of her sermons, academic publications, her dissertation, manuscripts from some of her speaking engagements, a chapter she authored about her preaching process, a dissertation chapter that highlights her as a case study of womanist preaching, and Hall's personal papers, which contain correspondence, sermon manuscripts, research, notes, legal documents, and photographs. This book utilizes photographs of Prathia Hall's papers from LaGretta Bjorn's private collection, used with her permission; those materials are referenced as PHP and numbered by box and digital file name. The SNCC Papers, including field reports and meeting minutes, illuminate Hall's work in the organization, augmented by Hall's FBI file and records from several civil rights cases involving Hall. Temple University Libraries' Urban Archive Special Collection have the full papers of Fellowship House, the civil rights organization in Philadelphia where Hall was involved as a high school and college student ("Fellowship House/Farm," acc. 723, Records, 1931–94, Temple University Libraries Urban Archives Special Collections). My work also utilizes dozens of oral history interviews with Hall's family, friends, and colleagues, which provide valuable information both supplementing and adding to hard-copy sources, all in the Prathia Hall Special Collection at the Baylor University Institute for Oral History, abbreviated as BU-PHP.

Introduction

1. Blackside and the Faith Project, *This Far by Faith*.
2. Holsaert et al., *Hands on the Freedom Plow*.
3. Even as civil rights historians have transitioned their focus beyond Martin Luther King Jr. to include groups like SNCC, only since about 2000 have scholars published widely on women in the Civil Rights Movement. Jo Ann Gibson Robinson's memoir, *The Montgomery Bus Boycott and the Women Who Started It*, reveals the critical work of women in organizing and sustaining the boycott. Other noteworthy titles include *Women in the Civil Rights Movement* (1990), edited by Vicki Craw-

ford, Jacqueline Anne Rouse, and Barbara Woods; *Gender and the Civil Rights Movement* (1999) by Peter Ling and Sharon Monteith; and *How Long? How Long?* (2000) by Belinda Robnett. Similarly, Lynne Olson's *Freedom's Daughters* (2001) describes the various political and social organizing of women toward gender and race equality. Rosetta Ross broke new ground with *Witnessing and Testifying* (2003). Danielle McGuire's *At the Dark End of the Street* (2010) analyzes the movement in light of gender oppression. Tiyi Morris's *Womanpower Unlimited and the Black Freedom Struggle in Mississippi* (2015) details Clarie Collins Harvey's organizing in Jackson as representative of the critical role local women's leadership played in the success of the movement.

Biographies of prominent women leaders emerged in the early 2000s. Both Kay Mills (*This Little Light of Mine*, 1993) and Chana Lee (*For Freedom's Sake*, 2000) have published biographies of Fannie Lou Hamer. Barbara Ransby's biography of Ella Baker, *Ella Baker and the Black Freedom Movement* (2002), and Cynthia Fleming's of Ruby Doris Smith Robinson, *Soon We Will Not Cry* (1998), are further examples of biographies of highly influential women leaders in the movement often ignored by movement literature.

Cheryl Greenberg's *Circle of Trust* (1998) includes three sections of Hall's reflections on her SNCC work, recorded at the twenty-fifth anniversary of SNCC in 1988. Several women of SNCC have collaborated to publish an edited volume of their memoirs, *Hands on the Freedom Plow* (2011), which includes chapters by Hall about her work in Albany and Selma. Blackside Inc., the production company of Henry Hampton, released *This Far by Faith* (2002), the fourth episode of which features Hall. Wesley C. Hogan's *Many Minds, One Heart* (2007) narrates SNCC's history angled around the organization's educational efforts; Hogan includes her name in a short list of influential preachers of the movement: Martin Luther King Jr., James Lawson, Charles Sherrod, and Prathia Hall.

4. Womanism is a liberation methodology that affirms the equal humanity of all people regardless of race, gender, or class. See chapter 5 for a more detailed description of womanism.

5. Blackside and the Faith Project, *This Far by Faith*; Fritts, "Most Famous American Sermon"; Haskins and Benson, *Black Stars*; Interdenominational Theological Center, "WPS Scholars—Dr. Prathia Hall," http://www.itc.edu/pages/wsp/WSPDrHall.htm, accessed September 29, 2008; Kinnon, "15 Greatest Black Women Preachers."

6. For further research of black women's intellectual history, see Cooper, *Beyond Respectability*; Waters and Conaway, *Black Women's Intellectual Traditions*; and Riggs, *Can I Get a Witness?*

Chapter 1. "I See Africa Rising"

1. Hall interview by Michaels.
2. Ibid.
3. Berkeley L. Hall Jr. to Jeremiah Wright, 1994, PHP 21:620–22; "Prathia Laura-Ann Hall," *Nelson County Virginia Heritage, 1807–2000* (Sebastian, FL: S. E. Grose Essbook, 2002), 133–34.
4. Hall interview by Michaels.
5. Now at 1609 W. Girard Avenue in Philadelphia, Mount Sharon Baptist Church formerly gathered on the first floor of the Hall family home, first at 1331 Jefferson Street and later at 1631 W. Girard Ave.
6. Hall interview by Michaels; Brown interview by Pace.
7. Prathia Hall Wynn, "PT 01 Introduction to Pastoral Care Final Paper," undated, PHP 6:269, 1.
8. Ibid.; Hall interview by Michaels.
9. Hall interview by Michaels.
10. Prathia Hall, "Profile of Ruby Hall," undated, PHP 6:149.
11. Brown interview by Pace.
12. Blackside and the Faith Project, *This Far by Faith*.
13. Hall interview by Michaels.
14. Ibid.
15. Brown interview by Pace.
16. "Addressing 'The Theological Scandal of Sexism,'" Women in Ministry Panel, *American Baptist* (July/August 1987), PHP 20:4–32, 16.
17. Blackside and the Faith Project, *This Far by Faith*.
18. Hall interview by Michaels.
19. Brown interview by Pace.
20. Hall interview by Michaels.
21. "Oratorical Winners," *Philadelphia Independent*, December 24, 1955, PHP 11:041.
22. Brown interview by Pace.
23. Hall interview by Michaels. The following description accompanies Prathia Hall's high school yearbook photo: "welfare representative, classical club, ping-pong club, social service club, president of debating club, tennis club. Prathia... keen social consciousness... artistic command of the English language... deep-rooted convictions." *Milestone: Philadelphia High School for Girls*, June 1958, 72.
24. Hall interview by Ransby; see also Hall, "Building between Heritage and Hope," PHP 23:1482–626.
25. Hall, "Freedom-Faith," 173.

Notes to Chapter One

26. Barrett interview by Pace.
27. Ibid.
28. Hall, "Freedom-Faith," 173.
29. Prathia Hall, draft of materials for *Hands on the Freedom Plow*, undated, PHP 23:154–209.
30. Ibid.
31. Hall interview by Michaels.
32. Brown interview by Pace.
33. E. Phyllis Grossman, "Marjorie Penney and Her Fellowship House," *Fellowship House History and Program*, Fellowship House Papers, acc. 723:5. Though originally biracial and exclusively Christian, by 1939, FH offered interfaith worship between Christians and Jews. By the mid-1940s, FH included Muslim, B'nai B'rith, Native American, Buddhist, and Hindu. Fellowship House Papers, acc. 723:5.
34. Charles E. Marshall and Amos Johnson, *Fellowship House History and Program*, Fellowship House Papers, acc. 723:5; "Fellowship House Farm," Fellowship House Papers, acc. 723:5; Lyons, "Burning Columbia Avenue."
35. Hall learned nonviolence philosophy from her father and the writings of African American leaders he discussed with her, such as Howard Thurman. She also learned about nonviolence philosophy through FH. When King popularized the approach, FH began calling its campaign Kingsway, though FH had been teaching nonviolence long before King's public activism. Fellowship House Papers, acc. 723:5.
36. Grossman, "Marjorie Penney"; Marjorie Penney, "Address—American Baptist Board of Education—Atlanta, Ga., February 4, 1966," Fellowship House Papers, acc. 723:7.
37. *Fellowship House History and Program*, Fellowship House Papers, acc. 723:5.
38. Untitled document, Fellowship House Papers, acc. 723:90.
39. Barrett interview by Pace.
40. "The History of Fellowship House," Fellowship House Papers, acc. 723:5.
41. Penney, "Address."
42. Barrett interview by Pace.
43. Fellowship House Papers, acc. 723:2.
44. "The Religious Fellowship of Fellowship House," Fellowship House Papers, acc. 723:1.
45. "History of Fellowship House," Fellowship House Papers, acc. 723:2.
46. "A Statement Regarding the Work of Dr. Herbert Haslam, Founder of the Religious Fellowship of Fellowship House," Fellowship House Papers, acc. 723:11.
47. M. L. King, *Stride towards Freedom*, 96.
48. Penney interview by Zimmerman.
49. Hall interview by Michaels.
50. Fellowship House Papers, acc. 723:26 and acc. 723:8.

51. Hall interview by Michaels.
52. "Racism," Fellowship House Papers, acc. 723:8.
53. "Units for Unity," Fellowship House Papers, acc. 723:11.
54. Untitled document, Fellowship House Papers, acc. 723:21.
55. "So You're Going to Speak for Fellowship House," Fellowship House Papers, acc. 723:1.
56. Archived copies of *Viewpoint* are not available.
57. "Fellowship House, Meeting of Directors, November 21, 1957," Fellowship House Papers, acc. 723:1.
58. Hall interview by Michaels.
59. Ibid.; Jeremiah Wright to Berkeley Hall Jr., June 13, 1994, PHP 21:624–27.
60. Hall, "Freedom-Faith," 177.
61. Untitled document, Fellowship House Papers, acc. 723:8.
62. Prathia Hall, "Peace in a Troubled World, John 14:27," undated, PHP 18:450–74; see also Prathia Hall, "Peace in a Troubled World," undated, PHP 23:1712–42.
63. Brown interview by Pace.
64. Zinn, *SNCC*, 18, 41.
65. Hall interview by Michaels.
66. Barrett interview by Pace. "Report from the South," Fellowship House Papers, acc. 723:1.
67. "Fellowship House, Meeting of Board of Directors, March 17, 1960," Fellowship House Papers, acc. 723:1; "Fellowship House," Meeting of Board of Directors, May 19, 1960," Fellowship House Papers, acc. 723:1.
68. Joyce Barrett to Jim Monsonis, January 23, 1962, and May 10, 1962; Jim Monsonis to Joyce Barrett, May 17, 1962, SNCC Papers, reel 6.
69. Hall, "Freedom-Faith," 173; "Report from the South" and "Fellowship House, Meeting of Board of Directors, March 16, 1961," both in Fellowship House Papers, acc. 723:1.
70. See note 35.
71. "Go No Further," *News of Delaware* (Upper Darby, PA), October 13, 1960; Barbara Murphy, "Drama, Tension, Tension Grip Skating Rink in Upper Darby's First Sit-In," Fellowship House Papers, acc. 723:1; Barrett interview by Pace.
72. Hall interview by Michaels; Barrett interview by Pace.
73. "'Civil Disobedience' Urged by Dr. King in Phila. Talk," *Evening Bulletin* (Philadelphia), October 24, 1961; Fellowship House Papers, acc. 723:1.
74. "Proclamation, Kingsway Day," Fellowship House Papers, acc. 723:37; Hall, draft of materials for *Hands on the Freedom Plow*.
75. "Fellowship House, Meeting of Directors, October 5, 1961," Fellowship House Papers, acc. 723:1.
76. Though the Eastern Shore demonstrations were called Freedom Rides, this

should not be confused with the 1961 Freedom Rides in the South, organized by CORE.

77. Barrett interview by Pace; Hall, draft of materials for *Hands on the Freedom Plow*.

78. Barrett interview by Pace.

79. Arsenault, *Freedom Riders*, 461.

80. "3 in Sit-In Turn Down Bail; 7 Released in Maryland," *Evening Bulletin* (Philadelphia), November 13, 1961; "Crowds Besiege Maryland Cafes: Day-Long Anti-Segregation Drive Brings 33 Arrests—300 Students Picket," *Evening Bulletin* (Philadelphia), "Three from City Refuse to Bail Selves Out of Maryland 'Sit-in,'" *Daily News* (Huntingdon and Mount Union, PA), November 14, 1961; "'Happy,' Say 3 Jailed in Bias Drive," *Baltimore News-Post*, November 14, 1961; "New Protest Is Slated at Restaurants," *Baltimore Sun*, November 13, 1961; "10 Demonstrators at Annapolis Diner Ask for Jury Trial," *Washington Post*, November 14, 1961; and "3 Decline Bail for Café Sit-In," Fellowship House Papers, acc. 723:90; Hall, draft of materials for *Hands on the Freedom Plow*.

81. Hall, draft of materials for *Hands on the Freedom Plow*.

82. Elizabeth Oliver, "'I Was in Cell 8,'" Fellowship House Papers, acc. 723:90.

83. "Fellowship House, Meeting of Directors, November 16, 1961," Fellowship House Papers, acc. 723:1.

84. Often the case with civil rights–related arrests and court proceedings, documentation can be difficult to locate, if it is even known to exist. Throughout the book, I have pieced together details from FBI files, court documents, county and municipal records, oral history interviews, historical archives, newspaper and magazine articles, and any other available sources to reconstruct what happened. Places where details seem to be lacking in the narrative point to where details lack in the sources, whether because researchers have not yet located them or because agents in history have intentionally withheld or destroyed them.

85. "3 Jailed 'Freedom Riders' Paint Cell at Annapolis," *Evening Bulletin* (Philadelphia), November 15, 1961; "8 Continue Hunger Strike: Refuse Bail In Maryland Sit-Ins," *Evening Bulletin* (Philadelphia), November 21, 1961.

86. Oliver, "'I Was in Cell 8'"; Barrett interview by Pace.

87. Hall interview by Michaels.

88. "Demonstrators Face Trials," *Evening Capital Annapolis*, December 19, 1961; AP, "Jury Chosen for Sit-In Trial of 9 from Fellowship House," *Evening Bulletin* (Philadelphia), December 18, 1961; "9 from Here Face Trial for Sit-in," *Evening Bulletin* (Philadelphia), December 19, 1961; Barrett interview by Pace.

89. Barrett interview by Pace.

90. Hall interview by Harding; Hall, "Freedom-Faith," 173; Barrett interview by Pace.

91. Hall, draft of materials for *Hands on the Freedom Plow*.
92. Hall interview by Harding, reel 3, 3.
93. Hall, "Freedom-Faith," 173.

Chapter 2. "Living in the Face of Death"

1. Carson, *In Struggle*, 23.
2. Lawson, who learned nonviolence while studying in India, trained the Nashville student movement volunteers in nonviolent workshops, learning resistance techniques like singing freedom songs in front of segregated businesses, sitting-in at counters where they were refused services, going limp when police tried to arrest them, and giving false names like Abe Lincoln, Super Snick, and Freedom Now, when police demanded identification. These workshops also trained SNCC workers in self-protection during mob violence and prepared them for the kind of rhetoric and vocabulary they would hear in the course of their work. James Lawson, "Statement of Purpose," *Student Voice* 1, no. 1 (June 1960), in Carson, *Student Voice*, 2.
3. "Report from the Office of SNCC," *Student Voice* 1, no. 3 (October 1960), in Carson, *Student Voice*, 16.
4. Hogan, *Many Minds, One Heart*, 40; Ransby, *Ella Baker*, 4, 88.
5. McDew interview by Pace. See also "Southwest Georgia Voter-Registration Project," undated, SNCC Papers, reel 8.
6. Holsaert et al., *Hands on the Freedom Plow*, 85; "Method of Revolution," undated, SNCC Papers, reel 8; see "In 'Terrible' Terrell: Night Riders Shoot Worker," *Student Voice* 4, no. 7 (December 1963), in Carson, *Student Voice*, 87, 89.
7. Bernice Johnson Reagon, "Uncovered and without Shelter," in Holsaert et al., *Hands on the Freedom Plow*, 122; Faith Holsaert, "Resistance U," in Holsaert et al., *Hands on the Freedom Plow*, 186; Howard Zinn, "Albany," January 8, 1962, SNCC Papers, reel 19.
8. Arsenault, *Freedom Riders*, 402–3, 449, 452; Sherrod quoted in Zinn, *SNCC*, 125.
9. Annette Jones White, "Expression of My Discontent," in Holsaert et al., *Hands on the Freedom Plow*, 116; DeLissovoy interview by Pace; White, "Expression of My Discontent," 107–8.
10. "Harris Family," SNCC Legacy Project, https://snccdigital.org/people/harris-family/, accessed September 9, 2018.
11. Prathia Hall, draft of materials for *Hands on the Freedom Plow*, undated, PHP 23:154–209.
12. Zinn, *SNCC*, 123.
13. Gordon Roberts, "Albany Student Penalty Stressed," *Atlanta Journal and Constitution*, January 7, 1962. See also Joan Browning, "Shiloh Witness" (37–84), and Casey Hayden, "Fields of Blue" (333–76), both in Curry et al., *Deep in Our Hearts*.

14. SNCC news release, Albany, Ga., March 22, 1962, SNCC Papers, reel 14; Zinn, *SNCC*, 130, 134; Claude Sitton, "202 More Negroes Seized in Georgia: Albany Jails Demonstrators on 2d Day of Protests," *New York Times*, December 14, 1961; Sitton, "202 More Negroes Seized."

15. "The Big Ambush," *Student Voice* 2 (January 20, 1962), in Carson, *Student Voice*, 48; Claude Sitton, "Guard Called Out in Racial Unrest: Georgia Parley Opens after Mass Arrests of Negroes," *New York Times*, December 15, 1961; Sitton, "202 More Negroes Seized."

16. Claude Sitton, "Negroes' Unrest Grows in Georgia: Talks Continue in Albany—Dr. King and Aides Arrive," *New York Times*, December 16, 1961; Arsenault, *Freedom Riders*, 471–72.

17. Sitton, "Negroes' Unrest Grows in Georgia."

18. Blackside the Faith Project, *This Far by Faith*; Claude Sitton, "Dr. King among 265 Negroes Seized in Albany, Ga. City Hall," *New York Times*, December 17, 1961.

19. Claude Sitton, "Negro Groups Split on Georgia Protest," *New York Times*, December 18, 1961.

20. Claude Sitton, "Rivalries Beset Integration Campaigns: Differences in the Protest Movement Tend to Stir Confusion but Center on Methods, Not Goals," *New York Times*, December 24, 1961. For more on the Albany movement in 1961, see Forman, *Making of Black Revolutionaries*, 247–62, and Carson, ed., *Autobiography of Martin Luther King, Jr.*, 151–69.

21. Claude Sitton, "Negroes Boycott Albany, Ga. Buses: Shift to Economic Weapons in Civil Rights Struggle," *New York Times*, January 28, 1962.

22. SNCC news release, Dawson, Ga., February 3 and 8, 1962, SNCC Papers, reel 14.

23. Claude Sitton, "Civil Rights Report Applauds Kennedy," *New York Times*, March 26, 1962.

24. See "Survey: Field Work, Spring 1963," SNCC Papers, reel 10. Claude Sitton, "Albany, Ga., Police Break Up Protest by 2,000 Negroes," *New York Times*, July 25, 1962.

25. Claude Sitton, "Dr. King Declares a Day of Penance," *New York Times*, July 26, 1962; Martin Luther King Jr. and W. G. Anderson, "Statement by Dr. Martin Luther King, Jr. and Dr. W. G. Anderson," July 25, 1962, SNCC Papers, reel 37.

26. Hall interview by Harding, reel 3; Hall interview by Michaels.

27. Hall interview by Harding, reel 3; Prathia Hall interview by Woods.

28. Hall, draft of materials for *Hands on the Freedom Plow*.

29. Hall interview by Michaels.

30. Hall, draft of materials for *Hands on the Freedom Plow*.

31. The 1960s civil rights project of SNCC in Albany is most commonly called the

Albany movement. The Southwest Georgia Project refers to the multidecade initiative in Albany and surrounding areas to promote racial and economic equality.

32. Hall interview by Michaels. Hall interview by Harding; Hall, "Freedom-Faith," 173–74.

33. Hall, draft of materials for *Hands on the Freedom Plow*.

34. Braden, "Images Are Broken"; Anne Braden to Charles Sherrod, October 24, 1962, SNCC Papers, reel 5; Barrett, interview by Pace.

35. Charles Sherrod at 50th Anniversary of SNCC, Shaw University, Raleigh, N.C., April 2010; Southwest Georgia Panel; Greenberg, *Circle of Trust*, xiii, 57.

36. Hall interview by Michaels. See also Aldon Morris, *Origins*, 221–23.

37. Braden, "Images Are Broken."

38. Hall interview by Michaels.

39. Holsaert, "Resistance U," 185.

40. Randy Battle, "SNCC Office: Sheriff 'Gator Johnson," in DeLissovoy, *Great Pool Jump*, 22–23; Hall interview by Michaels.

41. SNCC depended on donations and grants. SNCC suffered from severe financial difficulties and at times could not send any money to field-workers. In a letter to Martha Prescod, Julian Bond advised that "the best way to send money to SNCC is as soon as possible." See Julian Bond to Martha Prescod, December 13, 1962, SNCC Papers, reel 8. Support-raising efforts in the North provided critical financial and resource support for SNCC's work in the South, including money, food, awareness, and volunteers.

42. "They Lived in the Counties," *Student Voice*, 57–58.

43. Zinn, *SNCC*, 13.

44. Carawan, *Sing for Freedom*, 176.

45. Hall, "Freedom-Faith," 175; Hall interview by Kiburi, transcript at PHP 22:101–222.

46. Hall, "Freedom-Faith," 176.

47. Hall interview by Kiburi.

48. Hall interview by Michaels.

49. Hall "Freedom-Faith," 176.

50. Tuck, *Beyond Atlanta*, 163.

51. Powledge, *Free at Last?*, 343–44.

52. Hall, "Freedom-Faith," 174.

53. Holsaert interview by Pace.

54. Sherrod interview by Pace; Daniels interview by Pace. Sherrod interview by Pace.

55. Hall interview by Woods; Jack Chatfield, field report, March 1963, SNCC Papers, reel 5.

56. Hall interview by Woods.
57. Sherrod interview by Pace.
58. Faith Holsaert, "Staff Relationships or Personnel Politics," undated, SNCC Papers, reel 6.
59. Hall interview by Michaels.
60. Hall interview by Ransby.
61. Mary King to Burrelle's Press Clipping Bureau, November 6, 1963, SNCC Papers, reel 5; Ransby, *Ella Baker*, 345–46.
62. Harding, *Hope and History*, 74.
63. Sherrod interview by Pace.
64. Richardson interview by Pace.
65. Preacely interview by Pace; Sherrod interview by Pace. Richardson interview by Pace; Barrett interview by Pace; Hogan, *Many Minds, One Heart*, 73, 229.
66. Holsaert, "Resistance U," 187.
67. Noonan interview by Pace. Sherrod interview by Pace. Patch interview by Pace. Preacely interview by Pace.
68. Mary King interview by Pace.
69. Zellner interview by Pace.
70. Walker interview by Pace.
71. Preacely interview by Pace.
72. Mary Jane Doerr, "Civil Rights Advocate Speaks This Week at Voorhies Hall," *Northern Michigan Review*, undated, PHP 24:458–62.
73. "Support SNCC Today!" *Student Voice* 5, no. 8 (March 1964), in Carson, *Student Voice*, 131.
74. Hall interview by Michaels.
75. Holsaert interview by Pace.
76. For Hall, nonviolence was not just an activism tactic, but was truly a way of life, a fundamental philosophical and theological conviction.
77. Rubin interview by Pace.
78. Some in SNCC used to call Hall "the mother of the church" because of her deep religious convictions. Ransby interview by Hall.
79. Richardson interview by Pace; Rubin interview by Pace; Barrett interview by Pace; Preacely interview by Pace.
80. Bond interview by Pace; Hall quoted in Ransby, *Ella Baker*, 258; Mary King interview by Pace.
81. McDew interview by Pace.
82. Lewis interview by Pace.
83. Sherrod interview by Pace.
84. Robinson interview by Pace; Harris interview by Pace; Preacely interview by Pace.

85. Hall interview by Michaels.

86. Rubin interview by Pace; Braden, "Images Are Broken."

87. Preacely interview by Pace. Barbara Schwartzbaum, press release, Student Nonviolent Coordinating Committee, Albany, Ga., July 17, 1962, SNCC Papers, reel 19.

88. Holsaert, "Resistance U," 186; Chico Neblett, field report, undated, SNCC Papers, reel 8.

89. Sherrod quoted in Peter DeLissovoy, "Southwest Georgia in 1963," in DeLissovoy, *Great Pool Jump*, 50; Schwartzbaum, press release, Student Nonviolent Coordinating Committee, Albany, Ga., July 17, 1963, SNCC Papers, reel 19.

90. Hall quoted in Greenburg, *Circle of Trust*, 146; Hall interview by Michaels.

91. Hall interview by Michaels. See also Penny Patch, "Sweet Tea at Shoney's," in Curry et al., *Deep in Our Hearts*, 131–70.

92. Hall interview by Michaels; Prathia Hall, quoted in Robnett, *How Long?*, 124; Hall interview by Kiburi.

93. Hall interview by Kiburi.

94. Holsaert interview by Pace.

95. Hall interview by Ransby.

96. Executive Committee Minutes, September 4, 1964, SNCC Papers, reel 36, quoted in Robnett, *How Long?*, 109.

97. Robnett, *How Long?*, 111. For multiple perspectives of women in SNCC regarding gender discrimination, see Curry et al., *Deep in Our Hearts*, and Holsaert et al., *Hands on the Freedom Plow*.

98. Annette Jones White, "Expression of My Discontent," in Holsaert et al., *Hands on the Freedom Plow*, 114. Noonan interview by Pace.

99. Reagon, "Uncovered and without Shelter," 87, 127.

100. Prathia Hall, quoted in Robnett, *How Long?*, 123; Hall interview by Kiburi.

101. Prathia Hall, quoted in Robnett, *How Long?*, 42–43; Hall interview by Kiburi.

102. Lewis interview by Pace.

103. Preacely interview by Pace; Prathia Hall, quoted by Charles Wheeler, "Revealing Voices for Civil Rights," *Greensboro (NC) News & Record*, March 20, 2011.

104. Hall interview by Woods, 5.

105. Preacely interview by Pace. See also Patch, "Sweet Tea at Shoney's."

106. Prathia Hall, field report, February 23–March 8, 1963, SNCC Papers, reel 6.

107. DeLissovoy interview by Pace.

108. Hall interview by Harding.

109. Joanne Christian Mants, "Right Side Up," in Holsaert et al., *Hands on the Freedom Plow*, 130.

110. Blackside and the Faith Project, *This Far by Faith*; Hall, "Freedom-Faith,"

110. Hymn lining referred to the entire congregation singing as one person lined the song before the congregation joined.

111. Charles Cobb interview by Maegan Parker Brooks, September 25, 2012, quoted in Brooks, *Voice That Could Stir*, 108.

112. Greenburg, *Circle of Trust*, 125.

113. Hall, draft of materials for *Hands on the Freedom Plow*.

114. Hall interview by Woods; Hall interview by Harding; Reagon, "Laid My Burden Down," in Holsaert et al., *Hands on the Freedom Plow*, 150–51.

115. Hall interview by Woods.

116. Ibid.

117. Hall "Freedom-Faith," 178.

118. Carawan, *Sing for Freedom*, xx; "Freedom in the Air 'Rich with Immediacy' says Harper's," *Student Voice* 4, no. 3 (April 1963), reprinted in Carson, *Student Voice*, 66.

119. Hall, draft of materials for *Hands on the Freedom Plow*.

120. Daniels interview by Pace; Preacely interview by Pace.

121. Greenburg, *Circle of Trust*, 58.

122. Trezzvant W. Anderson, "Sheriff Scares Would-Be Voters," *Pittsburgh Courier*, August 4, 1962, SNCC Papers, reel 19.

123. Hall, "Freedom-Faith," 178–79; Claude Sitton, "Sheriff Harasses Negroes at Voting Rally in Georgia," *New York Times*, July 27, 1962.

124. Sitton, "Sheriff Harasses Negroes"; SNCC news release, Sasser, Ga., July 26, 1962, SNCC Papers, reel 14. Z. T. Mathews quoted in Zinn, *SNCC*, 138.

125. Hall, "Freedom-Faith," 178; Sitton, "Sheriff Harasses Negroes"; Claude Sitton, "2 Negro Churches Burned in Georgia: FBI Men Attacked: Robinson Visits Site," *New York Times*, September 10, 1962; Sitton, "Sheriff Harasses Negroes."

126. Hall quoted in Greenburg, *Circle of Trust*, 59.

127. "They Lived in the Counties: Churches Burned, Nightriders Attack SNCC Staff in Southwest Georgia Voter Registration Drive," *Student Voice* 3, no. 3 (October 1962), and "In 'Terrible' Terrell," both reprinted in Carson, *Student Voice*, 57, 87; Peggy Dammond, field report, July 9–16, 1962, SNCC Papers, reel 7; SNCC news release, Lee County, Ga., September 10, 1962, SNCC Papers, reel 13.

128. Kathleen Conwell, field report, July 10–14, 1962, SNCC Papers, reel 7.

129. Conwell, field report, July 10–14, 1962, and August 17–26, 1962, SNCC Papers, reel 7.

130. "Two Negroes," *Aiken (SC) Standard and Review*, September 10, 1962.

131. Blackside, and the Faith Project, *This Far by Faith*; National Archives file 44-HQ-20425, Federal Bureau of Investigation.

132. Blackside and the Faith Project, *This Far by Faith*; National Archives file 44-HQ-20425.

133. "S. W. Georgia Voter Program Continues Despite Legal Losses," *Student Voice* 4, no. 1 (April 1963), in Carson, *Student Voice*, 66; Hall interview by Harding.

134. "Two Negroes," *Aiken (SC) Standard and Review*, September 10, 1962; Hall, "Freedom-Faith," 177; National Archives file 44-HQ-20425.

135. "Klansmen Stage Albany, Ga., Rally: Tension Rises as Negroes Schedule School Move," *New York Times*, September 4, 1962.

136. National Archives file 44-HQ-20425; UPI, "Victims Pushed Voter Registration: Terrell Marshal Charged with Rights 'Violations,'" *Atlanta Daily World*, January 4, 1963, SNCC Papers, reel 37; (AP) "U.S. Accuses Sasser Officer of Harassing in Racial Case," *Atlanta Constitution*, January 4, 1963, SNCC Papers, reel 37.

137. National Archives file 44–HQ-20425; (AP) "U.S. Accuses Sasser Officer of Harassing in Racial Case," *Atlanta Constitution*, January 4, 1963, SNCC Papers, reel 37.

138. Greenburg, *Circle of Trust*, 60.

139. Chatfield interview by Pace.

140. Hall, "Freedom-Faith," 175; Chatfield interview by Pace. Other published accounts of the incident include "They Lived in the Counties," and "In 'Terrible' Terrell," in Carson, *Student Voice*, 57, 87.

141. Hall, "Freedom-Faith," 175; Preacely interview by Pace.

142. Hall, draft of materials for *Hands on the Freedom Plow*.

143. Carolyn Daniels, "We Just Kept Going," in Holsaert et al., *Hands on the Freedom Plow*, 155; "They Lived in the Counties," and "In 'Terrible' Terrell," in Carson, *Student Voice*, 57, 87; Chatfield, interview by Pace; SNCC news release, Terrell County, September 14, 1962, SNCC Papers, reel 13.

144. Hall, "Freedom-Faith," 175; Hall, interview by Michaels.

145. Hall, "Freedom-Faith," 175; Hall interview by Michaels; Sitton, "Negro Churches Burned."

146. Chatfield interview by Pace.

147. UPI, "2 Shot in Vote Try in Dawson," Dawson, Ga., SNCC Papers, reel 19.

148. Claude Sitton, "Voting Drive Met by Hope and Fear: Student Workers in Georgia Tell of Rights Campaign Hope for Negroes Seek Meaning in Lives U.S. Inquiry under Way," *New York Times*, September 11, 1962.

149. Hall, "Freedom-Faith," 175; Chatfield interview by Pace; Daniels, "We Just Kept Going," 155.

150. Daniels, "We Just Kept Going," 155; SNCC news release, "Nightriders Bomb, Shoot Registration Worker," Dawson, Ga., December 1963, SNCC Papers, reel 13.

151. Randy Battle and John Perdew, "One Tough Rooster," in DeLissovoy, *Great Pool Jump*, 219–20.

152. Daniels, "We Just Kept Going," 155; Daniels, interview by Pace.

153. "In 'Terrible' Terrell: Night Riders Shoot Worker," *Student Voice* 4, no. 8 (December 1963), in Carson, *Student Voice*, 94.

154. Tuck, *Beyond Atlanta*, 172.

155. Don Harris, field report, Americus, Ga., December 1963, SNCC Papers, reel 17.

156. Greenburg, *Circle of Trust*, 60; Rubin interview by Pace.

157. Daniels, "We Just Kept Going," 153.

158. Hall interview by Woods.

159. Ibid.

160. Conwell, field report, August 17–26, 1962, SNCC Papers, reel 7.

161. Hall, "Freedom-Faith," 179.

162. SNCC news release, Terrell County, Ga., September 14, 1962, SNCC Papers, reel 13.

163. Sitton, "2 Negro Churches Burned."

164. Rubin interview by Pace.

165. At this writing there is no known written proof that Hall used the phrase "I have a dream" in her prayer at the Mount Olive Baptist Church vigil, although there is substantial oral history evidence from eyewitnesses that she originated this phrase. For a complete analysis, see the appendix. See also Pace, "'Freedom Faith,'" and Richard Lischer to Prathia Hall, February 26, 1991, PHP 11:394–97.

166. Sitton, "2 Negro Churches Burned"; Rubin interview by Pace.

167. Hall interview by Hansen; Randy Kryn to Prathia Hall, October 28, 2000, PHP 11:85–90; Zellner interview by Pace.

168. SNCC news releases, Terrell County, Ga., September 14 and 17, 1962, SNCC Papers, reels 13 and 19.

169. UPI, "Urge President to Stop Terror in South Georgia," *Daily Courier* (Connellsville, PA), September 10, 1962; UPI, "Two Negro Churches Burned; White Man Held for Attacking an FBI Agent," *Albuquerque Journal*, September 10, 1962.

170. UPI, "Urge President"; UPI, "Two Negro Churches Burned"; Sitton, "2 Negro Churches Burned."

171. UPI, "Urge President"; UPI, "Two Negro Churches Burned."

172. UPI, "2 Churches Destroyed; FBI Agent Attacked," *Delta Democrat-Times* (Greenville, MS), September 10, 1962; UPI, "Two Negro Churches Burned."

173. UPI, "Two Negro Churches Burned"; SNCC news release, Dawson, Ga., September 10, 1962, SNCC Papers, reel 19.

174. "In 'Terrible' Terrell," 87, 89.

175. Roberts and Klibanoff, *Race Beat*, 266; UPI, "2 Churches Destroyed"; SNCC news release, Atlanta, Ga., September 13, 1962, SNCC Papers, reel 13; Claude Sitton, "Burned Churches Get $60,000 Gifts: Georgia Negroes Are Given Help Toward Rebuilding Terrell County Churches United Church Gift Greater Capacity Planned," *New York Times*, November 11, 1962.

176. Roberts and Klibanoff, *Race Beat*, 266; UPI, "2 Churches Destroyed." Nelson Rockefeller, Reinhold Niebuhr, and Harry Belafonte were also significant benefactors and supporters of SNCC's fund-raising efforts in Southwest Georgia. SNCC news release, Atlanta, Ga., September 13, 1962, SNCC Papers, reel 13; Sitton, "Burned Churches Get $60,000."

177. "In 'Terrible' Terrell," 87, 89; Claude Sitton, "President Chided Over Albany, Ga.: Fails to Guard Negro Rights, Southern Council Says," *New York Times*, November 15, 1962.

Chapter 3. "In Jail for a Just Cause"

1. Hall interview by Woods, 6–7.

2. SNCC news release, Terrell County, Ga., September 14, 1962, SNCC Papers, reel 13.

3. "Fellowship House, Meeting of Board of Directors, October 4, 1962," and "Fellowship House, Meeting of Board of Directors, November 15, 1962," Fellowship House Papers, acc. 723:1. Hall continued to attend meetings of the Director Board of Fellowship House during her organizing time in Philadelphia. She and Barrett were granted a one-year leave of absence from their FH staff duties to join—in Hall's case, continue—the movement in the South.

4. Jewish Labor Committee Activities Review, April 1963, SNCC Papers, reel 7.

5. Penney interview by Zimmerman.

6. National Archives file 44-HQ-20425.

7. Ibid.

8. Hall interview by Harding, reel 3; Hall interview by Michaels; Penny Patch, "Sweet Tea at Shoney's," in Curry et al., *Deep in Our Hearts*, 131–70.

9. Barrett interview by Pace.

10. Holsaert interview by Pace; James Forman to Mrs. E. L. Jackson of the Albany Movement, November 2, 1962, SNCC Papers, reel 37; Goldie Jackson to James Forman, November 9, 1962, SNCC Papers, reel 37.

11. UPI, "Victims Pushed Voter Registration: Terrell Marshal Charged with Rights 'Violations,'" *Atlanta Daily World*, January 4, 1963, SNCC Papers, reel 37.

12. SNCC news release, Sasser, Ga., January 3, 1963, SNCC Papers, reel 14; UPI, "Terrell Marshal Charged with Rights 'Violations,'" *Atlanta Daily World*, January 4, 1963, SNCC Papers, reel 19.

13. National Archives file 44-HQ-20425.

14. Ibid.

15. Ibid.

16. Hall, "Freedom-Faith," 177; William Paul Berrier, untitled document, undated, SNCC Papers, reel 37. Conversely, before the 1964 Democratic National Committee, Roy Wilkins expressed concern about Fannie Lou Hamer's decision not to "disguise her lower-class standing" by wearing, as he described it, an "ugly flowery thing." See Brooks, *Voice That Could Stir*, 100. Regardless of whether black women dressed up or down, whiteness disapproved of black women's bodies.

17. "Statements from SNCC Workers on Trial of D. E. Short," Americus, Ga., January 25, 1963, SNCC Papers, reel 37; William Paul Berrier, untitled document, undated, SNCC Papers, reel 37; (AP) "U.S. Accuses Sasser Officer of Harassing in Racial Case," *Atlanta Constitution*, January 4, 1963, SNCC Papers, reel 37.

18. Hall, "Freedom-Faith," 177.

19. Rubin interview by Pace.

20. SNCC news release, "Sasser Policeman Acquitted in 33 Minutes; SNCC Workers Decry Lack of Justice," Americus, Ga., January 26, 1963, SNCC Papers, reel 19.

21. Hall, "Freedom-Faith," 177.

22. Holsaert recollection quoted by William Paul Berrier, untitled document, undated, SNCC Papers, reel 37. Zinn, *On Race*, 74, 177–78.

23. "Survey: Current Field Work, Spring 1963," SNCC Papers, reel 10.

24. Braden, "Images Are Broken"; Claude Sitton, "Strict Law Enforcement Stifles Negroes' Drive in Americus, Ga: 4 Integrationists Face Death Penalty as Result of Riots and Demonstrations," *New York Times*, September 29, 1963.

25. Jack Chatfield, field report, March 1963, SNCC Papers, reel 5; Norma Collins to Dorothy Swisshelm, October 22, 1962, and Dorothy Swisshelm to SNCC, October 20, 1962, SNCC Papers, reel 7; Chatfield, field report, March 1963, SNCC Papers, reel 5; DeLissovoy interview by Pace; Faith Holsaert, field report, undated, SNCC Papers, reel 6; Chatfield, field report, April 16–25, 1963, SNCC Papers, reel 5; Holsaert, field report, February 19–March 7, 1963, SNCC Papers, reel 6; Harris interview by Pace.

26. Sitton, "Strict Law Enforcement."

27. "Fellowship House, Meeting of Board of Directors, March 21, 1963," Fellowship House Papers, acc. 723:1.

28. Holsaert, field report, February 19–March 7, 1963, SNCC Papers, reel 6.

29. John O'Neal, field report, February 23–March 6, 1963, SNCC Papers, reel 8.

30. Prathia Hall to SNCC, Albany, Ga., March 4, 1963, SNCC Papers, reel 37.

31. Ibid.

32. O'Neal, field report, February 23–March 6, 1963, SNCC Papers, reel 8; Holsaert interview by Pace.

33. Prathia Hall to SNCC, Albany, Ga., March 4, 1963, SNCC Papers, reel 37.

34. "Fellowship House, Meeting of Board of Directors, March 21, 1963," Fellowship House Papers, acc. 723, box 1.

35. Prathia Hall to SNCC, Albany, Ga., March 4, 1963, SNCC Papers, reel 37.

36. Ibid.

37. Holsaert interview by Pace.

38. Prathia Hall to SNCC, Albany, Ga., March 4, 1963, SNCC Papers, reel 37.

39. Prathia Hall, field report, February 23–March 8, 1963, SNCC Papers, reel 6; Holsaert, field report, February 19–March 7, 1963, SNCC Papers, reel 6.

40. Hall, field report, February 23–March 8, 1963, SNCC Papers, reel 6.

41. Holsaert, field report, February 19–March 7, 1963, SNCC Papers, reel 6; Prathia Hall to SNCC, Albany, Ga., March 4, 1963, SNCC Papers, reel 37.

42. Holsaert, field report, February 19–March 7, 1963, SNCC Papers, reel 6; Joyce Barrett to SNCC, March 4, 1963, SNCC Papers, reel 37.

43. Hall, field report, February 23–March 8, 1963, SNCC Papers, reel 6.

44. Ibid.

45. Ibid.; Holsaert, field report, February 19–March 7, 1963, SNCC Papers, reel 6.

46. Joyce Barrett, field report, March 2–10, 1963, SNCC Papers, reel 5.

47. Hall, field report, February 23–March 8, 1963, SNCC Papers, reel 6.

48. Ibid.

49. Holsaert, field report, February 19–March 7, 1963, SNCC Papers, reel 6.

50. Hall, field report, February 23–March 8, 1963, SNCC Papers, reel 6; Holsaert, field report, February 19–March 7, SNCC Papers, reel 6.

51. Hall, field report, February 23–March 8, 1963, SNCC Papers, reel 6; Faith Holsaert, February 19–March 7, 1963, SNCC Papers, reel 6.

52. Holsaert, field report, February 19–March 7, 1963, SNCC Papers, reel 6; Conwell, field report, July 1–9, 1962, SNCC Papers, reel 7.

53. Zinn, *SNCC*, 135; SNCC news release, "SNCC Workers 'Overjoyed' at Albany City Commission Vote to Repeal All City Segregation Ordinances," Albany, Ga., March 7, 1963, SNCC Papers, reel 19.

54. Ibid; Claude Sitton, "New Racial Technique: Trend in South Toward Flexible Laws Complicates Rights Cause City Is Off the Hook Convictions Thrown Out," *New York Times*, March 12, 1963; Chappell, *Inside Agitators*, 129.

55. Hall, field report, February 23–March 8, 1963, SNCC Papers, reel 6; Holsaert, field report, February 19–March 7, 1963, SNCC Papers, reel 6.

56. Hall, field report, February 23–March 8, 1963, SNCC Papers, reel 6; Holsaert, field report, February 19–March 7, 1963, SNCC Papers, reel 6. Ibid.

57. Holsaert, field report, February 19–March 7, 1963, SNCC Papers, reel 6.
58. Hall, field report, February 23–March 8, 1963, SNCC Papers, reel 6.
59. Holsaert, field report, February 19–March 7, 1963, SNCC Papers, reel 6.
60. "A Tribute to SNCC on Its Fifth Birthday," 1965, SNCC Papers, reel 22; Barrett, field report, March 2–10, 1963, SNCC Papers, reel 5; Holsaert, field report, February 19–March 7, 1963, SNCC Papers, reel 6.
61. Holsaert, March 9–22, 1963, SNCC Papers, reel 6.
62. Ibid.
63. Chico Neblett, field report, March 15–16, 1963, SNCC Papers, reel 8; Neblett, February 12–13, 1963, SNCC Papers, reel 8.
64. Neblett, field report, March 15–16, 1963, SNCC Papers, reel 8; Holsaert, March 9–22, 1963, SNCC Papers, reel 6.
65. Holsaert, field report, March 9–22, 1963, SNCC Papers, reel 6; "Tribute to SNCC."
66. Neblett, field report, February 12–13, 1963, SNCC Papers, reel 8.
67. Holsaert, field report, March 9–22, 1963, SNCC Papers, reel 6.
68. Ibid.
69. Ibid.; Barrett, field report, March 10–April 14, 1963, SNCC Papers, reel 5.
70. Chatfield, field report, March 1963, SNCC Papers, reel 5.
71. Neblett, field report, March 15–16, 1963, SNCC Papers, reel 8.
72. Chatfield, field report, April 16–25, 1963, SNCC Papers, reel 5.
73. Chatfield, field report, March 1963, SNCC Papers, reel 5.
74. Neblett, field report, April 16–23, 1963, SNCC Papers, reel 8.
75. Ralph Allen, field report, May 13–26, 1963, SNCC Papers, reel 37.
76. Joyce Barrett to Fellowship House, May 14, 1963, Fellowship House Papers, acc. 723:8.
77. "Fellowship House, Meeting of Board of Directors, May 16, 1963," Fellowship House Papers, acc. 723:1.
78. SNCC news release, May 21, 1963, Albany, Ga., SNCC Papers, reel 13; Ralph Allen, field report, May 13–26, 1963, SNCC Papers, reel 37.
79. Allen, field report, May 13–26, 1963, SNCC Papers, reel 37.
80. Annette Jones White, "Expression of My Discontent," in Holsaert et al., *Hands on the Freedom Plow*, 117.
81. Untitled document, SNCC Papers, reel 19.
82. William Cade quoted in Cathy Cade, "Caught in the Middle," in Holsaert et al., *Hands on the Freedom Plow*, 202, 204.
83. "Frustration, Bitterness Mount in Albany, Georgia," *Student Voice* 4, no. 2 (August 1963), in Carson, *Student Voice*, 72; White, "Expression of My Discontent,"

117–18; Claude Sitton, "Albany, Ga., Faces 3d Racial Crisis in 18 Months: Brutality Charged," *New York Times*, June 23, 1963.

84. Joann Christian Mants, "Right Side Up," in Holsaert et al., *Hands on the Freedom Plow*, 135–36.

85. Hall and Barrett quoted in "Frustration, Bitterness Mount."

86. Allen, field report, 1963, SNCC Papers, reel 37.

87. Ibid.

88. Ibid.

89. Ibid.

90. DeLissovoy, *Great Pool Jump*, 12.

91. Ibid., 11–15; SNCC news release, "Negroes Swim in White Only Pool," July 13, 1963, Albany, Ga., SNCC Papers, reel 13.

92. Allen, field report, 1963, SNCC Papers, reel 37.

93. Ibid.

94. Ibid.

95. Ibid.

96. Untitled document, SNCC Papers, reel 19.

97. Joann Christian Mants, "Right Side Up," 136; Faith Holsaert, "Resistance U," in Holsaert et al., *Hands on the Freedom Plow*, 193; Zinn, *SNCC*, 211–12; SNCC news release, "Attorney Questions Federal Concern for Law and Order," Albany, Ga., August 16, 1963, SNCC Papers, reel 13; Barrett interview by Pace; Ernest Goodman to James Forman, March 6, 1963, SNCC Papers, reel 8.

98. "In Americus, Georgia: Police Smash Demonstrators, Four Face Death Penalty," *Student Voice* 4, no. 3 (October 1963), in Carson, *Student Voice*, 74; Sitton, "Strict Law Enforcement"; Horace Julian Bond to Emanuel Coller, October 21, 1963, SNCC Papers, reel 1; "Georgia Jail Holds Denverite," *Denver Post*, September 4, 1963; SNCC news release, "3 SNCC Workers Face Death Penalty," August 20, 1963, Americus, Ga., SNCC Papers, reel 13; Special Report of the Student Nonviolent Coordinating Committee, Americus, Ga., August 8–15, 1963, SNCC Papers, reel 13.

99. Barbara Schwartzbaum memo to James Forman, "Long Overdue VR memo," July 20, 1963, SNCC Papers, reel 19; Peter DeLissovoy, field report, July 18, 1963, SNCC Papers, reel 6.

100. "In 'Terrible' Terrell: Night Riders Shoot Worker," in Carson, *Student Voice*, 89.

101. Joyce Barrett memo to SNCC, October 4, 1963, SNCC Papers, reel 5.

102. Don Harris, "Southwest Georgia," undated, SNCC Papers, reel 10; "King Campaign Spurs Voters," *Student Voice* 5, no. 18 (July 1964), in Carson, *Student Voice*, 175.

Notes to Chapter Three

103. Zinn, *On Race*, 79; SNCC, "Special Report: Selma, Alabama," September 26, 1963, SNCC Papers, reel 10; SNCC, "SNCC Work in Central Alabama," undated, SNCC Papers, reel 10.

104. SNCC, "Special Report: Selma, Alabama," September 26, 1963, SNCC Papers, reel 10.

105. Persons, *Sex and Selma*.

106. SNCC news release, "Alabama Vote Leader's Home Shotgunned Vows Drive Will Continue," Selma, Ala., April 17, 1963, SNCC Papers, reel 14.

107. SNCC, "Special Report: Selma, Alabama," September 26, 1963, SNCC Papers, reel 10; "SNCC Work in Central Alabama," undated, SNCC Papers, reel 10.

108. Rev. B. L. Tucker, field report, Selma, Ala., September 16–24, 1963, SNCC Papers, reel 10; SNCC news release, "Alabama Officials Arrest Negroes Trying to Get Vote," Selma, Ala., September 25, 1963, SNCC Papers, reel 13; SNCC news release, "Alabama Officials Arrest Negroes Trying to Get Vote," Selma, Ala., September 1963, SNCC Papers, reel 37.

109. Prathia Hall, "Keynote Address" (1998), PHP 7:326.

110. Chestnut and Cass, *Black in Selma*, 151–54; Forman, *Making of Black Revolutionaries*, 318.

111. SNCC, "Special Report: Selma, Alabama," September 26, 1963, SNCC Papers, reel 10; Rev. B. L. Tucker, field report, SNCC Papers, reel 13; Clarence Clyde Ferguson Jr. of the United States Commission on Civil Rights, letter to Julian Bond, October 10, 1963, SNCC Papers, reel 13.

112. Tucker, field report, SNCC Papers, reel 13.

113. SNCC, "Special Report: Selma, Alabama," September 26, 1963, SNCC Papers, reel 10.

114. Worth Long, field report, August 19, 1963, SNCC Papers, reel 5; Sandra Hayden to Patti Driscoll, September 25, 1963, SNCC Papers, reel 26.

115. Prathia Hall, quoted in Robnett, *How Long?*, 111.

116. "SNCC Work in Central Alabama," undated, SNCC Papers, reel 10, and Voter Education Project Newsletter, "Dallas County, Alabama," undated, SNCC Papers, reel 10.

117. Hall quoted in Robnett, *How Long?*, 112.

118. SNCC news release, "SNCC Chairman and Dick Gregory's Wife Convicted," Selma, Ala., October 1963, SNCC Papers, reel 13.

119. Zinn, *On Race*, 80–82.

120. Ibid., 85.

121. Seeger and Reiser, *Everybody Says Freedom*, 185–87; Zinn, *On Race*, 86–89.

122. Untitled document, October 7, 1963, SNCC Papers, reel 37; Mary King, *Freedom Song*, 218.

123. Zinn, *On Race*, 89.

124. WATS report, Selma, Ala., November 5, 13–15, February 12, 1963, SNCC Papers, reel 15.

125. SNCC news release, "Rights Workers to Appeal," Selma, Ala., February 20, 1964, SNCC Papers, reel 14; SNCC news release, "Two Beaten, Three Jailed as Selma Negroes Try to Register to Vote," Selma, Ala., October 1963, SNCC Papers, reel 37. See WATS line, December 7. Don Harris, field report, Americus, Ga., December 1963, SNCC Papers, reel 17.

126. Leslie Dunbar and Wiley Branton, "Second Annual Report of the Voter Education Project of the Southern Regional Council," fiscal year April 1, 1963–March 31, 1964, SNCC Papers, reel 10.

127. James Forman to Robert Kennedy, October 1, 1963, and Horace Julian Bond to David Marlin, July 1, 1964, SNCC Papers, reel 7.

128. James Forman to Wiley Branton, October 19, 1963, SNCC Papers, reel 10.

129. Hall quoted in Greenburg, *Circle of Trust*, 60; Prathia Hall, draft of materials for *Hands on the Freedom Plow*, undated, PHP 23:154–209.

130. Hall, "Freedom-Faith," 176; Ransby interview by Hall.

131. Hall, "Freedom-Faith," 176.

132. Ibid., 172. British SNCC volunteer John Papworth commented similarly in a field report, calling jail a "morale booster" John Papworth, field report, Albany, Ga., February 18–19, 1964, SNCC Papers, reel 37.

133. Hall, interview by Woods, 5–6.

134. Prathia Hall Wynn, "Freedom-Faith and the Leadership Dilemma," Independent Study with Dr. Gibson Winter, undated, PHP 21:161–77, 185–255.

135. Blackside and the Faith Project, *This Far by Faith*. For more on connection to Howard Thurman, see also Pace-Lyons, "Freedom Faith.'"

136. Hall, "Freedom-Faith," 180.

Chapter 4. "Equality Now"

1. Claude Sitton, "Atlanta Whites Act to End Crisis: But Negro Protest Leaders Get New Adult Support," *New York Times*, January 29, 1964. See also Brown-Nagin, *Courage to Dissent*.

2. PBS, "Prathia Hall," http://www.pbs.org/thisfarbyfaith/people/prathia_hall.html (accessed May 21, 2008); Mary King, *Freedom Song*, 218–19.

3. Dinky Forman, "Notes on Atlanta Arrests (From Dinky), December 21, 1963, SNCC Papers, reel 37. *Uhuru* is the Swahili word for *freedom*.

4. "Workers Spend Xmas in Jail," *Student Voice* 4, no. 10 (December 1963), in Carson, *Student Voice*, 97, 99; Dinky Forman, "Notes on Atlanta Arrests."

5. "Gregory in Ga.," *Tri-State Defender* (Memphis, TN), January 4, 1964; "Work-

ers Spend Xmas in Jail"; Forman, *Making of Black Revolutionaries*, 360; AP, "New Civil Rights Tactic—Buying Stock," *Daily Mail* (Hagerstown, MD), December 27, 1963; AP, "Stockholders Accused of Trespassing," *News* (Frederick, MD), December 27, 1963; AP, "New Tactic Used in C-Rights Court Hearing," *Post* (Frederick, MD), December 28, 1963; Sue Cronk, "Race Barriers Break Down over Coffee and Doughnuts: New Type of Woman in Civil Rights Work," *Winnipeg (MB) Free Press*, April 10, 1964.

6. Mary King, *Freedom Song*, 186.

7. Executive Committee of SNCC, John Lewis, and James Forman, telegram to Mayor Ivan Allen, December 26, 1963, SNCC Papers, reel 10.

8. SNCC telegram to Ivan Allen, January 18, 1964, SNCC Papers, reel 10.

9. SNCC telegram to Robert Kennedy, January 18, 1964, SNCC Papers, reel 10.

10. "Workers Spend Xmas in Jail," and "Agreement Reached with Dobbs Houses," *Student Voice* 5, no. 1 (January 1964), in Carson, *Student Voice*, 97, 99, 103–4.

11. UPI, "New Civil Rights Tactic."

12. SNCC news release, "Agreement Settles Atlanta Sit-Ins," Atlanta, Ga., January 6, 1964, SNCC Papers, reel 19.

13. SNCC news release, "Atlanta 'Open City' Drive Begins," Atlanta, Ga., January 11, 1964, SNCC Papers, reel 19; "Why We Protest," SNCC Papers, reel 19; Brown-Nagin, *Courage to Dissent*, 214.

14. "Ga. NAACP Presses Governor on Banning Bias in Hotels," *New Pittsburgh (PA) Courier*, January 18, 1964; "Agreement Reached with Dobbs Houses"; "Meeting Set to Air Atlanta Racial Dispute," *Kingsport (TN) Times*, Wednesday, January 29, 1964, 18; Claude Sitton, "Atlanta Whites Act to End Crisis: But Negro Protest Leaders Get New Adult Support," *New York Times*, January 29, 1964; SNCC news release, "Atlanta 'Open City' Drive Continues," January 16, 1964, SNCC Papers, reel 14.

15. "13 Arrested in Atlanta," *Student Voice* 5, no. 1 (January 1964), in Carson, *Student Voice*, 101, 103; "Atlanta 'Open City' Drive"; Judy Richardson, "Affidavit of Judy Richardson," 1964, SNCC Papers, reel 37; "Ga. NAACP Presses Governor"; U.S. District Court for the Northern District of Georgia, *The State of Georgia v. Prathia Laura Ann Hall*, "To the Judges of the United States District Court . . .," National Archives and Records Administration.

16. Phil Davis, field report, January 8–16, 1964, SNCC Papers, reel 5; "Atlanta Fact Sheet," SNCC Papers, reel 19; untitled document, 1964, SNCC Papers, reel 37.

17. "Agreement Reached with Dobbs Houses," and "Restaurant Chain Integrates," *Student Voice* 5, no. 2 (January 1964), in Carson, *Student Voice*, 103–4, 106; SNCC news release, "Agreement Settles Atlanta Sit-Ins," Atlanta, Ga., January 6, 1964, SNCC Papers, reel 19.

18. Untitled document, 1964, SNCC Papers, reel 37.

19. SNCC news release, "Dick Gregory to Arrive, Atlanta SNCC Head Announced," Atlanta, Ga., January 23, 1964, SNCC Papers, reel 37.

20. "Meeting Set to Air Atlanta Racial Dispute"; Sitton, "Atlanta Whites Act to End Crisis"; Mason, *Politics*, 114–15; untitled advertisement for January 28, 1964, "3:30pm Demonstration for Release of Demonstrators," SNCC Papers, reel 14.

21. "Meeting Set to Air Atlanta Racial Dispute"; Sitton, "Atlanta Whites Act to End Crisis"; Mason, *Politics*, 114–15; untitled advertisement for January 28, 1964, "3:30pm Demonstration."

22. Don C. White, assistant special counsel to the president, letter to James Forman, February 3, 1964, SNCC Papers, reel 10.

23. "Meeting Set to Air Atlanta Racial Dispute"; Sitton, "Atlanta Whites Act to End Crisis"; untitled notes from Atlanta Board of Education Meeting, January 20, 1964, SNCC Papers, reel 14; "Dick Gregory to Arrive."

24. Tuck, *Beyond Atlanta*, 119–20; M. Charles Bakst, "Atlanta: A Study in Strife: 'The City Too Busy to Hate' Begins to Realize It Cannot Wish Away Its Racial Unrest," *Brown Daily Herald* (Brown University), February 3, 1964, SNCC Papers, reel 19.

25. SNCC Executive Committee, "Statement of the SNCC Executive Committee," April 19, 1964, SNCC Papers, reel 10.

26. "'Open' Atlanta Still Closed," *Student Voice* 5, no. 5 (February 1964), in Carson, *Student Voice*, 119.

27. See "Ga. Judge Gives Coed 18 Months," *Student Voice* 5, no. 7 (February 1964), in Carson, *Student Voice*, 125, 128; "Shoofly Pye."

28. "Ga. Judge Gives Coed 18 Months"; "Shoofly Pye"; SNCC news release, "Judge Refuses to Grant Coed New Trial," Atlanta, Ga., July 9, 1964, SNCC Papers, reel 14.

29. Barrett interview by Pace; "Judge Refuses to Grant Coed New Trial"; "Ga. Judge Gives Coed 18 Months"; "Shoofly Pye"; SNCC news release, "White Girl Gets 18 Months, $1,000 Fine in Sit-In Case," Atlanta, Ga., February 20, 1964, SNCC Papers, reel 14.

30. The sources list only 12 names but say that 13 people were arrested. Multiple sit-in demonstrations resulted in more arrests than just the group of 13 in which Hall was a part, hence I refer to 17 total. The court docket itself lists 20 names of associated sit-in cases, so knowing exactly who is in which list of 13 or 12 is impossible.

31. "Shoofly Pye."

32. U.S. District Court for the Northern District of Georgia, *State of Georgia v. Prathia Laura Ann Hall*, "To the Judges."

33. Criminal docket, case 23886, *State of Georgia v. Prathia Laura Ann Hall*, United States District Court for the Northern District of Georgia, Atlanta Division;

John Herbers, "Atlantan Scores Conduct of Judge," *New York Times*, March 22, 1964; "Civil Rights Leader Free," *Gettysburg (PA) Times*, March 24, 1964; "Alabama Judge Yields 58 Cases: Rights Actions Are Recessed after U.S. Court Move," *New York Times*, March 25, 1964.

34. "In the Superior Court of Fulton County, Georgia," exhibit B, *State of Georgia v. Prathia Laura Ann Hall*, United States District Court for the Northern District of Georgia, Atlanta Division.

35. Julian Bond to Charles Waltner, April 6, 1964, SNCC Papers, reel 13.

36. U.S. District Court of the Northern District of Atlanta, *State of Georgia v. Prathia Laura Ann Hall*, "Response of Defendant, T. Ralph Grimes," "Response, and Motions to Remand Cases to Fulton County Superior Court," "Writ," March 21, 1964, and "Order," March 24, 1964, National Archives and Records Administration; Barrett, Interview by Pace, June 12, 2012.

37. "Shoofly Pye"; "In Atlanta, U.S. Court Forbids State to Try Sit-Ins," *Student Worker* 5, no. 9 (April 1964), in Carson, *Student Voice*, 139, 142.

38. U.S. District Court for the Northern District of Georgia, *United States v. Prathia Laura Ann Hall*, Appearance Bond, March 23, 1964, U.S. District Court for the Northern District of Georgia; John Herbers, "Atlantan Scores Conduct of Judge," *New York Times*, March 22, 1964; "Civil Rights Leader Free," *Gettysburg (PA) Times*, March 24, 1964; UPI, "State Judge Yields Cases to U.S. Court," *Independent* (London), March 23, 1964; AP, "One Dead in Florida Race Violence," *Burlington (NC) Daily Times-News*, March 24, 1964; UPI, "Groups Protest Segregation," *Billings (MT) Gazette*, March 23, 1964; UPI, "Southern Negroes Resume Race Campaigns," *Oakland (CA) Tribune*, March 22, 1964; AP, "Civil Rights Leader Free," *Gettysburg (PA) Times*, March 24, 1964.

39. *State of Georgia v. Prathia Laura Ann Hall*, U.S. District Court for the Northern District of Georgia.

40. "In Atlanta, U.S. Court Forbids State," 139, 142.

41. UPI, "State Judge Yields Case to U.S. Court," *Independent* (Pasadena, CA), March 23, 1964.

42. "Shoofly Pye"; "In Atlanta, U.S. Court Forbids State," 139, 142; *State of Georgia v. Prathia Laura Ann Hall* and U.S. District Court for the Northern District of Georgia, *State of Georgia v. Prathia Laura Ann Hall*, response of defendant, T. Ralph Grimes, NARA.

43. "Shoofly Pye"; "Sit-In Cases Near High Court Hearing," *Student Voice* 5, no. 14 (June, 1964), in Carson, *Student Voice*, 161; Judge Elbert P. Tuttle interview by Cliff Kuhn, Georgia Government Documentation Project, Georgia State University, April 10, 1992.

44. Cronk, "Race Barriers Break Down."

45. Hedgeman, *Gift of Chaos*, 98–99.

46. SNCC news release, "SNCC's Forman May Tour Africa," Atlanta, Ga., April 30, 1964, SNCC Papers, reel 14.

47. SNCC news release, "SNCC Chariman Visits African States," Accra, Ghana, West Africa, October 18, 1964, SNCC Papers, reel 14; John Lewis and Don Harris, "The Trip," December 14, 1964 SNCC Papers, reel 1.

48. Lewis and Harris, "Trip"; SNCC news release, "SNCC Head at Zambia Independence Celebration," Lusaka, Zambia, October 27, 1964, SNCC Papers, reel 14; John Lewis, *Walking with the Wind*, 284.

49. Brooks, *Voice That Could Stir*, 128.

50. Arthur I. Waskow memo, SNCC Papers, reel 1.

51. Don Harris memo to John Lewis, August 17, 1965, SNCC Papers, reel 1.

52. Naomi Bernstein to James Forman, May 31, 1963, SNCC Papers, reel 34.

53. Sandra Hayden to Jerry Bernstein, July 9, 1963, SNCC Papers, reel 34; Casey Hayden to Joyce Barrett and Prathia Hall, August 6, 1963, SNCC Papers, reel 34; Sandra Hayden to Harry Takiff, August 10, 12, 1963, SNCC Papers, reel 34.

54. Joy Takiff to James Forman, September 25, 1963, SNCC Papers, reel 34; James Forman to Harry Takiff, October 3, 1963, SNCC Papers, reel 34; Dinky Romilly to Diana King, October 11, 1963, SNCC Papers, reel 34; Diana King to Casey Hayden, October 18, 1963, SNCC Papers, reel 34; Patti Driscoll to Sandra Hayden, October 21, 1963, SNCC Papers, reel 34; Sandra Hayden to Patti Driscoll, October 23, 1963, SNCC Papers, reel 34; Naomi and Jerry Bernstein to Jim Forman, December 1, 1963, SNCC Papers, reel 34; Barbara Jones to Wallington & Cooper, November 16, 1964, SNCC Papers, reel 34.

55. A. Dudley Ward to SNCC, September 10, 1963, SNCC Papers, reel 25; Sandra Hayden to A. Dudley Ward, September 11, 1963, SNCC Papers, reel 25.

56. Ronald Ferguson to Prathia Hall, July 2, 1963, SNCC Papers, reel 25; Sandra Hayden to Patti Driscoll, September 25, 1963, SNCC Papers, reel 26; William Lovell to Prathia Hall, July 18, 1963, and Sandra Hayden to William Lovell, July 20, 1963, SNCC Papers, reel 26.

57. Sandra Casey Hayden to Anna Hedgeman, September 28, 1963, SNCC Papers, reel 8; Dr. Anna Arnold Hedgeman to James Forman, October 10, 1963, SNCC Papers, reel 25; Ed Boulton to Prathia Hall, October 11, 1963; Sandra Hayden to E. C. Boulton, September 28, 1963, SNCC Papers, reel 8; and Ed Boulton to Sandra Hayden, October 1, 1963, SNCC Papers, reel 8; "Religion, Race Speakers," *Daily Plainsman* (Lake Park, IA), October 20, 1963; "Huron Groups to Hear Race Leaders Monday," *Daily Plainsman* (Lake Park, IA), October 20, 1963. The National Council of the Churches of Christ in South Dakota and Nebraska so connected with Hall that they raised funds to aid her legal defense when she was being held by Judge Pye

in Atlanta. See AP, "Ask Funds to Aid Civil Rights Worker," *Daily Plainsman* (Lake Park, IA), January 5, 1964.

58. Ed Boulton to Prathia Hall, September 18, 1963, SNCC Papers, reel 8; "Racial Seminar Speakers Named," *Cedar Rapids Gazette*, November 8, 1963; UPI, "Seminars Scheduled for Iowa," *Ames (IA) Daily Tribune*, November 1, 1963; "Seminar on U.S. Racial Situation Set," *Globe-Gazette* (Mason City, IA), November 2, 1963. See J. Heber Miller to Prathia Hall, December 1, 1963, SNCC Papers, reel 25; "Travel Schedule for SNCC Staff to Student Meetings," undated, SNCC Papers, reel 25; James Shafer, "Students Attend BSM Confab," *Ottawa (KS) Campus*, December 11, 1963; Drew Pearson, "Washington Merry Go Round," *Atchison Globe*, December 8, 1963.

59. "SNCC Rally to Discuss 3 Workers," *Daily Times* (Delaware County, OH), July 7, 1964; "6 Members of Lake Park Senior M.Y.F. Attend Rally in Spencer Saturday," *Lake Park (IA) News*, April 9, 1964; "Clubs in Northeast Iowa Are Busy Meeting During April," *Waterloo (IA) Sunday Courier*, April 2, 1964; "District Meeting of WSCS Slated," *Globe-Gazette* (Mason City, IA), March 30, 1964.

60. Hilda Wilson to Philadelphia Friends of SNCC, September 23, 1964, SNCC Papers, reel 34.

61. Hilda Wilson to Betty Garman, February 7, 1965, SNCC Papers, reel 34. The letter includes more than five requests for Hall's availability to speak at the March 1, 1965, meeting. See also SNCC Calendar, March 1965, SNCC Papers, reel 25.

62. Betty Garman to Naomi Bernstein, February 9, 1965, SNCC Papers, reel 34; "SNCC Worker Visits at the College," *Bennington (VT) Banner*, March 29, 1965.

63. Julian Bond to Vincent Harding, February 9, 1964, SNCC Papers, reel 13; Mrs. Ernest Goertzen to Freedom Fighters, 1964, SNCC Papers, reel 13.

64. Margaret Shannon to Prathia Hall, April 3, 1964, SNCC Papers, reel 5; Margaret Shannon to James Forman, April 20, 1964; and Margaret Shannon to Prathia Hall, April 20, 1964, SNCC Papers, reel 5; Prathia Hall to Margaret Shannon, April 30, 1964, SNCC Papers, reel 5.

65. "Annual Spring Conference," March 27–29, 1964, SNCC Papers, reel 1; "Prathia Hall," SNCC Papers, reel 14. Ella Baker, Marion Berry, Julian Bond, Courtland Cox, Jim Forman, Don Harris, Bernard Lafayette, John Lewis, Bob Moses, Gloria Richardson, and Howard Zinn were also on the Executive Committee.

66. SNCC news release, "Volunteers Trained for Mississippi Freedom Summer," Oxford, Ohio, June 30, 1964, SNCC Papers, reel 14.

67. Hall interview by Kiburi.

68. Mary King, *Freedom Song*, 310.

69. Ibid., 314–15.

70. "Atlanta, June 10, 1964, Staff Meeting," PHP 11:4.

71. Mary King, *Freedom Song*, 314–15.

72. Notes of Executive Committee Meeting, Waveland Retreat, Waveland, Miss., November 1964, SNCC Papers, reel 12.

73. Jim Forman memo to All SNCC Staff Members, 1965, SNCC Papers, reel 10.

74. WATS report, Marion, Ala., February 5, 1965, SNCC Papers, reel 15.

75. Julian Bond to Robert F. Kennedy, May 22, 1964, SNCC Papers, reel 7.

76. SNCC news release, "Alabama Freedom Day Slated," Selma, Ala., June 30, 1964, SNCC Papers, reel 14; SNCC news release, "Selma Vote Drive, Rights Tests to Continue," Selma, Ala., July 9, 1964; WATS report, Selma, Ala., July 4, 1964, SNCC Papers, reel 15; SNCC news release, "Selma Vote Drive, Rights Tests to Continue," Selma, Ala., July 9, 1964; SNCC news release, "Selma, a Special Report," SNCC Papers, reel 14; WATS report, Selma, Ala., February 1, 3, 4, 5, 8, 10, 1965, SNCC Papers, reel 15.

77. Untitled document, February 4, 1965, SNCC Papers, reel 37.

78. Robinson interview by Pace.

79. Roberts and Klibanoff, *Race Beat*, 385.

80. Seeger and Reiser, *Everybody Says Freedom*, 193–94; SNCC news release, Selma, Ala., March 7, 1965, SNCC Papers, reel 14.

81. Roy Reed, "Alabama Police Use Gas and Clubs to Rout Negroes," *New York Times*, March 8, 1965, 20, quoted in Roberts and Klibanoff, *Race Beat*, 385.

82. Richardson interview by Pace; Hall interview by Ransby; WATS Report, Selma, Ala., March 7, 1965, SNCC Papers, reel 15; James Forman, "Report on Selma," March 7, 1965, SNCC Papers, reel 15.

83. Hall interview by Ransby.

84. Ibid.; Emilye Crosby, "That Movement Responsibility: An Interview with Judy Richardson on Movement Values and Movement History," in Crosby, *Civil Rights History*, 366–84, 378. In the same interview, Hall compared this incident of spiritual abuse to the larger problem of clergy abusing laity, "accepting monetary gifts from very poor people and not doing anything to significantly change the quality of life of the people."

85. "Julian Bond—Selma, 4:00," undated, SNCC Papers, reel 37.

86. Joyce Barrett to Fellowship House, May 28, 1963; Fellowship House Papers, acc. 732, box 7. The jail and its specific location are not identified in the documents.

87. Constance Curry, to Jean Fairfax, "A Report on a Trip to Middle Georgia, April 20–24, 1965," April 29, 1965, to June 15, 1965, Papers of the AFSC; Constance Curry to Francis Keppel, U.S. Commissioner of Education, May 6, 1965, Papers of the AFSC; Winifred Falls to Francis Keppel, July 1, 1965, Papers of the AFSC; Prathia Hall Wynn to Jean Fairfax, "Wheeler and Telfair Counties, Georgia, Report of Visits," July 16, 1965, Papers of the AFSC; Prathia Hall Wynn to Jean Fairfax, "Houston

County, Georgia—School Desegregation Trip—June 15, 16, 17, 1965," July 16, 1965, Papers of the AFSC; Constance Curry, to Jean Fairfax, "Houston County, Report of June 21–25," July 23, 1965, Papers of the AFSC. For various reasons personal to the family, gaps in information about the wedding, marriage, and eventual divorce of Prathia Hall and Ralph Wynn are unavoidable.

88. Curry, "Report on a Trip to Middle Georgia"; Curry to Keppel; Falls to Keppel; Wynn, "Wheeler and Telfair Counties"; Wynn, "Houston County"; Curry, "Houston County."

89. Curry, *Silver Rights*, 39, 23, 39.

90. The November 1964 SNCC annual staff retreat took place in Waveland, Mississippi. At that meeting, SNCC workers shared thirty-seven position papers reflecting on the direction in which SNCC should be headed for the future. The papers revealed several majors strands of tension: the role of nonviolence in the Movement, the interracial nature of SNCC, Black Nationalism, and sexism. The origins of the 1966 expulsion of white activists from SNCC can be traced back to that Waveland retreat. See Pronley, "Waveland."

91. Prathia Hall, quoted in Robnett, *How Long?*, 180; Hall interview by Kiburi.

92. Prathia Hall, quoted in Cronk, "Race Barriers Break Down."

93. Hall interview by Kiburi; Romily interview by Pace.

94. For various reasons personal to the family, gaps in information about the wedding, marriage, and eventual divorce of Prathia Hall and Ralph Wynn are unobtainable.

95. Noonan interview by Pace; Hall interview by Ransby.

96. Hall interview by Ransby.

97. Teach-In, October 28, 1965, New York University Friends of SNCC, Ella Baker Papers, Library of Congress Manuscript Division, F4, B8; Hall, interview by Kiburi.

98. Hall interview by Kiburi. See also Moody, *Coming of Age in Mississippi*.

Chapter 5. "Black, Preacher, Baptist, Woman"

1. Prathia Hall, "Biographical Sketch," 1978, Princeton Theological Seminary Student Record File—Prathia Hall.

2. Prathia Hall, resume, 1978, Princeton Theological Seminary Student Record File—Prathia Hall.

3. Ibid.

4. Prathia Wynn to Mayor Dalton Miller, July 14, 1977, PHP 4:94; Hall, resume.

5. Hall, resume. See PHP 7:932 for a flier of her campaign for Roosevelt School Board; speech for reelection, PHP 7:933–37.

6. Hall, "Biographical Sketch."

7. Prathia Hall, quoted by Dorothy Schneider, "Rev. Ms. Prathia Hall Wynn, Assoc. Dean for Spiritual and Community Life, Director of the Harriet L. Miller Women's Center, United Theological Seminary, Dayton, OH," Dorothy Schneider to Prathia Hall Wynn, September 8, 1994, PHP 23:599–635.

8. Ervin Dyer, "Heeding the Call of a Divine Mother," *Pittsburgh Post-Gazette*, undated; Ron Goldwyn, "Pastor Earns Acclaim as Lady of the House," *Philadelphia Daily News*, December 9, 1997.

9. "Addressing 'The Theological Scandal of Sexism,'" Women in Ministry Panel, *American Baptist* (July/August 1987), PHP 20:4–32, 14.

10. Prathia Hall, "Women in Ministry," Hampton University Ministers' Conference, June 5, 1984, PHP 24:309–39.

11. Hall, "Biographical Sketch"; Allen, "Toward a Womanist Homiletic," 51.

12. Prathia Hall, "Autobiographical Information," 1983, Princeton Theological Seminary Student Record File—Prathia Hall.

13. Prathia Hall correspondence with Arlo Duba, 1978–79, Princeton Theological Seminary Student Record File—Prathia Hall.

14. Ibid.

15. Ibid.

16. Ibid.

17. Prathia Hall Wynn, "PT 01 Introduction to Pastoral Care Final Paper," undated, PHP 6:269, 1, 1–2, 2, 9.

18. Prathia Hall Wynn, "The World in Whose Hands," undated draft, PHP 23:718–42.

19. Alider Bryant and John R. Curtis, to Friends of ASALH, December 23, 1987, PHP 7:640; Steering Committee Chair Ona Weldom, to Black Leadership Women, March 6, 1987, PHP 7:642; Harris Wofford, to Clergy Concerned about South Africa, September 21, 1986, PHP 7:660.

20. Urban League of Philadelphia New Brief, "Statement of the Urban League of Philadelphia to the State of Pennsylvania Senate Public Health and Welfare Committee on House Bill 20144," June 11, 1980, PHP 6:439; Pennsylvania General Assembly, Regular Session 1979–80, House Bill 2044, http://www.legis.state.pa.us/cfdocs/billinfo/billinfo.cfm?syear=1979&sind=0&body=H&type=B&bn=2044, accessed March 22, 2015.

21. Prathia Hall to Senate Committee, August 28, 1980, PHP 6:440–49.

22. Hall correspondence with Duba, 1978–79.

23. Prathia Hall correspondence with PTS Admissions Committee, 1982, Princeton Theological Seminary Student Record File—Prathia Hall.

24. Prathia Hall correspondence with Charles West, 1983, Princeton Theological Seminary Student Record File—Prathia Hall.

25. The Baptist Pastors and Ministers Conference of Philadelphia and Vicinity was founded in 1943 to facilitate cooperation and fellowship between Baptist pastors in Philadelphia and is most closely affiliated with the National Baptist Convention, USA. She was also appointed to the board of directors and the advisory committee of the Philadelphia Baptist Association in 1987. The *Philadelphia Tribune* published an article about Hall's selection; see Ruth Roland, "Baptists Pick First Woman," undated, PHP 11:347.

26. Prathia Hall, quoted in Kinnon, "Live Well."

27. Prathia Hall Wynn to Attorney Leslie Hill, Re: Divorce Complaint, July 16, 1984, PHP 16:54–89.

28. Prathia Hall to Ralph Wynn, June 29, 1980, PHP 15:258–62.

29. Prathia Hall to Leslie Hill, undated, PHP 6:207, 6:208; see also PHP 15:252–57.

30. Prathia Hall Wynn to Louise Robichaud, lawyer, May 9, 1986, PHP 4:707–15, 713. Hall might then have been keeping an apartment in New Jersey.

31. Prathia Hall Wynn, "Physical Violence," undated, PHP 16:896–914, 910; Prathia Hall Wynn, "Marital Relations," undated, PHP 16:915–20; Prathia Hall Wynn, "Financial Irresponsibility and Cruelty," undated, PHP 16:921–37.

32. Hall Wynn to Rochibaud, May 9, 1986; Prathia H. Wynn to Louise Robichaud, May 10, 1986, PHP 4:716–25; Mercer County Docket No. FM 05915-85.

33. Paul DeCoster to Prathia Hall, July 19, 2002, PHP 14:398–99; LaGretta Bjorn to Craig Feldherr, July 3, 2002, PHP 14:400; *Lincoln Savings Bank v. Ralph K Wynn and Parthia Wynn, Prathia Hall Wynn*, United States of America, State of New York, State Tax Commission, Manufacturers Hanover Trust Co., Supreme Court of the State of New York, County of Nassau, Index No. 16153/90, filed May 30, 2001, PHP 14:401–30; LaGretta Bjorn to Craig Feldherr, July 11, 2002, PHP 14:431–34.

34. Hall Wynn to Robichaud, May 9, 1986, 713.

35. Prathia Hall Wynn to the Honorable Bernard Rudd, July 23, 1985, PHP 5:176.

36. Prathia Hall Wynn, untitled document, PHP 4:760–69, 764–65.

37. Hall Wynn to Rudd.

38. Prathia Hall correspondence with Katharine Doob Sakenfeld, 1985, Princeton Theological Seminary Student File—Prathia Hall.

39. Prathia Hall, "Evaluation of Progress," April 22, 1985, Princeton Theological Seminary Student File—Prathia Hall.

40. Prathia Hall Wynn, personal statement, March 18, 1986, PHP 1:870.

41. Ibid., 1:871.

42. Barbara Simmons, Hugh Jemmott, Alja Small, and Prathia Wynn, "Working Draft: Statement of the African American Awareness Club Parent Support Group re Racism Within West Windsor Plainsboro Schools," undated, PHP 14:1–14.

43. Prathia Hall correspondence with Katharine Doob Sakenfeld, 1989–91, and

Jack Danton correspondence with Kathryn Sakenfeld, January 10, 1988, both in Princeton Theological Seminary Student File—Prathia Hall.

44. Prathia Hall to Dr. Ford and Dr. Paris, undated, PHP 4:298-99.

45. Katharine Doob Sakenfeld to Prathia Hall Wynn, January 12, 1988, PHP 7:093.

46. Albert Raboteau correspondence with Gibson Winter, 1984; Katharine Doob Sakenfeld correspondence with Prathia Wynn's Committee, 1987; Dick Fenn correspondence with Prathia Hall, 1991, all in Princeton Theological Seminary Student File—Prathia Hall.

47. Prathia Hall Wynn to Daryl Ward, October 24, 1988, PHP 3:287; Newell Wert to Prathia Hall Wynn, November 18, 1988, PHP 3:284.

48. Womanism is often described as a liberation methodology of black women committed to the survival, quality of life, and wholeness of all people through the critique of all forms of oppression, including sexism, racism, and classism. The term originated from Alice Walker's *In Search of Our Mother's Gardens*: "A black feminist or feminist of color.... Usually referring to audacious, courageous, or *willful* behavior.... Committed to survival and wholeness of entire people, male *and* female. ... Loves music. Loves dance. Loves the moon. *Loves* the Spirit. Loves love and food and roundness. Loves struggle. *Loves* the Folk. Loves herself. *Regardless*" (original emphasis; xi–xii). See also Cannon, *Black Womanist Ethics*, 6–9; Cannon, *Katie's Canon*, 34–56, 122–38; Coleman, *Making a Way*, vii–9, 31–38; Frederick, *Between Sundays*, 5–14; Gilkes, *If It Wasn't for the Women*, 184–211; Hayes, *Hagar's Daughters*, 49–54; Mitchem, *Introducing Womanist Theology*, ix; Riggs, *Awake, Arise, and Act*, 1–8; St. Clair, *Call and Consequences*, 1–12; Terrell, *Power in the Blood?*, 6, 134; Williams, *Sisters in the Wilderness*, 1–8; Turman, *Toward a Womanist Ethic*; and Gafney, *Womanist Midrash*.

49. David Kepple, "UTS Program Earns Rave Reviews Black Church Highlighted," *Dayton (OH) Daily News*, March 3, 1990.

50. Prathia Hall correspondence with Newell Wert, December 1990, Princeton Theological Seminary Student File—Prathia Hall.

51. Prathia Hall Wynn to Lealy L. Jones, associate for Fund for Theological Education, August 20, 1993, PHP 6:584.

52. The Interdenominational Christian Fellowship Union Appreciation Banquet Honoring Pastor Prathia Hall Wynn and Scholarship Award, November 6, 1993, PHP 11:601.

53. Daryl Ward, untitled, undated, included in the program for the Interdenominational Christian Fellowship Union Appreciation Banquet Honoring Prathia Hall Wynn, November 6, 1993, PHP 11:604. Air Jordans were a popular sneaker named for basketball legend Michael Jordan. Ward's joke about "Air-Wynn" analogized Hall as the Michael Jordan of preaching.

54. Jeremiah Wright, untitled, undated, in ibid., 11:605.

55. "Tribute to Prathia Hall Wynn," Interdenominational Christian Fellowship Union Appreciation Banquet, November 6, 1993, PHP 14:723–24.

56. Interdenominational Christian Fellowship Union Appreciation Banquet Honoring Prathia Hall Wynn, November 6, 1993, PHP 11:602–14.

57. Prathia Hall Wynn, "The African American Ministries Program: Perspectives and Possibilities," United Theological Seminary, undated, PHP 1:309.

58. Michael Nickerson, teacher placement form, April 24, 1998, and United Theological Seminary, news release, undated, Princeton Theological Seminary Student File—Prathia Hall; Prathia Hall, curriculum vita, Prathia Hall Papers; "Student Spiritual Life Committee," undated, PHP 1:51.

59. Newell J. Wert, Teacher Placement Form, March 18, 1998, Princeton Theological Seminary Student File—Prathia Hall; Prathia Hall Wynn to UTS African American Students, Staff and Faculty, "Re: Chapel Service April 27, 1994," PHP 3:86; Prathia Hall to Maxine Beach, June 29, 1994, PHP 3:156–58.

60. Ronald Peters (Pittsburgh Theological Seminary) to Richard Zimmerman and Prathia Hall (United Theological Seminary), March 12, 1996, PHP 1:401; Prathia Hall Wynn memo to UTS D.Min Mentors and African American Advisory Board Members, March 20, 1996, PHP 1:416; African American Ministries National Advisory Board Meeting Minutes, January 22–23, 1997, PHP 15:1–8.

61. United Theological Seminary, Faculty Seminar on Ecology, Theology, and Justice, PHP 3:112–15, 120–21; Bill Clinton to James Sweeny, August 3, 1994, PHP 3:115.

62. Charles Adams to Ronald Thiemann, May 9, 1992, PHP 21:48–49.

63. Peter J. Paris to Ronald Thiemann, February 3, 1993, PHP 21:51–58.

64. Brown interview by Pace; Bjorn interview by Pace.

65. Prathia Hall correspondence with Katharine Doob Sakenfeld, 1987–91, Princeton Theological Seminary Student File—Prathia Hall.

66. Peter Paris to Katharine Doob Sakenfeld, April 21, 1989, Princeton Theological Seminary Student File—Prathia Hall.

67. "Some Recommendations for Single Moms and Dads," undated, PHP 10:170–72.

68. Mass Rehabilitation Medicine, Initial Evaluation of Simone Wynn.

69. McMillian interview by Pace.

70. Simone Wynn, funeral program, March 11, 1992, Miller Memorial Baptist Church, Philadelphia, PA, PHP 14:464–501. After Michael turned four, he spent the summers with Hall but lived with his father, Henri McMillian.

71. Prathia Hall, "When Faith Trembles," *30 Good Minutes*, program 4318, February 6, 2000, http://www.30goodminutes.org/index.php/archives/23-member

-archives/648-prathia-hall-program-4318?tmpcomponent&print=1&page=/, accessed February 1, 2016.

72. Prathia Hall, correspondence with Katharine Doob Sakenfeld, 1992, Princeton Theological Seminary Student File—Prathia Hall.

73. Edward Wheeler to Prathia Hall Wynn, October 12, 1992, PHP 11:810–11.

74. United Theological Seminary Faculty Tenure Review Committee, March 18, 1996, PHP 1:412.

75. Leonette Vanderhost to Carol Sperling Allstate Insurance, June 9, 1993, PHP 4:775. The "closest friend" is presumably Simone.

76. Prathia Hall to Newell Wert, December 11, 1990, PHP 6:532; Newell Wert to Prathia Hal, December 13, 1990, PHP 6:536.

77. Leonard I. Sweet to Prathia Hall Wynn, May 1992, PHP 6:529; Prathia Hall Wynn to Newell Wert, March 27, 1992, PHP 6:530; Newell Wert to Prathia Hall, June 15, 1993, PHP 6:528.

78. Maxine Beach to Prathia Hall Wynn and Donetta Peaks, October 27, 1993, PHP 3:179.

79. Maxine Beach to Prathia Hall Wynn, November 16, 1993, PHP 3:174.

80. Prathia Hall Wynn to Maxine Beach, November 17, 1993, PHP 3:169.

81. Beach to Hall Wynn, November 16, 1993.

82. Maxine Beach to Prathia Hall Wynn, February 7, 1994, PHP 3:180.

83. Maxine Beach to Prathia Hall Wynn, May 12, 1994, PHP 3:236.

84. Prathia Hall Wynn to Maxine Beach, June 29, 1994, "Re: Observations and Commentary," 1 PHP 3:159.

85. Ibid., 1 PHP 3:159, 2 PHP 3:160, 3 PHP 3:161, 4 PHP 3:162, 4 PHP 3:162, 5 PHP 3:163.

86. Hall Wynn to Beach, June 29, 1994, 7 PHP 3:165.

87. Ibid.

88. J. T. Roberson to Prathia Hall Wynn, evaluation, October 30, 1995, PHP 3:260; Maxine Beach to Prathia Hall Wynn, June 5, 1995, PHP 3:245; Maxine Beach to J. T. Roberson, August 10, 1995, PHP 3:266; Daryl Ward to Prathia Hall Wynn, June 21, 1995, PHP 3:268; Prathia Hall Wynn to Daryl Ward, July 28, 1995, PHP 3:271; Prathia Hall Wynn to Maxine Beach, July 15, 1995, PHP 3:359.

89. Beach to Hall, June 5, 1995; Maxine Beach to Prathia Hall, July 18, 1995, PHP 3:304.

90. Maxine Beach to Prathia Hall Wynn, August 8, 1995, PHP 3:269.

91. Prathia Hall to Davis-Putter Scholarship Fund, May 3, 1995, PHP 7:243.

92. James Howard to Prathia Hall-Wynn, March 30, 1995, PHP 4:313–14.

93. "3rd Senatorial District Humanitarian Service Award," February 9, 1997, PHP 24:463.

94. Higginbotham, *Righteous Discontent*.

95. Hall, "Religious and Social Consciousness," vii.

96. Ibid., ," vii–viii; Crenshaw, "Mapping the Margins."

97. Prathia Hall, Peter Paris, and Katharine Doob Sakenfeld correspondence, 1994–96, and J. A. Danton, November 21, 1994, Princeton Theological Seminary Student File—Prathia Hall; Jeremiah Wright to Ruby Johnson, February 22, 1995, PHP 7:37; Jeremiah Wright to Prathia Hall Wynn, March 11, 1996, PHP 21:615; Bjorn interview by Pace.

98. Prathia Hall to Cheryl Townsend Gilkes, April 17, 1997, PHP 4:80.

99. Otis Moss to Maxine Clark Beach, April 23, 1997, PHP 4:121; Gale Poindexter to Maxine Beach, April 23, 1997, PHP 4:106; Susan Newman to Michael Nickerson, April 21, 1997, PHP 4:107–8; Robert Jones to Maxine Beach, April 23, 1997, PHP 4:109; Thomas Hoyt to Maxine Clark Beach, April 22, 1997, PHP 4:110; Pamela June Anderson to Maxine Clark Beach, April 22, 1997, PHP 4:112–13; Carlyle Stewart III to Maxine Beach, April 22, 1997, PHP 4:114; Jacquelyn Grant to Maxine Beach, April 23, 1997, PHP 4:115–16; M. Shulligan Haney to Maxine Beach, April 23, 1997, PHP 4:117; Ella Pearson and Henry Mitchell to Maxine Beach, April 22, 1997, PHP 4:118; Charles E. Booth to Maxine Clark Beach, April 22, 1997, PHP 4:119–20; Daryl Ward to Maxine Beach, April 23, 1997, PHP 4:121; Samuel Dewitt Proctor to Maxine Beach, April 22, 1997, PHP 4:125; Kevin Cosby to Okechukwu Ogbonnaya, April 22, 1997, PHP 4:126; Molly Longstreth to Maxine Beach, April 21, 1997, PHP 4:127–28; H. Beecher Hicks to Maxine Clark Beach, April 23, 1997, PHP 4:129; Linda Hollies to Maxine Clark Beach, April 21, 1997, PHP 4:130.

100. Otis Moss to Maxine Clark Beach, April 23, 1997, PHP 4:121.

101. Molly Longstreth to Maxine Beach, April 21, 1997, PHP 4:127.

102. Samuel Dewitt Proctor to Maxine Beach, April 22, 1997, PHP 4:125.

103. Prathia Hall to Carlyle Fielding Stewart, September 17, 1997, PHP 14:92–94.

104. United Theological Seminary Press Release, August 19, 1997, PHP 6:380.

105. Michael Nickerson to Prathia Hall, September 2, 1997, PHP 11:799; severance agreement, PHP 11:800–803; Prathia Hall to Michael Nickerson, undated, PHP 11:804–5, also 14:219–29; LaGretta Bjorn to Prathia Hall, September 12, 1997, PHP 14:210–13; Prathia Hall to Michael Nickerson, September 31, 1997, PHP 14:216–17; LaGretta Bjorn to Prathia Hall, undated, PHP 14:218; Michael Nickerson to Prathia Hall, January 22, 1998, PHP 14:230–33.

106. McMillian interview by Pace.

107. LaGretta Bjorn to Prathia Hall, December 27, 1997, PHP 15:89–101.

108. Ruby Hall to LaGretta Bjorn, PHP 11:453.

109. McMillian interview by Pace, May 4, 2016.

110. Brown interview by Pace.

111. Anonymous reviewer, report 2, e-mailed to author by Walter Biggins, April 20, 2018. I am grateful to my reviewer for suggesting this similarity. It is beyond the scope of the present work to delve more into Hall's influence on landmark legislation.

Chapter 6. "I'm 5'6" but I Should Have Been Taller"

1. Hall, "Working on the Building," PHP 23:269–314.
2. Hall Wynn, "Faith and Freedom," PHP 1:713, 1:748.
3. Hall, "African American Church at the Crossroad," PHP; Hall, "Working on the Building." Hall, "African American Religious Experience," PHP 19:360–497, 460–61.
4. Hall, "African American Church at the Crossroad."
5. Ibid.
6. Prathia Hall Wynn, untitled document, PHP 7:811; Hall Wynn, "Faith and Freedom."
7. Hall, "Building between Heritage and Hope."
8. Hall, "African American Religious Experience," PHP 19:360–497, 407.
9. Hall Wynn, "Faith and Freedom"; Hall Wynn, "Convergence and Crisis," DS 57, Dr. Lois Livezy, undated, PHP 1:867.
10. Prathia Hall, untitled, undated, PHP 8:195–86 (this may be an earlier draft of Prathia Hall Wynn, "Faith and Freedom").
11. Hall, "Church at the Crossroad."
12. Hall, "Working on the Building."
13. Hall Wynn, "Faith and Freedom"; Hall Wynn, "Convergence and Crisis," 23.
14. Hall Wynn, "Convergence and Crisis," 21.
15. Hall, "Working on the Building." Michele Wallace, *Black Macho and the Myth of the Superwoman* (New York: Dial, 1978), 15, quoted in Hall Wynn, "Convergence and Crisis," 25. Hall Wynn, "Convergence and Crisis," 25.
16. Hall, "Building between Heritage and Hope."
17. Hall, "Church at the Crossroad"; Hall, "Womanist Moral Leadership."
18. Untitled notes, undated, PHP, box 1, 30s and 40s.
19. Hall, "Dilemma," PHP 1:045.
20. Hall, "Womanist Moral Leadership"; Hall, "Religious and Social Consciousness," 181.
21. Prathia Hall Wynn to Jeremiah Wright, September 13, 1996, PHP 21:601–5.
22. Sékou Touré quoted in Hall, "Child as Prophet, Jeremiah 1," PHP 18:31–57. Prathia Hall, untitled sermon, Genesis 1, undated, PHP 18:58–132.
23. Hall, "Convergence and Crisis," 35, PHP 1:889; Hall Wynn, "Theological/Educational Foundations," PHP 1:924, 18.

24. Ibid., 18–19.

25. Ibid., 19.

26. Ervin Dyer, "Heeding the Call of a Divine Mother," *Pittsburgh Post-Gazette*, undated. Hall-Wynn, "Challenge of True Kinship," 121.

27. Prathia Hall, quoted in Ray Waddle, "Pastor Says Sexism Sin That Defies God," *Tennessean* (Nashville), October 21, 1992; Prathia Hall, quoted in Ray Waddle, "Black Churches Harbor Sexism, Minister Charges," *St. Petersburg (FL) Times*, October 24, 1992; Hall Wynn, "Theological/Educational Foundations," 12; Prathia Hall, untitled paper on domestic violence, undated, PHP 23:1119–27.

28. Hall, untitled paper on domestic violence; Hall Wynn, "Theological/Educational Foundations," 12.

29. Hall Wynn, "Theological/Educational Foundations," 16–17, 17.

30. Hall Wynn, "Convergence and Crisis," 38.

31. Ibid. Hall Wynn, "African American Faith/Freedom Struggle," PHP 1:939.

32. Hall, "Convergence and Crisis," 45.

33. Hall, "Challenge of True Kinship: Sisters and Brothers in Church and Community," undated, PHP 10:15.

34. Hall, "Challenge of True Kinship," PHP 10:14.

35. Prathia H. Wynn, "Term Project," submitted to Dr. Lois Livesay, Princeton Theological Seminary, undated, PHP 21:66–160, 90, 90, 95, 146.

36. Ibid., 95, 146, 158, 146.

37. Ibid., 152–53.

38. Hall, "Challenge of True Kinship," PHP 10:16.

39. Ibid., 10:9.

40. "How to Close the Widening and Dangerous Gap between Black Men and Black Women," *Ebony*, 1985, 62, cited in Hall Wynn, "Convergence and Crisis"; Hall Wynn, "Convergence and Crisis."

41. Hall Wynn, "Convergence and Crisis," 23; Marian Wright Edelman, to Prathia Hall, November 24, 1998, PHP 5:477.

42. Hall, untitled sermon.

43. Hall, "Challenge of True Kinship," PHP 10:15.

44. Congress of National Black Churches, to Prathia Hall, June 19, 1995, PHP 10:259.

45. Prathia Hall Wynn, "A Call to the 1995 Black Church Leadership Conference," PHP 10:260.

46. Hall, "Working on the Building."

47. Prathia Hall Wynn, "Abolitionist Religion" and "Additional Pages," UTS Doctoral Studies, November 9, 1994, PHP 17:218–39.

48. Hall, "African American Religious Experience," 383; Hall, "Music from the Rubbish Heap," PHP 23:1417–64.

49. Derek Ali, "Activists: Civil Rights Movement Still Vital," *Dayton Daily (OH) News*, February 21, 1995, PHP 7:263–64. Hall, "Building between Heritage and Hope."
50. Hall, untitled sermon.
51. Hall, "Building between Heritage and Hope."
52. Hall, untitled sermon.
53. AP, "Civil Rights Act Failed, Movement Veterans Say," *New York Times*, November 6, 1994, PHP 17:261–62; Brigitte Greenberg, AP, "Rights Leaders Mourn Failures of Movement," *Advocate* (Stamford, CT), November 5, 1994, PHP 17:265–68; Ellen Nakashima, "There's Still Work to Be Done: Civil Rights Activists Meet 30 Years Later," *Hartford Courant*, November 6, 1994, PHP 17:272–74; Hall, untitled sermon.
54. Hall, "Working on the Building". See also Hall, "Building between Heritage and Hope," PHP 23:1482–626.
55. Hall, untitled sermon. Hall, "Working on the Building." Hall Wynn, "Abolitionist Religion" and "Additional Pages." Hall, "Working on the Building."
56. Hall, untitled sermon. Hall, "Building between Heritage and Hope."
57. Hall, "Working on the Building." See also Prathia Hall, "Proclaimer."
58. Hall, "Evaluating, Reviving, Revisioning the Meaning," PHP 24:695–722.
59. Hall Wynn, "Abolitionist Religion" and "Additional Pages."
60. Hall, "Working on the Building."
61. Hall, "Building between Heritage and Hope."
62. Hall, "In Search of a Society," PHP 7:443; also in PHP 19:664–752.
63. Melanie Turner, Office of the Vice Chancellor for Undergraduate Education at Indiana University–Purdue University at Indianapolis, to Dr. Hall-Wynn, February 20, 1991, PHP 23:113–14; Bernadine Grady, Afro-American Studies Program at University of Pennsylvania, January 31, 1999, PHP 23:115; Peter T. Nash, the Church and the Black Experience at Garrett-Evangelical Theological Seminary, to Dean Prathia Hall Wynn, December 9, 1991, PHP 23:140.
64. Hall, "In Search of a Society"; also in PHP 19:664–752.
65. Ibid.
66. Hall, "Baccalaureate Address" (1992).
67. Hall, "In Search of a Society."
68. Ibid.
69. Ibid.

Chapter 7. "The Living God Is Not a Bigot"

1. Hall, "Foreword" (1985), 9–10.
2. Pace Lyons, "Breaking through."
3. Ibid.
4. Hall Wynn, "Foreword" (1995), ix–x.

5. Prathia Hall, quoted by Dorothy Schneider, "Rev. Ms. Prathia Hall Wynn, Assoc. Dean for Spiritual and Community Life, Director of the Harriet L. Miller Women's Center, United Theological Seminary, Dayton, OH," Dorothy Schneider to Prathia Hall Wynn, September 8, 1994, PHP 23:599–635.

6. Hall, "Journey with Jesus."

7. Hall Wynn, "Foreword" (1995), x.

8. Hall, "Encountering the Text," 66. Hall, "Religious and Social Consciousness," vii, vii–viii.

9. Hall, "Between the Wilderness." PHP. Hall's sermon "Between the Wilderness and a Cliff" was transcribed by Hall's graduate student LaGretta Bjorn sometime in the late 1990s or early 2000s. See Bjorn interview by Pace. A published version of the sermon appears in *Preaching with Sacred Fire: An Anthology of African American Sermons, 1750 to the Present* (2010), 687–95.

10. Hall, "Proclaimer."

11. Allen, "Toward a Womanist Homiletic," 67.

12. Prathia Hall, quoted in ibid., 52.

13. Wright interview by Pace; Bjorn interview by Pace.

14. A. J. W. James, "Tenth Anniversary Celebration Honors Rev. Wynn as Pastor," *Philadelphia Tribune*, March 4, 1988.

15. Charles Adams, quoted in ibid.

16. Michael Eric Dyson, "Freedom Was Foremost for Philly Activist. Like King She Inspired, Gifted Minister Fought Oppression Wherever She Found It," *Chicago Sun-Times*, August 20, 2002.

17. Hall, "Encountering the Text," 65.

18. Hall, "Between the Wilderness," PHP.

19. Hall, "Journey with Jesus"; she used a similar device at the end of this sermon, about Jesus's journey to earth, to the cross, and then risen.

20. Hall interview by Allen, quoted in Allen, "Toward a Womanist Homiletic," 50–51.

21. Hall, "Encountering the Text," 63–64.

22. Ibid., 60–61.

23. Ibid., 68.

24. Hall, "Encounters with Jesus, Mark 5:21–34," PHP 19:563; various handwritten manuscripts of the same sermon are found in PHP 22:1975–2074.

25. Hall, "Encountering the Text," 60–61.

26. Hall, "Encounters with Jesus, Mark 5:21–34," PHP 19:570.

27. Hall, "Encounters with Jesus," 70.

28. Ibid., 71.

29. Hall, "Encounters with Jesus, Mark 5:21–34," PHP 19:584–85.

30. Hall, "Crippled by a Spirit."
31. Hall, "Burden Bent."
32. Hall, "When Jesus Tells Her Story."
33. Ibid.
34. Prathia Hall, "When the Hurts Do Not Heal" (1989). A published version appears in *Those Preaching Women: More Sermons by Black Women* (1987), 2:95–102.
35. Hall, "Between the Wilderness" (2010), 691–92.
36. Ibid., 694.
37. Hall, "Journey with Jesus."
38. Hall, "When the Hurts Do Not Heal" (1989).
39. Hall, "When the Hurts Do Not Heal" (1987).
40. Hall, "Outrageous Assertion." This sermon was transcribed by LaGretta Bjorn in the late 1990s and was included in a collection of three transcribed sermons in Prathia Hall's papers.
41. Hall, "Encountering the Text," 65.
42. Hall, "Partnership in Ministry," PHP 23:781.
43. Hall Wynn, "Theological/Educational Foundations," PHP 1:920.
44. Hall, "Letter to the Church," PHP 23:896–932.
45. Prathia Hall, "Beyond Eden," undated, typed MS from audiocassette, PHP; Hall Wynn, "Theological/Educational Foundations," PHP 1:905; see also Hall, "Garden of Eden."
46. Hall, "Garden of Eden," PHP 24:432–33.
47. Ibid., 24:438–39.
48. Hall, "Beyond Eden."
49. Ibid.
50. Hall Wynn, "Theological/Educational Foundations," PHP1:917–18. See also Lerner, *Creation of Patriarchy*.
51. Hall, "Beyond Eden."
52. Ibid.
53. Ibid.
54. Ibid.
55. Hall, "Partnership in Ministry," PHP23:798–800.
56. Hall, "Beyond Eden."
57. Ibid. Hall Wynn, "World in Whose Hands," PHP23:735; Hall, "Partnership in Ministry," PHP23:785.
58. Hall, "Beyond Eden."
59. Prathia Hall, title illegible, undated, though likely in preparation for Kelly Miller Smith Institute, PHP 1:305; Hall, "Garden of Eden," PHP 24:451.
60. Hall, "Dialogue on Black Theology," PHP 24:212.

61. Hall, "Encounters with Jesus" (2002), 70. This sermon can also be found as Hall, "Children: A Suffering Sister, Frantic Father, Dying Daughter: Encounters with Jesus" (sermon given at Third Annual Center for Congregations and Family Ministries Conference, Louisville Presbyterian Theological Seminary, Louisville, Ky., 1999).

62. Hall, "Encounters with Jesus" (2002), 72–73.

63. Ervin Dyer, "Heeding the Call of a Divine Mother," *Pittsburgh Post-Gazette*, undated; Hall, untitled sermon, Genesis 1, undated, PHP 18:58–132.

64. Hall, "Baccalaureate Address" (1998), PHP 23:1077–78.

65. Hall, interview by Allen, in Allen, "Toward a Womanist Homiletic," 58–59.

66. Prathia Hall, "Captivity's Capture" (undated).

67. Ibid.

68. Hall Wynn, "Captivity Is a Lie," 54.

69. Ibid.

70. Ibid.

71. Hall, "Partnership in Ministry," 54.

72. Ron Goldwyn, "Pastor Earns Acclaim as Lady of the House," *Philadelphia Daily News*, December 9, 1997.

73. Hall, "Partnership in Ministry," 764.

74. Hall Wynn, "World in Whose Hands," PHP 23:727, 738, 737.

75. Hall, "Preaching a Liberating Word."

76. Ibid.

77. Hall, "Partnership in Ministry." Hall Wynn, "World in Whose Hands"; Hall, "Partnership in Ministry."

78. Hall, "Deliverance for the Captives."

79. Ibid.

80. Ibid.

81. Ibid.

82. Ibid.

83. Ibid.

84. Ibid.

85. Ibid.

86. Hall, "Letter to the Church."

87. Ibid.

88. Hall, "Between the Wilderness and a Cliff," PHP.

89. Ibid. Betty Garman Robinson remembered seeing Hall preach in Baltimore sometime in the late 1990s or early 2000s. When Robinson heard that Hall would be in town, she made a point to attend the service. The neighborhood was steeped in drug trade and a strong cultural tendency toward "external symbol[s] of importance" such as gold teeth, gold chains, and gold rings. Robinson remembered Hall's sermon

speaking against materialism, inviting the congregation to a deeper spirituality and embrace of values and character (Robinson, interview by Pace).

90. Hall, "Proclaimer."

91. Hall, "Nightmare," PHP.

92. Hall, "Broken by the Blessed," PHP. Typical of her merging of eloquence with colloquialism, Hall said: "They loved a high time in the Lord, but when the substance of their faith was tested by the evidence of their Christian living, it was found to be tissue paper thin."

93. Hall, "Broken by the Blessed."

94. Ibid.

95. Hall, "Keynote Address" (1998), PHP 7:329; John Stewart to Prathia Hall, April 21, 1998, PHP 11:550.

96. Dorothy Rowley, "Women Urged to Get Involved to Combat Imprisonment of Men," undated newspaper clipping, PHP 4:625.

97. Hall, "Church under Construction."

98. Hall, "Outrageous Assertion."

99. Ibid.

100. Hall, "Building between Heritage and Hope."

Chapter 8. "The Baptist Church Is Going to Have to Deal with Me"

1. Hall affiliated with the Progressive National Baptist Convention and the American Baptist Convention, USA, though this section refers to her engagement with black Baptists at large. Underneath her engagement with black Baptists also lies her correction to white Baptists guilty of racism, sexism, classism, and other oppressions against which her womanist hermeneutic compelled her to proclaim.

2. Ron Goldwyn, "Pastor Earns Acclaim as Lady of the House," *Philadelphia Daily News*, December 9, 1997.

3. Hall, "Power over Power," PHP 16:206.

4. Wynn, "Accepting the Call to Leadership."

5. Ervin Dyer, "Heeding the Call of a Divine Mother," *Pittsburgh Post-Gazette*, undated.

6. Hall, "Working on the Building."

7. Ibid.

8. Hall Wynn, "Foreword" (1995).

9. Wynn, "Accepting the Call to Leadership," 24–25, 27.

10. Hall-Wynn, "Challenge of True Kinship," 118–19.

11. Ibid., 120.

12. Daryl Ward, letter ("To Whom It May Concern") January 12, 1996, PHP 5:499; Barry Hopkins to Prathia Hall, June 18, 1990, PHP 11:886; Tyrone S. Pitts to Prathia Hall, December 31, 1990, PHP 13:034.

13. Tyrone Pitts to Prathia Hall, October 10, 1991, PHP 11:889.

14. Jualynne E. Dodson to President Rev. Charles Adams and General Secretary Rev. Tyrone Pitts, November 26, 1991, PHP 1:128.

15. Ibid.

16. John Hewitt to Prathia Hall, December 20, 1992, 1:120 PHP; Jualynne Dodson to Prathia Hall, undated, PHP 1:143; Ken Sehested to Prathia Hall, November 27, 1991, PHP 1:166; Ken Sehested to Participants in the BPFNA Friendship Tour to Cuba, November 27, 1991, PHP 1:167–68.

17. Appendix to letter from Jualynne E. Dodson to President Rev. Charles Adams and General Secretary Rev. Tyrone Pitts, November 26, 1991, PHP 1:129–30.

18. John Hewitt to Prathia Hall, December 20, 1992, PHP 1:120; Jualynne Dodson to Prathia Hall, undated, PHP 1:143.

19. "Statement of the 1991 Delegation to Cuba of the Presbytery of New York City," October 1–11, 1991, PHP 1:137–39.

20. Appendix 2, "Statement of the position of the Methodist Church with respect to the blockade against Cuba," June 19, 1991, Havana, PHP 1:140–42.

21. Hall, "Captivity's Capture" (1994).

22. Thelma Chambers-Young to LaGretta Bjorn, February 19, 1998, PHP 11:544; George E. Young to Prathia Hall, November 25, 1997, PHP 11:781.

23. William R. Macklin, "Black Church Lags in Women Leadership—Fiscal Problems Take Precedence for Baptists," *Star-Ledger* (Newark, NJ), September 12, 1999.

24. Robert Tiller to Prathia Hall, October 1, 1982, PHP 1:652; Atha J. Baugh to Prathia Hall, March 23, 1983, PHP 3:015.

25. "Amendments to the Report of the Statements of Concern Committee, Section II," Biennial Meeting, American Baptist Churches/USA, June 19, 1987, PHP 7:989–95.

26. "Reporting from Racial Ethnic Groups," ABCUSA Racial/Ethnic Women in Ministry Consultation, Menlo Park, Calif., June 1–3, 1988, PHP 7: 838–43.

27. Rich Schramm, American Baptist Churches USA, press release, "Racial/Ethnic Women in Ministry Unite to Pursue Placement and Visibility," July 1, 1988, PHP 8:229.

28. Rev. Kathryn Choy-Wong to Prathia Hall, May 9, 1988, PHP 8:212.

29. Holly Vincent Bean to Prathia Hall, February 2, 1988, PHP 8:234–35.

30. "Categorization of Initial Issues and Concerns from the Racial/Ethnic Women in Ministry Consultation," Racial/Ethnic Women in Ministry Consultation, ABCUSA, Menlo Park, Calif., June 1–3, 1988, PHP 7:832–37.

31. "Transcription of Initial Issues and Concerns," Racial/Ethnic Women in Ministry Consultation, ABCUSA, Menlo Park, Calif., June 1–3, 1988, PHP 7:835.

32. Holly Vincent Bean to Prathia Hall, August 11, 1988, PHP 8:216.

33. "Time-Line, Women in the American Baptist Churches," undated, PHP 7:882–97; Holly Vincent Bean to Prathia Hall Wynn, February 2, 1988, PHP 7:848–49; Rev. Ms. Valentine B. Royal to Rev. Dr. Prathia Hall, October 3, 1967, PHP 11:779–80.

34. Kate Harvey and Valentine Royal to Dr. Prathia Hall, September 15, 1998, PHP 7:336.

35. Robert Fisher to Prathia Hall, April 18, 1990, PHP 1:202.

36. Mary O. Ross to Prathia Hall Wynn, July 28, 1993, PHP 11:628.

37. Mary Jones to Prathia Hall, April 17, 1987, PHP 7:912.

38. Elmorie Miller to Prathia Hall, June 15, 1984, PHP 7:918.

39. "They were all filled with the Holy Spirit," Spiritual Life Commission, Woman's Convention Auxiliary to the National Baptist Convention, USA, Inc., Consecration Service, September 4, 1985, Atlanta, PHP 7:925.

40. Prathia Hall, quoted by Dorothy Schneider, "Rev. Ms. Prathia Hall Wynn, Assoc. Dean for Spiritual and Community Life, Director of the Harriet L. Miller Women's Center, United Theological Seminary, Dayton, OH," Dorothy Schneider to Prathia Hall Wynn, September 8, 1994, PHP 23:599–635.

41. Ibid.

42. Ibid.

43. J. Richard Butler of Riverside Baptist Church to Prathia H. Wynn, June 24, 1988, PHP 4:246; J. Richard Butler of Riverside Baptist Church to Prathia H. Wynn, September 19, 1988, PHP 5:033–35; Prathia Hall Wynn to Carl E. Flemister of American Baptist Churches of Metro New York, April 12, 1988, PHP 4:248; Carl E. Flemister to Prathia Hall Wynn, July 12, 1988, PHP 4:249; Prathia Hall to Fred Jones of First Baptist Church Capitol Hill, September 23, 1999, PHP 7:603.

44. Goldwyn, "Pastor Earns Acclaim as Lady." Dyer, "Heeding the Call"; Goldwyn, "Pastor Earns Acclaim as Lady"; Ron Goldwyn, "Big Churches Hear but Don't Hire Popular Black Female Preacher," *Fort Worth Star-Telegram*, December 13, 1997. An alternative explanation for Hall never moving beyond Mount Sharon was her mother Ruby's ("Mother Hall") controlling hold on Hall. Presttonia Brown remembered Mother Hall pressuring Hall to stay at Mount Sharon to preserve what Hall's father had built and stay close to her extended family. See Brown, interview by Pace.

45. Goldwyn, "Pastor Earns Acclaim as Lady."

46. Significant correspondence in this regard in PHP 7:900s–1000s, extending into the 8:000s; also 11:629, 11:652, 11:668.

47. Hall, "Women in Ministry," PHP 24:309–39.

48. Mr. Clay to Prathia Wynn, September 4, 1984, PHP 7:998; Lee Coppernell to Prathia Hall, August 27, 1984, PHP 7:999.

49. Yvonne Delk and Joan Campbell to Rev. Wynn, November 24, 1987, PHP 7:973–74.

50. Ona Weldon to Black Women Leadership, March 6, 1987, PHP 8:28; Jettie D. Newkiri to Black Women Leadership, February 17, 1988, PHP 8:33.

51. "And They Shall Rise: Afro-American Women Scholars in Religion," University of Virginia Office of Afro-American Studies and Department of Women's Studies, Program, April 6–7, 1989 PHP 10:242–45.

52. Hall, "Dialogue on Black Theology," PHP 24:199–215.

53. Ibid.

54. Forrest Harris to Michael Battle, Prathia Hall Wynn, Janes Cone, Roscoe Cooper, and Samuel Proctor, June 16, 1992, PHP 1:288–89; Forrest Harris memo to James Cone Samuel Proctor and Prathia Hall Wynn, "Re: National Dialogue: What Does It Mean to Be Black and Christian Hampton Minister's Conference," April 9, 1992, PHP 1:290; Forrest Harris to Prathia Hall-Wynn, June 11, 1991, PHP 1:291–92; Forrest Harris, Progress Report, November 21, 1991, Kelly Miller Smith Institute, Vanderbilt University, PHP 1:296.

55. Ray Waddle, "Black Churches Harbor Sexism, Minister Charges," *St. Petersburg (FL) Times*, October 24, 1992.

56. Hall-Wynn, "Challenge of True Kinship," 116.

57. Ibid., 121; see also Hall, "Dialogue on Black Theology."

58. Hall-Wynn, "Challenge of True Kinship," 121.

59. Prathia Hall, title illegible, undated, though likely in preparation for Kelly Miller Smith Institute document, PHP 1:304.

60. Hall-Wynn, "Challenge of True Kinship," 119.

61. Ibid., 120.

62. Hall, "What Does It Mean to Be Black and Christian?" (1992).

63. Hall-Wynn, "Challenge of True Kinship," 115.

64. Ibid., 113, 112–14.

65. Ibid., 114.

66. Ibid., 116, 122, 121.

67. Ibid., 117. Waddle, "Black Churches Harbor Sexism."

68. Jacquelyn Grant to Think Tank Participants, "Think Tank—October 14, 1999," September 28, 1999, PHP 11:934–36; Jacquelyn Grant to Think Tank Participants, "Thursday's Process," October 12, 1999, PHP 11:937–40.

69. Sullivan Robinson to Prathia Hall, October 8, 1999, PHP 11:456–57; Sullivan Robinson to Prathia Hall, November 4, 1999, PHP 11:465; LaGretta Bjorn to Dorothy Height, undated, PHP 11:462; Prathia Hall, Address to the National Council of Negro Women, December 4, 1999, PHP 23:1052–64.

70. Hall-Wynn, "Transcendent Power."

71. Ibid.; Hall, "God, Is There Any Difference?," PHP 22:1282–301.

72. Hall, "God, Is There Any Difference?"

73. Dyer, "Heeding the Call"; Hall, "Partnership in Ministry."

74. William Banks to Prathia Hall, September 11, 1984, PHP 1:700.

75. Hall interview by Ransby, 18.

76. Lerone Bennett Jr. to Prathia Hall Wynn, July 1, 1997, PHP 15:231–32; "Great Women Preachers," submitted by Prathia L. Hall to Editorial Board, EBONY, undated, PHP 15:221–30.

77. Prathia Hall to Leroy Bennett Jr., August 4, 1997, PHP 15:218–20.

78. Renita Weems to Prathia Hall, November 19, 1982, PHP 1:436; Cheryl Dudley to Prathia Hall, December 18, 1982, PHP 1:437.

79. Prathia Hall to Larry Waltz, Mary 24, 1986, PHP 14:604–6; Alan Berg to Rev. Larita Wilson, May 1, 1986, PHP 14:607; Prathia Hall to Larry Waltz, undated, PHP 14:608–10.

80. Miniard Culpepper to Praethia Hall-Winn [sic], October 26, 1989, PHP 1:237; Donnie Woods to Prathiaa [sic] Hall Wynn, September 6, 1991, PHP 1:207.

81. Judy Fentress to Prathia Hall Wynn, November 27, 1989, PHP 1:220; Jonathan Staples to Prathia Wynn, January 25, 1990, PHP 1:214; Prathia Hall Wynn to Jonathan Staples, February 3, 1990, PHP 1:212–14; Prathia Hall to Cain Hope Felder, October 6, 1989, PHP 1:255.

82. Miniard Culpepper memo to Cain Hope Felder, October 30, 1989, National Association of Black Seminarians, PHP 1:239.

83. Conference Program, PHP 11:447–48.

84. Daryl Ward to Davis-Putter Scholarship Fund, undated, PHP 7:250.

85. Prathia Hall to Maxine Beach, June 29, 1994, "Re: Update Regarding January 3 Memo," PHP 3:155–56.

86. Prathia Hall to Betty Shields, Marsha Foster-Boyd, Sally Carpenter, Sue Glash, Katie Paredes, Lisa Wolfe, Holly Longstreth, Carolyn Bohler, and Diane Pivarnik, December 15, 1992, "Update Since Our Women's Center Brunch in September," PHP 6:526.

87. MacLeod, *Word in Edgewise*.

88. Prathia Hall to President Leonard I. Sweet, Dean Darryl Ward, Professors Correll, Schrodt, and Proctor, undated, PHP 6:524; Prathia Hall to Betty Shields, Marsha Foster-Boyd, Sally Carpenter, Sue Glash, Katie Paredes, Lisa Wolfe, Holly Longstreth, Carolyn Bohler, and Diane Pivarnik, December 15, 1992, "Update Since our Women's Center Brunch in September," PHP 6:526.

89. Wright interview by Pace; Prathia Hall Wynn to Cheryl Townsend Gilkes, December 14, 1994, PHP 10:222; Prathia Hall Wynn to Susan Brooks Thistlethwaite, December 14, 1994, PHP 10:219; Prathia Hall Wynn to Jeremiah Wright, Decem-

ber 16, 1994, PHP 10:218; Prathia Hall Wynn to Provost Maxine Clarke Beach, January 12, 1995, PHP 10:226; Prathia Hall Wynn to UTS Doctor of Ministry Participants, December 16, 1994, PHP 10:231.

90. "Concerns and Questions Raised by Female Faculty and Administrative Staff," undated, PHP 7:430–31.

91. Frances Frazier to Rev. Prathia Wynn, March 3, 1994, PHP 11:647–50.

92. "'We Shall Not Be Moved': The Life and Times of the Student Non-violent Coordinating Committee, 1960–1966," April 14–16, 1988, Trinity College, Hartford, Conn., PHP 7:648–59.

93. Duminani Kumalo to Prathia Hall, May 19, 1989, PHP 7:024; "Churches Ask Boycott of Shell Oil Co," undated news clipping, PHP 7:025.

94. Harris Wofford, Chair of the Pennsylvania Democratic State Committee, to Clergy Concerned about South Africa, September 21, 1986, PHP 8:46; additional documents extend through PHP 8:48.

95. Louis S. Brown to Prathia Hall Wynn, August 30, 1994, PHP 11:657–60.

96. Invitation to 70th Birthday Celebration to Honor Jim Forman, October 3, 1998, PHP 14:313; Jim Forman 70th Birthday Celebration Committee, "70th Birthday Celebration of Civil Rights Activist Jim Forman," September 22, 1998, PHP 14:355–66. Jim Forman to Prathia Hall, October 14, 1998, PHP 14:316–17; "Jim Forman Celebrations 70th Birthday," *Washington Afro-American*, October 10, 1998, PHP 14:324–29; Bill Clinton to James Forman, October 2, 1998, PHP 14:330; Hamil Harris, "Celebrating a Birthday and the History of Civil Rights: Former Activists Reunite, Reminisce," *Washington Post*, October 4, 1998, PHP 14:331–42. Charles Sherrod to Prathia Hall, August 2001, PHP 7:343.

97. Blackside and the Faith Project, *This Far by Faith*"; Frazier Moore, "Exploring Role of the Sacred in the Lives of Black Americans," *Philadelphia Inquirer*, June 24, 2003.

98. "Black Church Advisory Committee Meeting," undated, PHP 13:172.

99. "The Ford Foundation's African American Church Program," undated, PHP 13:174; Lynn Huntley and Robert Franklin to Prathia Hall-Wynn, January 11, 1995, PHP 13:177–80.

100. Marian Wright Edelman to BCCC Advisory Board Members, "A September 28th Celebration of Self Help and a Special Evening of Hope from the Black Community Crusade for Children," August 4, 1995, PHP 6:603–5.

101. Marian Wright Edelman and Barbara Kelley-Sease to S. 10 Forum January 27–28 Participants, February 4, 1998, "Re: S. 10 The Violent and Repeat Juvenile Offender Act: You Made a Difference!," PHP 6:589; Kim Wade to Marian Wright Edelman, "Re: Update on S. 10, the Violent and Repeat Juvenile Offender Act," July 29, 1998, PHP 6:01; PHP 6:589–601.

102. Prathia Hall, personal notes from a conference call, with Fred Lofton, Otis Moss, and Prathia Hall, "Re: Collaboration Between CNBC and CDF on Black Church Initiatives for Children," February 16, 2000, PHP 11:940–45; Prathia Hall, "Omega B Church Dayton," PHP 11:946–48; Prathia Hall, untitled summary of this collaboration, undated, PHP 11:950–54.

103. Hall, untitled summary.

104. Hall, "CDF Black Community Crusade," PHP 6. Hall, "CDF Black Community Crusade."

105. Prathia Hall Wynn to Sullivan Robinson, Executive Director of the CNBC, September 23, 1999, PHP 6:365; Marian Wright Edelman and Prathia Hall to Advocate for Children, May 18, 1999, PHP 6:370; Prathia L. Hall to Sullivan Robinson, September 23, 1999, PHP 6:371; Prathia Hall to Barbara Kelley Duncan, March 15, 1999, PHP 11:959; Prathia Hall to Barbara Kelley Duncan, December 23, 1999, PHP 11:958.

106. Hall, untitled summary.

107. Hall, "CDF Black Community Crusade."

108. Hall, untitled summary; Hall, "CDF Black Community Crusade."

109. Hall, "Heritage," PHP 23:50–80.

110. Sullivan Robinson to Prathia Hall, October 8, 1999, PHP 11:456–57; Sullivan Robinson to Prathia Hall, November 4, 1999, PHP 11:465; LaGretta Bjorn to Dorothy Height, undated, PHP 11:462; Hall, "Heritage."

111. Hall, "Heritage."

112. Ibid.

113. Ibid.; Hall Wynn, "Theological/Educational Foundations," 18; Hall, "Heritage."

114. Prathia Hall, curriculum vitae, PHP. Among the other awards Hall won were these: Womanist Scholar Award, International Theological Center, 1999–2000; Davis-Putter Scholarship Fund, 1995; Ebony African American Achievement Award, Honorable Mention, 1994; American Baptist Churches, USA Ellen Cushing Scholar Award, 1985 and 1986; Black Doctoral Scholarship, Fund for Theological Education, 1983, 1984, 1993; Hawkins Memorial Award for Scholastic Excellence, 1982, Princeton Theological Seminary; Blizzard Memorial Award for Social Ministry, 1982, Princeton Theological Seminary; Jasow Preaching Award, 1981, Princeton Theological Seminary; Benjamin E. Mays Fellowship, 1981, Fund for Theological Education; Roosevelt Board of Education Service Award, 1976; International Theological Center Womanist Scholar Award and Visiting Professorship, 1999–2000.

115. Goldwyn, "Pastor Earns Acclaim as Lady." *Ebony*, "15 Greatest Black Preachers"; Kinnon, "15 Greatest Black Women Preachers."

Chapter 9. "One of the Founding Mothers of the New America"

1. Ron Goldwyn, "She Spreads Word about Donating," *Philadelphia Daily News*, June 7, 2001; Brown interview by Pace; Jeremiah Wright to Mother Ruby Johnson Hall, October 22, 2001, PHP 21:816–18.

2. At times, those involved in Hall's care had significant conflict with each other. This team was managing Hall's care across several state lines, and miscommunications, undiscussed assumptions, and differences of opinion occurred, particularly given how strongly each one cared for Hall. Almost all of those involved in her care expressed lament that DuBois was not more involved. Their correspondence often included the phrase "what a son should do," positively comparing themselves to DuBois and his apparent nonengagement with his mother's care. See Correspondence between LaGretta Bjorn, Echol Nix, and Evelyn Brooks Higginbotham, PHP 10:473–507.

3. Cheryl Townsend Gilkes was a reader on Prathia Hall's dissertation committee at Princeton Theological Seminary and remained her close, personal friend.

4. McDew interview by Pace.

5. DuBois's daughter was born during Hall's final illness. Hall was able to hold her granddaughter before she died.

6. Dorothy Hartsfield Adams, Daphne Waters, and Teresa Hall Darden, to "All Who Are Concerned," December 31, 2002, PHP 19:354–58.

7. Fry-Brown, *Can a Sistah Get a Little Help?*

8. Susan Newman to Michael Nickerson, April 21, 1997, PHP 4:108.

9. Otis Moss III to Prathia Hall, August 21, 1998, PHP 11:561.

10. Pamela June Anderson to Maxine Beach, April 22, 1997, PHP 4:112–13.

11. Bjorn interview by Pace. Because Bjorn had been a practicing lawyer before returning to seminary, she was more mature than many of her fellow students. Bjorn spoke of Hall the way Hall spoke of Ella Baker as a young woman in SNCC.

12. Fry-Brown interview by Davenport.

13. Vanessa Ward, quoted in Dale Huffman, "Powerful Speech a Pivotal One," *Dayton (OH) Daily News*, February 25, 2006.

14. Daryl Ward, letter (no addressee), March 7, 1990, PHP 3:282.

15. Davenport, "Dispatches from the Wilderness."

16. Thimas, "Prathia Hall."

17. Peter Paris to Maxine Beach, April 14, 1997, PHP 4:097.

18. Charles Adams to Maxine Beach, April 11, 1997, PHP 4:102.

19. Charles Adams to Harold Shapiro, November 8, 1988, PHP 5:024.

20. Nobeu Christensia to Prathia Hall, undated, PHP 7:466–67.

21. Ed Wheeler to Prathia Hall, October 10, 2001, PHP 23:218–19; Lewis interview by Pace; Walker interview by Pace; Dyson, "Freedom was Foremost."

22. Mariann Taylor Malone, "Profile of Rev. Prathia Hall-Wynn," Submitted to Dr. Samuel Dewitt Proctor's Leadership in the Black Church course, Princeton Theological Seminary, September 26, 1990, PHP 16:647–52.

23. Wright interview by Pace.

24. Preacely interview by Pace.

25. John F. Morrison, "Prathia Hall, Preacher, Theology Teacher," *Philadelphia Daily News*, August 19, 2002.

26. Prathia Hall, "Rekindling the Spirit," PHP 23:980–1018.

Appendix. Who Had the Dream?

1. Lewis, *Walking with the Wind*, 214, 221–22, 233.

2. See Hansen, *Dream*, and Sundquist, *King's Dream*. For rhetorical and oratorical analysis of King's speech, see Vail, "'Integrative' Rhetoric"; Miller, "Voice Merging and Self-Making"; Martha Solomon, "Covenanted Rights: The Metaphoric Matrix of 'I Have a Dream,'" 66–84, and John H. Patton, "'I Have a Dream': The Performance of Theology Fused with the Power of Orality," 104–26, in Calloway-Thomas and Lucaites, *Martin Luther King, Jr.*); and Al Weitzel, "King's 'I Have a Dream' Speech." A transcript of the full speech is available at https://www.archives.gov/files/press/exhibits/dream-speech.pdf.

3. Sundquist, *King's Dream*, 14.

4. Chatfield interview by Pace.

5. Claude Sitton, "2 Negro Churches Burned in Georgia: FBI Men Attacked: Robinson Visits Site," *New York Times*, September 10, 1962.

6. Rubin interview by Pace.

7. Though there are no written sources verifying that Hall used the phrase "I have a dream" in her prayer at the Mount Olive Baptist Church vigil, there is substantial oral history evidence from eyewitnesses that she originated the phrase "I have a dream." Three studies of King's sermons, discussed later in this appendix, mention Hall's potential involvement with the phrase due to oral history evidence. See my collection of oral history interviews on the subject, Prathia Hall Special Collections Project at Baylor University Institute for Oral History, Waco, Tex., which are the most extensive research on this idea to date.

8. Sitton, "2 Negro Churches Burned in Georgia."

9. Rubin interview by Pace.

10. Hall interview by Hansen.

11. Bernice Johnson Reagon comment to author, postpresentation discussion, "The Religious Leadership of African American Women," Association for the Study of African American Life and History, September 26–30, 2012, Pittsburgh, Pa.

12. Miller, "Voice Merging and Self-Making," 23–31, 24. Richard Lischer labeled

King's corpus of written material, including his dissertation, as plagiarized and most of his work as "derivative." Further, Lischer placed King fully within the Western intellectual tradition, explicitly stating that in so doing, King had left the African American intellectual tradition, to which he returned later in his career "with his horizons considerably widened" by the vocabulary and theological values of Western intellectualism. At the same time, Lischer placed King's preaching firmly within the African American tradition, particularly his use of allegory and typology and his delivery style. Because King was both African American and trained in the Western intellectual tradition, he was able to communicate prophetically with mainstream American society in language that mainstream white society could understand and appreciate. Lischer called this King's "gift of metaphor," which should be appreciated regardless of what we know about King's sources. See Lischer, *Preacher King*, 7, 10.

The question of King's cultural understanding of knowledge ownership has also raised significant questions about King's primary theological and preaching influences. King scholars such as David Garrow, Stephen Oates, and Taylor Branch have often described King as a product of his seminary education, emphasizing the Western theologians whose liberal Protestant ideas influenced him, namely, Reinhold Niebuhr, Paul Tillich, Walter Rauschenbusch, and Harry Emerson Fosdick, whom he read in graduate school. Those who cite liberal white Protestant influences typically find King guilty of plagiarizing. See Garrow, *Bearing the Cross*; Oates, *Let the Trumpet Sound*; and Branch, *America in the King Years*.

Clayborne Carson's work as editor of the Martin Luther King Jr. Papers, rejected traditional white interpretations of King's influences and work. If King was most deeply influenced by "the Great White Thinker," meaning Western white theologians, Carson argued, then so was the African American Civil Rights Movement. Carson argued for the origination of the Civil Rights Movement and its liberation impulses from within the African American community itself, a conclusion of the collective wisdom and spirituality of African Americans. Scholars like Carson typically do not blame King for plagiarism, even when he repeats others' words verbatim without citation. See M. L. King, *Papers of Martin Luther King, Jr.*, and Carson, *Autobiography of Martin Luther King Jr.*

Keith Miller's work acknowledged that King was influenced by liberal white preachers like Niebuhr, Tillich, and Rauschenbusch, but sided with Carson that African American folk preaching was ultimately the most influential for King. While in school, King learned to navigate intellectual print culture out of necessity, and that the ideas of Western White liberal Protestantism did shape his theology, but once graduated, he returned to his African American folk preaching roots. Particularly as King developed his preaching voice in southern African American churches, Miller argued that African American folk preaching remained the most formative influence on his preaching: "Resisting his professors' rules about language and many notions of the Great White Thinkers, King crafted highly imaginative, persuasive discourse through the folk procedures of voice merging and self-making" (123). See Miller, "Redefining Plagiarism," A60. See also Keith D. Miller, "The Roots of the Dream: The Papers of Martin Luther King, Jr.," *New York Times*, March 15, 1992, BR13.

13. Kenneth L. Smith and Ira G. Zepp suggested that King used personal pronouns while quoting biblical prophecy to parallel his role in the movement with biblical prophets. See Smith and Zepp, *Search for the Beloved Community*, and Vander Lei and Miller, "Martin Luther King, Jr.'s 'I Have a Dream' Speech." King quoted from Amos 5:24 and Isaiah 40:4–5.

14. Douglass, *Life and Writings*, 1:276–77. W. E. B. Du Bois, *Autobiography*, 422–23. Mays quoted by an anonymous reviewer during the review process. Brown quoted in *Atlanta Daily World*, June 9, 1948, 1; my thanks to an anonymous reviewer who pointed this out to me. Langston Hughes, "Let America Be America Again" (1935). Thurman, *Jesus and the Disinherited*, 21, 35. Lillian Smith, *Killers of the Dream*, 20.

15. Miller suggested that King's "dream" set piece emerged from the biblical language of "dream" and "vision" evident from his use of Amos and Isaiah. See Vander Lei and Miller, "Martin Luther King, Jr.'s 'I Have a Dream' Speech"; Miller, "Second Isaiah"; Vail, "'Integrative' Rhetoric," 51–78; and Miller, "Martin Luther King, Jr."

16. Hansen, *Dream*, 70. Lischer's homiletical study of King importantly distinguished King's sermons from his set pieces, which King "patched together in a bewildering number of combinations under a variety of sermon titles." While King did construct some of these set pieces, many were derived or borrowed; Lischer qualified this statement with a note that even when using borrowed material, King did make them his own. King's genius, according to Lischer, was not necessarily in his ability to compose phrases or sermons but in his ability to recognize pregnant phrases and piece them together into a sermon with captivating delivery, which Lischer credited to the legacy of oral tradition within the African American church. In other words, "His originality was an originality of effect, not composition." For more about King's formation, use of sources, and development as an orator, see Lischer, *Preacher King*, 8–9, 93–118.

17. King rarely used a manuscript or notes of any kind when speaking. Instead, his preaching and speaking relied heavily on the arrangement and adaptation of memorized set pieces and extemporaneous speech, rather than manuscripted text. King was required to submit a manuscript for the March on Washington because of the television broadcast. See Garrow, "King," 31.

18. The speech was originally titled for the "bad check" set piece but later changed

to "I Have a Dream" because of the overwhelming popularity of that section. King's opening reference to the Emancipation Proclamation was strikingly similar to President Kennedy's "Radio and Television Report to the American People on Civil Rights," June 11, 1963. Both began with references to the unfulfilled promises of Abraham Lincoln's Emancipation Proclamation. Mark Vail suggested that the three documents—the "Letter from Birmingham Jail," Kennedy's civil rights speech, and King's "I Have a Dream" speech—share a call and response relationship. See Vail, "'Integrative' Rhetoric," 60.

19. M. L. King, "I Have a Dream," in Hansen, *Dream*, 75–76.

20. Note the identical phrasing between King's speech and the Fellowship House campaign to promote King's methods in 1962. See chapter 1.

21. M. L. King, "I Have a Dream," 75–76.

22. Garrow, "King," 31, 35; Carson, ed., *Autobiography of Martin Luther King, Jr.*, 223.

23. David Garrow echoed Drew Hansen's argument that King's speech up until this point had been good but unremarkable; when King switched to his extemporaneous preacher voice with "I have a dream," America was able to see his preaching power. Garrow, "King," 35; Hansen, *Dream*.

24. Especially given the accusations abetted by J. Edgar Hoover's FBI that King was a Communist, and given the intentional setting of his speech to connect 1963 with the 1863 Emancipation Proclamation, King connected his message of civil rights with the founding principles of the United States. This shrewd tactic was certainly reminiscent of Frederick Douglass and W. E. B. Du Bois, who frequently did the same. See Vander Lei and Miller, "Martin Luther King, Jr.'s 'I Have a Dream' Speech," 91–93; Sundquist, *King's Dream*, 49, 184–86.

25. M. L. King, "I Have a Dream," 81.

26. Ibid., 75, 85.

27. Thurman, *Jesus and the Disinherited*, 50–51.

28. King conflated Lincoln's Gettysburg Address and the Emancipation Proclamation in his introduction: "Fivescore years ago, a great American, in whose symbolic shadow we stand today, signed the Emancipation Proclamation." For a thematic biography of King as a radical, see Sitkoff, *King*.

29. For more detail on the connections King made between Abraham Lincoln and the Civil Rights Movement, see Sundquist, *King's Dream*, especially the "Lincoln's Shadow" chapter.

30. James Bevel was a leading student activist in SNCC who later transitioned into SCLC leadership, but his personal and legal difficulties later in life have called into question his veracity.

31. Lischer, *Preacher King*, 93.

32. Ibid., 93, 287; Richard Lischer, e-mail to author, March 16, 2009.

33. Hansen, *Dream*, 249–50.

34. Sundquist, *King's Dream*, 22; Fritts, "Most Famous American Sermon.". Lischer's study of King's Dream speech acknowledged multiple sources behind King's "I Have a Dream" set piece. Lischer acknowledges Hall as likely one of these sources, in addition to the biblical connection of dreams with prophecy. Lischer, *Preacher King*, 9.

35. Zellner interview by Pace.

36. Ibid.

37. Lewis interview by Pace.

38. Sherrod interview by Pace.

39. Richardson interview by Pace; Hampton et al., *Eyes on the Prize*; June Cross, Dante J. James, Lorraine Toussaint, Lulie Haddad, Alice Markowitz, Valerie Linson, Leslie D. Farrell, and W. Noland Walker, 2003. *This Far by Faith: African American Spiritual Journeys* (Boston: WGBH).

40. Rubin interview by Pace.

41. Johnson, "Student's Surprising Discovery"; M. L. King, "Negro and the Constitution."

42. Euchner, *Nobody Turn Me Around*, 5–6.

43. King gave a sermon titled "The Negro and the American Dream" in September 1960 in Charlotte, North Carolina, in which he compared America to a dream since its promises for equality were not yet reality. However, the use of dream was more of an unfulfilled hope, used in the biblical prophetic sense, than the repetitious use of the word in the 1963 "I Have a Dream" speech. For more, see Sundquist, *King's Dream*, 27.

44. Sundquist, *King's Dream*, 22.

45. Hansen, *Dream*, 114–15.

46. Ibid., 109–10, 114–15.

47. Ibid., 115–16, 249–51.

48. Ibid., 116.

49. King certainly did make something of Hall's phrase. Most traditionally, scholars like Mark Vail have noted the integrative effect of the speech by suggesting "two pivotal rhetorical events" leading up to the March: because of King's notoriety and the momentum of success in Birmingham, combined with Kennedy's sanction of the March on Washington, King's sermon framing the Civil Rights Movement as protection of core American values was an instant success. Moreover, the march was well-attended and had a "friendly and easygoing tone," which contributed to the success of its speakers' messages. Vail has also suggested that the close link between the "Letter from Birmingham Jail" and "I Have a Dream" evidenced his argument for

the integrative rhetoric as key to the success of "I Have a Dream." Strictly as text, the Birmingham letter "lacked the potency and power that only King's orality could supply" (59). The March on Washington gave King a platform to voice the rhetoric established by the Birmingham letter, aided by the momentum of national attention from Birmingham and support from the Kennedy administration.

50. Malcolm X, in his response to the March on Washington, independently echoed the dichotomy Hall coined the phrase to transcend: "Yes, I was there. I observed that circus. Who ever heard of angry revolutionists all harmonizing 'We Shall Overcome... Suum Day...' while tripping and swaying along arm-in-arm with the very people they were supposed to be angrily revolting against? Who ever heard of angry revolutionists swinging their bare feet together with their oppressor in lily-pad park pools, with gospels and guitars *and 'I Have A Dream' speeches? And the black masses in America were—and still are—having a nightmare*" (emphasis added). Malcolm X and Haley, *Autobiography of Malcolm X*, 281.

51. Hall interview by Hansen.

52. Ibid.

53. Ibid.; Dyson, *I May Not Get There*, 143, 280.

54. Noonan interview by Pace; Higginbotham interview by Pace; Zellner interview by Pace; Nix interview by Pace.

55. Bjorn interview with Pace.

56. Evelyn Brooks Higginbotham is chair of the Department of African and African American Studies at Harvard University and author of *Righteous Discontent*, for which Prathia Hall's dissertation functions as a sequel.

57. Higginbotham interview by Pace.

58. Noonan interview by Pace.

59. Hansen, *Dream*, 250.

60. Hall interview by Hansen.

BIBLIOGRAPHY

Primary Sources

ARCHIVAL COLLECTIONS

Papers of the American Friends Service Committee. American Friends Service Committee. Philadelphia, Pa.

National Archives File 44-HQ-20425. Federal Bureau of Investigation. National Archives and Records Administration. Washington, D.C.

Fellowship House Papers. Temple University Libraries Urban Archives Special Collections, Philadelphia, Pa.

Film and Media Archive. Washington University, St. Louis, Mo.

Papers of the Student Nonviolent Coordinating Committee, 1959–72. Ann Arbor, Mich.: University Microfilms, 1994. Microfilm. Abbreviated in the notes as SNCC Papers.

Prathia Hall Papers. In Prathia Hall Special Collection. Baylor University Institute for Oral History, Waco, Tex. Abbreviated in notes and bibliography as BU-PHP.

Prathia Hall Papers. In the private collection of LaGretta Bjorn. Ewing, N.J. Abbreviated in notes and bibliography as PHP (followed by box number).

Student Record File—Prathia Hall. Princeton Theological Seminary.

PRATHIA HALL AND PRATHIA HALL WYNN

Multiple versions in multiple media exist of some works, notably Hall's sermons. The notes contain references to additional versions not listed in this bibliography.

"Abolitionist Religion." UTS Doctoral Studies. November 9, 1994. PHP, box 17.

[Wynn, Prathia.] "Accepting the Call to Leadership." *American Baptist*, (July–August 1987): 22, 24–25.

"Additional Pages." UTS Doctoral Studies. November 9, 1994. PHP, box 17.

"Addressing 'The Theological Scandal of Sexism.'" Women in Ministry Panel, *American Baptist* (July/August 1987), PHP 20:4–32, 16.

"The African American Church at the Crossroad: Facing the Moral Challenge of Gender." Undated. PHP.

"The African American Faith/Freedom Struggle: Historical Dimensions and Current Problems: The Power of Song." Senior Thesis Project. Undated. PHP, box 1.

"The African American Religious Experience as Contemporary Resource for a Community in Crisis." Paper for Sociology of Religion Seminar by Richard Fenn at Princeton Theological Seminary. Undated. PHP 19:360–497.

"Baccalaureate Address." Stanford University. June 13, 1992. PHP 24:174–95.

"Baccalaureate Address." Vassar College. May 23, 1998. PHP 23:1065–78.

"Between the Wilderness and a Cliff." In *Preaching with Sacred Fire: An Anthology of African American Sermons, 1750 to the Present.* Edited by Martha Simmons and Frank A. Thomas. New York: W. W. Norton, 2010: 687–95.

"Between the Wilderness and a Cliff." Undated transcript. PHP.

"Beyond Eden." 1989. PHP.

"The Bible in the African American Context." In *Called to One Hope—The Gospel in Diverse Cultures*, edited by Christopher Durasingh, 158–65. Geneva: World Council of Churches Press, 1996.

"Bloody Sunday." In *Hands on the Freedom Faith: Personal Accounts by Women in SNCC*, edited by Faith Holsaert, Martha Prescod Norman Noonan, Judy Richardson, Betty Garman Robinson, Jean Smith Young, and Dorothy M. Zellner, 470–73. Chicago: University of Illinois, 2010.

"Broken by the Blessed." 1997. Audio tape. PHP.

"Building between Heritage and Hope." Undated. PHP, box 23.

"Burden Bent." Undated. PHP 24:565–88.

"Called but Not Chosen Review of Righteous Discontent: The Women's Movement in the Black Baptist Church, 1880–1920." *Women's Review of Books* 11, no. 12 (September 1994): 31–32.

"Captivity's Capture." Freedom Night of the 33rd Annual Session of the Progressive National Baptist Convention. Memphis, Tenn. August 12, 1994. PHP, box 10.

"Captivity's Capture." Sermon preached at Omega Baptist Church, Dayton, Ohio. Undated. Audio tape. PHP.

"Captivity Is a Lie." *Other Side* 33, no. 3 (May–June 1997): 44–47, 54.

"CDF Black Community Crusade for Children Outreach in the African American Religious Community." PHP, box 6.

"The Challenge of True Kinship." In *What Does It Mean to Be Black and Christian?: Pulpit, Pew, and Academy in Dialogue*, edited by Forrest E. Harris Sr., 111–24. Nashville: Townsend Press, 1995.

"The Challenge of True Kinship: Sisters and Brothers in Church and Community." PHP, box 10.

"The Child as Prophet, Jeremiah 1." Undated. PHP, box 18.

"Children: A Suffering Sister, Frantic Father, Dying Daughter: Encounters with Jesus." Sermon preached at Third Annual Center for Congregations and Family

Ministries Conference. Audio recording. Louisville Presbyterian Seminary. Louisville, Ky. 1999.

"The Church at the Crossroad." PHP.

"Church under Construction." Grace Church. September 22, 1988. PHP.

"Convergence and Crisis: The Impact of Racism and Sexism on the African American Community." Undated. PHP.

"Crippled by a Spirit." Undated. PHP 22:2100–36.

"Deliverance for the Captives." Sermon at Interdenominational Theological Center, Atlanta, Ga. October 18, 2001. PHP 11:410–28.

"Dialogue on Black Theology." Hampton University 78th Ministers Conference. 1992. PHP 24:199–215.

"Dilemma." Undated. PHP 1:045.

"Encountering the Text." In *Power in the Pulpit: How America's Most Effective Black Preachers Prepare their Sermons*, edited by Cleophus J. Larue, 59–66. Louisville, Ky.: Westminster John Knox Press, 2002.

"Encounters with Jesus from Dying to Life." In *Power in the Pulpit: How America's Most Effective Black Preachers Prepare Their Sermons*, edited by Cleophus J. Larue, 67–74. Louisville, Ky.: Westminster John Knox Press, 2002.

"Encounters with Jesus from Dying to Life, Mark 5:21–34." Undated. PHP 22:1964–74 and PHP 19:551–86.

"Evaluating, Reviving, Revisioning the Meaning of the African American Church." Undated. Vanderbilt Divinity School. PHP, box 24..

"Faith and Freedom—Common and Constant Struggle." Master's thesis, Princeton Theological Seminary. May 1, 1982. PHP, box 1.

"Foreword." In *A Costly Obedience: Sermons by Women of Steadfast Spirit*, edited by Elizabeth Smith Bellinger, ix–x. Valley Forge, Pa.: Judson, 1995.

"Foreword." In *Those Preachin' Women: Sermons by Black Women Preachers*, edited by Ella Pearson Mitchell, 9–10. Valley Forge, Pa.: Judson, 1985.

"Freedom-Faith." In *Hands on the Freedom Faith: Personal Accounts by Women in SNCC*, edited by Faith Holsaert, Martha Prescod Norman Noonan, Judy Richardson, Betty Garman Robinson, Jean Smith Young, and Dorothy M. Zellner, 172–81. Chicago: University of Illinois, 2010.

"Garden of Eden: A Mission of Discovery." Undated. PHP 24:427–56.

"God, Is There Any Difference between the Million Man March and the CNBC Conference?" Undated. PHP, box 22.

"Heritage, The Primary Asset of the Black Church and the African American Community: Implications and Imperatives for the 21st Century." Congress of National Black Churches. Los Angeles, Calif. December 8, 1999. PHP, box 23.

"In Search of a Society Where Freedom Rings and Justice Reigns: The Martin Luther King Model." Keynote Address for Martin Luther King Jr. Day Celebration. Boston University. 2000. PHP, box 19.

"A Journey with Jesus." Sermon preached at Trinity United Church of Christ. May 15, 1990. Chicago, Illinois. Audio tape.

"Keynote Address." A Celebration of the Civil Rights Revolution. April 29, 1998. John F. Kennedy Library. PHP 7.

"A Letter to the Church in Tough Times." Undated. PHP, box 23.

"Music from the Rubbish Heap." Undated. PHP, box 23.

"A Nightmare in Broad Daylight." Sermon preached at Allen Temple Baptist Church. Oakland, Calif. March 29, 1998. Audio tape. PHP.

"An Outrageous Assertion." Undated transcript. PHP.

"Partnership in Ministry: Christian Ethics Then Flows from Who We Are!" Undated. PHP 23:746–812.

"Power over Power." Undated. PHP box 16.

"Preaching a Liberating Word to a Dying World." Urban Outreach. October 3, 1996. PHP 14:95–118.

"The Proclaimer, the Proclaimed, and the Proclamation." Undated. Duke University School of Divinity. osc>php 23:1666–703.

"The Religious and Social Consciousness of African American Baptist Women." PhD diss., Princeton Theological Seminary, 1997. Ann Arbor, Mich.: UMI.

"Rekindling the Spirit." Alex Haley Farm. March 21, 1999. PHP, box 23.

"Theological/Educational Foundations for the Black Church's Ministry to Families." December 7, 1984. PHP 1:905–26.

"Toward a New Starting Point." *Women's Review of Books* (1991): 25–26.

"Transcendent Power: A Black Woman's Perspective on the Million Man March." *Sojourners*, January–February 1996, 23.

"What Does It Mean to Be Black and Christian?" In *A Call to National Dialogue: The Challenge of a Black Theology to the African American Church*, 14–16. Nashville, Tenn.: Kelly Miller Smith Institute on African American Church Studies, 1992.

"When Jesus Tells Her Story." Undated. Delivered to American Baptist Women in Ministry. PHP 23:1198–244.

"When the Hurts Do Not Heal." In *Those Preaching Women: More Sermons by Black Women*, vol. 2, edited by Ella Pearson Mitchell, 95–102. Valley Forge, Pa.: Judson Press, 1985.

"When the Hurts Do Not Heal." Sermon preached at Hartford Memorial Baptist Church. March 22, 1987. Detroit, Mich. Audio tape. PHP.

"When the Hurts Do Not Heal." Sermon preached at Trinity United Church of Christ. May 21, 1989. Chicago, Ill. Audio tape.

"Womanist Moral Leadership and Ecclesial Integrity, or, The Silencing of Women and the Crisis of Morality in the Church." Womanist Consultation of the Womanist Approaches to Religion and Social Group at the American Academy of Religion, November 21, 1997. PHP.

"Women in Ministry." Hampton University Ministers' Conference. June 5, 1984. PHP, box 24.

"Working on the Building." 16th Annual B. Moses James Colloquium on African American Religion. 1990. PHP, box 23.

"The World in Whose Hands." Undated draft. PHP 23:718–42.

OTHER PRIMARY SOURCES

Blackside and the Faith Project. *This Far by Faith*. Episode 4, "Freedom Faith." Directed by Alice Markowitz, Blackside Inc., 2002.

Braden, Anne. "The Images Are Broken: Students Challenge Rural Georgia." *Southern Patriot* 20, no. 10 (December 1962).

Carson, Clayborne. *The Student Voice 1960–1965: Periodical of the Student Nonviolent Coordinating Committee*. Westport, Conn.: Meckler, 1990.

Curry, Constance, Joan C. Browning, Dorothy Dawson Burlage, Penny Patch, Theresa Del Pozzo, Sue Thrasher, Elaine DeLott Baker, Emmie Schrader Adams, and Casey Hayden. *Deep in Our Hearts: Nine White Women in the Freedom Movement*. Athens: University of Georgia Press, 2000.

DeLissovoy, Peter, ed. *The Great Pool Jump and Other Stories from the Civil Rights Movement in Southwest Georgia*. Lancaster, N.H.: You Are Perfect Press, 2010.

Douglass, Frederick. *The Life and Writings of Frederick Douglass*. Edited by Philip S. Foner. 5 vols. New York: International, 1950.

Du Bois, W. E. B. *The Autobiography of W. E. B. DuBois: A Soliloquy on Viewing My Life from the Last Decade of Its First Century*. New York: International, 1986.

Forman, James. *The Making of Black Revolutionaries*. Seattle: University of Washington Press, 1997.

Greenberg, Cheryl Lynn, ed. *A Circle of Trust: Remembering SNCC*. New Brunswick, N.J.: Rutgers University Press, 1998.

Holsaert, Faith, Martha Prescod Norman Noonan, Judy Richardson, Betty Garman Robinson, Jean Smith Young, and Dorothy M. Zellner, eds. *Hands on the Freedom Plow: Personal Accounts by Women in SNCC*. Chicago: University of Illinois, 2010.

Kennedy, John F. "Radio and Television Report to the American People on Civil Rights [June 11, 1963]." *Public Papers of the President of the United States, 1963*. Washington, D.C.: U.S. Government Printing Office, 1964.

King, Martin Luther, Jr. "The Negro and the Constitution." *Cornelian* (1944). http://

mlk-kpp01.stanford.edu/index.php/kingpapers/article/volume_i_april_1944/. Accessed January 21, 2013.

———. *The Papers of Martin Luther King, Jr.* 7 vols. Edited by Clayborne Carson, Stewart Burns, Susan Carson, Adrienne Clay, Peter Holloran, Ralph E. Luker, Dana Powell, Virginia Shadron, Penny A. Russell, and Kieran Taylor. Berkeley: University of California Press, 1994–2007.

———. *Stride towards Freedom: The Montgomery Story.* New York: Harper and Row, 1958.

King, Mary. *Freedom Song: A Personal Story of the 1960s Civil Rights Movement.* New York: Quill, 1987.

Lewis, John. *Walking with the Wind: A Memoir of the Movement.* New York: Mariner, 1990.

Moody, Anne. *Coming of Age in Mississippi: The Classic Autobiography of Growing Up Poor and Black in the Rural South.* New York: Dell, 1992.

United States District Court for the Northern District of Georgia, Atlanta Division. Criminal Docket, Case 23886. *The State of Georgia vs. Prathia Laura Ann Hall.* United States District Court for the Northern District of Georgia, Atlanta, Ga.

Philadelphia High School for Girls. *Milestone: Philadelphia High School for Girls.* 1958.

Princeton Theological Seminary. Prathia Hall—Student Record File. Princeton Theological Seminary. Trenton, N.J.

Oral History Sources

Barrett, Joyce. Interview by Courtney Pace. June 12, 2012. Compact disc. BU-PHP.

Bjorn, LaGretta. Interview by Courtney Pace. June 19, 2012, in Philadelphia, Pa. Compact disc. BU-PHP.

Bond, Julian. Interview by Courtney Pace. May 3, 2010. Compact disc. BU-PHP.

Brown, Presttonia Davis. Interview by Courtney Pace. June 20, 2012, in Philadelphia, Pa. Compact disc. BU-PHP.

Chatfield, Jack. Interview by Courtney Pace. June 3, 2011, in Albany, Ga. Compact disc. BU-PHP.

Churchville, John. Interview by Courtney Pace. February 14, 2011. Compact disc. BU-PHP.

Darden, JaiOliver. Interview by Courtney Pace. June, 2012, in Philadelphia, Pa.

Daniels, Carolyn. Interview by Courtney Pace. May 24, 2010, in Atlanta, Ga. Compact disc. BU-PHP.

DeLissovoy, Peter. Interview by Courtney Pace. April 16, 2010, in Raleigh, N.C. Compact disc. BU-PHP.

Fry-Brown, Teresa. Interview by Jessica Davenport. March 31, 2010. http://prathiasdaughters.wordpress.com/2010/07/22/remembering-rev-prathia-an-interview-with-rev-dr-teresa-fry-brown/. Accessed October 10, 2013.
Gilkes, Cheryl Townsend. Interview by Courtney Pace. April 2012.
Goodman, Janice. Interview by Courtney Pace. April 16, 2010, in Raleigh, N.C.
Hall, Prathia. Interview by Donna Allen. November 18, 1997. Cited in Allen, "Toward a Womanist Homiletic," 2005.
——. Interview by Drew Hansen. November 15, 2001. Private documents of Drew Hansen.
——. Interview by Vincent Harding. June 25, 1997. "Interview with Prathia Hall." Ghandi-Hamer-King Center. Washington, D.C.
——. Interview by Lalia Kiburi. "Professor Belinda Robnett's Research." November 9, 1992. PHP.
——. Interview by Joy Bennett Kinnon. "Live Well—Wear Your Own Shoes." *Ebony*, November 2002.
——. Interview by Richard Lischer. Undated. Cited in Lischer, *Preacher King*, 1995.
——. Interview by Sheila Michaels. February 25, 1999. Film and Media Archive.
——. Interview by Barbara Ransby. June 25, 1997. PHP.
——. Interview by Meredith Woods, October 4, 1999. Film and Media Archive.
Harris, Don. Interview by Courtney Pace. April 16, 2010, in Raleigh, N.C. Compact disc. BU-PHP.
Higginbotham, Evelyn Brooks. Interview by Courtney Pace. March 21, 2012. Compact disc. BU-PHP.
Holsaert, Faith. Interview by Courtney Pace. May 19, 2010. Compact disc. BU-PHP.
King, Mary. Interview by Courtney Pace. April 15, 2010, in Raleigh, N.C. Compact disc. BU-PHP.
Kunstler, Karen. Interview by Courtney Pace. April 16, 2010, in Raleigh, N.C.
Lewis, John. Interview by Courtney Pace. August 11, 2009, in Atlanta, Ga. Compact disc. BU-PHP.
Lyon, Danny. Interview by Courtney Pace. April 16, 2010, in Raleigh, N.C.
McDew, Chuck. Interview by Courtney Pace. June 3, 2011, in Albany, Ga. Compact disc. BU-PHP.
McMillian, Henri. Interview by Courtney Pace. May 4, 2016.
Nix, Echol. Interview by Courtney Pace. March 21, 2012. BU-PHP.
Noonan, Martha Prescod Norman. Interview by Courtney Pace. June 3, 2011, in Albany, Ga. Compact disc. BU-PHP.
Paris, Peter. Interview by Courtney Pace. 2009.
Patch, Penny. Interview by Courtney Pace. April 16, 2010, in Raleigh, N.C. Compact disc. BU-PHP.

Penney, Marjorie. Interview by Rosa King Zimmerman. July 20, 1976. West Chester State College Oral History Program. Fellowship House Papers, acc. 723:5.
Perdew, John. June 3, 2011, in Albany, Ga. Compact disc. BU-PHP.
Preacely, Peggy Dammond. Interview by Courtney Pace. April 16, 2010, in Raleigh, N.C. Compact disc. BU-PHP.
Richardson, Judy. Interview by Courtney Pace. June 25, 1997. Compact disc. BU-PHP.
Robinson, Betty Garman. Interview by Courtney Pace. May 4, 2010. Compact disc. BU-PHP.
Romily, Constancia Dinky. Interview by Courtney Pace. January 30, 2017.
Rubin, Larry. Interview by Courtney Pace. November 18, 2010. Compact disc. BU-PHP.
Sherrod, Charles. Interview by Courtney Pace. April 16, 2010, in Raleigh, N.C. Compact disc. BU-PHP.
Six-Means, Horace, Sr. Interview by Courtney Pace. January 28, 2010.
Smith, Frank. Interview by Courtney Pace. May 18, 2010.
Tuttle, Elbert P. Interview by Cliff Kuhn. April 10, 1992. Georgia Government Documentation Project. Georgia State University.
Walker, Wyatt Tee. Interview by Courtney Pace. May 1, 2012. Compact disc. BU-PHP.
Ward, Daryl. Interview by Courtney Pace. June 19, 2012.
Ward, Vanessa. Interview by Courtney Pace. June 19, 2012.
Weems, Renita. Interview by Courtney Pace. May 10, 2012.
Wright, Jeremiah. Interview by Courtney Pace. April 3, 2012. Compact disc. BU-PHP.
Wynn, DuBois. Interview by Courtney Pace. June 21, 2012.
Zellner, Bob. Interview by Courtney Pace. April 15, 2011, in Raleigh, N.C. Compact disc. BU-PHP.

Secondary Sources

Allen, Donna. "Toward a Womanist Homiletic: Katie Cannon, Alice Walker, and Emancipatory Proclamation." Ph.D. diss., Vanderbilt University, 2005.
Arsenault, Ray. *Freedom Riders: 1961 and the Struggle for Racial Justice*. New York: Oxford University Press, 2006.
Branch, Taylor. *America in the King Years, 1954–1968*. 3 vols. New York: Simon and Schuster, 1988–2006.
Brooks, Maegan Parker. *A Voice That Could Stir an Army: Fannie Lou Hamer and the Rhetoric of the Black Freedom Movement*. Jackson: University of Mississippi, 2014.

Brown-Nagin, Tomiko. *Courage to Dissent: Atlanta and the Long History of the Civil Rights Movement*. New York: Oxford University Press, 2011.

Calloway-Thomas, Carolyn, and John Louis Lucaites, eds. *Martin Luther King, Jr., and the Sermonic Power of Public Discourse*. Tuscaloosa: University of Alabama Press, 1993.

Cannon, Katie G. *Black Womanist Ethics*. Atlanta: Scholars Press, 1988.

———. *Katie's Canon: Womanism and the Soul of the Black Community*. New York: Continuum, 1997.

Carawan, Guy, and Candie Carawan. *Sing for Freedom: The Story of the Civil Rights Movement through Its Songs*. Montgomery, Ala.: New South Books, 2007.

Carson, Clayborne, ed. *The Autobiography of Martin Luther King, Jr*. New York: Warner Books, 1998.

———. *In Struggle: SNCC and the Black Awakening of the 1960s*. Cambridge: Harvard University Press, 1995.

Chappell, David. *Inside Agitators: White Southerners in the Civil Rights Movement*. Baltimore: Johns Hopkins University Press, 1994.

Chestnut, J. L., Jr., and Julia Cass. *Black in Selma: The Uncommon Life of J. L. Chestnut, Jr*. New York: Farrar, Straus and Giroux, 1990.

Coleman, Monica A. *Making a Way Out of No Way: A Womanist Theology*. Minneapolis: Fortress Press, 2008.

Cooper, Brittney. *Beyond Respectability: The Intellectual Thought of Race Women*. Champaign: University of Illinois Press, 2017.

Crawford, Vicki L., Jacqueline Anne Rouse, and Barbara Woods. *Women in the Civil Rights Movement: Trailblazers and Torchbearers, 1941–1965*. Bloomington: Indiana University Press, 1990.

Crenshaw, Kimberlé Williams. "Mapping the Margins: Intersectionality, Identity Politics, and Violence against Women of Color." *Stanford Law Review* 43, no. 6 (July 1991): 1241–99.

Crosby, Emilye, ed. *Civil Rights History from the Ground Up: Local Struggles, a National Movement*. Athens: University of Georgia Press, 2011.

Curry, Connie. *Silver Rights*. Chapel Hill, N.C.: Algonquin Books, 1995.

Davenport, Jessica. "Dispatches from the Wilderness: Welcome to Prathia's Daughters." July 21, 2010. http://prathiasdaughters.wordpress.com/2010/07/21/dispatches-from-the-wilderness-welcome-to-prathias-daughters/. Accessed January 16, 2014.

Dyson, Michael Eric. *I May Not Get There with You: The True Martin Luther King, Jr*. New York: Free Press, 2000.

Ebony. "The 15 Greatest Black Preachers." *Ebony*, November 1997, 156.

Euchner, Charles. *Nobody Turn Me Around: A People's History of the 1963 March on Washington*. Boston: Beacon, 2010.

———. *Soon We Will Not Cry: The Liberation of Ruby Doris Smith Robinson*. Lanham, Md.: Rowman and Littlefield, 1998.

Frederick, Marla F. *Between Sundays: Black Women and Everyday Struggles of Faith*. Berkeley: University of California Press, 2003.

Fritts, Roger. "The Most Famous American Sermon of the 20th Century." Sermon given at Cedar Lane Unitarian Universalist Church. Bethesda, Md. January 13, 2002. http://www.cedarlane.org (dead). Accessed September 29, 2008.

Fry-Brown, Teresa. *Can a Sistah Get a Little Help? Encouragement for Black Women in Ministry*. Boston: Pilgrim Press, 2008.

Gafney, Wilda C. *Womanist Midrash: A Reintroduction to the Women of the Torah and the Throne*. Louisville, Ky.: Westminster John Knox Press, 2017.

Garrow, David. *Bearing the Cross: Martin Luther King, Jr., and the Southern Christian Leadership Conference*. New York: William Morrow, 1986.

———. "King: The Man, the March, the Dream." *American History* (2003): 26–35.

Gilkes, Cheryl Townsend. *If It Wasn't for the Women: Black Women's Experience and Womanist Culture in Church and Community*. Maryknoll, N.Y.: Orbis Books, 2001.

Hampton, Henry, Judith Vecchione, Steve Fayer, Orlando Bagwell, Callie Crossley, James A. DeVinney, and Madison Davis Lucy. *Eyes on the Prize*. Alexandria, Va.: PBS Video, 2006.

Hansen, Drew D. *The Dream: Martin Luther King, Jr., and the Speech that Inspired a Nation*. New York: Harper Collins, 2003.

Harding, Vincent. *Hope and History: Why We Must Share the Story of the Movement*. Maryknoll, N.Y.: Orbis Books, 1999.

Haskins, Jim, and Kathleen Benson. *Black Stars: African American Religious Leaders*. San Francisco: John Wiley and Sons, 2008.

Hayes, Diana L. *Hagar's Daughters: Womanist Ways of Being in the World*. New York: Paulist Press, 1995.

Hedgeman, Anna Arnold. *The Gift of Chaos: Decades of American Discontent*. New York: Oxford University Press, 1977.

Higginbotham, Evelyn Brooks. *Righteous Discontent: The Women's Movement in the Black Baptist Church, 1880–1920*. Cambridge: Harvard University Press, 1994.

Hogan, Wesley. *Many Minds, One Heart: SNCC's Dream for a New America*. Chapel Hill: University of North Carolina Press, 2007.

Hughes, Langston. "Let America Be America Again." In *The Collected Poems of Langston Hughes*, edited by Arnold Rampersand and David Roessel, 189. New York: Knopf, 1996.

Interdenominational Theological Center. "WPS Scholars—Dr. Prathia Hall." http://www.itc.edu/pages/wsp/WSPDrHall.htm. Accessed September 29, 2008.

Johnson, Lacey. "A Student's Surprising Discovery about Martin Luther King Jr.'s Dream for America." *Chronicle of Higher Education* 58, no. 8 (2011): A25.

Kinnon, Joy Bennett. "15 Greatest Black Women Preachers." *Ebony*, November 1997, 102.

———. "Live Well—Wear Your Own Shoes." Sisterspeak interview. *Ebony*, November 2002.

Lee, Chana Kai. *For Freedom's Sake: The Life of Fannie Lou Hamer*. Chicago: University of Illinois Press, 2000.

Lerner, Girda. *The Creation of Patriarchy*. New York: Oxford University Press, 1987.

Ling, Peter, and Sharon Monteith, eds. *Gender and the Civil Rights Movement*. New Brunswick, N.J.: Rutgers University Press, 2004.

Lischer, Richard. *The Preacher King: Martin Luther King, Jr., and the Word that Moved America*. New York: Oxford University Press, 1995.

MacLeod, Heather. *A Word in Edgewise*. [Halifax]: Women and Video Exploration, 1986. Videocassette.

Malcolm X and Alex Haley. *The Autobiography of Malcolm X*. New York: Ballantine Books, 1964.

Mason, Herman, Jr. *Politics: Civil Rights, and Law in Black Atlanta, 1870–1970*. Charleston, S.C.: Arcadia, 2000.

McGuire, Danielle L. *At the Dark End of the Street: Black Women, Rape, and Resistance—A New History of the Civil Rights Movement from Rosa Parks to the Rise of Black Power*. New York: Alfred A. Knopf, 2010.

Miller, Keith D. "Martin Luther King, Jr., and the Black Folk Pulpit." *Journal of American History* 78 (1991): 120–23.

———. "Redefining Plagiarism: Martin Luther King's Use of an Oral Tradition." *Chronicle of Higher Education*, January 20, 1993,: A60.

———. "The Roots of the Dream: The Papers of Martin Luther King, Jr." *New York Times*, March 15, 1992, BR13.

———. "Second Isaiah Lands in Washington, D.C.: Martin Luther King, Jr.'s 'I Have a Dream' as Biblical Narrative and Biblical Hermeneutic." *Rhetoric Review* 26, no. 4 (2007): 409.

———. "Voice Merging and Self-Making: The Epistemology of 'I Have a Dream.'" *Rhetoric Society Quarterly* 19 (1989): 23–31.

Mills, Kay. *This Little Light of Mine: The Life of Fannie Lou Hamer*. New York: Plume, 1993.

Mitchem, Stephanie Y. *Introducing Womanist Theology*. Maryknoll, N.Y.: Orbis Books, 2002.

Morris, Tiyi. *Womanpower Unlimited and the Black Freedom Struggle in Mississippi*. Athens: University of Georgia Press, 2015.

Oates, Stephen. *Let the Trumpet Sound: The Life of Martin Luther King, Jr.* New York: Harper Perennial, 1994.

Olson, Lynne. *Freedom's Daughters: The Unsung Heroes of the Civil Rights Movement, 1830–1970.* New York: Scribner, 2001.

Pace Lyons, Courtney. "Breaking through the Extra-Thick Stained Glass Ceiling: African American Baptist Women in Ministry." *Review and Expositor* 110, no. 2 (winter 2013): 77–92.

———. "Burning Columbia Avenue: Religious Undertones of the 1964 Philadelphia Race Riots." *Pennsylvania History: A Journal of Mid-Atlantic Studies* 77, no. 3 (2010): 324–48.

———. "'Freedom Faith': The Civil Rights Journey of Rev. Dr. Prathia Hall." PhD diss., Baylor University, 2014.

PBS. "Prathia Hall." *This Far by Faith*, PBS. http://www.pbs.org/thisfarbyfaith/people/prathia_hall.html. Accessed May 21, 2008.

Persons, Albert C. *Sex and Selma: The True Selma Story.* Birmingham, Ala.: Esco, 1965.

Powledge, Fred. *Free at Last? The Civil Rights Movement and the People Who Made It.* Boston: Little, Brown, 1991.

"Prathia's Daughters." http://www.prathiasdaughtersvoices.ning.com (dead). Accessed January 23, 2014.

Pronley, Matthew. "Waveland: Mississippi, November 1964: Death of SNCC, Birth of Radicalism." Thesis, University of Wisconsin, 2008.

Ransby, Barbara. *Ella Baker and The Black Freedom Movement: A Radical Democratic Vision.* Chapel Hill: University of North Carolina Press, 2003.

Riggs, Marcia. *Awake, Arise, and Act: A Womanist Call for Black Liberation.* Cleveland: Pilgrim Press, 1994.

———. *Can I Get a Witness? Prophetic Voices of African American Women: An Anthology.* Maryknoll, N.Y.: Orbis Books, 1997.

Roberts, Gene, and Hank Klibanoff. *The Race Beat: The Press, the Civil Rights Struggle, and the Awakening of a Nation.* New York: Alfred A. Knopf, 2007.

Robinson, Jo Ann Gibson. *The Montgomery Bus Boycott and the Women Who Started It.* Knoxville: University of Tennessee Press, 1990.

Robnett, Belinda. *How Long? How Long? African-American Women in the Struggle for Civil Rights.* New York: Oxford University Press, 1997.

Ross, Rosetta. *Witnessing and Testifying: Black Women, Religion, and Civil Rights.* Minneapolis: Fortress Press, 2003.

Seeger, Pete, and Bob Reiser. *Everybody Says Freedom.* New York: W. W. Norton, 1989.

"Shoofly Pye: The Bench." *Time*, April 17, 1964.

Sitkoff, Harvard. *King: Pilgrimage to the Mountaintop.* New York: Macmillan, 2009.

Smith, Lillian. *Killers of the Dream*. Rev. ed. 1961. Reprint New York: Norton, 1978.

Smith, Kenneth L., and Ira G. Zepp. *Search for the Beloved Community: The Thinking of Martin Luther King, Jr.* Lanham, Md.: University Press of America, 1986.

St. Clair, Raquel A. *Call and Consequences: A Womanist Reading of Mark*. Minneapolis: Fortress Press, 2008.

Sundquist, Eric. *King's Dream*. New Haven: Yale University Press, 2009.

Terrell, JoAnne Marie. *Power in the Blood? The Cross in the African American Experience*. Maryknoll, N.Y.: Orbis Books, 1998.

Thimas, Natasha. "Prathia Hall." http://prezi.com/dfbaxhee4a6h/prathia-hall/. Accessed October 10, 2013.

Thurman, Howard. *Jesus and the Disinherited*. New York: Abingdon-Cokesbury, 1959.

Tuck, Stephen. *Beyond Atlanta: The Struggle for Racial Equality in Georgia, 1940–1980*. Athens: University of Georgia Press, 2001.

Turman, Eboni Marshall. *Toward a Womanist Ethic of Incarnation: Black Bodies, the Black Church, and the Council of Chalcedon*. New York: Palgrave Macmillan, 2013.

Vail, Mark. "The 'Integrative' Rhetoric of Martin Luther King Jr.'s 'I Have a Dream' Speech." *Rhetoric and Public Affairs* 9, no. 1 (2006): 51–78.

Vander Lei, Elizabeth, and Keith D. Miller. "Martin Luther King, Jr.'s 'I Have a Dream' Speech in Context: Ceremonial Protest and African American Jeremiad." *College English* 62 (1999): 83–99.

Walker, Alice. *In Search of Our Mother's Gardens*. San Diego: Harcourt Brace Jovanovich, 1983.

Waters, Kristen, and Carol B. Conaway. *Black Women's Intellectual Traditions: Speaking Their Minds*. Lebanon, N.H.: University Press of New England and University of Vermont Press, 2007.

Weitzel, Al. "King's 'I Have a Dream' Speech: A Case Study of Incorporating Orality in Rhetorical Criticism." *Communication Reports* 7 (1994): 50–56.

Williams, Delores. *Sisters in the Wilderness: The Challenge of Womanist God-Talk*. Maryknoll, N.Y.: Orbis Books, 1993.

Zinn, Howard. *On Race*. Introduction by Cornel West. New York: Seven Stories Press, 2011.

———. *SNCC: The New Abolitionists*. Cambridge, Mass.: South End Press, 2002.

Newspapers

Aiken (S.C.) Standard and Review.
Albuquerque Journal.
Ames (Iowa) Daily Tribune.
Atchison (Kans.) Globe.

Atlanta Constitution.
Atlanta Daily World.
Atlanta Journal and Constitution.
Baltimore News-Post.
Baltimore Sun.
Bennington (Vt.) Banner.
Billings (Mont.) Gazette.
Brown Daily Herald (Brown University).
Burlington (N.C.) Daily Times-News.
Cedar Rapids Gazette.
Chicago Sun-Times.
Daily Courier (Connellsville, Pa.).
Daily Mail (Hagerstown, Md.).
Daily News (Huntingdon and Mount Union, Pa.).
Daily Plainsman (Lake Park, Iowa).
Daily Times (Delaware County, Ohio).
Dayton (Ohio) Daily News.
Delta Democrat-Times (Greenville, Miss.).
Denver Post.
Evening Bulletin (Philadelphia).
Evening Capital Annapolis.
Fort Worth Star-Telegram.
Gettysburg (Pa.) Times.
Globe-Gazette (Mason City, Iowa).
Greensboro (N.C.) News & Record.
Independent (London).
Independent (Pasadena, Calif.)
Kingsport (Tenn.) Times.
Lake Park (Iowa) News.
New Pittsburgh (Pa.) Courier.
New York Times.
News (Frederick, Md.).
News of Delaware (Upper Darby, Pa.).
Oakland (Calif.) Tribune.
Ottawa (Kans.) Campus.
Philadelphia Daily News.
Philadelphia Independent.
Philadelphia Inquirer.
Pittsburgh Courier.

Pittsburgh Post-Gazette.
Post (Frederick, Md.).
St. Petersburg (Fla.) Times.
Star-Ledger (Newark, N.J.).
Tennessean (Nashville).
Tri-State Defender (Memphis, Tenn.).
Washington Post.
Waterloo (Iowa) Sunday Courier.
Winnipeg (Man.) Free Press.

INDEX

Adams, Charles, 189, 203, 212; on Prathia Hall's preaching, 157, 211, 216–217
Adams, W. T., 64
Aelony, Zev, 80
African American Awareness Club Parent Support Group (West Windsor-Plainsboro, N.J.), 119
African American Baptist Women's Consortium, 203
African American National Anthem, 149
African independence, movement for, 97–98
Albany State University (Ga.), 27–28, 32
Alexander, Raymond Pace, 14
Allen, Chris, 55–57
Allen, Donna, 112–113, 156
Allen, Ivan, 90–91, 92–93
Allen, Ralph, 231; Prathia Hall's description of, 32; work in Southwest Georgia, 51–57 passim, 64–66 passim, 69, 77–80 passim
Alliance of Baptists, 188–189
Alton, Joseph W., 22
American Baptist Churches of the USA, 3, 188, 190–192, 211, 275n1; Concern Committee for, 190; Ellen Cushing Scholar Award of, 281n114; presidency of, 192; Racial/Ethnic Women in Ministry Conference of, 190–192; Women and Men in the Community of Faith of, 190; Women in Ministry of, 191–192; Women of Color in, 191
American Baptist Theological Seminary (Nashville, Tenn.), 81
American Friend Service Committee (aka Quakers), 11, 13, 83; on Prathia Hall's work with, 98–99, 106–107, 109; school desegregation work of, 106–107
Anderson, Pamela June, 69, 129, 214
Anderson, William G., 27, 75, 98
Anemia, aplastic, 212–213
Anti-Semitism in Philadelphia, 12
Association for the Study of African American Life and History (ASALH), 114, 120
Atlanta Summit Leadership Conference, 91

Baker, Ella, 5, 221–222, 236n3; comparison with Prathia Hall, 40; mentorship of Prathia Hall, 108–109; work with SNCC, 26, 31
Baldwin, David, 84
Baldwin, James, 84
Baptist Minister Conference of Philadelphia and Vicinity (Philadelphia, Pa.), 3, 115, 121, 194, 203, 264n25
Baptist Peace Fellowship of North America, 189
Barnes, Mitzy Jacoby, 16
Barrett, Joyce: attending founding of SNCC, 17; connection with Fellowship House, 16, 66–67; description of Prathia Hall's preaching, 37, 39; participation in Eastern Shore Freedom Rides, 20–22; relationship with Prathia Hall, 63; working in Atlanta, Ga., 91, 94; working in Southwest Georgia, 66–69, 74–80 passim, 106
Barry, Marion, 206
Battle, Randy, 78
Baylor University Institute for Oral History (Waco, Tex.), 235n1

Beach, Maxine, 125–127
Belafonte, Harry, 14, 61, 97, 105
Bell, L. Henderson, 208
Bell, Mrs. (Albany, Ga.), 70–71
Bell, Peggy, 70
Bellinger, Elizabeth, 187
Bernstein, Naomi and Jerry, 98, 100
Berrien, Willie Paul, 53, 64
Bethune, Mary McLeod, 14
Bevel, James, 228, 230–231, 286n30
Bjorn, Akil, 131
Bjorn, LaGretta, 235n1; on assisting Prathia Hall, 122, 128, 130–131, 272n9; on Prathia Hall's origination of "I Have A Dream," 233; on Prathia Hall's preaching, 212–214
Black churches: Prathia Hall's advocacy for bone marrow donors within, 212–213; historical heritage of, 133–152 passim, 158–159, 175–177, 183–184, 208–214 passim; moral crises facing, 134–152 passim, 159, 166–211 passim, 217–219; preaching tradition of, 157–159, 223–225; relationship between religion and politics, 144–145, 179, 204–211; women in ministry in, 153–155, 164–184 passim, 185–204 passim, 213–219 passim; Women's Days, 201. *See also* Womanism
Black Leadership Women, 114, 194–195
Black Nationalism, 107, 262n90
Black Power, 107–108, 109, 230
Black women's intellectual history, 4–5, 236n6
Blackwell, Unita, 97
Bond, Julia, 31
Bond, Julian, 31, 39, 100, 206, 243n41
Boston University School of Theology, 3, 131, 204, 212
Boynton, Amelia, 84–85
Boynton, Sam, 84
Boynton family, support for Selma, Ala., movement, 84

Brotherhood of Sleeping Car Porters, 221
Brown, Kenneth, 224
Brown, Mrs. (Albany, Ga.), 71
Brown, Presttonia "Prestie," 212; on Prathia Hall's speaking, 10, 122; on Ruby Hall, 9
Browne, Eddie, 68–69, 91
Buber, Martin, 35
Buford, Floyd M., 64
Bunche, Ralph, 14
Burroughs, Nannie Helen, 5, 9, 128, 149
Bush, George W., 151

Cade, Cathy, 76
Cade, William, 76
Carawan, Guy, 50
Carmichael, Stokely, 107, 230, 262n90
Carson, Clayborne, 223–224, 284n12
Carter family (Drew, Miss.), 107
Cary, Mary Shadd, 4
Castro, Fidel, 80
Center for Cuban Studies (New York, N.Y.), 189
Challis, William, 64
Chaney, James, 100
Chatfield, Jack, 231; Prathia Hall's description of, 32; work in Southwest Georgia, 54–57, 66, 74, 222–223
Cherry, W. B., 56
Chestnut, J. L., 85
Children's Defense Fund (CDF), 3, 151, 206–210; Black Church Initiative Committee of, 207–210; Black Community Crusade for Children, 206–210 passim; Edelman and, 143, 205–206; Alex Haley Farm of, 207, 218–219
Choy-Wong, Kathryn, 191
Christensia, Noubeu, 217
Christian, James, 77
Churchville, John, 57, 66, 71
Civil Rights Bill (1964), 96, 132, 146, 205
Clark, Jim, 82–85 passim, 103–105

Clark, Septima, 14
Clergy Concerned about South Africa, 114
Clinton, William (Bill), 122, 206
Cobb, Charlie, 48
Colby College (Waterville, Maine), 213
Conference of National Black Churches (CNBC), 200
Congress of National Black Churches (CNBC), 120, 144, 207–210; Project Spirit of, 207–208
Congress of Racial Equality (CORE), 19, 221
Connecticut College (New London, Conn.), 205
Conwell, Kathleen, 32, 52, 231–232
Conwell School of Theology (Philadelphia, Pa.), 31, 110
Cooper, Anna Julia, 5
Coppin State Teachers College (Baltimore, Md.), 7
Cotton, Dorothy, 231–232
Council of Federated Organizations (COFO), 101–102
Cox, Courtland, 97
Cox, Leon, 91
Crenshaw, Kimberlé, 128
Crozer Theological School (Upland, Pa.), 13
Cullen, Countee, 9
Curry, Connie, 43, 107

Dallas County Voters League (Selma, Ala.), 85
Daniel, James, 47
Daniel, Roy (aka Roychester Patterson), 53–55
Daniels, C. Mackay, 208
Daniels, Carolyn: attacks on home of, 54–58; on Prathia Hall's relationship with Sherrod, 35; on support for SNCC workers, 50–51, 65–73 passim, 86, 98
Davenport, Jessica, 215–216
Davis, Lehman, 54
Davis, Phil, 78

Davis-Putter Scholarship Fund, 127
Day, Dorothy, 14
DeLissovoy, Pete, 32, 47, 78
Delta Sigma Theta, 135–136
Democratic National Convention (1964), 97, 250n16
Dilworth, Richardson, 19
Doar, John, 107
Dobbs House, 91–92
Dodson, Jualynne, 189, 195
Domestic abuse: Prathia Hall as survivor of, 115–118; Prathia Hall preaching about, 138–140, 165–166, 175–176
Donaldson, Ivanhoe, 97
Douglas, Kelly Brown, 195
Douglass, Frederick, 87, 135, 224, 286n24
Du Bois, W. E. B., 224, 286n24
Dunaway, R. M., 52
Dunbar, Paul Laurence, 9
Dyson, Michael Eric, 157, 206, 217

Ebony, 115, 143; African American Achievement Award, 281n114; Fifteen Greatest Black Women Preachers List, 3, 193–194, 202, 210–217 passim
Edelman, Marian Wright, 143, 205–206. See also Children's Defense Fund
Einstein, Albert, 12
Elliot, James Robert, 65
Euchner, Charles, 230–231
Evers, Medgar, 13, 226

Fairfax, Jean, 107
Farmer, James, 103
Fauntroy, Walter, 103
Felder, Cain Hope, 203
Fellowship Baptist Convention in Cuba (La Fraternidad), 189–190
Fellowship House (Philadelphia, Pa.), 11–22 passim, 38, 249n3; interfaith work of, 238n35; involvement with SNCC, 62–67 passim, 75, 99; papers of, 235n1

Fellowship of Reconciliation (FOR), 72
Ford Foundation: African American Church Program Advisory Committee of, 206; Rights and Social Justice Program of, 127
Forman, James, 205–206; on fundraising for SNCC, 50, 62–63, 98, 100; on meeting Prathia Hall, 31; on Mississippi Freedom Summer, 101–103; on SNCC's strategy generally, 79; on SNCC's work in Africa, 97–98; on SNCC's work in Atlanta, Ga., 92–93; on SNCC's work in Selma, Ala., 78, 81–85 passim, 105–106; on SNCC's work in Southwest Georgia, 61; on women in movement, 44
Forum for Theological Education, 124
Fosdick, Harry Emerson, 284n12
Freedom Rides: in Albany, Ga., 27; along Eastern Shore, 19–22, 239n76; 1960–1961 bus rides, 15, 17, 32, 50, 240n76
Freedom Singers, 50, 62. *See also* Reagon, Bernice Johnson
Fry-Brown, Teresa, 214–215
Fund for the Rehabilitation of Burned Churches, 61
Fund for Theological Education, 120, 281n114
Furrow, Harold D., 91

Gaines, Monroe, 77
Gandhi, Mahatma, 13, 218
Georgia Education Commission, 93
Giddings, Paula, 140
Gilkes, Cheryl Townsend, 129, 195, 204, 213
Goodman, Andrew, 100
Gore, Albert (Al), 151
Graham, Charles, 63
Grant, Jacquelyn, 129
Greensboro, N.C., sit-ins, 17, 23
Gregory, Dick, 84, 90
Gregory, Lillian, 90–91
Grimes, T. Ralph, 95

Hall, Berkeley, Jr. (brother), 6, 16, 128
Hall, Berkeley, Sr. (father), 1, 6–11 passim, 87, 112, 137, 234
Hall, Betty (sister), 6, 8, 63, 213
Hall, Ruby (mother), 6–11 passim, 123, 130–131, 146, 154; on Prathia Hall going South, 30, 63; on Prathia Hall's medical care, 213
Hall-Darden, Teresa (sister), 6, 8, 213, 218
Hamer, Fannie Lou, 97–98, 236n3, 250n16
Hampton Ministers' Conference, 112, 146, 194–195
Hansen, Bill, 64
Hansen, Drew, 228–229, 231, 234, 286n23
Harding, Vincent, 36, 100
Harper, Frances E. W., 4
Harris, Don, 41, 66, 77, 80, 97–98
Harris, Isaiah, 28
Harris, McCree, 76
Harris, Rutha, 50
Harris family, support for Albany, Ga., movement, 27–28, 54
Harvard Divinity School (Cambridge, Mass.), 122, 288n56
Haslam, A. Herbert, 13
Hayden, Casey, 108
Heart of Atlanta Motel, 91, 94, 96
Hedgeman, Anna Arnold, 96–97, 99
Height, Dorothy: collaboration with Prathia Hall, 199, 205; as leader in civil rights movement, 14, 103, 140, 221–222
Heschel, Abraham, 14
Higginbotham, A. Leon, 21–22
Higginbotham, Evelyn Brooks, 128, 212, 233, 288n56
Hill, Norman, 103
Holloway, Fannie B., 10, 146
Holloway, Lucius, 52
Holloway, Mrs. (Albany, Ga.), 69–70
Holsaert, Faith, 231; description of Prathia Hall's preaching and character, 36–37, 39; Prathia Hall's description of, 32; on

SNCC's interracial nature, 42–44; work in Southwest Georgia, 66–74 passim, 77
Hoover, J. Edgar, 286n24
Hopkins, Pauline, 4
Howard University (Washington, D.C.), 13
Hubbard, Alfonzo, 66
Hughes, Langston, 9, 224

"I Have a Dream" speech, 59–60, 287n34, 287n43, 287–288n49; as delivered, 225–227, 286n23; Prathia Hall's origination of, 222–223, 227–233, 248n165, 283n7; organization of, 221–222; original manuscript for, 225–226, 285–286n18; precedent for, within black heritage, 224–225. *See also* King, Martin Luther, Jr.; March on Washington for Jobs and Justice
Interdenominational Theological Center (ITC; Atlanta, Ga.), 3, 31, 100, 131, 199; Visiting Womanist Scholars Program at, 131, 212, 281n114
Interfaith Ministerial Alliance (Albany, Ga.), 75
Interstate Commerce Commission ruling against segregated public transportation (November 1961), 28

Jackson, Mahalia, 221–222, 226
Jackson, Mattie Mae, 73
James B. Moses Colloquium on African American Religion, 186–187
Jewish Labor Committee, 62
Johnson, Lyndon, 90, 92
Johnson, Mordecai, 9, 13, 14
Johnson, Violet, 5
Jones, Charlie, 27, 51
Jones, Mr. (Drew, Miss.), 107
Jordan, Clarence, 66
Jordan, Florence, 66

Kennedy, John F., 29, 60, 69, 90, 221, 286n18; Library and Museum of, 181

Kennedy, Robert, 61, 66, 91
Kimbrough, Edith, 189
King, Barbara, 195
King, C. B., 64, 69; congressional candidacy of, 80, 106; leadership in Albany, Ga., movement, 27, 78
King, Coretta Scott, 14, 150
King, Diana, 12, 20
King, Marion, 64, 67
King, Martin Luther, Jr., 235n3; comparison with Prathia Hall, 1, 38, 149–150; on Prathia Hall's preaching, 1, 232–234; hearing "I have a dream" from Prathia Hall, 222–223, 227–234; involvement with March on Washington for Jobs and Justice, 221–222; involvement with SNCC's work in Albany, Ga., 29–30, 59–60, 63, 222–223; involvement with SNCC's work in Atlanta, Ga.; involvement with SNCC's work in Selma, Ala., 104–106; "Letter from Birmingham Jail" of, 286n18, 287–288n49; on nonviolent direct action, 12, 13–14, 72, 150–152; papers of, 284n12; preaching/speaking of, 223–227, 230–234; preaching/speaking style analysis, 282n7, 283n7, 283–285nn12–13, 285n16, 285–286nn17–18; relationship with Fellowship House, 13–14, 63; relationship with Prathia Hall, 38, 59–60, 99, 150, 232–234. *See also* "I Have a Dream" Speech; March on Washington for Jobs and Justice; Southern Christian Leadership Conference
King, Martin Luther, Sr., 38
King, Mary, 44, 108; on Prathia Hall's preaching, 37, 40, 101–102
King, Slater, 27–29 passim, 69, 75, 91
King family, support for Albany, Ga., movement, 27–28
Kingsway (also King's Way), 15, 19–20
Kinnon, Joy Kennedy, 115
Knight, Carolyn, 211

Knit Goods Workers Union, 67
Koinonia Farm (Americus, Ga.), 66–67
Ku Klux Klan (KKK), 12, 54, 77, 85

Lafayette, Bernard, 81–84
Lafayette, Colia, 83
Laubach, Frank, 14
Lawson, James, 236n3; involvement with SNCC, 25–26, 72; training students for nonviolent direct action, 15, 241n2
Lee, Bernard, 222
Lewis, John, 206; description of Prathia Hall, 40, 217, 229; involvement with March on Washington for Jobs and Justice, 221–222; involvement with SNCC's work in Africa, 97–98; involvement with SNCC's work in Atlanta, Ga., 91; involvement with SNCC's work in Selma, Ala., 104–106; on women in movement, 46
Lincoln, Abraham, 227, 286n18, 286n24, 286n29
Lincoln, C. Eric, 206
Lischer, Richard, 228–229, 231, 283–284n12, 285n16, 287n34
Little Rock, Ark., school desegregation, 17
Lofton, Fred, 207–208
Long, Worth, 83
Longfellow, Henry Wadsworth, 9
Longstreth, Molly, 129
Love, John, 104
Lyon, Danny, 39

Maier, Claire, 18, 66–67
Malcolm X, 97, 104, 107, 288n50
Mallory, Catherine, 65
Malone, Mariann Taylor, 217–218
Mamiya, Lawrence, 205
Mants, Joann Christian, 77
March on Washington for Jobs and Justice, 96, 221–222, 225–226, 232, 288n50. *See also* "I Have a Dream" speech
Marshall, Burke, 64

Marshall, Thurgood, 10
Martin, Clarice, 195
Mathews, Z. T., 57, 60–61
Maxwell, Joan, 52
Mays, Benjamin, 224, 281n114
McDew, Chuck, 40, 60, 213
McKenzie, Vashti, 211
McMillian, Henri, 123, 130
McMillian, Michael, 123, 130, 131
Meade, Margaret, 14
Mercer School of Theology (Garden City, N.Y.), 113
Methodist Conference on Human Relations, 99
Michaels, Sheila, 36
Michaelson, Benjamin, 22
Miller, Keith, 223, 284–285n12
Million Man March (1995), 200
Mississippi Freedom Summer, 101–103, 106
Mitchell, Ella, 129, 204
Mitchell, Henry, 129
Mitchell, Juanita Jackson, 20, 22
Monastery of the Holy Spirit (Conyers, Ga.), 61
Montgomery, Ala., bus boycott, 17
Moore, Howard, 91
Moore, Susan Newman, 214
Morehouse College, 123, 149, 210, 224; Martin Luther King College of Preachers and Scholars of, 210
Morris, Richard, 91
Morsell, John, 103
Moses, Robert (Bob), 36, 101–102
Moss, Otis, Jr., 129, 207–208
Moss, Otis, III, 214
Motley, Constance Baker, 10
Mt. Sharon Baptist Church (Philadelphia, Pa.): appreciation for Prathia Hall, 157; Berkeley Hall Sr. founding of, 7, 188; Prathia Hall's calling to, 114; Prathia Hall's commitment to, 121–122, 126, 193;

Prathia Hall's membership at, 113; ministry of, 7–11 passim, 145–146, 237n5; support for women in ministry, 201, 203
Murphy, William, 230
Murray, Pauli, 5, 221–222

Nannie Helen Burroughs National Training School for Women and Girls, 128
Nash, Diane, 205
National Association for Black Seminarians, 203
National Association for the Advancement of Colored People (NAACP), 13, 20–22, 27; involvement with March on Washington for Jobs and Justice, 221; work with black churches, 145; work with other civil rights organizations, 91–93, 106
National Baptist Convention of America, Incorporated, 7, 190, 192, 208, 264n25; relationship with Women's Convention Auxiliary, 132, 136. *See also* Black churches
National Coalition of 100 Black Women, 181–182
National Council of Churches (NCC), 13, 96, 99, 101
National Council of Churches of Christ, Racial Ethnic Women in Ministry Consultation of, 195; Women in Ministry Program of, 191–192
National Council of Negro Women (NCNW), 111, 199–200
National Organization for Women (NOW), 96, 109
National Revolutionary Council, 97
National Urban League, 209–210, 221
Neblett, Carver (Chico), 66, 69–74 passim
Neblett, Chuck, 50
Niebuhr, Reinhold, 14, 61, 284n12
Nix, Echol, 212
Noble, Aurelia, 76

Noonan, Martha Prescod Norman, 243n41; on Prathia Hall's preaching, 37, 233; on women in movement, 44–45
Northern Seminary (Lisle, Ill.), 192

Odinga, Oginga, 89–90
Ohio Baptist Convention, 192
Ohio Commission on African American Males, 205
Ohio Department of Human Services, 205
Oliver, Elizabeth, 21
One Church / One Child, 114
One Church Ten Families, 207, 210
O'Neal, John, 74
Opportunities Industrialization Center (OIC; Philadelphia, Pa.), 23

Page, Edith, 65, 69
Paris, Peter, 122, 186, 203, 216
Paschkis, Victor, 12
Patch, Penny, work in Southwest Georgia, 51–52; on Prathia Hall's preaching, 37
Peacock, Willie, 102
Penney, Marjorie, 11–22 passim, 38, 62–67 passim, 75; relationship with Martin Luther King, Jr., 13–14. *See also* Fellowship House
Pennsylvania Baptist State Convention, 188
Pennsylvania Democratic State Committee, 205
Perdew, John, 80
Perry, Mrs. (Dawson, Ga.), 73
Phalen, Dale, 16
Philadelphia Baptist Association, 264n25
Philadelphia Commission on Human Relations, 19
Philadelphia High School for Girls, 10, 16, 237n23
Post-traumatic stress syndrome (aka post-traumatic stress disorder), 109
Powell, Adam Clayton, 23, 87

Prathia's Daughters, 215–216
Preacely, Peggy Dammond: Prathia Hall's description of, 32; on Prathia Hall's preaching, 36, 38, 39, 41; on SNCC's interracial and interregional nature, 42; work in Southwest Georgia, 46, 52
Princeton Theological Seminary (Princeton, N.J.), 3, 113, 281n114; Association of Black Seminarians at, 3, 120, 202–203; Prathia Hall's course of study at, 114–115; Prathia Hall's dissertation at, 122, 124, 127, 130; Prathia Hall's experiences as black student at, 118–119
Pritchett, Laurie, 29, 71, 76–77
Proctor, Samuel DeWitt, 129–130, 196–197, 199, 204, 217–218; Institute of, 208
Progressive National Baptist Convention, 3, 122, 188–190, 211, 216, 275n1; executive committee of, 188; Prathia Hall's strategic vision for, 208–210; ministry in partnership with La Fraternidad (Fellowship Baptist Convention in Cuba), 189–190; Women's Department of, 208. *See also* Black churches
Progressive Oklahoma Baptist State Convention, 190
Project Womanpower, 109, 110–111
Pye, Durwood T., 93–96

Rabinowitz, Joni, 66, 75, 80
Rabinowitz, Victor, 80
Randolph, A. Philip, 103, 221
Ransby, Barbara, 202, 236n3
Rauschenbusch, Walter, 284n12
Reagan, Ronald, 145
Reagon, Bernice Johnson, 45, 50, 205–206, 223
Reagon, Cordell, 27, 50
Reeb, James, 107
Richardson, Judy, 105; on Prathia Hall's preaching, 36–37, 39, 229
Ricks, Willie, 230

Roberson, J. T., 127
Robeson, Paul, 9
Robichaud, Louise, 116
Robinson, Betty Garman, 100, 104; on Prathia Hall's preaching, 39, 41, 274–275n89
Robinson, Gary, 91
Robinson, Jackie, 61
Robinson, Reggie, 213
Robinson, Ruby Doris Smith, 31, 97–98, 103, 236n3
Rockefeller, Nelson, 61
Romily, Constancia Dinky, 109
Roosevelt, Eleanor, 14
Rubin, Larry: description of Prathia Hall's preaching and character, 39, 59–60, 65–66; on Prathia Hall's origination of "I have a dream," 223, 229–230; on SNCC's interracial nature, 42; work in Southwest Georgia, 71, 74
Rudd, Bernard, 117
Rustin, Bayard, 72, 103

Sanders, Mary, 73
Sanders, Mrs. (Dawson, Ga.), 73
Schneider, Dorothy, 192–193
Schomburg Center for Research in Black Culture (New York, N.Y.), 131
Schwerner, Mickey, 100
Sehested, Ken and Nancy, 189
Shaw, William, 208
Shaw University (Raleigh, N.C.), 25
Sherrod, Charles, 36, 205, 236n3; beaten in prison, 29; description of Prathia Hall, 36–37, 40–41, 51, 229; on leading SNCC's work in Albany, Ga., 27, 67–77 passim; on recruiting Prathia Hall for Southwest Georgia, 31; relationship with Prathia Hall, 35–36, 63, 222; strategy with interracial activism, 32, 42–46, 55–57, 79; on women in SNCC, 43–46
Short, D. E., 53–54, 60, 64–67, 159

Shuttlesworth, 14
Sinatra, Frank, 14
Sirizotti, Larsine, 20
Sitton, Claude, 51, 55–59 passim, 71, 222–223
Sloan, Boyd, 94–95
Smith, Amanda Berry, 4
Smith, Kelly Miller Institute (Nashville, Tenn.), 148, 196–197, 273n59
Smith, Lillian, 224
Southern Baptist Convention, 175
Southern Christian Leadership Conference (SCLC), 26–30 passim, 91, 228; compared with SNCC, 26, 35, 92, 150; involvement with March on Washington for Jobs and Justice, 221–222; Montgomery Bus Boycott of, 230–231, 235n3; work in Birmingham, Ala., 287–288n49; work in Selma, Ala., 105–107. *See also* King, Martin Luther, Jr.
Southern Regional Council, 61
Spearing, Florence, 5
Spelman College (Atlanta, Ga.), 17
St. Benedict's College (St. Joseph, Minn.), 99
Stanford University, 150–152
Stewart, Maria, 4
Stewart, Mary Watson, 10, 201
Strickland, Bill, 31
Student Nonviolent Coordinating Committee (SNCC), 207, 225, 234, 235n3; adult advisors of, 17; annual staff retreat of, 262n90; archived papers of, 235n1; compared with SCLC, 26, 35, 92, 150; executive committee of, 90, 92, 100, 103, 229; expulsion of white members of, 107–108, 262n90; founding of, 18; Friends of, 99, 100, 109, 243n41; interracial nature of, 32, 41–47 passim, 79, 262n90; involvement with March on Washington for Jobs and Justice, 221–223, 231; Legacy Project of, 205; listserv of, 205; mass meetings of, 48–50, 222; Mississippi Freedom Summer, 101–103; northern students in, 41–47 passim, 96, 99; relationship with other civil rights organizations, 26, 35, 72–73; reunions of, 205; trip to Africa (1964), 97–98, 137; Waveland retreat of, 107–108, 262n90; women in, 2, 43–46, 108, 233, 235n3, 262n90; work in Albany, Ga., 2–4, 25–80 passim, 206, 242n31; work in Atlanta, Ga., 89–96 passim; work in Selma, Ala., 2–4, 78–86 passim, 103–107, 206
Sullivan, Leon, 14, 23–24
Summit Conference on Apartheid, 205
Sundquist, Eric, 228, 286n29
Sweet, Leonard, 120, 124–126

Taylor, Gardner C., 206
Taylor, Susan, 140
Temple University (Philadelphia, Pa.), 16–18, 31, 92; Urban Archive Special Collection at Libraries of, 235n1
Terrell, Mary Church, 5
Terrell County White Improvement Association, 74
Thimas, Natasha, 215–216
Thistlethwaite, Susan Brooks, 204
Thomas, Clarence, 179
Thomas, Norman, 14
Thurman, Howard, 14, 23, 224, 227, 238n35
Tillich, Paul, 35, 284n12
Toddle House, 90–92
Toliver, Mrs. (Dawson, Ga.), 72
Touré, Sékou, 97, 137
Trapp, H.J., 111–112
Trinity College (Hartfield, Conn.), 32, 205
Truth, Sojourner, 4, 135
Tubman, Harriet, 4, 135
Tucker, B. L., 83
Tuskegee University (Tuskegee, Ala.), 16, 123
Tutu, Desmond, 205

United Negro College Fund (UNCF), 209–210
United Theological Seminary (Dayton, Ohio), 3, 120–130 passim, 192; African American Ministries Program at, 121, 127–130, 214; Faculty Study on Ecology, Theology, and Justice at, 121–122; Harriet L. Miller Women's Center at, 121, 125–126, 203–204, 214; Interdenominational Christian Fellowship Union at, 120; potential merger with Northern Seminary, 192
University of Virginia (Charlottesville, Va.), 195

Vanderbilt Divinity School (Nashville, Tenn.), 25, 148, 196
Vanderhost, Leonette, 124
Vandiver, Ernest, 28
Vassar College (Poughkeepsie, N.Y.), 172
Vietnam War, veterans of, 109
Voting Rights Act (1965), 132

Wake Forest University, 230
Walker, Alice, 265n48
Walker, Wyatt Tee, 38, 91, 205, 217, 231–233
Wallace, George, 82, 104
Wallace, Michele, 140
Ward, Daryl, 120, 126–129, 215
Ward, Vanessa, 215
Warren, Repsie M., 128
Weems, Renita, 195
Wells, Samuel, 68, 76
Wells-Barnett, Ida B., 5
Wert, Newell, 124
Western College (Oxford, Ohio), 101
WHAT 1340 (Philadelphia, Pa.), 63
Wheeler, Ed, 123–124, 196–197, 217
White Citizens Council (Selma, Ala.), 80–81, 85

Williams, Delores, 203
Williams, Hosea, 104
Williams, Myrlie Evers, 145
Williams Mandate (1939), 136–137
Wilson, Hilda, 100
Womanism, 4, 236n4, 265n48; black women's intellectual history, 4–5, 236n6; critique of feminism, 142, 201–202; Prathia Hall as professor of, 120; Prathia Hall's dissertation using methodology of, 128, 136–137; Prathia Hall's "dream" as, 222–225, 227, 232–234; Prathia Hall's involvement in founding of, 142; Prathia Hall's leadership rooted in, 185–211 passim, 213–219, 275n1; Prathia Hall's preaching using methodology of, 153–184 passim; Prathia Hall's social research using methodology of, 128–152 passim, 155; Interdenominational Theological Center's Womanist Scholars Program, 131, 212, 281n114; Alice Walker and, 265n48. *See also* Black churches
Women, in civil rights movement, 2, 43–46, 108, 233, 235n3
Women's Convention Auxiliary of the National Baptist Convention, Incorporated, 128, 132, 136–137. *See also* National Baptist Convention of America, Incorporated
Women's International League for Peace and Freedom, 98
Women's memoirs, on civil rights movement experiences, 2, 235n3
World Council of Churches, 188, 195
Wright, Jeremiah, 137, 204, 206, 212, 214; on Prathia Hall's preaching, 121, 157, 211, 218
Wynn, DuBois (son), 115–118, 123, 130–131, 212–213, 282n2
Wynn, Ralph (husband), 108–109, 113–118 passim, 130

Wynn, Simone (daughter), 109, 123, 124, 131, 267n75; on parents' divorce, 115–118

Yancey, Roberta, 90–91
Yores, Aura, 66–67
Young, Whitney, 103

Zellner, Bob, 36; on Prathia Hall's preaching, 37–38, 229–230
Zellner, Dottie, 44
Zinn, Howard, 17, 28, 61, 66, 205; on Prathia Hall, 84–85

www.ingramcontent.com/pod-product-compliance
Lightning Source LLC
Chambersburg PA
CBHW011754220426
43672CB00018B/2957